PATRIARCHY;

OR,

THE FAMILY:

ITS

CONSTITUTION AND PROBATION;

BY

JOHN HARRIS, D.D.

PRESIDENT OF NEW COLLEGE, LONDON, AND AUTHOR OF "PRE-ADAMITE EARTH," "MAN PRIMEVAL," "GREAT TEACHER," "GREAT COMMISSION," ETC.

BOSTON:
GOULD AND LINCOLN,
59 WASHINGTON STREET.
NEW YORK: SHELDON, LAMPORT & BLAKEMAN,
115 NASSAU STREET.
1855.

PREFACE.

In "Man Primeval," the constitution and probation of individual man were traced. The Family is the unfolding of the individual—the development of social man. In the following pages an attempt is made to exhibit the family in its constitution and probation.

The First Part is devoted to the Laws or Method of the domestic constitution. And although the Patriarchal character of the antediluvian community, as a form of government and a dispensation, is never lost sight of, yet, as the constitution of the family itself is as fixed as that of the individual, all that is here advanced on the subjects of marriage, of domestic government, and of education, is of permanent and perpetual application.

The Second Part indicates the stages and changes through which the Patriarchal community may have passed in the course of its probationary history. Had the Biblical narrative of these changes been as full as it is of the stages through which the Theocracy subsequently passed, we should have been able to affirm and exemplify where now we can do little more than suggest. Owing, however, to the permanent character of the domestic constitution, its post-diluvian history down to the present day supplies ample data for indicating all the probabilities of that primitive period. And the distinct and decisive language of the sacred historian, respecting the fullness of the trial, justifies the inference that not one of all these probabilities was unknown to that ancient community, as far as it was necessary to make their probation complete.

As far as the Reasons, exhibited in the Third Part, relate to the constitution of the Family, they are as much in force now as ever. As far as they account for the probation of the Family, they belong to the present only as history. Patriarchy itself was not suited for permanence. But, though failing of its high end, its failure was far from entire. It prepared for postdiluvian man an unknown amount of material civilization with which to begin the new world. It developed much of the real nature of good and evil, and placed them in vivid contrast. It showed the insufficiency of Nature for man, even when it was yet all but paradisiacal. And it exhausted one class of possibilities in man's great experiment to do without God. So that its failure was not on the great scale, and for God; but for man, or as a rich possibility which he ought to have made actual.

In the Fourth Part, it is shown that Patriarchy, though failing as a Dispensation calculated to be a manifestation of God *by* man, was not less a manifestation of God *to* man. Not only was it based on a scheme of Mercy—an aspect of the Divine character before unknown; it placed the sufficiency of the Divine long-suffering in a light so strong that the finger of inspiration points to it as a fact settled for all time.

CONTENTS.

FIRST PART.

THE DIVINE METHOD.

CHAPTER I.

A NEW STAGE OF THE DIVINE MANIFESTATION.

CHAPTER II.

THE MEANS OF DIVINE MANIFESTATION IN THE PRECEDING STAGE BROUGHT ON INTO THIS.

CHAPTER III.

THE NEW ASPECT OF THE DIVINE CHARACTER, AND THE MEANS OF ITS MANIFESTATION; A REMEDIAL ECONOMY THROUGH THE FAMILY.

CHAPTER IV.

THE DEVELOPMENT OF THE FAMILY CONSTITUTION, AND OF THE MEANS OF MERCY DURING THE PATRIARCHAL ECONOMY.

CHAPTER V.

THE ACTIVITY WHICH THE LAW OF DEVELOPMENT PRESUPPOSES, AND WHICH THE FAMILY PUTS IN MOTION.

CHAPTER VI.

THE CONTINUITY OF THIS DEVELOPMENT AND ACTIVITY IN THE MEANS OF DIVINE MANIFESTATION.

CHAPTER VII.

THE FAMILY RELATIONS WHICH THE PRECEDING LAWS BRING TO LIGHT.

CHAPTER VIII.

LAWS WHICH THE RELATIONS OF THE FAMILY CONSTITUTION PRESUPPOSE.

CHAPTER IX.

OBLIGATIONS CONSEQUENT ON THE RELATIONS AND LAWS OF THE DOMESTIC CONSTITUTION.

CHAPTER X.

THE WELL-BEING OF THE DOMESTIC CONSTITUTION MEASURED BY THE DISCHARGE OF ITS OBLIGATIONS.

CHAPTER XI.

THE ORDER OF THE LAWS OF THE FAMILY CONSTITUTION IMPLIED IN ITS WELL-BEING.

CHAPTER XII.

THE SUBORDINATION IMPLIED IN THE ORDER AND WELL-BEING OF THE DOMESTIC CONSTITUTION.

CHAPTER XIII.

THE LAW OF INFLUENCE IMPLIED IN THE ORDER, WELL-BEING, AND DESIGN OF THE FAMILY CONSTITUTION.

CHAPTER XIV.

DEPENDENCE OF THE FAMILY CONSTITUTION, AND OF THE REMEDIAL SYSTEM WHICH UNDERLIES IT, ON THE GOOD PLEASURE OF GOD.

CHAPTER XV.

ULTIMATE FACTS AND NECESSARY TRUTH INVOLVED IN THE DEPENDENCE OF THE DOMESTIC CONSTITUTION.

CHAPTER XVI.

THE CONSTITUTION OF THE FAMILY AND OF THE MEANS OF MERCY IN ANALOGY WITH EVERY PRECEDING PART OF THE DIVINE CONDUCT.

SECOND PART.

CHAPTER XVII.

THE LAW OF CHANGE; OR, HISTORY OF THE PROBATION OF THE FAMILY.

THIRD PART.

THE REASON OF THE METHOD AND OF THE HISTORY.

CHAPTER XVIII.

SECTION I.—THE REASON WHICH BELONGS TO MAN'S CONSTITUTION AND INVOLVES HIS WELL-BEING.

SECTION II.—THE REASON WHICH RELATES TO THE MANIFESTATION OF THE DIVINE ALL-SUFFICIENCY, AND SO INCLUDES MAN'S DESTINY.

FOURTH PART.

THE ULTIMATE END OF THE FAMILY PROBATION AND ECONOMY AS A MEANS OF DIVINE MANIFESTATION.

CHAPTER XIX.

SECTION I.—POWER.

SECTION II.—WISDOM.

SECTION III.—GOODNESS.

SECTION IV.—HOLINESS.

SECTION V.—MERCY.

SECTION VI.—LONG-SUFFERING.

FIRST PART.

THE DIVINE METHOD.

CHAPTER I.

A NEW STAGE OF THE DIVINE MANIFESTATION.

Man's first sin a foreshadowing.

By the creation of man the earth itself may be said to have been transfigured; for its new inhabitant consciously radiated the Divine image. In his constitution, his dominion, and his far-reaching relations, he stood forth the embodiment of a Divine idea—"the type of Him that was to come." His probation raised the earth into a scene of moral government. Sinai itself was anticipated and even surpassed in him; for his constitution was a living court of Divine judicature. His temptation announced that he had joined the solemn march of events in the government of God at a period when the great conflict between good and evil had already begun; and that, as a moral agent, he could not but take part in it. His first sin may be regarded as a foreshadowing, for all time, of the kind of contest which he would be likely to wage;—presuming on his sufficiency for himself, he brought his will into selfish collision with the Supreme will. And the first great lesson taught him by experience—that the well-being of the creature lies in loving obedience and dependence—may be regarded as a prophecy of the *moral* of man's entire history. Henceforth, no second fall of man, as a sinless being, is possible. His probation, in this sense, can never be repeated.

And the occasion of a new stage of his self-manifestation.

But not on account of his fall was the unfolding of the Divine character to pause, or man's career to terminate. His nature, unlike that of any of the animal races which had here preceded him, admits of a prolonged process of development; and, from this point, a new stage of his eventful history was to begin, and a new aspect of the Divine character to be disclosed. According to the poet of Paradise, it was while bending over the stream that Eve first caught sight of her physical beauty; and it is more than poetically true, that it was by falling man first beheld the reflection of his mortal image. While standing as in the vertical radiance of the Divine complacency, he cast no shadow; but his guilty fall revealed him to himself in dark and ominous outline. The fountains of the great human deep were broken up. It was the commencement of a course of self-manifestation which is still in progress.

As the head of a family.

Man himself was now to become a moral governor, and the new family constitution was to be the scene of his jurisdiction. In a new, an official sense, he was now again promoted to be the image of God; for, within limits, his will is to be law to beings to whom he stands in the relation of subordinate creator. While still charged with the duties of self-government, he was to enter on the high office of forming the character, and pointing to the destiny, of creatures, indebted to him instrumentally for their existence. The scenes of Eden were to be repeated virtually, and on a small scale, in the circle of the family. The probationer there was now to conduct the probation of others in an Eden of his own; to issue prohibitions and restrain self-will; and to learn new lessons of obligation to his Father in heaven, while encouraging the obedience of his own children.

The family on probation.

The Family constitution itself was now, in a deep and solemn sense, to be placed on probation. And with the Divine announcement of the promise of a SEED the new dispensation commenced. Not, indeed, that individual probation was at an end. The probation of the first man himself had ended in one form, only to begin in another. As a representative and a sinless being, there could not be "another fall of man;" for never again could there be a first man, insulated from all the influences of his race, yet representatively related to the race. Never, in this sense, can probation be repeated. But as the subject of a new economy, which recognizes man as fallen and provides for his recovery, every man is on personal probation. And the institution of the family, as the medium through which the Promise was to find fulfillment, secured the means for rendering such probation successful. The event proved that it had a collective character and function; and a period of time was assigned for its trial. The chief occasion of its failure is specified; and the reprieve of a hundred and twenty years shows that it had, in the Divine mind, its own appropriate fullness of time." Indeed, to ignore its probationary character, would be to take it out of all vital connection with the two economies between which it stands; and to hold it as purely exceptional. But there are no dropped links in the chain of the Divine procedure.

Period of its probationary existence.

The period of probation for the Family extended, not exclusively, but specifically, and as a dispensation, from the Fall to the Flood. Not exclusively; for its natural constitution preceded its dispensational form and use. The conjugal union, and the Divine command, "increase and multiply," preceded man's first sin. And being founded in nature, it survives its dispensational application. To the end of time, every family, like every individual, will pass through a probation of its own, with duties and obligations commensurate with its means and advantages. But specifically; for it then existed alone, with no national organizations encompassing it, no governing influences from without to control it. It enjoyed certain peculiar advantages—in the longevity of man, for example—never enjoyed subsequently. And it existed as an all-connected whole: the very root of the great genealogical tree, surviving for nearly a thousand years—a human banyan-tree—gradually taking possession of Central and Western Asia. It was charged with the duties of a dispensation; and the Flood was its judgment-day. The stage of Divine procedure which commenced with the calling of Abraham (popularly, but erroneously named "*the* Patriarchal Dispensation") supplies a further confirmation of this view. For his knowledge of God, his sacrificial worship, and all that was evangelical in the promises made to him, belonged to the religion of the antediluvian patriarchy. Saved in the ark with Noah, the existence of the whole was once more threatened by the rising flood of postdiluvian idolatry. The office of the Abrahamic family was to receive and mark, for a time, the ancient and rescued treasure; while their jealous separation and supernatural guardianship showed that the human family, as a whole, had not only lost sight of its high, original destiny, but had even become hostile to the means of attaining it.

As a universal dispensation, then, the Patriarchal economy may be regarded as having terminated with the deluge. Soon after that event, its dispensational form began to be absorbed in other modes of government, or entirely subverted from its original design. The prophetic, priestly, and kingly offices fell off from the paternal relation, and even separated from each other. Noah's denunciation of Canaan predicted a condition of society incompatible with the *idea* of Patriarchal rule. The Divine enactment of a law respecting the murderer, immediately after the Flood,* was an implied impeachment of Patriarchal government, and a virtual institution of magistracy—of an authority extra-Patriarchal. With Nimrod commenced a form of wide-wasting despotism, which defied alike paternal rule and moral law, and acknowledged no superiority but that of brute force. Even where the primitive Patriarchal form was retained—as among some of the descendants of Shem—it could not have been entirely exempt from these external influences. The calling of Abraham, and the promise of Canaan to his posterity, made him prospectively the father of a new economy; while the promise, that through him all the families of the earth should be blessed, retained him in vital connection with the antediluvian dispensation, for it was the original promise of "a seed" renewed in a more specific form.

Its antediluvian state sufficiently known to us.

The constitution of the family is essentially as fixed as that of the individual. And, owing

* Genesis, ix. 5, 6. *By man shall his blood be shed;* which the Chaldee paraphrases, "With witnesses by the sentence of the judges shall his blood be shed."

to the unchanging habits of Patriarchal life, not only may the families of Jacob and of Job be regarded as copies of the antediluvian type, repetitions of these copies are still extant among the nomadic tribes of Arabia and the steppes of Northern Asia. However few and fragmentary, therefore, the notices of antediluvian life transmitted to us in the Bible, we need be at no loss to conceive of its great characteristic outlines. But it is with the moral history of that early period that we are chiefly concerned. And in looking for its traces we shall find the few Biblical hints as significant and suggestive as a fossil bone is of the entire skeleton of some extinct species, or as the disinterred fragment of a sphynx is of the proportions of the temple whose entrance it guarded. We shall find striking points of analogy between the fall of the individual and what may be called the fall of the family. And while admiring the frame-work of the domestic constitution—the new garden of the Lord—we shall find the trail of the serpent, the self-willed spirit of the first sin, reappearing in every stage of the period, and with ever-increasing aggravation of consequences; till, at length, Forbearance itself grows weary, and the world's destruction prepares the way for the second birthday of the human race.

Patriarchy adapted only for an early stage of civilization.

It is not to be supposed that the Patriarchal form of government, even if it had answered its high intention, would have continued to exist alone. By itself, it was adapted only to an early stage of civilization. But in the exact proportion in which it fulfilled its Divine design, it would have prepared the way for a larger form of government; a form, for example, akin to that of the Jewish theocracy. And that second form, accomplishing its holy purpose, might only have opened the way for the Divine introduction of another superior still. The domestic constitution, meanwhile, would not only have co-existed with these enlarging and advancing stages of government, but would have risen in importance at each successive step, and have become the ministering angel of each.

Its commencement introduced a new stage of the Divine manifestation.

But the possibility of the family constitution, and of its prolonged trial, pre-supposes the introduction of a new stage of the Divine manifestation. Nothing of the kind had occurred in the history of the angelic order of offenders. Some of them having "kept not their first estate, but left their own habitation, everlasting chains" received them "unto the judgment of the great day."* The bolt of justice followed close on their sin, taking direct and full effect. Man also had sinned. And as his own history, up to the present point, had run strictly parallel with that of the angels, illustrating the power and wisdom, the goodness and holiness of God, what shall hinder but that the parallel extend also to unmixed Divine justice? It could not be pleaded in arrest of judgment that man had been coerced into evil against his will by a power *without* him. Had his will remained loyal to God, Omnipotence could have crushed the coercing power, and have set man at liberty. But he had consented to sin; his will had yielded, and become the leader of the revolt. Had he fallen into evil through some unavoidable misapprehension of the Divine will, he would have only required to be set right in his judgment in order to be restored to happiness. But it was his informed will which had yielded and which was now in danger of drawing all the powers of his nature after it, and of arming them in

* Jude, vi. 5.

the cause of sin. Objectively and subjectively, then, he had undergone a change. While the whole external universe remained the same, he had undergone a change in himself, and a consequent change in relation to every other being and object. What can or will be the momentous result? The following appear to be the only hypothetical alternatives:

Hypothetical alternatives; man's annihilation.

That the Almighty, in the exercise of unlimited authority, should reduce man to annihilation. But this result is opposed by the consideration that it would be in violation of rectitude—would be effected by rendering might superior to right—or allowing arbitrary will to overrule the claims of justice, which require that man should not be dismissed beyond the reach of punishment, but be subjected to it. His annihilation would seem to subvert moral government to its foundations.

His entire reconstruction.

That God, by an act of omnipotence, should reconstruct and alter man's constitution, placing it in such relation to the external universe as to render sin impossible. So that if, for example, he look on a forbidden object, it shall fail to excite desire; or, that no amount of attention to the visible, should divert him from the invisible. But his faculties and susceptibilities remain numerically and physically as they were before he sinned. The annihilation of any of his existing powers, the addition of new faculties, or the essential change of any part of his constitution, then, is open to the same objection as the preceding hypothesis—that it could be effected only by an act of arbitrary power counteracting the demands of justice. And further, it would be a virtual repeal of the existing scheme as a probationary constitution. It would be a constructive admission on the part of the Divine Creator that He had not, at first, adapted the constitution of man to his condition, and therefore could not, in justice, inflict the penalty. Nor would such a change be a remedy for the evil introduced and experienced by the identical creature, man. His identity would be lost in the change; and, in effect, another being would take his place.

The reconstruction of the external universe.

That man's constitution remaining as sin had made it, the external universe should be altered and adapted to it. That is, that although the laws of nature remain as they were, in harmony with the will of God, they shall be so changed that sensual excesses shall cease to injure health, or to incapacitate for intellectual effort, and shall be made as conducive to man's moral well-being as the government of the appetites is; that the earth shall bring forth spontaneously because man may dislike labor; in a word, that all the physical laws shall be so adjusted to man's newly-acquired tendency as that disobedience shall enjoy all the immunities and advantages of obedience. This would be, however, not to remedy, but to perpetuate the evil of sin, and even to reward it. For as all the requirements of moral law are only the demands of justice, the repeal of these demands would be to legalize injustice, and to make the holy Lawgiver himself the Patron of sin. As in the last hypothesis, too, this abatement in the Divine requirements would tacitly imply that the original claim had exceeded the demands of justice, and that the law consequently required revision; which would be taking the blame from man, and casting it upon God. But the laws of moral government are simply the expression of the immutable nature of the Lawgiver; and the laws of nature are the harmonious expressions of His will. To expect, therefore, that the external universe should be adapted to man's altered state is as if we should expect that because a small celestial globe needed rectifying, the earth should alter its position, or the whole material universe should move and adjust itself to that little globe; and inconceivably more irrational. It would be the error of the Ptolemean system of astronomy repeated in the sphere of moral government. Man's nature, and not the nature of the Diety, would be the standard of law.

Man's punishment.

That the law be allowed to take its direct course, and man endure the just penalty of his transgression. Tremendous consequence! yet as just as tremendous. Man himself expected it. As a self-infliction it had even commenced. Had it actually taken place, every holy intelligence might have united in saying, "True and righteous art Thou, O God, because Thou hast judged thus!" But this alternative, perhaps, would have been answering only one great end—the vindication of the Divine government. The nature of man would still be left at variance with itself, with creation, and with the nature of the Blessed God. Yet how can this dreadful alternative be avoided? Why is it not actually carried into effect?

The Divine adoption, instead, of a compensative and remedial arrangement.

That a compensative and remedial arrangement be, in some manner, effected, which shall preserve the authority and control of the moral government of God over its subjects, as truly and fully as it would have been by the personal punishment of the transgressor; and in consequence of which the transgressor himself may be restored, in a manner consistent with his free agency, to a state of harmonious obedience to the will of God. For if man is to be saved from the consequences of sin, the arrangement by which it is effected must obviously possess a twofold bearing—a personal and a relative, or a subjective and an objective. As he has taken himself out of harmony with the Divine government, and has incurred its penalty, the arrangement must provide an objective remedy—the Divine government, that is, must be vindicated and satisfied. And as his own nature is deranged and depraved, the arrangement must provide a subjective remedy, or, his constitution must be restored to harmony with the government of God. If only the former were provided, man might be exempted from inflicted punishment, but his personal depravity would prevent him from being happy; the provision would suit him only as the being *to* whom the Divine manifestation was to be made. On the other hand, were it possible that only the latter should be provided, it would suit him only as the being *by* whom, instrumentally, the Divine manifestation was to be made; while his external relations would render him miserable, for he would have to endure death, the displeasure of God, and whatever may be included in the inflicted penalty of transgression. In the hypothetical event, too, of either provision being made alone, the Divine all-sufficiency would remain unknown. For, in order to its display, provision must be made both for the personal and relative exigence; in which case it will be adapted to man both as the being by whom, and the being to whom, the Divine all-sufficiency is revealed. And still more would the all-sufficiency appear, if the same provision which remedied the relative or objective evil were made the occasion and means for the removal of the personal evil.

Disclosing a nattribute before unknown—mercy.

The bare possibility of such a provision, however, supposes the existence and exercise of an attribute of the Divine character hitherto unknown to the history of creation. For "every Divinely-originated object and event is a result, the supreme and ultimate reason of which is in the Divine Nature." This principle—the first illustrated in the "Pre-Adamite Earth," and in "Man Primeval"—here comes forth with peculiar luster. For if the question be asked, in relation to the twofold provision which man's recovery requires, which part will be made first? our theory, based on Revelation, enables us to reply without hesitation—the objective. If the ultimate reason of every thing which God does is to be found in Himself, then, before man's character is restored, and even in order to it, we may confidently expect that his condition will be remedied; or, that provision will be made in virtue of which the moral government of God will retain that authority which the unconditional forgiveness of sin would tend to destroy. Besides which, the movement for making the provision must be not only first, but entirely, on the part of God. And it is only as His Sovereignty can make that provision in harmony with the requirements of His equity that His infinite sufficiency will be brought to light. Now, that God, in the exercise of His rich and sovereign *mercy*, and in perfect consistency with every principle of moral government and of human freedom, has made such a provision, is the great subject of Divine revelation. And that this mercy was implied in the first Promise, and the means of the fulfillment of the promise symbolized in the first Sacrifice, is our deep, grateful, and admiring conviction.

Man's history recapitulates all the Divine perfections previously displayed.

Here, then, an aspect of the Divine character rises on our view which every prior dispensation had left undisclosed. Immeasurable ages had elapsed since first the Power of God proclaimed itself in the origination of matter. At an unknown period afterward, Wisdom proceeded to employ inorganic phenomena as means for the development of the new and sacred principle of organic Life as an end. A subsequent fiat went forth, and Goodness transformed the earth into a scene of animal enjoyment. But if Power, Wisdom, and Goodness are not to perpetuate their manifestation by multiplying physical creations alone, some other Perfection must now appear, which shall render the continuation of such additions unnecessary. Now, it is an incidental disclosure of Revelation that, elsewhere, a race of beings had come on the field of the Divine manifestation bright with the luster of a new attribute. In their creation, Power had put forth its mightiness; in their intellectual endowments, Wisdom had shone with unwonted splendor; Goodness had surpassed all its prior displays in their enlarged capacity for enjoyment; and Holiness—the new and crowning characteristic of their nature—had, in their creation, now first prepared a throne of moral government, around which they were assembled as accountable creatures. Some of their number sinned, and Justice appeared, clothed in terrors for their punishment. But here, as far as they are concerned, the manifestation of the Divine character paused. In the constitution and history of the new-made man, however, all these perfections have been recapitulated. On the principle of progressive manifestation, then, might it not have been expected that, if another attribute remains to be disclosed, the new race will be the medium of its revelation? Coming, as man does, on the stage of the Divine procedure at a period when Power, and Wisdom, and Goodness, and Holiness, and Justice, are already developed, we are led to expect that the great design of another stage of creation will be the display of another Divine perfection. Accordingly, he not only exhibits an epitome of all that has gone before: the unfolding of God's nature is actually resumed in the history of man's nature, and is carried forward. A new constellation appears in man's moral firmament—compassion, long-suffering, mercy, love. Man is honored to occupy an advanced post in the sublime march of the Divine manifestation. He has sinned, but is to be saved. The very heart of Love is to be put in stress for his pardon and recovery.

His family nature implies properties analogous in the character of God.

We speak not now of the extent of Divine mercy, but of its existence, as of a new thing in the earth, and, for any thing we know, new in the universe. Nor do we speak of its means, but of its *promise* and its *type.* And on the principle we are now illustrating—that every thing Divinely originated expresses some property in the great Originator—we recognize in this gracious disclosure an entirely new aspect of the Divine Nature. On the same principle, we are led to inquire, what, in God, does the new family constitution itself denote? Every effect in nature is, not indeed formally, but virtually, a manifestation of some property of the Creator. Every idea which is truly suggested and represented in creation points to a spiritual correspondence, infinitely greater, in the Divine Nature. The first man was not only a compendium of the preceding stages of creation, and as such an exponent of all which they had displayed of their Maker, but, by the addition of a moral constitution, he became a distinct and solemn utterance of the moral character of God. Every thing else had only disclosed a part or property of their Creator; here, at length, was His character—His *Image.* And if man's moral nature found its infinite counterpart in the Divine holiness, shall the fathomless mysteries of his social or family nature, with all its warm gulf-streams and ocean-currents of emotion, be supposed to denote no resembling property in the Deity? While every other part of man's nature is a spiritual index, shall this alone point away into an objectless infinite void? We speak not now of its suggestive power relative to any social distinctions in the internal economy of the Godhead, but of its analogous relations to the Divine character. And we believe that, so far from being a shadow, to which there is nothing answering in the great Substance, the love in which the family constitution is founded, and all the deep affections which it develops and by which it is administered, are designed to aid man in the conception of the Fatherhood, the unknown benevolence of God toward His sinning human family, and in which the great Promise of deliverance through the self-subordination and voluntary suffering of another, originated. The child obtains life, and all that makes life desirable, through another. Indeed, the whole of parental duty is a system of mediation; often attended with suffering and self-denial, but always impelled by love. And the first promise of man's deliverance, as the result of a conflict, was a Family promise. Thus early was the great principle of mediation taught—inwoven into the texture of the family economy.

In treating of the antediluvian period, however, we have to do with mercy, as a revelation to man, only in promise and symbol. The objective fullfilment of the promise, and the means of mercy in the actual coming of "the second man, the Lord from heaven," belong to a subsequent dispensation. An intimation of mercy to the race introduced the family economy, but that feature of the Divine character which the history of the economy itself brought to light was Long-suffering. Man occupied himself for about two thousand years in seeing what Nature could do for him under circumstances the most favorable to the development of its resources. But his guilty experiment could not arrest the advance of the Divine manifestation; for, while voluntarily disregarding the mercy which would have saved him, he was involuntarily magnifying the forbearance which spared him.*

* I have spoken of the period extending from the Fall to the Flood as "about two thousand years." Dr. Bunsen asks "ten thousand years, or very little more;" Philosophy of Universal History, vol. ii. p. 12. It is well that the certainty of events does not depend on our knowledge of their precise dates. (See Man Primeval, pp. 190, 191.) The different dates assigned to the period in question gives an extreme difference of 1142 years. I adopt the chronology of the Septuagint, which is that of Josephus, as exhibited substantially by Vossius, Jackson, Hales, and Russell. I do this on the evidence there is that the chronology of the Bible was corrupted by the Jews (as to the ages of the Patriarchs at the births of their eldest sons), in order to *put back* the dial of Time for the coming of the Messiah; leaving it to be inferred that the computation of the Septuagint is the true transcript of the original Hebrew chronology. This reckoning makes the deluge to have occurred, A.M. 2256.

CHAPTER II.

THE MEANS OF DIVINE MANIFESTATION IN THE PRECEDING STAGE BROUGHT ON INTO THIS.

The law stated.

THE means of education and of Divine manifestation enjoyed by primeval man consisted of external nature, of his own constitution and condition, and of supernatural communications from the Creator. And in relation to these means, we have now to verify the law which leads us to expect "that they will all be found brought forward"* from the paradisiacal into the family economy.

The first means; external nature.

Accordingly, the first of these—the new-made world—still lay expanded before the eye of man. None of its ancient laws had been repealed. None of its beauties, nor of its wonders, had been blotted out. Power was here with all the demonstrations of its activity and greatness. And Wisdom, with its endless adaptations of means to ends. And Goodness, spreading a continual banquet for the creatures, and filling them with enjoyment. Not that these laws and objects of nature were continued by any inherent and independent necessity. As their existence, at first, was entirely dependent on the will of God, and in order, partly, to answer a specific end in the history of man, so, now that sin had brought a crisis in

* Pre-Adamite Earth, p. 60, and Man Primeval, p. 10.

that history, it was dependent on the same will whether or not these means should receive any modification. Much of the paradisiacal in external nature might have been withdrawn, and the place which it occupied have been left a blank. But the whole had been devised by Him who "seeth the end from the beginning;" and it was now continued to answer the end of its original appointment. Not less brightly did "the heavens declare the glory of God," after the Fall, than they did before. For nine hundred and thirty years did the human eye which had first gazed on Paradise in its primal freshness, and the ear which had there listened to the opening burst of its melodies, continue to be regaled by the same music and the same vernal beauty. Even the "thorn and the thistle"* did not less eloquently speak of the perfections of God, because they served at the same time as memorials of the sin of man. "He left not Himself without witness, in that" man still found himself in a world, not of mere coincidences, but of speaking signs; a worshiper in a temple whose every object and event possessed a symbolic value, and where the service paused not day nor night. And thus "the invisible things of God from the creation of the world" continued to be "clearly seen, being understood by the things that are made, even His eternal power and Godhead."† The illuminated volume of natural theology continued to invite the attention of mankind till the flood came and quenched in death the eyes that should have read it.

* Gen., iii. 13: *Thorns also and thistles shall it bring forth to thee*—including all kinds of weeds. Not that they were now called into existence for the first time, but that man should now first become acquainted with them. Leaving the garden, he should go forth into the common wilderness.

† Romans, i. 20.

Secondly; man's constitution and condition.

The *constitution and condition* of man, also, as the subject of moral government, continued to manifest all they had ever disclosed of the Divine perfections. Sin, indeed, had involved him in guilt, and had depraved his nature, but the susceptibilities and powers with which he left Paradise, were numerically the same as when he entered it. And, consequently, his sensitive, intellectual, and moral relations to the objective universe were not numerically diminished. Whatever the loss which he sustained, or the moral change which he had undergone, he still retained a natural capacity for subserving the ends of the Divine manifestation, and for this he was held responsible.

Man's degeneracy reproduced.

But this statement involves certain points of vital importance; and the law now under consideration requires us to examine them. It implies that the character of fallen man will re-appear in each of all his descendants, and that it will appear in them natively, and as his descendants. Were it otherwise, a breach of continuity would exist of the most radical kind. The stream would rise higher than its source. The tree would no longer be known by its fruits. Man and his posterity would form two species in the highest or moral sense.

Universally.

Accordingly, *first*, the degeneracy and depravity of universal man are undeniable. There is no man who does not believe that every man he knows might be somewhat better than he is. The records of history forbid us to think of any man who has ever lived, that he never failed in a single duty to God or man. Every man's consciousness attests the truth of the appeal that there is "none that doeth good and sinneth not." And the testimony of Scripture respecting antediluvian man is that "all flesh had corrupted its way before God;" that evil increased in proportion to the multiplication of the species, and that there existed a depravity which connected every man with the entire race.

Natively.

The *second* part of our proposition is, that there is a degeneracy of character native to man. Accordingly there is a sense in which every human being is conscious of this defectiveness as soon as he is capable of moral agency. I employ the term *degeneracy*, negatively, to denote the state of the young human being before he comes to distinguish between good and evil; and the term *depravity*, positively, to denote his state as soon as he has become conscious of evil. It should be observed that I am not speaking of this native imperfection as if it consisted of a Divine *infliction*. Nor do I believe it to be any thing inserted from without—an entity—or a *positive* cause of evil in the heart. Nor do I view it as any thing actually blameworthy or simple, until the subject of it has become a moral agent—has come to distinguish between right and wrong—for until then he can not be said to have a moral character. And this is a sufficient reply to those who object to our view of the native defectiveness of the human being, that the Scriptures represent little children as patterns of innocence and humility; for until such defectiveness has developed itself in actual sin, they can not be regarded as blameworthy on account of it, while their humility and innocence—mere negative virtues in them—render them models to the positively proud and vicious. Nor, remembering that the young of the brute creation, incapable of moral evil, often exhibit impulses very nearly approaching to vanity, rage, revenge, and stubborn self-will, would I interpret all the similar phenomena of the human infant as indications of a sinful nature. Nor, lastly, when the child has reached the state of moral accountability, should he be spoken of as "totally" depraved in the sense of being as bad as he can be; but meaning, that in a constitution all-related, the defect of one part, especially if that part be the highest, must necessarily involve the derangement of the whole. A moment's consideration will place this subject in the proper light.

This degeneracy ungodliness.

The *morality* of conduct depends on the motives which lead to it. Motives are distributable into the following classes—those of the appetites and passions, of self-love, of the affections or dispositions toward others, and a regard to the will and character of God, each class being alike of Divine origination. These motives range in an ascending scale, our obligation to God being paramount. Now, as there is no duty which we owe to ourselves, or to our fellow-men, which we do not owe partly and chiefly because God has willed it as inherently right, to omit all reference to Him in the performance of it, is to lay ourselves open to the charge of *ungodliness*. An adequate answer this to those who object to our view of the native imperfection of man, that he naturally produces good fruit as well as bad. For we are not now speaking of outward acts, but of the motives which determine their moral character. Now, a man may spend life in the performance of acts outwardly right; and he may even perform many of his social duties, not merely from a native kindliness (in which there may be no more morality than in the gentleness of the lamb), but because he deems the performance socially right. Yet these very acts may be wanting in a whole order of motives, and that the highest—a regard to the will of God. True morality is the practical recognition of *all* the obligations arising out of *all* the relations we sustain. Now, as God, the Being to whom we sustain all-comprehending relations, has enjoined those very acts toward our fellow-men, to perform them irrespective of His will on the subject, from no conscious regard to Him, is to be found wanting in the highest obligation. For as the regulation of the appetites would not acquit a man from the charge of sin, who should yet indulge in selfishness; and as the due limitation of the appetites and of self-love would not absolve him from immorality if he yet neglected his social duties, so neither can his attention to these three classes of duties exempt him from the charge of ungodliness if he discharge them irrespective of the will of God on the subject. The inferior classes of motives hold and rule the man to the exclusion of the highest—a moral vacuum this of the worst description—God is wanting. So that even if no one of these three inferior classes predominate strongly, so as to characterize the man, to the exclusion of the other two, *ungodliness* must yet be regarded as vitiating his whole conduct. Indeed, the very rightness and excellence of his actions—considered, that is, apart from his motives—is likely to be made by him the occasion of forgetting God, and of virtually trying to do without Him.

Example will not account for it.

Regarding the faultiness in question, then, in this least and lowest sense, as ungodliness, or as the want of a due respect to the character and will of God, I return to the proposition that this defectiveness is native to man. Every human being is conscious, or may be made conscious, that he is chargeable with this defectiveness as soon as he is capable of moral agency. It is presupposed in his first act of sin. Depravity in the concrete, or personal transgression, presupposes this defectiveness in the abstract. And, hence, *example* alone will not account for depravity. The prodigious influence of example on the outward conduct, indeed, is admitted; so that if the question related to actions only, and if all actions good and bad were equally imitated, the difficulty could be explained by resolving the whole affair into instinctive imitation. But the points to be noticed are, first, that the very first generations were universally depraved: to ascribe this to example is to assign the evil itself as the cause of the evil. Secondly, that *evil* example is incomparably more operative than good, often counteracting any amount of good. This preponderating power of evil is the very thing to be explained; and can be accounted for only by supposing that a peculiar affinity for it exists within. Thirdly, that while example may influence actions and even thoughts, the depravity of which we speak supposes a defectiveness of motives, an imperfection which imitation will not account for. *Principles* of action are not thus amenable to example. And, fourthly, that evil example is, more or less, universally imitated, so that no one escapes it absolutely. Were the action of an infectious disease universal, it would be ascribed to the universality of the predisposing causes in the patients; and in the same manner, the universal influence of bad example pre-supposes a universal readiness to yield to it, a readiness which dates beyond the reach of memory.

Nor the early development of the passions.

Neither will the early and rapid development of the passions, as compared with the later and more tardy development of the reason, account for the evil of which we speak. It is perfectly true that the passions are the first in the field; that, at the very period when the appetites are strong, the counteractive judgment and reason are feeble; that the self-regulating powers are slow in acquiring authority; and that, let them ascend the throne as early as they may, antagonist habits are already begun. But this is the very fact to be accounted for. Instead of being itself an ultimate fact, it requires us to look for such fact. Here is depravity, of some kind, already in actual process; and our theory is that it pre-supposes something defective in the state of the human constitution. Here is a practical result; we only affirm that there must be something anterior to account for it. Here is a uniform event; we only decline the absurdity of ascribing it to nothing. Of all the myriads of the posterity of Adam that have lived to reach the period of moral agency, it is affirmed that every individual has in some sense "gone astray;" that each has done this in virtue of his human descent; that sin is "his own" in a sense in which nothing else is; and that it is a distinctive quality identifying him with the species.

The degeneracy hereditary.

The third part of our proposition remains to be noticed—that the character of fallen man not only reappears in his posterity, that it so appears natively, but also that it appears in them as his descendants. Here certain previous questions arise:—What was the loss which the progenitor of the race sustained, or what the change which he underwent? Could any part of such loss be entailed on his posterity, or such change be transmitted, yet leaving man free? And, provided this were possible, would such entailed loss or transmitted change be sufficient to account for the sinfulness of every moral agent of the race?

The loss experienced by the first man.

In reply to the first question, respecting the nature of the loss or change experienced by the first man as a sinner, the teaching of the Bible appears to be this—that man was created sinless, *potentially* perfect, and capable of maintaining his will in strict coincidence with the will of God.

As a creature, man could not be otherwise than dependent; dependent *in proportion* to his high endowments as a spiritual and immortal being; dependent, therefore, as a spirit on a connatural spiritual Being—on the favor of the infinite Spirit, and on loving and confiding intercourse with him.

Man's well-being depended on his habitual recognition of his dependence; for on such recognition depended the maintenance of a loving and obedient state of mind toward God corresponding with his dependent condition. Any other state of mind could only be a practical falsehood.

The powers requisite for recognizing the fact of his dependence, in order to the maintenance of the appropriate state of mind, belong to man's constitution, or are natural to him. As such, they form the subjective ground of his responsibility, or render him responsible for living in the constant recognition of his dependence.

But as the power of obedience implied the power of disobedience, God was pleased, instead of leaving man to the mere exercise of his own powers, as He justly might have done, to superadd a direct Divine influence disposing and determining man, in a way consistent with his moral freedom, to maintain the loving harmony of his own will with that of his Father in Heaven.

This predisposing influence extended to the whole of man's conduct, one solitary act excepted. For surely it is not to be understood that man was left at liberty to violate every obligation, except the probationary law, with impunity. Neither could it have meant that, if left to himself, there was no other liability to which he was exposed than the one specified. Apart from a special provision to the contrary, his liabilities as a free agent were co-extensive with his multiplied obligations. This Divine provision, then, is to be regarded as reducing his thousand liabilities to one; but as leaving him, at that one, to the sense of his responsibility alone. Just as if a youth whose father had marked out for him his whole course of conduct, should enjoy, in addition, the companionship of one who constantly placed his father's character before him in the most attractive light, and reminded him of his father's will in every particular except one; leaving him in that one, in which he well knew his father's mind, to his own sense of right and duty.

Man's retention of that gratuitous provision, or superadded influence, was made contingent on his obedience in that one particular. Continuing in his state of inward and outward conformity to the Divine will, he would enjoy the threefold result—in the continued expression of the Divine complacency—the growing excellence of his character—and the corresponding improvement of his outward condition; or, in his relation to God, to himself, and to nature. But voluntarily failing in obedience to the one probationary law, he would experience a change answering to this threefold relation—his consciousness of guilt would be the signal that he had *forfeited* that mark of the Divine favor which consisted in the superadded influence of which we have spoken; that his own nature had become *defective* and *depraved;* and that a change of outward condition would ensue answering to this change of character and relations, or that he would, in some sense, die.

Now, in relation to the one easy law in which man was left to his own sense of duty, as he might have been left in regard to every other law, man failed.* Losing sight of his dependence and obligation, he lost the appropriate state of mind toward God, and fell; and his fall incurred the first of the three evils named—the *loss* of the superadded influence which had been hitherto accorded to him.

But the very act which incurred this loss from without denoted a loss within—the loss of that consciousness of the soul's dependence which is essential to the maintenance of a right state of the affections toward God. In other words, the external loss denoted, and was occasioned by, an internal *change*. This is the second of the three evils in question. Now this change itself, be it remarked, was twofold; it was both negative and positive; or, as I have said, it denoted defect and depravity. Man's non-recognition of his dependence implied the voluntary suspension or absence of the only act or habit which could maintain his affections in the right state toward God. Here was *defect*. But this defect itself can be accounted for, in an adult human being, only as it is seen to imply the presence and predominance of another's will—man's own will asserting and aiming at self-subsistence: and here was *depravity*.

Deferring, for the present, our consideration of the other evil referred to—the change in man's condition, as not immediately bearing on the question before us, we are already in possession of three forms of evil. Here are loss, defect, and depravity; the loss of the auxiliary influence graciously superadded to man's already responsible powers; defect, or negative evil, in the non-recognition of his profound and vital dependence on God, and in the consequent absence of love to Him; and depravity, or positive evil, in the replacement, or, rather, displacement of love to God by the su-

* See Man Primeval, p. 423, etc.

preme love of self—the substitution of self for God; a change which could not fail to impair his sense of responsibility. And of course, in a being already responsible, like the first man, the defect must be held to be sinful, as well as the depravity.

The consequent loss or change experienced by his posterity.

Man having sinned, then, the question arises, what part of his consequent loss or of his twofold change could be shared in by his posterity? No reflecting mind can be startled by such an inquiry as if all such participation were a novelty. We are all hourly experiencing effects, natural, civil, and moral, which can be traced back to remote generations. "The shallower the man, so much the more isolated will every thing appear to him, for upon the surface all lies apart. He will see, in mankind, in the nation, ay, even in the family, mere individuals, where the act of the one has no connection with that of the other. The more profound the man is, so much the more do these inward relations of unity, proceeding from the very center, force themselves on his notice." *

The subject, indeed, has been invested with a repulsiveness which does not properly belong to it, by the extreme theory of those who assume that the posterity of Adam personally share in the *guilt* of the first transgressor—are guilty, that is, of the first transgression in the same personal sense as he was. As if the judgment of God could be otherwise than according to fact and truth. As if infants could be regarded by Him before they themselves sin as guilty in the same sense in which they will be after they have become actual transgressors. But who of all his descendants ever felt the consciousness of such guilt? It is a

* Prof. Stahl, quoted by Olshausen in Comm. Rom. v. 12.

commutation which the constitution of the human mind makes impossible. The error consists in confounding *culpa* with *reatus;* the inherent blame-worthiness of sin with the evil consequences inseparably connected with it. In the nature of things, the *guilt* of the sin is and must be the sinner's own alone. In *this* respect, our relation to the first man is the same as if the sin had been committed in his own private or individual capacity, and quite irrespective of any special probationary law.

But it by no means follows that because we do not partake of the guilt of an act committed before we existed (an impossibility), therefore we are related to it in no substantial sense whatever. In the language of Julius Muller "it is a superficial view of human nature which regards the race as being, in a moral respect, a mere aggregate of individual personalities, morally connected with each other, and dependent on each other, only in so far as in the progress of their development they receive, one from another, discipline, doctrine, example. Behind this division into atoms may be discerned a native substantial unity, in which the moral life of the individual is rooted as in its maternal soil. . . . If the community in which he lives is not a mere artificial one, but has a firm ground in nature, he is not only born into it, but breathes a common life with it." Events which are occuring to-day will affect the character and condition of the men of future ages. The great system to which we belong is interlaced in all its parts, and the first moment connected with the last; and the very fact, that all the race have derived life from Adam, renders it antecedently probable, or at least not improbable, that they have derived from him something more. Certainly, life is not the only thing which we have derived from any of our immediate ancestors.

In answering the question, then, respecting the possible loss or change derivable to us from the progenitor of the race, I reply, first, that the original transgression incurred the *forfeiture* of that superadded influence by which we might have been secured in a state of holy obedience. The provision was gratuitous and conditional. It was superinduced on a nature already endowed with all the elements of responsibility. When, therefore, man sinned, this superinduced provision was simply withdrawn; its special object had been defeated. Man was now to be left, in respect to every other law, as he had been left in relation to the probationary law—to his own responsible powers as a being fitted for moral government. Thus he might have been left from the first, as far as equity was concerned; and thus he now was left. Now, that his posterity should be destitute of this provision also, follows, as far as he is concerned, as a matter of course. Unless he could have transmitted that which he no longer possessed, the consequence was inevitable. Superior as our condition might have been then, if our representative had maintained his standing, and had secured for his posterity the enjoyment of this superadded provision, I do not regard it as worse now that he has fallen than it would have been if such a prospect had never been placed within his reach; but he had been left to fail, and had failed, in an ordinary manner. On him the deprivation fell as a *punishment;* on his posterity it comes simply as the *loss* of a possible good; but leaving us no more just ground of complaint, than as if it had never existed, but man's failure had taken place when left to his own moral resources.

Secondly, we have seen that man's original transgression implied a personal change of a twofold nature—defect and depravity. Abundant evidence exists to show that "the likeness of children to their parents extends beyond the features of their body;" that there are not only hereditary diseases, but hereditary tendencies to certain vices, and that such particular tendencies often run through a family for many generations. But these are mere specialities, transmissible by propagation, and dependent for their particular forms, it may be, on localities, varieties of organization, states of civilization, and on circumstances accidental to humanity; and the proximate origin and fluctuation of which are bounded by limits. They belong in their specific forms to families, and not to the race. Our first father stands in no relation to such transmission different, in kind, from that which every other parent sustains. Underlying these specific forms of evil, indeed, and making them physiologically possible, there exist the organic effects of the first sin, by the shock of which bodily perfection was forfeited; the most exquisite organization being no longer strictly normal, but only an approximation to it.

Our present question relates, however, not to the specific degeneracy of a family or a community, but to the generic change of a race. And since this change is of a kind which is felt to be alien to our idea of man as made by God, calls for incessant conflict, and is subversive of his well-being, but is yet pervasive of the entire race, the Scriptural account is the only adequate one—that this universal degeneracy commenced in the apostacy of our first parents from God. But what is the nature of this transmitted change? I believe it to consist of *defect*, or rather *degeneracy*, such as I have previously described, and of an impaired sense of responsibility attendant on such defect. The voluntary defect of the first man becomes the involuntary degeneracy of his posterity. I regard the evil, as transmitted, as negative, reserving the term *depravity* for that positive evil into which it grows.

That the change is of a nature which invariably leads to moral depravity, if the subject of it live to the point of moral agency; that it then assumes the second and positive form of the first sin, self-assertion as opposed to the Divine will, I not only admit but contend for. But that *as* and *when* transmitted it is moral—moral in the same sense in which it afterward becomes moral when the will has accepted it—seems inadmissible on these grounds. It is opposed to the plain declaration of Scripture, that "sin is the transgression of the law;" for the infant human being, as yet unconscious of moral obligation, is incapable of such transgression. It implies, consequently, that moral evil is not an affair of the will, but is constitutional and involuntary, and a part of our nature in the same sense as the appetites and passions are; a view inconceivable, and subversive of every sound theory of responsibility. It implies further, that (as the blessed God can not be the author of sin) souls are not successively created by Him, and connected according to a general law, with a material organization, at the proper period,* but that they are propagated like and with the body; or else, that if they are successively created, the body itself, as matter, is, according to the old Manichæan principle, inherently evil, and possesses the power of corrupting the soul. But whichever of these views be adopted, the theory of a transmitted moral de-

* The affirmative of this view was called by the schoolmen *Creationism;* the theory that souls are propagated, *Traducianism.*

pravity appears to involve the further difficulty of loosening the very foundations of man's accountability; for if the nature we inherit be, in any intelligible sense, morally depraved—if it actually comes to us inevitably burdened with a debt of personal guilt—the voluntary and the involuntary, the necessary and the free, are confounded in a manner which destroys all our conceptions of moral government. The guilt in question must, in that case, be held to be mere calamity. And hence the theory further implies that the atonement of Christ is little more than an expedient to remedy the misfortune. The very attempt to silence complaint at the supposed arrangement of transmitted guilt, by pointing to the mediatorial dispensation, is to ascribe that dispensation to justice rather than to grace.

That part of the twofold change, then, which the fall of our first father exhibited, and which descends to his posterity, is an evil of degeneracy. Some would call it physical depravity; not meaning thereby material, bodily, or physiological, as if it were wholly an affair of the organization, but simply to denote that it is not moral. If I spoke of it as depravity, I should designate it *involuntary*, to denote that the action of our personal will having had nothing to do with it, the very element is wanting necessary to constitute it guilt. For the sake of distinctness, however, and, as I believe, of truth, I prefer speaking of it as degeneracy. Here, then, are two of the evils derived from our first transgressor:—the *loss* of the special influence originally accorded to his already responsible powers; and the *degeneracy* which early shows itself in our non-recognition of dependence on God, and in the consequent absence of love to Him. Now, of these two effects, my conviction is that the former alone is entailed by Adam, in his *represent-*

ative capacity, on his posterity; that, to them, the direct and immediate result of his failure is one of deprivation. Of the transmission of the second effect, in any sense *peculiar* to the first man—except the numerical fact that he was the *first* man—I find it impossible to conceive. In other words, I regard it as transmitted *paternally* from generation to generation.

Will it account for the universality of depravity?

And now comes the third of our inquiries: Whether such inherited loss and transmitted degeneracy be sufficient to account for the universality of human *depravity?* As to the loss of the special provision, it is obvious that if its absence at a solitary point was followed by the fall of the first man at that point, the failure of every other human being might have been apprehended, inasmuch as the withdrawment of that provision leaves us exposed to danger at every point. The consequent disadvantage, indeed, at which we begin our moral life is not so great as at first sight we may be apt to suppose. For while the first man might plead that he was betrayed into a state of which he could previously know nothing, we, however numerous our points of danger, encounter only one at a time. We commence life, too, in the hands of those whose office it is to protect us from each danger in succession, till we have acquired the power of self-government. Similar inequalities of danger, moreover, exist in every state of society, without at all affecting our responsibility; just because the greatest amount of such disadvantage lies within limits which leave man's moral agency complete. Still the mere deprivation of that special provision was, considering man's circumstances, ominous of the universal deprivation, which has actually ensued. For although this, I conceive, is the only spiritual loss resulting to us directly from the sin of the first man, and although had this provision been retained, antagonistic influences might have assailed us in vain, yet, being withdrawn, the will, the cause of moral action, is left exposed to the threefold influence of whatever evil may be occasioned by the parental transmission of abnormal temperaments and organizations—by an imperfect and even pernicious example—and, especially, by the early development and irregular action of the inferior principles of our nature. In addition to the loss which leaves us simply to our responsible powers, our nature itself is in a state of *degeneracy.* "That which is born of the flesh is flesh." Even supposing this to mean that the *voluntary* products of our unregenerate nature can not be otherwise than sinful, there is an underlying truth presupposed, namely, the great law of natural production, that like begets like; that no generative power can impart any thing which is not contained in its own nature. And if every man in succession from the Fall is naturally characterized by a want of disposition to recognize his dependence on God, this is only saying that every human being is born in this state and transmits it.

Degeneracy issues in depravity.

Now to be born in this merely negative state toward God is itself an adequate solution of the positive *depravity* in which it uniformly issues. The only alternative to a non-recognition of dependence on God, is an undue or exclusive recognition of self. The vacuum arising from the absence of love to God is filled up by nothing but the love of self—of a fragmentary, godless self. This love has nothing to displace. It has merely to take possession of a vacant throne.

Now what form of sin is not ultimately resolvable into

All forms of depravity resolvable into selfishness.

this principle of selfism?* What is *worldliness*, whether as covetousness or sensuality, but the aim of a being who has lost the infinite good to substitute and appropriate the finite? *Hypocrisy* is the mask he wears to conceal his aim; *anger* and *impatience* the results of impediment and disappointment; *envy* and *malice* the emotions excited at the superiority or the success of others; and *hatred* and *cruelty* the reaction of thwarted self-will. *Ambition* is an attempt at lofty self-isolation; *pride* the feeling that we have achieved, or can achieve, such distinction; and *despondency* and *moroseness* the offspring of disappointed desire. Detached from God, man's relation to every other object is false; he himself is a moral falsehood; and every *breach of veracity* is but a particular form of the great falsehood. Living out of harmony with God and with himself, *variance* with his fellow-man follows of course. *Lawlessness* of every kind is but the result of man's attempting to be a law to and by himself. All human governments are still occupied in reconciling law and liberty—in restraining the fierce *collisions* of human wills. And "whence come *wars* and *fightings* among you? come they not hence, even of your lusts that war in your members? Ye lust and have not; ye kill and desire to have, and can not obtain. Ye ask and receive not, because ye ask amiss, that ye may consume it upon your lust." *Impenitence* is self-satisfaction unwilling to submit to God; the choice to remain at variance with Him. *Unreasonableness* is self-will substituted for reason and conscience. And *unbelief* is self-trust as opposed to trust in God.

"But is not self-love of moral obligation?" Undeniably:

* See J. Müller's Christian Doctrine of Sin, vol. i. p. 187.

it is to be the measure of our love to others. But the ground of the obligation to love ourselves, remarks Müller, is the same as that on which we are required to love our fellow-man—our relation to God. My moral worth consists in my having been made in the image of God, capable of entering into His plans, and of sharing in His glory. But if God be lost from my soul, I can not be said strictly to love my integral and proper self, but only the ungodly remains of myself. The act is essentially different in *kind*, for it is directed toward an essentially different *object*. A moral element is wanting in the love answering to the element wanting in the object. It is the idolatry of a self from which God is absent. An object of self-compassion I may rightly be; but this implies a desire of self-restoration, and of restoration to God. And it is only as I "lose myself,"* surrender my self-predominance, and welcome God back again to His throne within, that my regard for myself can be morally good.

But how does this view of self-predominance, as the characteristic of all sin, accord with the existence of those benevolent affections which are admitted to belong to our moral constitution? And may not guilt be incurred by the misdirection of our benevolent affections, as well as by the excess of our self-regard? One reply will meet these two questions; and may, possibly, supply the defect with which Müller's answer is thought to be chargeable. Man *is* capable of disinterested deeds as far as his fellow-man is concerned; deeds which have not self, as opposed to another human being, for their object. The first sin of Adam appears to have consisted partly of mistaken sympathy with Eve. But the question is not one merely between man and

* Matt. xvi. 25.

man, or one of ordinary selfishness; it is a question between God and man, or one of self-assertion to the exclusion of God. All man's actions capable of a moral quality are either deliberate and voluntary or spontaneous and impulsive. If voluntary, the charge is that however right they may be in relation to his fellow-man, they have no relation whatever to God. They are the offspring only of a human will which confesses no allegiance to the Divine will; so that, in relation to God, they are selfish. But the *disinterested* class of actions are those commonly which are impulsively performed, and which are susceptible of moral approbation, and of being consciously placed in relation to the Divine will, only *after* their performance; and the charge is that this is not done. The performer does not trace them beyond himself, but absorbs the admiration they excite. Until performed, they can possess no moral character whatever, for they are instinctive or impulsive; and when performed, he takes the entire credit to himself. Here, then, are two classes of actions: the small class in which he regards himself as his own beginning; and the large remainder, in which he is both beginning and end. God is in neither. Self, as distinct from God, prevails in both.

Two half views of sin.

All profound views of sin have regarded it either negatively as the privation of good, or positively as selfishness. "Evil (says Augustine) has no nature of its own; but the loss of good has received the name of evil."* "The principle of excessive self-love (says Plato) is the cause of all the errors which every man at various times falls into."† These are the two halves of one truth, corresponding to the twofold change denoted by the

*Quia nec illa effectio est, sed defectio. (de Civ. Dei, xii. 7.)

†Laws, 371. E.

first sin, and answering to the degeneracy and the depravity disclosed by every subsequent transgression. Primarily, and in relation to God, evil is the non-recognition of our dependence on Him, and the consequent privation or absence of love to Him; and secondarily, in relation to man, it attains a substantive existence as selfishness, directing his life, and sustaining a conflict with the Divine will, in a course of actual disobedience. Man becomes to himself a new center of action. "The relation of the subject to itself intead of to God (remarks Müller) being the point in which all the efforts and tendencies of sin centralize, sin thus becomes not merely disorder but a *perverted order*, not merely dissolution of unity but a false concentration of human existence, a perverted totality. It dissolves the true unity in order to erect a false one in its place." The negative conception of evil alone would lead to defective views of human responsibility and guilt; the positive conception alone would generate superficial views of man's depravity. Truth requires the combination of the two. Augustine, indeed, more than hints at this union, when he says, "the first act of our evil will was rather a defection from the work of God to its own work, than any real work; and the fruit of such a tree could not but be evil, because it was connatural with itself, and not according to the will of God."*

Man's early consciousness of evil.

Our third question, then, is answered: man's transmitted degeneracy is sufficient to account for the universality of his depravity. And will it not also account for the earliness of his consciousness of evil? Even at the time of his transition from the instinctive to the accountable state, the mind of the young human being is far from being a *tabula rasa* destitute of all *tendency* to evil.

* De Civ. Dei, xiv. 11.

Like the mere animal he comes into a system of fixed relations in respect to which his every movement and desire is right or wrong.* He is wrong a thousand times before he is capable of being guilty. Even the first man himself, had he not been Divinely instructed, could have arrived at the knowledge of right respecting many of those relations only by first violating them. The infant can be taught this knowledge only by slow degrees. Much of it comes to him by painful experience. During the time he is acquiring it, he lives amid sensuous objects, in the domain of the appetites and passions. Here, the animal side of his constitution, the part which is rooted in nature and subject to its necessary laws, is daily acquiring strength. Tempers, propensities, and appearances very similar to those which in after-life he feels to be sinful, are as yet only wrong. Every tripping step, every pain, every check, every perception that he is wrong, awakens in him a sense of self-dissatisfaction and discord, and forms part of that training by which he will soon become conscious of a moral emotion. Hitherto, however, his history is only a history of effects. He himself has not truly and properly caused. Now, all the effects and impressions of which he has been the recipient, and all the tendencies which the inferior part of his nature has been receiving, are taken with him when he passes into the sphere of moral responsibility. And hence, let him begin his contest with moral evil as early in life as he may, he will yet be conscious of something wrong anterior to all his efforts. And this will account for that sense of inward contradiction, that collision of freedom and necessity, which is felt when that which had been known only to be wrong is first felt to be guilty. As it comes from the earthly side

* Man Primeval, pp. 274–279.

of his constitution, it is subject to the laws of nature, and appears to be inevitable; but as it is adopted by the free will—the very ground of his personality—it is felt to be resistible. In adopting that which he might have resisted, he feels that he has put forth a power—has become a cause. So that while the act, as a temptation, originated in the dark, fixed, irresponsible part of his constitution, as a sin, it truly and properly springs from his will. Wherever, and however, it may have taken its rise as a desire, as a sin it has a distinct beginning, and that beginning caused by the will. Beyond this new, this spiritual cause, it can not, as sin, be traced. Here, the individuality of the man links on to the race. The degeneracy is derived, the depravity in which it issues is consciously his own. In other words, our sinfulness is not caused by our degeneracy, though it is the consequence of it.

Doctrine of derived degeneracy defensible.

If our exposition of the subject required that we should also vindicate that constitution of our nature by which its degeneracy is transmitted, we might enlarge on such facts as the following:—first, that, according to our view, guilt is in no real sense ascribed to the young human being until he himself has willed and accepted evil. His personal responsibility begins only when he himself becomes a consciously voluntary agent. Secondly, that the invariableness of depravity in every one who has reached the state of voluntary agency is not to be confounded with inevitableness in the sense of physical necessity. If the certainty of its existence in every moral agent is a fact of history, so also is the voluntariness of its existence a fact of consciousness—a proof this that the will is left free. Were it not so, depravity could not be felt to involve guilt, and repentance and improvement would be no duties.

Thirdly, that the universality of human depravity betrays only the universal absence of the right dispositions, or, at least, of the proper strength of the right dispositions. Now all that God owes to accountable beings are the powers essential to accountability, implying, of course, the absence of all necessarily overpowering force. He can not owe to them also a disposition to employ these powers aright, so as infallibly to secure obedience. This would be either to make failure impossible, or else to remove all responsibility from the creature, and to devolve it entirely on the Creator. For the presence of such dispositions man is held responsible, just because the power and means of acquiring and exercising them are among the grounds of his accountability. He is blameworthy, not for being destitute of any of the elements of responsibility, but for possessing without employing them aright.

Fourthly, that while the invariableness of depravity discloses an ultimate law of the creature's dependence, it no more casts a doubt on man's responsible adequacy than the fall of Adam did. For he sinned, not owing to any degeneracy, or to the withdrawment of any such provision from the point at which he fell. *There* he had been left to his own responsible powers. The withdrawment of the special provision from every other point took place *in consequence* of his failure in that particular. So that the difficulty with which we are now dealing is only the recurrence of the original difficulty respecting the entrance of sin. The depravity of every separate individual is only an additional aspect of the general question respecting "the *origin* of evil." Explain (we might say) how sin is possible in a sinless being, and we doubt not we shall be in a condition to explain and vindicate that constitution of things by which man's original loss and his transmitted degeneracy are permitted to result in universal depravity.

As a fact, it needs no defense in peculiar from us.

In reality, however, the vindication of such a constitution—if, indeed, any vindication be necessary—devolves alike on all who believe in a personal God and the fact of the universality of sin. Our acceptance of the Biblical account of the subject, loads us, in this respect, with no peculiar responsibility. Even if we reject that account, the *fact* of human sinfulness remains. The Bible only finds it. The call to explain the fact belongs as much to the Deist, who believes only in the existence of moral government, as it does to us. While, as we think, the view which we take, in the light of Scripture, gives us the advantage of seeing the nature of the required remedy, and of being prepared to welcome it. The "Second Adam," by introducing himself into the line of transmitted humanity, so as to become truly related to all its inheritors, can not only restore our disturbed relations to God, but, by recovering for us a Divine influence more abiding than that which was originally lost, can heal alike our degeneracy and the depravity in which it results.

Man's constitution is still a means of Divine manifestation.

Resuming our proposition, that the constitution of man continued after the Fall unimpaired, as a means of Divine manifestation, we have merely to point to the fact that he was still the subject of moral government. No power was lost from the soul. His emotions retained their susceptibility, though diverted from their highest object. His power of moral discrimination was not destroyed, though overruled. His will remained as active and energetic as before. His chosen motives came now, indeed, from an inferior domain; the right disposition of his powers was gone, each being placed in a new and a false relation to the others, but all remained. Man's second sin was as free as his first.

His individuality not merged in the family.

It is important to remember, also, that, owing to the indestructibleness of man's responsible nature, his *individuality* is not merged in his social relations, but is carried on into them. The individual is made for the family only in a subordinate sense. The family exists for the individual in this respect, that it attains its own and best by enabling him to attain his end, and only as it helps him to attain it. It is here that the first crude and overbearing impulse of his personality to assert itself in all directions begins to be restrained. Other personal beings are here found to enter into the sphere of his personality, limiting and defining its activity. His blind wishes and aims are reduced to personal rights as the only form in which they can dovetail in with the rights of others. And every step of the process renders his consciousness of his own accountableness more wakeful and profound.

Condition of fallen man is the condition of his posterity.

We are led to expect, further, that the *condition* of the first man, as exposed to suffering and death, will be the condition of all his posterity. And it is so. Long as had been the lives of his antediluvian successors, and varied as had been their moral character, concerning each of those whose names are on record (with a single exception) it is said—"and he died." "Death reigned from Adam." And, as if to put the question at rest, that their death was not the result of their own personal transgression, we find that infants, incapable of personal transgression, died also. "In Adam *all* die."

"But are not the young of animals, though unconnected with man, subject to the law of mortality also?" Yes, and the young of both die by the operation of the same natural law, though not for the same moral reason. The animal dies in consequence of the operation of a law from which it was never exempt; but the infant in consequence of the operation of the same law from which the father of the race was conditionally exempt; but which exemption, on the violation of that condition, was repealed, and the pre-existing law of death in the animal kingdom was allowed to prevail universally. Man was recalled to the condition *above* which for a time he had been raised, and was allowed to fall down as a sinner to the level of the more ancient law of animal suffering and death. Such, indeed, would have been our condition if no probationary law had existed, but the first man had been guilty of some other act of disobedience. Then, as now, death would have been introduced objectively by Adam, and would have been continued as a law of sentient existence, from which our race had never known exemption. Notwithstanding the perverting tendency of sin, then, man still retained the natural capacity with which he had been originally endowed for knowing, appreciating, voluntarily promoting, and enjoying the Divine manifestation. Not less did his constitution and condition illustrate the power, and wisdom, and goodness of God than on the day of his creation. And even more strikingly than at first did they disclose the holiness and justice of which they were designed to be the special manifestation.*

Thirdly, direct Divine communications.

The law now under consideration leads us to expect that the third means of human education and of Divine manifestation enjoyed

* Man Primeval, pp. 471, 472.

by innocent man—namely, direct supernatural communications—will be brought forward into this succeeding economy. If no power had been lost from the human constitution, neither had any law of moral government been repealed, nor any perfection of the Divine character obscured. The theology of unfallen man, as implied especially in the primal law, was—a powerful, wise, and beneficent Creator; that Creator his equitable moral Governor; and immortal happiness in prospect as the reward of his obedience; and a threatened death or loss as the deserved penalty of disobedience. And this was no less the theory of fallen man.

The new revelation of Mercy involved no withdrawment of the claims of Justice; and this perhaps, in the present connection, is the only point calling for remark. The sin of man was no frustration of moral government; for that government showed itself capable of enforcing its sanctions. With man's first moment of conscious guilt commenced a process of self-punishment, for that very consciousness involved suffering. The external sentence only interpreted his fears, and ratified his self-pronounced condemnation. Nor was he less a subject of moral government after Mercy had arrested him in his guilty descent than he was before. That mercy involved no relaxation of law, no apology for the government under which man had fallen. So far from arraigning the equity of that rule, mercy supported it, forgiveness proclaimed it. Sacrifice and expiation were the methods of indemnifying and celebrating it. Mercy left man in the hand of justice still, and only rescued him from its punishment; and just so much of mercy as there was in the rescue was there of justice in the punishment. Hence, the original government was still in force. Cain found himself under law not less than Adam. Each man, as he sinned, incurred the penalty. The judgment of the flood announced that justice had abated none of its requirements; that law, "holy, just, and good," as at the beginning, was as strong to vindicate itself against the last transgression as against the first.

Whatever was implied in the original institution of the Sabbath, continued to be implied, for the Sabbath, "made for *man*," continued to be obligatory. To what extent it was observed, is not at present the question; though there is strong probable evidence, from the practice of measuring time by weeks,* that it was never entirely lost sight of, and that in certain families, at least, it continued to be applied to holy purposes. Not only did the original reason of the Sabbatic appointment remain; it increased with every addition which was made to man's knowledge of God. The impartation of such knowledge to the young would form part of the appropriate employment of the patriarchal Sabbath, as it did subsequently of the Jewish Sabbath, into which probably it was copied. For the pious among the patriarchs could not fail to perceive that the highest design alike, of the Sabbath and of the family economy, was, "'that they should make (such truths) known to their children; that the generation to come might know them, even the children which should be born, who should arise and declare them to their children, that they might set their hope in God, and not forget the works of God, but keep His commandments;" that the knowledge of the laws and purposes of the Divine manifestation might be carried forward from age to age. In other words, the Divine Procedure in the

* Gen. vii., 4; viii., 10, 12.

past is never lost to the present or the future. A new stage of Divine manifestation is not a commencement *de novo*, standing in isolation from all that has gone before, but presupposes, includes, and even promotes it.

CHAPTER III.

THE NEW ASPECT OF THE DIVINE CHARACTER, AND THE MEANS OF ITS MANIFESTATION; A REMEDIAL ECONOMY THROUGH THE FAMILY.

Law stated.

A THIRD Law of the Divine manifestation leads us to expect that the present stage will be found in advance of the preliminary or Paradisiacal constitution, and "will exhibit the evolution of new laws, facts, or means of manifestation."

Nature an ever-unfolding revelation.

External *nature* would for ages continue to present to antediluvian man a preternatural aspect. In emerging from the garden into the great Edenic region—comprehending probably large portions of Asia and Africa*—he took possession, in effect, of a "new world;" and, for him, it was boundless. Experience was then taking its first lessons. Every step into the wilderness brought to light a new creation. Every discovery was virtually the imposition of a new law. Even the succession of day and night, the vicissitudes of the seasons, and the annual renewal of the face of the earth, had yet to be classed among the uniformities of nature. The phenomena of nature, regular and familiar as they at length became, would all appear, as they arose first into the hori-

* Man Primeval, p. 18.

zon of human observation, to be so many wonders. The progress of civilization would be constantly multiplying and magnifying wonders. And even to the last, probably, the phenomena of the heavens would continue to possess, for antediluvian man, the exciting and alarming interest of preternatural interpositions of the Deity.

Direct Divine manifestation must now precede the unfolding of man's constitution.

Had man's career been unimpeded by sin, the original order of the Divine procedure would have led us to look, secondly, for an advance in the means of manifestation afforded by the natural constitution and social condition of man. But sin had interposed an obstacle to this orderly progression. Between man individual and man social the Fall had intervened. In order to the resumption of the great plan, therefore, and as a part of it, a direct interposition is necessary—an interposition which shall meet the twofold exigency of the case, by both remedying man's objective condition in relation to God, and by restoring his character to holiness.* Apart from such a provision, the Divine manifestation can not proceed, and man's earthly history is at an end. Our order of inquiry, therefore, is now reversed. Man must now stand aside till God has spoken. Before we can resume our investigation of the human being as a means of Divine manifestation, we must await a new and direct unvailing of the Divine character. The manifestation of God by man must wait a Divine manifestation to him.

Accordingly, the law which is now guiding our inquiries warrants us in expecting such advance in the direct means of Divine revelation. This might have been now looked for even if man had not fallen, but had come out of his

* *Supra*, p. 14.

probation without a stain; for progressiveness is a law of the Divine procedure. But the fact of his having sinned and fallen—virtually essaying to displace God, and to make himself the end of creation—supplies a new and a most urgent reason, entirely distinct from the designed progressiveness of the plan, why, if he is to be spared, an additional revelation should now be made. His mere punishment, indeed, would have been just; but, elsewhere—in the doom of the sinning angels—the fires of Justice were already kindled; so that even if the earth had been left to career through immensity, a stricken and "a wandering star," it would have been only re-proclaiming an attribute already known. But if the law of progressiveness is in force, and if, besides, the Divine manifestation is to be continued *to* man, as well as by him, then new and peculiar means are necessary, both in order to vindicate the various stages through which the manifestation has already been carried —indeed, to vindicate its commencement at all, when such a crisis as sin has brought was fully and clearly in the Divine view—and also to vindicate its continuance still, and visibly to place the continuation of the great process on an adequate basis. Accordingly, the course which the infinitely blessed God was pleased to take, and which had ever formed a part of His all-comprehending plan, was one of MERCY;—a course, the details and wonders of which are still only in the process of evolution.

Means fundamental to the economy to be distinguished from those added afterward.

In specifying the truths and facts belonging to this new stage of the Divine procedure, it is proper to distinguish between those which are coeval with, and fundamental to, the economy, and those which were superadded from time to time, as man needed or was prepared for them. The truths fundamental to the preceding dispensation, were essential also to this new economy, were presupposed by it, and assumed into it; namely, a powerful, wise, and beneficent Creator, the object of man's worship; that Creator his equitable moral Governor; and immortal life in prospect as the reward of his obedience, and death, standing for all that is opposed to life, as the deserved penalty of disobedience. The new means of revelation made necessary by man's changed relations, consisted in a remarkable Promise, and in the institute of Sacrifice significant of the manner in which the promise would be fulfilled; and these were laid at the basis of the dispensation. All the other disclosures and events which we shall have to notice, were either the natural illustrations and developments of this primary theology, or else were accorded by God as man's condition appeared to require them. These belong to the law of development.

The first Promise.

The First Sin was immediately followed by the First Promise—the promise of deliverance. "I will put enmity between thee (the serpent) and the woman, and between thy seed and her seed; he shall bruise thy head, and thou shalt bruise his heel."*

Serpent and his seed.

But who, or what is to be understood by the *serpent* and his *seed?* Our reply to this question will depend on the light in which we view the Biblical account of the Fall. From the time of Philo,† and of the Grecian Jews in general, it has been received by many, in every age, as a sacred *allegory;* and we are free to admit that, provided the doctrinal import of the account is retained—namely, the trial of man's obedience to the will of God, and its guilty and judicial issue—the great

* Gen. iii. 15.

† Sacrarum Legum Alleg. Lib. iii.

point, as to this particular representation, is secured. According to Coleridge, who agrees substantially with Origen's hypothesis,* the serpent "is the pervertible understanding (as distinguished from the Reason), the *sophistic* principle, the wily tempter to evil by counterfeit good, the pander and advocate of the passions and appetites; ever in league with, and first applying to, the *Desire*, as the inferior nature in man, the *woman* in our humanity; and through the desire prevailing on the will." And his seed is "the same serpentine and perverted understanding, . . . henceforth sentenced and bound over to the service of the animal nature, its needs, and its cravings, dependent on the senses for all its materials, with the world of sense for its appointed sphere:" "upon thy belly shalt thou go, and dust shalt thou eat all the days of thy life."†

Is the account allegorical?

The reason for giving the narrative an allegorical interpretation—namely, that if it were found in any other work of Eastern origin, it would be so construed—admits of easy reply. For, first, if this be an adequate test by which to distinguish the allegorical from the historical, *all* the *supernatural* of the Bible (the element which makes the Bible what it is) must be regarded as allegorical also, for such it would be regarded if found in any other work not Divinely authenticated. Secondly, it forgets that the very fact that other books actually contain some such accounts, implies that at some time, and in some form, the reality itself has truly existed. Thirdly, it ignores the peculiar character and claim of the Book in which the account is given, and degrades it to an equality with other books. Fourthly, it overlooks the unique and

* De princ. iv. 16. Contra Cels. iv. 40.

† Aids to Reflection; First Edition, pp. 251–253.

tremendous nature of the occasion on which the instrumentality in question is said to have been employed, and lets it down to the level of an ordinary occasion. Fifthly, if the difficulty arises from erroneously supposing the *natural* serpent to have spoken, it should disappear the moment the presence and agency of an evil spirit are recognized; or if it arises from the preternatural character of the event, the answer is, that to suppose "the first sin could come about in a natural manner, is to regard that sin itself as a natural thing; while, on the contrary, it was just that kind of thing which is most unnatural, and which has only *become* natural." Sixthly, the permission of evil at all under the government of the All-perfect is the great mystery, compared with which the present and every similar question is but as the light dust of the balance; and if it be admitted that the introduction of sin into a new race of intelligences be an object likely to call forth the activity of beings already evil, the only question which remains is, whether the instrumentality said to have been employed was suited to the end aimed at. In addition, it is to be remarked that the allegorical view does not recommend itself by conveying any superior instruction, for all the lessons which it teaches are equally deducible from the literal interpretation.

Or historical?

The reasons for regarding the Biblical account of the Fall as historical, are these: It is organically united with the narrative of the creation, which takes the usual formula of Hebrew history—"these are the generations." It appears in a Book which by uniformly and distinctly recognizing one living and personal God, and by distinctly defining man's moral relation to Him, leaves no room for a mythology. The fact that, while every other nation had a series of myths or a system of mythology, no one has ever pretended to find more than single and detached myths in the Hebrew Scriptures, casts discredit on such pretense. It is recorded in the old, simple, objective style of historical narrative; reminding us of the significant fact that, unlike other nations of antiquity with whom the poetic element preceded the historical, Hebrew poetry always looks back to Hebrew history. While the mythological, moreover, is always national, local, and particular, the Biblical account, both of the Creation and the Fall, has the character of true universality. Besides, it would have been deeply revolting to the reverential piety of an Israelite to represent his own figments as Divine history. The account also, in connection with that of the creation, forms the introduction to an acknowledged history—that of the Theocracy. It is the only account which, from its view of sin, assumes and really possesses a historical character. In all the ancient accounts, apart from Biblical influence, sin is either an unreal or an eternal thing. Pantheism, as in the Egyptian, Phenician, and Babylonian traditions, by treating sin as an unreality, renounces its historical existence. Dualism, of which Parseeism, Brahmaism, and the later Manichæism, are forms, by regarding it as eternal, make a first sin, as the act of a free being—impossible. It is only where both the finitude and the individual liberty of man are apprehended, as they are in Genesis, that the nature of sin is recognized, and a first sin is possible.* The Biblical account, too, is full of historical details and facts. Thus, it contains a minute geographical description of Paradise: the condition of mankind, threatened in this narrative as a punishment, actually exists: and the account of the same human progenitors,

* Hävernik's Introduction to the Pentateuch, § 15, p. 100.

here brought into view, is continuously carried forward as history. Then, again, sin and salvation—the two fundamental ideas of the narrative—form the germ of which the entire Bible is the development. In addition to all which, the historical character of the narrative is repeatedly recognized in the New Testament.*

Receiving the narrative of the Fall, then, as historical, and applying to it those rules of interpretation which its optical and anthropopathic nature obviously demands, we arrive at the following conclusions: that a certain *natural* serpent appeared on a particular occasion to surpass in sagacity every animal nature with which our first parents were at that time acquainted; that this serpent, selected by an invisible agent for its pleasing and attractive motion, color, and form, appeared even to speak—although, as the serpent is destitute of the organs of speech, the voice must have proceeded from the unseen Tempter, of whom at that time they knew nothing; and that, in the same manner, when the temptation had succeeded, the apparent serpent and its race were denounced, although the denunciation fell, in reality, not on the visible instrument, but on the unseen agent of evil; and it should be remembered that the sentence was addressed, not to them, but to the unseen intelligence whom it concerned, and who could well penetrate through the symbolical language in which his doom was pronounced. In the New Testament, indeed, the presence of this spiritual agent in the natural serpent is distinctly recognized.† Even the earlier writings of the Apocrypha point to the same

* Rom. v. 12–19; 1 Cor. xv. 21, 22; 2 Cor. ii. 3; 1 Tim. ii. 13, 14, etc.

† 1 John, viii. 44; 2 Cor. xi. 3–14; Rev. xii. 9; xx. 2.

fact.* And, probably, our first parents themselves soon afterward came to the right general conclusions on the subject. But at the period of the Fall, when their deep sense of injury demanded that the *occasion* of their transgression should not go unpunished, and when the punishment to be inflicted on the invisible foe could not be made obvious to them, the sentence *appeared* to them to fall where it was due (although no change in the structure or habits of the serpent actually took place,† only its peculiar reptilian habits became symbols of deep disgrace)—thus gratifying their sense of right, developing their feeling of the evil of sin, and inculcating the great doctrine that every tempter to evil shall be punished.‡

The seed of the woman.

Who or what is to be understood by the *seed* of the woman? That it has a collective

* Wisdom, ii. 24. The same doctrine is taught in the Zend-Avesta, the ancient and sacred book of the Parsees, Th. 3, pp. 84, 85.

† Is it not remarkable, as a coincidence, that there should have been a period in the ancient history of animal life when reptiles were not the degraded class which they now are? During "the reptile dynasty" of the secondary ages, the shrunken and footless serpent of later times was unknown. "The Iguanodon must have been quite as tall as the elephant; the Megalosaurus must have at least equaled the rhinoceros; the Hylæosaurus would have outweighed the hippopotamus. And when reptiles that rivaled in size our largest mammals inhabited the land, other reptiles, Icthyosaurs, Plesiosaurs, and Cetiosaurs possessed the sea. * * * Nor did the Hand that makes no slips in its working 'form the crooked serpent,' footless, groveling, venom-bearing—the authorized type of a fallen and degraded nature—until after the introduction of the mammals."—Hugh Miller's Footprints of the Creator, pp. 294–298.

‡ On this subject see Hengstenberg's Christology, vi. c. 2. *Art.* Adam in Kitto's Bibl. Cyclo. Knapp's Theology, § 75. Storr's Comment. de Protevangelio in his Opuscula, tom. II.; and Bishop Horsley's Sermons, vol. ii. 38–54.

and secondary reference to the entire body of the faithful, there can be no doubt; for the triumph of the Deliverer is the virtual triumph of all whom he delivers. And hence the cheering declaration of the Apostle, "The God of peace shall bruise Satan under your feet shortly."* But that its primary and principal reference is to a single individual among the posterity of Eve—however dimly this fact was apprehended at first—appears from several New Testament allusions. Even two of the ancient Jewish paraphrases—the Targum of Jonathan and that of Jerusalem—while interpreting the *seed*, of the Jews collectively, expressly refer the fulfillment of the promise to "the days of the King Messiah." Indeed, if the term *seed* is only to be considered collectively, of the *posterity* of Eve, both of our first parents are excluded from the benefit of the promise. For, although the conduct of some of their posterity might operate beneficially for those who came after, it is not conceivable how it could so operate retrospectively. It is only by supposing, then, that the Deliverer should be an unique individual, and his deliverance of a nature calculated to benefit all alike, in every age, from "the foundation of the world,"† who might desire to avail themselves of it, that our progenitors could be regarded as included in the promise. And though this might not have occurred to them at first, the longer they lived, and especially as death approached, this was the only view of the promise which was calculated to console them. In harmony with this interpretation, we read that, "when the fullness of the time was come, God sent forth His Son made of a woman."‡ And "for this purpose the Son of God was manifested, that He might destroy the works of

* Romans, xvi. 20. † 1 Peter, i. 20; Romans, iii. 25.

‡ Galatians, iv. 4.

the devil."* He was the SEED so pre-eminently that, for the bearing of it, woman was continued, and that but for the bearing of it, the race would have been discontinued: so pre-eminently, that of all who would be born prior to His advent the most distinguished would be, at best, only partial types; and of all born after, the greatest and the best would be only His imitators and servants.

Import of the promise.

Here, then, was projected a dim shadow of the great plan of mercy. What was the cheering intimation which it was calculated to convey to the minds of our first parents? To say that they could not recognize in it a distinct prophecy of a Redeemer as we do, is only saying that as new light has been poured on it in successive ages, its full import has been more clearly developed, and more comprehensively understood. "This promise, as it is the first, is also the most indefinite." But, even to their minds, it must have forcibly conveyed the impression that their sin and suffering would certainly be remedied; that this deliverance would be the result of a struggle in which the seed of the woman would sustain only partial injury; that their enemy or enemies would sustain final and fatal defeat; and, perhaps, that this triumph would be achieved by a Being who should be, in a peculiar sense, the offspring of the woman.

That this promise was especially seasonable and necessary for our first parents, is evident from the self-abased and trembling condition in which it found them. That the figure of a conflict and a triumph in which the promise was conveyed was eminently suitable, will appear when it is remembered that they themselves had just been conscious of

* 1 John, iii. 8. Also Heb. ii. 14; Gal. iii. 16. On the latter passage, see Tholuck on the Hebrews, App. to Diss. I.

a struggle—of a mental and moral conflict—in which they had sustained a fearful defeat, and that they were probably filled with indignation against the supposed occasion of their transgression. That it was of vast importance in the Divine estimation of Him who announced it may be inferred from the circumstance, that no sooner had He convicted man of his guilt than He uttered it, even before He announced the impending penalty. Not only "in the midst of wrath did He remember mercy;" but by the precedence, in the order of time, which He gave to the promise, MERCY rejoiced against judgment even in this first moment of her advent. It gave man a moral horizon, and kindled in it a star. Its power of awakening expectation and inspiring hope appears from the fact that, having been once dropped, like a seed of the tree of life, into the human mind, it never ceased to germinate and flourish, though the product speedily and extensively degenerated.

In close connection with the giving of this PROTEVANGELIUM, or First Gospel, an event is recorded,* from which we infer that it was immediately followed by the Divine institution of Sacrifice. And our object will be to show that the institute is related to the promise in meaning as closely as it is in time—that, together, they form consistent and organic parts of a great system of revelation. But in order to this we must first determine the special truths which sacrifices were designed to express; and prior to this we must ascertain the nature of their origin.

Institution of sacrifice, was it Divine?

Now, that sacrifices were not of human invention, but of Divine institution, appears morally certain, we think, from such considerations as these:—That it is not antecedently probable that

* Genesis, iv. 2–8.

God would leave man in ignorance of the manner in which he should acceptably worship Him; and yet the first act of acceptable worship which we find man performing is that of animal sacrifice. That this improbability is greatly increased by the fact that God had not only inspired man with hope by the language of promise, but had even condescended to instruct him to clothe his body with a skin-vesture; and surely He who thus condescended to meet man's bodily wants would not abandon him to his own inventions respecting the cravings of his higher nature. That the *universality* of expiatory offerings* proves man's deep consciousness of such a want; and yet, if they were not Divinely appointed, no provision was made to meet the exigence. That if God had left man uninstructed, it is not likely that man would have *so early* devised *any* settled method of his own for approaching God; yet here we find the first members of the first family coming before the Lord with offerings as their *familiar*, *established*, and *only* mode of worship. That of all methods of worship, that of shedding blood—of *sacrificing an animal*—is one of the least likely to have originated in the human mind; and yet here we find a member of the first family—one who had probably never slaughtered an animal for himself†—reject-

* See Magee's Disc. on Atonement and Sacrifice, No. v. xxxviii. lvi. Prof. Ernst von Lasaulx on the Expiatory Sacrifices of the Greeks and Romans; Bibliotheca Sacra, vol. i. p. 368, etc.

† The fact that Abel was "a keeper of sheep" suggests the question, For what purpose did he keep them, if not chiefly for *sacrifice?* For surely they would not be slain solely for their skins. The notion that a portion of the victim was eaten by the offerer is opposed by the fact that the *holocaust*, or "whole burnt offering," was *entirely* consumed on the altar, and that the word so translated, עֹלָה, is used to designate the car-

ing the more simple and natural oblation of fruits and flowers, and confidently calculating on pleasing God by putting an animal to death. That the *Divine acceptance* of the first sacrifice on record confirms the conviction that the rite was instituted by God; for as it is a fundamental rule in the worship of God that "in vain do they worship me, teaching for doctrines the commandments of men,"* if the first sacrifice on record was not offered in vain, but was honored with the Divine acceptance, it follows that it was not a human invention, but a Divine appointment.† And that the acceptance of Abel's offering, and the rejection of Cain's, was not owing merely to a difference in the worshipers, but also to *a difference in their offerings;* for not only is the Divine approbation of Noah's offering attributed to its sacrificial nature,‡ but as the faith which the Apostle celebrates, when speaking of Abel, was a faith which led the patriarchs to acts of obedience,§ who can doubt that the faith of Abel consisted also in obedience to a Divine appointment? On these grounds we conclude that the institution of sacrifice was of Divine origin.

Significance of sacrifice.

Additional reasons for this conviction will appear in proceeding to consider the *significance* or *symbolical nature* of sacrifice. What, then, is the

liest recorded sacrifices after that of Abel, Gen. viii. 20; xx. 7, 8, 13; leaving it to be inferred that Abel's sacrifice was of the same kind; although, in relation to it the more general term *offering* is employed, which is applied also to that of Cain. There is no ground to believe that animal food had then been thought of; indeed, it is unknown in many parts of Asia to this day. See also Magee, No. lxiv. vol. ii. pp. 230, 231.

* Mark, vii. 7.

† *Hallett* on Heb. xi. 4, in his *Continuation of Peirce on the Epistle to the Hebrews;* and *Faber's Prim. Sacrifice*, p. 183.

‡ Gen. viii. 20, 21.

§ Heb. xi.

fundamental idea of sacrifice? It can not be that of a gift merely, as an expression of gratitude. Such an offering man might have presented, while yet unfallen, denoting by it how entirely he felt himself to belong to God, how perfectly his own will harmonized with the will of God, and how profoundly conscious of joy he was on account of it. But "before Adam sinned, he was himself an offering, and hence had no need of an offering."* Where total union of will exists, where all that belongs to man belongs to God in a yet higher sense, the special consecration of a part would have been felt to be inadequate and unsatisfactory. But this union of the will of man with the will of God no longer existed; sin had disturbed it, and rebelled against it. Any offering, therefore, which ignored the fact of this awful rupture, or which rated it at less than fatal, would have been an acted falsehood—a repetition of the original offense with aggravation—an indignity to the Divine nature. Nor could the offering embody mere external and material conceptions, or be irrespective of the mind and *will* of the offerer. This man's own nature forbade. For, having revolted, he could not conceal from himself a deep-seated sense of guilt; and having, by the same act which dissevered him from God, broken up the harmony of his own nature, he could not but carry about with him a restlessness for restoration. Every sigh for self-restoration was a sigh for return to God; and the converse. The only offering, therefore, which could now be relevant, was one by which man might plead guilty to his disturbed relationship with God, and earnestly aim at reparation. Hence, the idea lying at the foundation of all sacrificial worship was

* Quoted by *Thobuck on the Ep. to the Heb.* vol. ii. p. 252, from a work of Rabbi Jacob, of Metz.

that of self-surrender, by substitution, and in the hope of pardon—a deep consciousness of having merited the death inflicted on the vicarious animal, and an intense desire that the insulted Deity would accept the immolation as a means of compensation. It was an acted deprecation, for a reason. The will which had offended was seen symbolically supplicating, on expiatory grounds, the will which had been violated. In each of the two parties, the *will* was the supreme point; for it was an affair of will—of personality and government—which had made the sacrifice necessary. Springing from the requirements of holiness in the Divine nature, it responded to the cries of conscience in the human nature. The two natures could not be satisfied with less. Deep called unto deep, "without the shedding of blood is no remission of sins." And, hence, the *purest* sacrifice was preferred, not only as the most worthy of the recipient, but also as the furthest removed from the guilty condition of the offerer, and most condemnatory of it; and the *costliest* sacrifice, as most expressive of the fact that there was nothing which he had not forfeited, and which might not have been demanded; and the most *voluntary*, as that alone which could express the idea of self-abnegation—of the offerer "divesting himself of his own subjectivity" and surrendering his "innermost" to God;—all vividly denoting the idea which forms the essence of true religion—the offering up of self—the readjustment once more, by subordination, of our will to the Divine will, and the consequent recovery of a Divine life. Subjectively, then, the institution of sacrifice finds its reason in man's deep consciousness of guilt and desire of reunion with the Supreme will; and, objectively, in a Divine appointment of holiness and mercy which made such restoration possible.

Was sacrifice piacular?

Now, that the patriarchal and primitive sacrifices were regarded as *piacular* is established by all the evidence of which the case admits. Thus, of Job it is recorded that "he offered burnt-offerings" for his sons, for he said, "*it may be that my sons have sinned.*"* When "Noah builded an altar unto the Lord, and offered burnt-offerings upon the altar, the Lord smelled *a savor of rest* [or *propitiation*]; and the Lord said, I will not again curse the ground any more."† He was appeased. So also, of the first recorded offerings, it is said, that Cain brought of his *fruits* and Able of his *flock;* "and the Lord had respect unto Abel and to his offering, but unto Cain and to his offering He had not respect."‡ But why this distinction? Considered merely as eucharistic offerings, Cain's fruits, the products of his own tillage, were not less appropriate than the firstlings of Abel's flock. Regarded in the light of covenant pledges—of which a portion was eaten by the offerer—the oblation of Cain was even preferable to that of Abel, for animal food was yet unknown. The only inference is, that the reason of the Divine preference of Abel's sacrifice lay in its piacular nature; but that Cain, though sinful like his brother, and needing forgiveness, ignored the awful fact of his guilt, and thus converted his professed homage into an act of impenitence and insult. Still further is the expiatory nature of primitive sacrifices to be inferred from the Divine reply to Cain's anger at his rejection. "And the Lord said unto Cain, Why art thou wroth? and why is thy countenance fallen? If thou doest well, shalt thou not be accepted? And if thou doest not well, a sin-

* Job, i. 5; see also xlii. 7, 8.

† Gen. viii. 21, 22; comp. Lev. xxvi. 31.

‡ Gen. iv. 4–7.

offering coucheth at thy door."* Here is clearly the statement of a grand alternative; and it is implied that with neither member of it could Cain be justly dissatisfied. Let him render sinless obedience, and he shall find Divine acceptance as a perfect being; or else let him come as a penitent transgressor, suing for mercy through an expiatory sacrifice, and, like Abel, he shall be accepted. Thus early was redemption through a piacular medium appealed to as an already-established principle of the Divine administration.

The sentiments it was calculated to develop.

What, then, were the sentiments which sacrifices were calculated to develop in the mind of primeval man? Let the thrilling scene of the first sacrifice be imagined. Let the offerer be pictured, recent from his guilty fall, and with the last accents of his Maker still sounding in his ear. Let him be seen inflicting on the selected victim the fatal stroke—now, first, looking on death by violence—death inflicted by his own hand. Let him be traced through all the stages of the service, until the last palpitation of the animal has ceased—the life-blood has poured its last drop—the consuming flame has burnt out—and nothing but the ashes of the animal remain. How eminently was the impressive rite calculated to awaken sentiments such as these:—"No more can I come before God in the simple glow of gratitude and the confidence of innocence; I have sinned, I have sinned; the purpose for which life was bestowed upon me I have frus-

* The rendering of the last clause of this passage in the English version amounts to a truism. *Chattath*, translated "sin," denotes in the law a "sin-offering," Lev. vi. 19; ix. 15; Hosea iv. 8; etc.; and *rabatz*, translated "lieth," describes the recumbency of a beast. Lightfoot's Works, vol. vii. p. 209. Faber's *Origin of Expiatory Sacrifice*, p. 85, *Horæ Mosaicæ*, B. ii. § 3, c. 2.

trated; the only condition on which I could hope to retain it I have violated; I have brought my will in collision with the Supreme will; my offense is heinous, death its only proper punishment; I am unable, by any thing I can do, to merit exemption from the penalty; and, like this sacrifice, I deserve to die; but in the appointment of this awful rite, God has shown Himself to be full of mercy; the way of forgiveness may be through the substitution of an expiatory victim; but, whatever that way may be, I desire cordially to acquiesce in it; and, therefore, in faith and obedience I present this sacrifice; offering myself as I offer this blood; surrendering my forfeited life, that I may receive it back again as the free gift of God." How many of these reflections were present to the mind of Adam or of Abel, we know not. It is not to be supposed that every offerer could give to himself so distinct an account of what he was doing. But the fact that Abel sacrificed "by faith," determines that his *state of feeling* was in harmony with this Divine strain, and gave to the act this significance.

Promise and Sacrifice parts of a whole.

Now, as might have been expected, these primary means and movements of Mercy—the Promise and the Institute—are found united as integral parts of the same plan. If the one verbally announced deliverance, the other symbolically indicated the manner in which it would be effected. If the one pointed for its instrumental fulfillment to the woman, the other looked for its performance to the man. Each alike affirmed and respected man's free agency; for the promise which is addressed to faith, man may believe or reject; and the sacrifice which calls for obedience, he may perform or neglect—he is not forced to either. But, chiefly, both the promise and the institute strikingly unite in the production of this one effect—to impress man with a sense of his increased dependence on God. Related to God as he was previously at every point of his nature, and through every moment of his being, their special office is to keep him in the habitual recognition of his new and still profounder relationship. They find him guilty, and in that state they arrest and fix him; or rather, they require from him a permanent acknowledgment of the fact. They find him depraved; and they lead him in that state into the presence of God, as a being on whom the eye of Holiness can not rest complacently except through a medium of Divine origination. They find him helpless and self-condemned; and in proportion as he enters into their spirit and design, he confesses that his hope of deliverance is derived directly from God. His first sin was an effort at independence; his first acceptable act of worship, as a sinner, must be a profound acknowledgment that he is more dependent than ever. His first sin was an action; his first expression of sorrow must be an act of self-condemnation. And such is sacrifice—self-immolation "in a figure." His sin was a virtual diversion of all the kingdoms of nature which had been given into his hand that he as their interpreter and minister might give the glory of the whole to God; in his first sacrifice, he is to bring them all back again—for in the altar, the wood, and the victim, they were all present—and is thus to take them as the witnesses of his guilt in abusing them, and of his penitence and dependence in restoring them again to the Great Proprietor.

And thus the first promise and the first institute, like the first prohibition, were designed to impress man with a sense of his entire dependence, and to augment his motives of obedience; so that they belong, in this respect, to the one great system of means—proclaiming the same truths, and promoting the same end. And this principle, we repeat, we may expect to find pervading the whole economy of the Divine manifestation; exhibiting the blessed God as taking occasion from man's guilty and helpless condition to unfold a new aspect of his own all-sufficiency.

Arrest removed from man's evolution.

With this grand remedial arrangement on the part of God, the arrest was removed from the evolution of man. The God of holiness had appeared as the God of mercy, and therefore the manifestation of man individual was allowed to proceed to that of man social. Now, supposing sin had not intervened, we should surely have been justified in looking for a new illustration of the Divine character in the constitution of social man, on the same grounds in which we were led to expect it in the individual; for the command, "increase and multiply," preceded the Fall. The end proposed by the existence of man and his race was one; and every onward step in his history—and therefore his social development—was to be a step toward the attainment of that end. But the ground for expecting such progress now, so far from being diminished by the new arrangement of Mercy, is greatly increased. Every previous reason continues in force, and this new ground has been added to them—that the proposed remedy for man individual is to come instrumentally through the family. The very step in advance which sin had threatened to cut off is actually converted into the means of indefinite progress. On the highest ground, therefore, we are warranted to expect an advance in the means of the Divine manifestation in the constitution of the human family, on all that had preceded it in the animal kingdom.

Antecedent questions.

Prior to the existence of the first human family, the questions might, hypothetically, have been asked, What will be the nature of the relations between man and wife, between them and their descendants, and among these descendants themselves? What will be the strength, the tendency, the duration, and the distinctive characteristic of these relations? What will be the order of their importance? How will they modify each other; and how will they affect the multitudes that will be born? Will man live in isolation like some of the animal tribes? or in gregarious juxtaposition like others? or in a state of social intercommunion different from any thing which the earth has yet exhibited? This last might have been expected, as we have seen, from the essential difference both of man's constitution and of his destiny. Accordingly, we here find the evolution and existence of the domestic constitution; a constitution which was evidently contemplated at the institution of marriage, and subsequently pre-supposed in the giving of the first Promise, but the peculiar nature of which was yet to be developed.

Basis of the family laid in marriage.

The foundation of this new constitution was laid in the Divinely-instituted union of husband and wife. "Have ye not read (saith our Lord)* that He who made them [man and wife] at the beginning, made them [a] male and [a] female; [as intending to prevent both polygamy and divorce] and said [as the formal authentication of the great law of marriage already inserted in the constitution of human nature], For this cause [or, on account of entering into the married state] shall a man leave his father and mother [the nearest relation he had previously sustained], and cleave unto his wife, and

* Matthew, xix. 4–6, referring to Genesis, ii. 24.

they twain shall be one flesh. Wherefore, they are no more twain, but one flesh." A union this so intimate, that every other is to yield to it; so sacred, that the Divine proclamation concerning it is, "What God hath joined together let no man put asunder;" so indissoluble, that nothing is to separate it but that which separates the soul from the body; so spiritual in its ultimate relations and aims, as to find its antitype only in that Divine union which, as the fruit of redemption, is to survive every other, and to attain its consummation in heaven.*

The institution unique.

Now, here was not only "a new thing in the earth," but an immeasurable advance on every previously existing arrangement in the animal kingdom, as well as the occasion of the grand development of the individual man. Duality in unity, indeed, is a principle pervading even inanimate nature. The botanical kingdom brings us acquainted with the antithesis of sex, and even with so-called social plants. Very different, however, is this antithetical unity in the more advanced classes of the animal kingdom; and especially as seen in its results among the few labor-dividing and *apparently* social species. But it is to be borne in mind that the nearer the animal appears to approach to man in these respects, the more distinctly the phenomena proclaim themselves to be purely instinctive. Not only are the same phenomena in the human sphere different in degree, but also in *kind*. The acts are estimated by the agent himself; the ends are deliberated on and proposed by an act of freedom.

Divine idea of the family.

If man's destiny, regarded as an individual, is different from that of all the rest of animated nature, it was to be expected that every part of his

* Ephesians, v. 32.

constitution would point to this difference, and in some way subserve it. And our examination, in a preceding volume, presented man to view as a being capable of enjoying and subserving the highest ends of the Divine government, and therefore as held accountable for it; leaving us to the conclusion that the conjugal union is not necessary as the *moral* complement of either sex, but that such accountable completeness is pre-supposed by marriage. But if every part of the individual man is thus found to be relative to his high spiritual destiny, there is still stronger ground to expect that the union which makes of two individuals one, will point to the same end; and stronger still is the ground for expecting it, when it is viewed as a union in which, by the birth of offspring, man becomes instrumentally an exponent of that life-giving, creative power by which he himself was made in the Divine image. Why can he have been invested subordinately with the prerogative of multiplying his own image, but in order that he might transform his offspring into the likeness of the Creator? Procreation itself is not an end; nor is his own character the standard of perfection. Education is only the continuation and complement of procreation, and the end of both is to assimilate the human to the Divine.

Its high purpose.

For this profound conception of the conjugal union, we are indebted exclusively to the Bible.* The derivation of the woman, and of only one woman, from the man—the domestic supremacy of the man—the entireness or oneness of the union—and its sacred indissolubility—all point to this high spiritual aim as the normal idea of marriage. Only on this ground have two beings, made for God, any right to give themselves up to

* Tholuck's Exposition of the Sermon on the Mount, p. 319.

each other in a union of love. But the fact that the union is one by which the Creator actually admits man into fellowship with Himself in the accomplishment of His highest ends, makes the mutual surrender, otherwise inexplicable, consistent with human dignity by consecrating it to the Divine glory. In the primal union, all the foreshadowings of nature on the subject were interpreted and fulfilled. The instinctive affections acquired the sacredness of moral principles. Animal appetites became the means of religious improvement. The gregarious instinct was exchanged for a sociality whose tendency is to become perpetual. That which, in the lower creation, had been only sexual and transitory, now became sacramentally related to the spiritual and eternal. The paternal will found itself enthroned over other wills. Man was the representative of God. The family became the seat of moral government—the very image of the Divine. As its members multiplied, its relations became diffused and attenuated, till they even ceased to be specifically named; but still an indestructible network of affinity held them all in union, and from every relation sprang a corresponding obligation. To individual man, the first table of the law only would have been known; with the family, came the second table. Aspects of the Divine character, hitherto unknown, were now unvailed; and the family constitution, rightly understood, became a new volume of Divine Revelation.

The germ of society.

In the bosom of this primal union lay the germ of the great genealogical tree of the human race. "Individuals (says Howe)* are elements of families; families are elements of which both Churches and kingdoms or commonwealths are made up; and as the one

* Vol. v. p. 511.

of these is purely civil, the other purely sacred, that which is elementary to both must be both." So that here we find ourselves looking in on the elements of all the forms of human society. And this constitution—unique as compared with all that had gone before it—will be found pre-eminently to characterize that stage of the Divine manifestation which stretches from the Fall to the Flood. We may call it, interchangeably, the Domestic Constitution, the Family Economy, or the Patriarchal Dispensation; the last name being especially descriptive of the Domestic Constitution in its state of utmost development, and of its dispensational aspect as distinguished from the Mosaic economy and the Christian Church.

With the family came mediation.

Finally, with the rise of the family, there come into view a new aspect of the sacrificial institute—that of *mediation;* for, if the offering up of the animal symbolized the idea of substitution, equally did the offerer, as the father of the family, express the idea of mediation. Even from the first, man stood not alone. Not one of all his progeny can be truly viewed as an isolated individual. He is a member of a race. His individual life is connected with the life of the collective race. In that collective capacity, worship is due from the race to God. How significantly would this great truth be embodied as often, and as long, as the father of the race himself continued to officiate at the altar in his representative capacity! For centuries, the unity of the race could not be doubted, for there, at the place of sacrifice, the first man was seen interceding for his human family. Having instrumentally originated their bodily existence, and having, by his fall, vitiated their normal condition, it was now his high office to represent them all at the altar of propitiation. They who from sex and age were incapacitated for offering, and they who, as heads of younger families, were entitled personally to sacrifice, were all alike present in the person of the officiating patriarch. The life-blood of the victim flowed for the "one blood" of humanity. Thus early the human family was seen symbolically drawing near to God, as one living organic whole, through a mediator. And, in a similar manner, Abraham, and Noah, and every antediluvian patriarch, represented their offspring and dependents at the place of sacrifice, transacting with God on their behalf. And the idea which lay at the root of primeval mediation corresponded with that at the basis of sacrifice—a deep sense of guilt and of estrangement from God on the part of those represented—making it necessary that he who represented them should himself be a holy, accepted, consecrated worshiper, concerned alike for the honor of God and for the acceptance of those for whom he mediated. Surely it might have been said, the blood-relationship of the human family, thus represented and consecrated at the altar, will prove too strong for the exploding selfishness of sin! Love will triumph!

CHAPTER IV.

THE DEVELOPMENT OF THE FAMILY CONSTITUTION AND OF THE MEANS OF MERCY DURING THE PATRIARCHAL ECONOMY.

Law of development.

We have seen that the threefold means of human education and of Divine manifestation enjoyed by paradisiacal men—namely, external nature, his own constitution and condition, and direct communications from the Creator—have all been brought forward into the family economy. The law of development leads us to expect that these means, "besides being brought forward, will be here Divinely expressed in higher forms, or applied to higher purposes, or else that it will be in the power of the human being so to express or apply them." It will be remarked that so far from favoring the popular error of human perfectibility as a fact of inherent necessity, we view man's progress as made possible only by the progress of the means Divinely supplied to him. All history is a protest against the notion of man's advance on any other condition. Since the world began, History might have written alternate chapters on man's material perfectibility, and his moral corruptibility.

Its antediluvian theater.

"Man (says Montesquieu) is born in society, and there he remains." Even the first man was made for the associate which the Creator provided.

Nor was the region which they came forth from Eden to occupy less adapted, after its kind, to become the theater of the development of the family constitution than they themselves were adapted to each other. Of antediluvian topography we can of course do little more than form conjectures. The *garden* of Eden was, as we have elsewhere stated,* probably situated on the southern slope of Armenia. But Eden itself may have embraced the fairest portion of Asia and a part of Africa. Over large tracts of this widely extended territory, especially of that comprehending the lands lying between 25° and 40° N. latitude, and between 30° and 80° E. longitude, the antediluvian families may have been diffused. But it would aid us little toward verifying our views, even if we were able to determine the precise boundaries of the districts inhabited, unless we could also ascertain their physical condition at that time, as compared with the changes which they may have since undergone. The probability is, indeed, that the physical geography of those portions of the earth did not then materially differ from what it was in, at least, the early portions of their postdiluvian history.† Doubtless, they were wisely adapted to be the theater of the great transactions for which Providence had destined them.

Means of development waiting to be employed.

And who that had seen the primeval pair come forth from paradise to take possession of their new world, could have pictured to himself the amazing degree in which it was to become the occasion of human development, and to be filled with the indications of "what was in man," or of his self-manifesta-

* Man Primeval, p. 18.

† See an admirable *article* on *the Physical Geogr. of W. Asia* in the *Penny Cyclo.*

tion! True, the elements of the whole race were slumbering within them; and some of those elements were already in a state of incipient activity and development. Already they had been, to a certain extent, Divinely instructed in the knowledge of *nature*. But before them now lay a vast domain to which such knowledge had never yet been applied, and where it would be receiving perpetual accessions. There were the cattle upon a thousand hills, yet unherded and untamed; the fields and forests yet unclaimed, and intelligently untrod; its mineral and other resources yet unemployed; its still unexhausted treasures yet to be intelligently looked on for the first time. Yet, with its still unnumbered objects, and its changes of times and seasons, the whole, even to the atom too light to fall to the earth, was under law. And by his study of this diversified law, and his growing perception of its all related operation, man was to be led in adoring wonder to the Law-giver, and to increase his knowledge of natural theology. Already had our first parents been Divinely taught to anticipate the subsequent multiplication of their species. But at present they stood childless and alone. The tender names of father and mother had yet to be uttered for the first time; the endearing relations of brother and sister, yet to exist; the first shelter yet to be provided, and the first couch spread, for infantine weakness. And as they stood yet thus alone, look where they would, "the world was all before them where to choose." "There was much land to be possessed;" and wherever they chose to abide, and on whatever they chose to lay their hand, it was their own. No landmark yet existed. The laws of property were not yet expressed. The whole system of social ethics had yet to be evolved; and thus to increase their knowledge of *hu-*

man nature. And already had a *special revelation* of mercy been made to them in the first promise, and in the institution of sacrifice. But the various effects of these on different classes of character had yet to be seen. The deep and hallowed emotions they would excite had yet to find their images in the objects around. The first Edenic altar had yet to arise. And in all the widely-extended solitudes which lay before them, they were the only worshipers. If, from some Pisgah height, they surveyed the goodly prospect which stretched on all sides round, what did they behold but a world filled with the selected and arranged manifestations of the Deity, all of which were as yet undisturbed and untouched; and awaiting their descent to become the scene of their own activity, and the occasions and means of human manifestation.

Now had it been our privilege, as beings of a different order, to have gazed with them on that virgin earth; and if then, after an absence of about two thousand years—on the eve of the Flood—we could have looked on the same region from the same spot, how strangely revolutionized should we have found the scene! Might we not have supposed that it must, in the interval, have been taken possession of by colonies from other worlds? Civilization, in many of its most transforming processes, would be seen to have changed its active face; an ever-active being to have left marks of his presence every where.

Nature; why had the creative process paused?

In proceeding to illustrate the development which took place in the means of manifestation during the period in question, we have to begin with those of *external nature.* The inquiry may sometimes arise in the mind, Why did the *creative* process stop when it did; or, why do not the Divine perfections continue to be displayed by additional exhibitions of creative glory? To which it might be replied that, in other parts of the universe, such creative displays may, not improbably, continue to be made; and many a holy being, once an inhabitant of this world, may now be looking on. In relation to this earth, the process has *not* reached its final termination. That it has paused for a few thousand years—as it did probably during its earlier stages—we admit. But after awhile the pause will probably cease, and the process be resumed again, when the earth shall have passed through its regenerating fires. Meantime, the questioner may properly be met with the counter question, Why should the creative process be, for the present, continued? Surely, he would not assign any reason for his wish inferior to that of being afforded an opportunity of admiring the power, and wisdom, and goodness of God. But the earth is still stored with unclassed and unexplored illustrations of *these* perfections. Till these are exhausted, therefore, *the glory of God* does not need that any such new illustrations should be added, whatever man's curiosity and frivolity might desire; besides that it may be for the honor of the Divine regard to our welfare, as free beings, to withhold them. But the direct and sufficient reply to the question is this, that the very production of a creature such as man—capable of reading aright the signs of power, and wisdom, and goodness, which the objective universe already displays, and of making the right use of them—would form, in his own person, so perfect a complement of mere *creative* manifestation, as to render further additions of the creative kind, for the present at least, unnecessary. A mere irrational creation, however enlarged and diversified, could not carry the manifestation of the Deity beyond the point which it has already reached—the illustration of Goodness. While a rational and responsible being, such as man, not only requires the display of the *moral* perfections of his Maker, but actually constitutes such a moral manifestation, and, as such, desires, and is prepared to appreciate, whatever other and higher disclosures of moral excellence God may be pleased to grant.

Nature meant for man's improvement.

What, then, are the media through which man is to express his need of such higher manifestations; or, what the vehicle through which God is to impart them? The constitution of man might have led us antecedently to expect that "the things which are *seen*" would, in some way, be employed to suggest and to signify the invisible, and the material to subserve the spiritual. And when we remember that, previous to creation, the selection of the planet which man should inhabit, the choice of the form, the appearance, and the complicated relations of every object on it, was entirely dependent on the will of God, it is only rational to expect that the whole would be made conducive, in some way, to one chief and ultimate end, as well as variously contributive to the principal means subsidiary to that end. Accordingly, on the coming of man, nature assumed a new aspect, and showed that she had been awaiting his presence, by forthwith presenting him with the occasions and materials appropriate to his comfort and improvement.

Arts successively developed.

Starting from a point far in advance of the savage state, man's first easy occupation in Eden had been "to dress it and to keep it." But now he had left the garden for the field, the plain, and the wilderness. Nothing was absolutely ready to his hand, but every thing offered itself to his use. The cultivable nature of the soil, and the knowledge which had been Divinely imparted on the subject, made *agriculture* possible; and "Cain was a tiller of the ground." The habits of certain animals invited man to practice the art of *animal domestication;* hence pasturage arose, and "Abel was a keeper of sheep." One animal seemed to offer to man its fleece, and another its milk; one became his companion, and another contentedly bore his burdens. The properties of certain ores made *metallurgy* possible; and Tubal-Cain was "a smiter or hammerer in brass and iron." The laws of form and friction,* which characterize some materials, made *architecture* possible; and hence arose the first "city," or collection of stationary buildings; and, afterward, the construction of the stupendous ark, and the attempt to rear the tower of Babel. The nomadic habits of some tribes made *tent-making* desirable, and the skins of animals made it possible; and "Jubal was the father of such as dwell in tents." The tenacity† and pliability of some substances made *platting* and *weaving* possible; and the intertwining of leaves by our first parents for a covering renders it highly probable that textile fabrics, hand-made, early came into use. The apparent motions of the heavens made *chronology* and elementary *astronomy* possible; and the exact manner in which the ages of Seth and his descendants are recorded, together with the precise statement of the year, month, and day, in which the ark was both entered and left, imply an acquaintance both with the lunar and the solar year.‡ The constitution of the atmosphere made

* See an interesting chapter on *Friction* in Whewell's *Astronomy and General Physics.*

† J. S. Mill's Principles of Political Economy, vol. i. p. 31.

‡ The Hebrew word for year, שׁנה—*repetition, iteration,* a return to the

music objectively possible; and "Jubal became the father of all such as handle the harp and pipe." Owing to the same provision, *poetry* (as far as the rhythmical arrangement of sounds is concerned) was known as well as music —indeed, as the music of the feelings, poetry would precede instrumental harmony, and create the want of it; and hence the poetical address of Lamech—the effusion of excited emotions. Nature itself, besides being a grand hieroglyphic and suggestive picture for man's deciphering eye, presented him with materials for transcribing her records; and, having received an impulse from the same beneficent power which had endowed him with speech, he early practiced some art of *writing*—recording events by, most probably, alphabetic signs.* Thus, the objects and powers of

same point, favors this conjecture. For even if it be not the precise vocable which was employed in the antediluvian computations of time, it most likely corresponds in signification with that which was employed.

* The antediluvian origin of alphabetic writing is thought to be probable from reasons such as these:—That the genealogies of the patriarchs are recorded with an exactness superior to that of tradition: that the poetical address of Lamech possesses no internal recommendation to be preserved, during a tract of centuries, by tradition, and "yet differs essentially from all the specimens of known ideagraphic poetry:" that the Mosaic account of the Flood has the air of a description derived from an eye-witness, or placed on record by him: that the formulæ, "This is the book of the generations of Adam," and "These are the generations of Noah," imply a transcript from authentic genealogical tables regularly kept in the patriarchal families: that the earlier part of the Book of Genesis is marked by differences of style denoting distinct compositions, from which Moses, under Divine direction, compiled his history, and that these archives were authentic memorials of and from antediluvian families: that (even supposing alphabetic signs were not the result of Divine suggestion like articulate sounds) the longevity of the antediluvians was highly favorable to the discovery; that we "never heard of

nature gradually took rank in the service of man. One after another they came into his presence, owned his dominion, and received their commission. Things, before apparently useless and even evil, disclosed "a soul of goodness;" secret affinities came to light; laws and relations every where sprang up; startling adaptations presented themselves; objects apparently slumbering and inert became instinct with life; "the trees of the field clapped their hands." And as time advanced, these ministries went on multiplying, till Nature appeared full of the objective conditions of art and science.*

Development of natural theology. The laws and objects of Nature served a higher purpose still, in supplying the materials of a *natural theology*. At this altar they began to minister even in the *garden* of Eden. Primeval man, indeed, had not been then left to learn the Divine existence and government from this source. To say nothing of the Divine communion which he there enjoyed, the fact of his own immediate creation was, for him, an ever-resounding proclamation of the Creator; and his subsequent history had kept him conscious of his amenableness to natural law. As time advanced, and the race multiplied, the first faint intimations of nature on the subject grew louder and more distinct, until ten thousand voices united in the acclaim. Proofs of

any society which had made such progress in the arts as the antediluvians certainly did, without being acquainted with the use of letters:" and that it is favored by the traditions of the most widely separated nations and of almost all religions. See *Dr. Wall* on the origin of alphabets; *Hale's* Analysis of Chronology, vol. i. pp. 369–373. Edinburgh Cyclopedia, article *Antediluvian*. *Faber's* Pagan Idolatry, vol. ii. pp. 150, 151. *Cory's* Ancient Fragments, pp. 23–29, 57. *Smith's* Sacred Annals, pp. 52–86.

* Man Primeval, chapters vii. and xvii.

the wisdom and goodness of God increased with every new adaptation which came to light; and natural law, in its application to man, went on accumulating precedents, and establishing its authority. Man, in his wilfullness, might resist it, and, in his ignorance, arraign it, but not the less eloquently did it reason with its pretended judge "on righteousness, temperance, and judgment to come, until he trembled." The earth gradually became a great justice-court, in which the administration of law was constantly and consciously going on.

Of language.

In the department of *language*, nature was found supplying man with images of the moral, the spiritual, and the Divine. Every thing in creation represents a thought of God, for it must have been *thought of* by Him. Nature is a great system of Divine thoughts eternalized, and externalizing themselves in things. Man came therefore to find that things, as the exponents of a universal mind, were here before him; and here to be the vehicles of his own thoughts—the exponents of his own mind. Whatever the subject which might occupy his thoughts, he found Nature had so spoken on the theme before him as to provide the very prototypes of the words he wanted. As a poet, a world of impressive images lay around him; if he reasoned, analogies crowded to his aid; if he theorized, prolific suggestions met his eye; if he worshiped, the finite and the visible referred him to the Infinite invisible. With the new ideas of Revelation, came a new demand on the materials of language. Besides the new words which would be thus called into existence, language would be exalted by the secondary or derivative sense in which it would be now extensively employed. That man was already in possession of a portion of *natural* knowledge was pre-supposed in the very fact of his being capable of receiving supernatural additions to it; for to that previous knowledge of Nature the supernatural must appeal, and on it must be grafted. Names, besides being descriptive of the natural qualities and uses of objects, extended their illustrative power to Divine things. Spiritual ideas had to be translated into human language; and thus terms which, before, had only a natural meaning, acquired a metaphorical and theological value also. *Ruach*,* for example, signifying *breath*, came to mean also life, soul, spirit, Spirit of God; *aor*,† light, was extended to mean knowledge, and security as resulting from knowledge, and happiness as flowing from both. Thus language was progressively molded and enriched by Revelation. As things were emblematical, possessing a value beyond their material forms and uses, so the words describing them, besides their primitive signification, developed a succession of senses, in proportion as man's horizon was lifted up and enlarged. Words became "figures of the true." Man could not even speak on earthly subjects, without employing terms, some of which had acquired also a consecrated sense, and were consequently ever suggestive of loftier conceptions. He "who seeth the end from the beginning" had forelaid the entire plan, and it proceeded with the uniformity of law.

Material objects raised to religious symbols.

Here we come to the principle which lies at the basis of all Biblical symbols—or representation of truth by object or action. The Creator had so adapted external nature to man's prospective constitution, that all its phenomena should serve as exponents or signs of loftier correspondences—indexes of the spiritual and the Divine. If Nature is spirit translated into

* רוח † אור

matter, in religion, matter is translated back again into spirit. On this principle, the same material universe whose *objects* first served to illustrate the power of God; whose complicated *relations* and exquisite adaptations, next, set forth His wisdom; and whose peculiar *sentient endowments*, afterward, proclaimed His goodness; had, subsequently, in Paradise, shown their susceptibility of receiving a new and a higher application to a new and a loftier order of truth. The Being who, with infinite foresight, had surrounded man with a world of things emblematic of thoughts, was there pleased to *appoint* one of these to be the symbol of a great principle. The tree in the midst of the garden was the chosen symbol and instrument of moral government. Other trees might speak to man of goodness, but this proclaimed Divine Supremacy and Equity. So easily might this symbolic arrangement be pictured to the eye, that some have actually supposed, with Rosenmüller,* that the Biblical narrative is derived from a hieroglyphic or pictorial representation transferred to alphabetic signs. And now that man's altered moral relation required the impartation of new knowledge from God, is instruction by symbol to be disparaged and dismissed? That nothing in Nature can, of itself, suggest *remedial* truth is admitted. The directness with which the new revelation came from God himself, implied that, as a *source* of instruction for *sinful* man, Nature was dumb. So far, however, from being superseded as a *channel* of Divine instruction, it now took a wider range, and discharged a higher office. Symbolism was not only called to minister at the gate of Paradise; at the altar of sacrifice it might be said to have been consecrated with blood.

* Repertor. th. i. s. 160; see Knapp's Theology, § lxxv.

Symbols become types.

Besides the development of symbolism which now took place, *types*, or acted predictions, were Divinely appointed. In going to the altar of sacrifice, a thousand wayside objects might have suggestively appealed to his emotions, owing to the general harmony of man with Nature. But, arrived at the altar, the death of the victim impressively symbolized his own deserts; while, as a means of expiation, it typified a nobler victim yet to be offered up. In each instance, his emotions were appealed to; but, in the first, the appeal was made chiefly through his imagination; in the second, through his understanding; and in the third, through his faith. The first pre-supposed nothing more than man's power of interpreting natural signs and latent affinities by sympathetically communing with Nature; the second implied this to be an explicit Divine *appointment* in addition; the third implied both these, and pre-supposed besides the Divine promise or *prediction* of an antitype. While the first was only *suggestive*, and might awaken very different trains of thought at different times, the symbol *figured* fixed specific truth—was a scenic representation of the worshiper's penitence and of the Divine acceptance; and the type, advancing still beyond, *pre*-figured the great sacrifice on which that acceptance rested. If the first implied that the temple of Nature was filled with objects suggestive of truths beyond themselves; the second implied that, in the Divine hand, they could be made vividly to symbolize truths which they could never have possessed the power to reveal; and the third denoted that they belonged to a grand scheme of things in which the present is not more certainly related to the past than the future is to the present.* Here was development—the

* Bishop Marsh's *Lectures on the Criticism and Interpretation of the Bible*, pp. 374, etc.; and Fairbairn's *Typology of Scripture*, chap. ii.

lifting of another fold in the vail which concealed the Divine purposes—the disclosure and adoption of an arrangement which had never been absent from the Divine plan, although now first made present to the mind of man.

Man's own development.

In the preceding chapter, we have seen the progress which the family constitution exhibits as compared with every previously-existing arrangement in the animal kingdom; here, we have to illustrate the development of social man as we saw him "brought forward," in the second chapter, as a means of Divine manifestation.

Prior to the Fall, man himself was a revelation. He had been made in the image of God, that he might be to himself a manifestation of God. He, the subject, was to become indirectly his own object, and to behold in that object the brightest reflection within his horizon of the Divine likeness. And even now, though morally defaced by sin, his natural capacity for excellence remains. He still retains the Divine image in this high and indestructible sense—that, unlike all the orders of creation which preceded him, he is a *personal* being; one *by* whom God is revealed that He may be also revealed *to* him. "But has not sin arrested forever the process of his development?" We have already had occasion to admire the arrangement by which the same promise which intimated that the Divine manifestation was to proceed signified also that the family constitution was to unfold; for it taught that the progress of the former was to be secured instrumentally through the medium of the latter.

In developing nature Man unfolds himself.

The earth, we have seen, presented a grand system of objective means for man's development. Accordingly, every advancing step which we have marked in man's employment of them, implied that his own development was in progress. While occupied in cultivating the earth, he was cultivating himself. In training the animals for his use, he was learning the art of self-government. While interpreting Nature, he was interpreting himself. Even when transforming some natural substances for his use till no trace of their original form was left, he was still more transforming himself by the process. Nature, indeed, supplied him with more than materials—with powers; but even when he had to do least for the attainment of his ends, that little involved a conscious assertion of will, a revelation of mind. The remoteness of the starry heavens might seem to have almost withdrawn them from his range of study; but while yet he could do little more than gaze at the sublime spectacle, the apparent whirl subsided, and took order under his eye; "Arcturus appeared with his sons, and the bands of Orion, and Mazzaroth (the zodiacal signs) in his season."* In the process of unvailing Nature, man developed his own resources, externalizing and painting himself on the face of the midnight sky, and peopling it with the creations of his own imagination.

Now, as a being capable of such development, the family provided for man's constant progress. He came into it, not like the animal, to begin and end where all his progenitors did, but to inherit all the past, and to add to it something of his own for all the future. He came, generation after generation, to find many experiments in art and Nature already completed, and the results laid up for his use; many of the ways of error explored, and a warning placed over the entrance for the benefit of future travelers; many

* Job, xxxviii. 31, 32.

proverbs, the generalized results of hard-won experience, "floating on the lips of the wise;" and many facts observed and collected, and waiting only the arrival of some generalizing mind to classify them—thus rendering them useable, and a step to higher and wider generalizations still.

This favored by longevity.

These, indeed, are advantages of a nature still enjoyed; but the longevity of antediluvian life added to them, in various ways, tenfold. It enabled men to acquire inconceivable dexterity in many of the mechanical arts. In this department, the proverb that "practice makes perfect" emphatically applies. How great, then, must have been the tact and proficiency resulting from the continued practice of centuries! The prospect of such longevity would encourage men to lay out comprehensive plans, and to enter on vast undertakings with the expectation of completing them, and of enjoying the fruits. Added to which, that in proportion as this longevity was physiologically dependent on superior climatic influences, it would be also conducive to bodily and mental exertion.*

* On the great age of the Patriarchs, *physiology* is of necessity silent. Haller speaks of it as a *problema ob paucitatem datorum insolubile.** Buffon regards it as possible.† But what says *history?* Josephus writes, "I have, for witnesses to what I have said (respecting the great length of patriarchal life), all those who have written antiquities, both among the Greeks and Barbarians; for even Manetho, who wrote the Egyptian history, and Berosus, who collected the Chaldean monuments, and Mochus, and Hestiæus, and those who composed the Phœnician history, agree to what I here say; Hesiod also, and Hecatæus, Hellanicus, and Acusilaus; and besides these, Ephorus and Nicolaus, relate that the ancients lived a thousand years."‡ Diodorus, Pliny, and Plutarch, indeed,

* Elem. Physiol. viii. p. 21. † Hist. Nat. iv. p. 353. ‡ Antiq. book. i. chap. 3.

Theological development is self-development.

The gradual development of the means of natural theology implied the development of the *theologian* himself. To give a single illustration;—the family constitution, viewed in connection with the prolonged duration of antediluvian life, supplied pre-eminent advantages for observing the consequences of actions, and of courses of action, and of thus ascertaining the will of God as expressed in the laws of Nature. The abbreviation of human life has greatly diminished our opportunities in this respect. Otherwise, we should often see early tendencies of character, almost too minute to be noticed, ultimately leading to consequences almost too vast to be measured. But the knowledge we inherit—the accumulated results, in an important sense, of the experience of all the past—renders the enlargement of our actual opportunities

would make the ancient year of the Egyptian to consist of one month. But this attempt of theirs (says Ideler)* rested on no information, but was a mere hypothesis invented to explain the long duration of life assigned by history to the earliest men.† The Institutes of Menu state that, in the first age, men lived four hundred years. And, according to M. De Guignes, the early annals of China represent the eight emperors of their first dynasty as reigning 695 years, which is only seventy-seven years less than what may be called the patriarchal reign of the first eight postdiluvian Patriarchs. A singular coincidence. Not only do instances of great *comparative* longevity still occur in every country,‡ statistics show that they occur in constant proportions. What does this imply, but that our constitution includes certain possibilities and properties, of which longevity is one (gigantic stature and extraordinary strength might be named as others), which are not often permitted fully to evolve, and to attain their utmost limits? During the early period of the world's history this development was, for wise purposes, allowed to take place to a much greater extent than at present.

* Handbuch d. Chron. i. p. 93. † Hävernick's Introduction, § 16, p. 107.

‡ Sharon Turner's Sacred Hist. of the World, vol. iii., letter 23.

unnecessary. In an antediluvian family, however, the natural laws had time to work themselves out in the history of the individual and the family. As to the laws of health, for example, slight infractions which might be persevered in with comparative impunity for the limited period of fifty or sixty years, could not be multiplied by five or six hundred without beginning to vindicate and avenge themselves. The deposition of a single seed of disease by some early excess, would have time, like the aloe, fabled to bloom only once in a century, to blossom again and again, till it even "brought forth fruit unto death." As to self-will and self-indulgence of various kinds, leading to peculiarities of temper and perversities of conduct, and which, owing to their now being so early arrested by death, are known to us only under the names of idiosyncracies and harmless eccentricities—many of these would have time to ripen into their proper forms of insanity and madness. The same of the various degrees of industry, veracity, and benevolence;—how certainly a very slight error in either of these respects, admitted into the character in very early life, and allowed to go on self-multiplying by practice, would be found, at the close of five hundred years, to have involved the violator in social ruin. And thus man would come to find that his history was an ever-advancing argument for the being and government of God.

Linguistic development implied intellectual progress.

The progress of language proclaimed the progress of man. Every new thought is a creation—a spiritual emanation, calling for a body to clothe it. In the infancy of language, every such body is an image fresh from the treasury of Nature. The first word which is recorded to have burst from the lips of Adam, after the voice which announced the Promise had ceased, was of this description:—and he "called his wife's name Eve* [Life] because she was [to be] the mother of all living." Every such appropriation from Nature was a new synthesis between it and the human mind; or rather between the mind of man and the universal mind underlying the objects of Nature. Every time a word, besides its primary and physical signification, became the representative of a moral idea, a new stage was reached. How limited the conception awakened in the mind of Adam by the term, *nachash*†—serpent, prior to the Fall, compared with the host of painful associations which it was calculated to suggest afterward, when it had become the opponent of the great spiritual Foe, and stood for the ever-increasing faction of evil, which divided, until it almost engrossed, the human family. How contracted the notion which the word *minchah*‡—offering, would convey to the mind of Cain, who contented himself with the presentation of fruits and flowers, suitable only for a sinless being, compared with the volume of theology which it would lay open to the mind of Abel, who regarded it as synonymous with sacrifice, and whose faith it pointed to a true expiation. Thus, words which at first had only a specific sense, came to be generic; and, in that generalization included ideas of heaven as well as earth. "Enoch (it is said) walked with God; and he (was) not, for God took him." In the first clause, the familiar phrase *he walked*, by being connected with *God*, is made to denote piety of the highest order; but in the latter part, as if language as yet had received no term to express even by metaphor the *translation* of the Patriarch, a

* חוה. † נחש. These may not have been the identical vocables employed; but the same statement would equally apply to their equivalents.

‡ מנחה.

negation is employed, *he was not*, and this receives the explanation that *God took him*. The event was a prodigy for which language had not yet prepared a descriptive term. Similarly would language be taxed, with the rise of every new relation in the family, and in order to give utterance to the world of feeling belonging to each relation. The origination of music—the inarticulate language of the heart—denoted that man was conscious of depths of feeling which no words could reach. Music came to the aid of speech—told of emotions which had not yet become thoughts—which were greater than all his thoughts—and which made him feel allied to the infinite.

As the descendants of common parents, too, the antediluvian population spoke a common language. Slight dialectic peculiarities might have begun to appear, but the uniformity was such that the one language, as it measured from time to time the progress of some, might have been the means of improvement to all.

Sin remedied, the occasion of religious development.

In a similar manner, the Divine appointment of religious *symbols* was the creation of a new scene in the world *without*, denoting that man had become conscious of an entirely new world within, which nothing previously existing in Nature, as Nature, could represent. The predictive character of the *type* pointed man away from the present, and showed him capable of the greatness of inheriting and even anticipating the distant future. But both these Divine appointments, as parts of the new scheme of mercy, remind us of the far-reaching action of *sin* as an occasion of human development. Of man's capacity for progress—on the hypothesis of his having remained unfallen—there can be no question. Equally certain is it that sin is an arrest of man's progress in one direction—the highest—and an acceleration of the development of his inferior nature. The law of development which should be diffused through the whole man, concentrates its force on a part. But we speak now of sin as itself arrested, or of man as living under a remedial economy. And who can question that as sin became the occasion of a new manifestation of the Divine character, so, owing to that restorative manifestation, it became the grand occasion of man's development? Powers previously hidden below the depths of his consciousness, now emerged and were evolved. Susceptibilities were awakened which, otherwise, would have slumbered on forever. He stood as in a new world. His dependence on God was unutterably more profound than ever. New and more affecting relations to God surprised him; and obligations, unknown before, claimed him. A whole order of sensations awoke—the hopes and apprehensions, the joys and sorrows, of pardon and penitence. The events immediately subsequent to man's transgression—the sentence, the expulsion, the flaming sword, the dying victim, the accepted sacrifice—were all re-enacted in his breast, or pictured what was passing there. His fearful recoil and fall, on coming into collision with the Divine will, disclosed to him the measure of power which he had put forth, and told him that he could exert the same, and incomparably greater, in a pursuit after holiness; that, advancing from that original freedom, in which he was conscious only of the power of resisting evil, he could attain to that high state of excellence which excludes the practical possibility of evil. The sinfulness of the race supplied new occasions and incitements to his piety. The state of protest and antagonism which his holiness had to maintain, strengthened it. The surrounding ignorance and depravity opened the fountains of his compassion. Every instance of misery presented a new field for his activity, a new occasion for intercession; and, in the event of his success, a new source of gratitude and joy. And thus an event, which God had not seen fit to prevent, He had been pleased so to remedy as to bring forth new aspects of man's moral being, and to show him capable of attaining a degree of holiness and happiness which might otherwise, perhaps, have remained unknown.

The family, a society for the same—a church.

The paternal relation, viewed in connection with the remedial scheme, and indeed as a part of it, afforded a still deeper insight into the human constitution. In the family, the first man himself would receive lessons on self-government such as even the garden of Eden did not supply, and perpetual occasion for its exercise. In what a variety of ways would he have to repeat to his children the substance of the Divine prohibition to himself, "Thou shalt not eat of it!" How soon would he who had Paradise for a home discover that if he would convert home into a Paradise, he must guard his offspring at this point—subordinating their lower propensities to their superior powers! At first, the parental attention has nothing else to occupy it. As if to intimate that this is the deep groundwork of the child's subsequent well-being, the earliest ardor of parental solicitude and love is left to concentrate and expend itself on this point alone. The parent has to advance the Divine glory by subserving the great end of creation, and by what arrangement could he enjoy a greater opportunity for so doing, than by that which the family constitution affords him? It gives him, in addition to his own individual relations, a young immortal to train for the service of God, and facilities for the process such as can not be exceeded. How could the circle of objects which his eye surveys be more enriched than by the introduction into it of a young mind which is to expand under his own observation, so that he may study and aid it in its progress? How profound the satisfaction of a Patriarch who could regard himself as the channel of his children's double life—temporal and spiritual! To be the means of securing their earthly well-being would yield him exquisite delight, but to have succeeded in training them up for the life which is unending, and to see them occupied as agents for advancing the great scheme of Providence, comprehending time and the race, would yield him a satisfaction truly godlike. It at once revealed to him his vast capacity for happiness, and occupied and enlarged that which it revealed. How dignified and ennobling his position—the very copy of that which his heavenly Father had sustained to unfallen man in Paradise! For, placed at the head of the family, the Patriarch shadowed forth more definitely than any other image, the Divine supremacy. Engaged in the religious training of his family, he was still the representative of God on earth. Officiating in intercession, or as a priest at the altar of sacrifice, he was both symbolizing a great evangelical truth, and typically mediating between God and man. From the moment that the first Adam sinned, he sunk to the office of becoming a type of the second Adam;* rather, in becoming that type, he found his true position and his highest dignity. And each of all his posterity rose in the scale of true nobility in proportion as he intelligently relied on the ultimate appearance of the great antitype, and was so brought "to the obedience of faith."

* Romans, v. 14.

Social man in advance of the first individual man.

In this manner, the family constitution would develop and exhibit the social man in advance of the same properties and powers in the first individual man. His appetites would be found to have taken a wider range, and yet to have become subservient to nobler purposes. His self-love would be found to have projected itself to a greater distance of time and place, and to have included in its calculations other objects as parts of self. His affections would be found to have multiplied its objects, and to have often subordinated self-interest to their happiness. And each of these three springs of action would be found, in every instance in which the laws of the human constitution were duly developed, to have been subordinated by the will of God, and ennobled by love to Him.

If the first man, for example, became the subject of penitence and progressive holiness, what an immense difference would there be between the Adam leaving Paradise, and the Adam of about nine hundred years after! It would be hardly correct to institute a comparison between him and a man who should have lived, hypothetically, from the close of the tenth century of the Christian era to the present time; nor indeed, between him and any man who might be supposed to have lived during a similar lapse of centuries. Still, the allusion may serve to suggest the vast development which must have taken place in his intellectual and moral character in the course of that time. Think of the man whose very knowledge of *material* life, Divinely communicated, had as yet, with very slight exceptions, to be practically applied, compared with the same man standing in the midst of a busy population, and a comparatively reclaimed and cultivated region. Think of the man who left

Paradise childless, as compared with the same man when the Patriarch of wide-spread families and distant tribes! Think of the man who yielded to a temptation to eat of a forbidden tree, as compared with the same individual authoritatively warning the human race—and that race his own family—to flee temptation, and affectionately pointing them to the way of life! And then imagine the ever-widening and deepening stream of thought and feeling daily pouring through his mind, enlarging its channel, and forming his character.

Enoch in advance of Adam.

Still greater would be the opportunity for the development of the mind and character of Enoch. The advanced point of time at which he commenced life, as compared with Adam, would enable him to survey material civilization from a more commanding position, and to take a more comprehensive view of the relations and influences of social life. He recognized some of the first traces of a providential scheme. He saw some of the minor and earlier purposes of that scheme attained. Divine manifestations multiplied. "He walked with God," and his assimilation to the Divine image was quickened. Year after year he became conscious of higher spiritual attainments; acts of piety became confirmed habits; his views of the Divine character became more enlarged and ennobling, and his increasing endeavors to ameliorate the condition of the world, brought and kept him more in communion with God, and thus rendered him more godlike.

Noah in advance of Enoch.

The advantages enjoyed by the Patriarch Noah for mental and moral development were greater still. From his advanced post, he could watch the coming of the great crisis, gradually resulting from all the past. The very fact that man had been spared and the race continued, proclaimed aloud to the world, and, perhaps, for the first time, to the universe, the great doctrine of the Divine long-suffering. Every sinful inhabitant of earth might have borne about on his forehead, through his life of centuries, the inscription—"I am a monument of the Divine forbearance." Of that forbearance Noah became the minister. And yet the certainty of retribution at a given point of time was believed in by him not less confidently than the continuance of long-suffering up to that point. "By faith Noah being warned of God of things not seen as yet, moved with fear, prepared an ark to the saving of his house; by the which he condemned the world, and became heir of the righteousness which is by faith."* He was heir already of a greater knowledge of material life, and of human nature, than any of his predecessors had the opportunity of possessing; and now, standing near the awful point where forbearance would cease and judgment commence, his own character revealed to him the transforming and developing influence of the character and government of God.

Each generation might have been in advance of the preceding.

It hardly need be stated that the birth of every individual from the first-born of Adam and onward, afforded an opportunity for a new development of the capabilities of human nature. Every man might have exhibited the modified excellence of a Seth, an Enoch, or a Noah. Each patriarchal family might have displayed its own distinctive phase of excellence; while it yet stood in harmonious relation with the great whole. Every succeeding year, from the first man to the flood, might have added a new page to the volume of Divine manifestation transcribed from the character of man.

* Heb. xi. 7.

Each human being, differing as he necessarily would, in some respects, from all the rest, might have presented, in his own character, a distinct exposition of the Divine excellence; and thus each might have presented a study for all the rest, and for angelic beings. There was no necessitating reason why the day that poured down the deluge on a world already drenched with evil, did not see it flooded with heavenly light in approbation of its spiritual proficiency.

Religious means themselves developed.

The remaining class of means of which we have to speak consists of what we have called the secondary means employed in illustration and development, both of the primary truths which were laid at the foundation of the new economy of mercy, and of the preceding revelations of Paradise. Of this class, we may speak first of "the cherubim placed at the east of the garden of Eden." What were they? What did their particular occasion denote? And why was it so denoted?

Cherubim; what were they?

What is to be understood by the cherubim? The popular notion is that, as they here appear at the gate of Eden, they were angels; that they were armed with burning weapons; and that they occupied their station solely to bar the way to the tree of life. The Biblical account of this Divine arrangement, however, is as follows: "So he drove out the man: and he caused to dwell [stationed] at the east end of the garden the Kerubim,* and the flame of the sword [*i. e.*, a flaming sword] which was [continually] turning itself to guard the way to the tree of life."† Here, the presence of the article before *cherubim* denotes that, when the narrative was written, their appearance, whatever it was, was

* The Hebrew word in English letters. † Gen. iii. 24.

sufficiently well known to those who were addressed to render any description unnecessary beyond that of their mere name. On the next occasion in which they are spoken of,* when Moses is directed to make cherubim for the ends of the mercy-seat, the same familiar acquaintance with their form is assumed, for the Divine directions which he receives relate exclusively to the material and the position of the figures. When, at length, however, their actual appearance is given as they were seen in vision,† it is evident that they could never have been viewed otherwise than as unreal, emblematic beings. In the book of the Revelation, they are carefully distinguished from angelic beings‡—the order with which they were most likely to be confounded. Indeed, as if to make it impossible that they should be regarded as beings of another world, all the characteristic parts of which they are compounded are derived from the earth. While their merely figurative existence is demonstrable from considerations such as these—they are described as uniting the attributes of several beings of dissimilar *kinds*—each having the faces of a man, a lion, an ox, and an eagle—that is, of the highest beings of the highest divisions of animated nature; besides four wings with hands under the wings—denoting the predominance of the human element; and as covered with ever-wakeful eyes, and having a motion unique and incessant. They are sometimes spoken of anonymously and anomalously as *living creatures*§—creatures of no specific or existent order, but whose office it is to represent the idea of life in its height and intensity. Their form, so far from being definite and permanent, varied from time to time; in-

* Exod. xxv. 18–22.

† Ezek. cc. i.–x.

‡ Rev. v. 6–14; vii. 11.

§ Ezek. i. 5, etc.; Rev. iv. 6.

deed a progressive development is traceable both in their complexity of appearance and in their office,* indicating at once their unreal existence, and providing against the danger of their becoming objects of idolatrous veneration. And, notwithstanding the stringent and oft-repeated Mosaic prohibition of making any likeness of any being in heaven, earth, or ocean,† the cherubic figures were yet to be placed, by Divine command, on the ends even of the mercy-seat—the symbolic throne of Jehovah; and, as such, they could be regarded only as ideal beings.

What their particular location denoted.

What, then, did the presence of the symbolic group at the east of the garden of Eden denote? From the concluding cause of the verse—"to guard the way of the tree of life"—it has been hastily assumed that this was the office—the only office—assigned to the cherubim. Doubtless, this was one of the effects which their presence was intended and calculated to produce. But it is quite consonant with the construction of the verse, and more in harmony with all the requirements of the case, to regard the flaming weapon alone as placed there specifically for this purpose. For it is to be observed, that although there was more than a single cherub stationed there, yet only one weapon is spoken of. Nor are the cherubim represented as wielding even that single weapon; on the contrary, the awful sword-flame is expressly described as self-brandished and self-revolving (*hammithhappeketh*, continually turning itself) to guard the way of the tree of life.

The question returns, then, respecting the ulterior and emblematic design of the Edenic cherubim. To the sancti-

* Exod. xxv. 20; Ezek. i. 6: Rev. v. 6–14.

† Exod. xx. 4; Levit. xxvi. 1; Deut. iv. 16, etc.

fied imagination the sublime spectacle would doubtless be ever appealing in favor of the unearthly and Divine. It pointed man away to the regions of the possible. It gave him a visible starting-point from which to ascend to the invisible. It reminded him of the voluntary subserviency of other orders of beings to that supreme will which he had violated, and of the glory they found in obedience.

But we speak not now of the mere suggestive power of this Divine arrangement: our question relates to its symbolic design. Now, on taking the question to every other instance in which the cherubim are spoken of, it is found that they form the invariable symbol of the Divine presence, or else are attandants on it. That such was their recognized office under the Jewish economy can not be questioned. In the construction of the tabernacle and the temple, they formed the awful focus, and reflected the very splendor, of the Divine glory. He that "dwelleth between the cherubim," came to be one of the Biblical titles of the manifested God.* So closely was their presence associated in the Hebrew mind with the Divine presence, that the verb *shakan*, which is employed to denote their stationing or dwelling in Eden, was appropriated by the Talmudists to express the dwelling of the Divine glory in the temple as the *Shekinah*.† And not without reason, therefore, is it supposed that the Apostle John purposely employed the word *Skenoun*—*to erect a tent, to dwell*—in order to represent our Lord as the true Shekinah, the embodiment of the Divine presence. The only just conclusion is, then, that the same symbol had the same significance from the beginning; and that the Jewish Targum correctly pharaprases the verse thus: "He drove out the man, and caused the

* 1 Sam. iv. 4; 2 Sam. vi. 2; Ps. lxxx. 1. † See Gesenius *in voce.*

glory of his presence to dwell of old, at the east of the garden of Eden, above the two cherubim."

Now, if the appearance of the Edenic cherubim denoted the reality of the Divine presence, the following are some of the great truths which the arrangement significantly expressed: That although God had shown himself justly offended with sinful man, and that He could not be disobeyed with impunity, yet He had not withdrawn from the world, but was still "a God near at hand and not afar off." That restoration to immortal life was not impossible. Such impossibility might have been emphatically signified by destroying the *sign* of immortality—the tree of life. But *that* being allowed to stand, the thing signified by it might be supposed to remain also. The presence of the sword-flame in the way which led to the sacred pledge, however, denoted man's utter forfeiture of the blessing, and that if it ever became his, it could only be by an act of sovereign mercy. And thus the ever-speaking symbol proclaimed both the justice and the grace of God, and tended to keep alive in the human breast the emotions of penitence for the past and of hope for the future. It formed, in connection with the first promise and the institute of sacrifice, an organic part of the new outline of the Divine manifestation.

But besides being *symbols*, to the Divinely-instructed mind they may have been *types;* not only "figures for the time then present;" but prefigurations of "good things to come." Here were "Living Ones,"—collections and concentrations of life—of life in its essence and idea; might not man himself, at length, prove to be its antitype? They are allied to man, for, in their complex form, the human prevails; and they are equally allied to God, for it is with His life they are supposed to be preternaturally instinct, and His presence which they symbolize; might not this alliance point to some sublime union, in the future, between Divinity and humanity of a kind unknown at that time to the universe?

Why so denoted.

To the third inquiry, respecting the reason of their employment, we may reply, generally, that as a symbol, they only constituted a new hieroglyphic in the great emblematic roll which man was just beginning to read, and by which, partly, he was to decipher his Maker's will. All nature was to be to him a disclosure of the supernatural; the actual, a manifestation of the ideal; the visible, of the invisible. So that here was only a new sign inscribed on a page already instinct with significance. Here was only the insertion of a new emblem in a Divinely-instituted system of symbols; just as the truths which it implied formed part of a great scheme of Divine revelation. Reasons may be suggested also for the adoption of this particular symbol, always bearing in mind, however, that the unknown may be far more important than those which are apparent. How easy and natural the transition, for example, from the contemplation of the animals on which the first man had so recently bestowed descriptive names, to the consideration of the same forms as they were seen compounded in the cherubic vision. And yet how much loftier the order of truth to which, in the latter instance, they directed his mind! Then he looked on them as the living signs of the Maker's power, and wisdom, and goodness, but now they impressively symbolized His ever-wakeful Providence, and His blended justice and grace. Then, the very act of their coming into the presence of man was a sign of homage to their earthly lord, but now their symbolic office proclaimed that, were it the will of the Supreme, creation in all its beings and elements, would instantly arm to avenge their Maker. They taught him that though by a single act of sin he had threatened the coherence and well-being of nature—"showing that all material beauty and blessedness is but, as it were, the clothing of one good thought, which, if it become evil, straightway all departs like the shadow of a dream"—yet that he was now encircled by a system in which the moral should transmute and exalt the material, and nature become a ministering angel, subserving and sharing in his highest interests.

Local manifestation of the Divine presence.

There is evidence of the local manifestation of the Divine presence as the scene of patriarchal worship. "And Cain said unto Jehovah . . . Behold, thou hast driven me out this day from the face of the land [from the region which I have hitherto inhabited and cultivated] and from thy face shall I be hid. . . . And Cain went out from the presence of Jehovah, and dwelt in the land of wandering, on the east of Eden."* The only inference to be drawn from this language is, that there was a place to which the visible indications of the Divine presence had been hitherto accorded and confined. Now, such a spot the presence of the cherubic vision actually designated. That place might have been a field, a mount, or a district: judging from the imagery of Ezekiel—"thou hast been in Eden, thou art the anointed cherub, thou wast upon the holy mountain of God"†—the hallowed scene was an elevation, attracting the eye, and inviting the approach of penitent man—"another morn risen on mid-day." And the mode of special Divine manifestation, when he did approach, might have been by oracle, by the consumption of the sacrifice

* Genesis, iv. 13, 14, 16.

† Ezekiel, xxviii. 12–17.

laid upon the altar by a heaven-descending flame, or by the brightening glow of the cherubim. But however this may have been, it is clear from the language of the fratricide, that communion with God had been hitherto maintained in a given locality—that in that scene of the Shekinah he now expected his complaint to be heard and answered, but that, if exiled beyond its precincts, he should be driven forth beyond the circle sacred to the worship of God, and to the visible displays of His presence. Upward of a century had then elapsed from the hour of the Fall, and numerous children had probably been born to Adam meanwhile, besides the fratricide and his brother, and here, during the long interval, God had graciously met with His first human worshipers, "from between the cherubim," and "communed with" them.

Moral government.

Events occurred to develop and illustrate the doctrine of an all-encompassing Providential government, administered in equity, but based on mercy. Already, in the fearful results of the Fall, the grand disclosure had been made for all time, that to sin is to suffer. In the detection of the fratricide, the proclamation again went forth through all his posterity, "Be sure your sin will find you out." The question, "Where is Abel thy brother?" showed that "to smite a saint on earth, is to create a commotion in heaven." The declaration, "thy brother's blood crieth to me from the ground," was more than metaphor; it implied that nothing is dumb to God; that every thing man thinks on or touches, carries up an appeal on high, either for him or against him; that, already, materials for the final assize were collecting. His actual punishment taught him that "God is no respecter of persons;" that an eternal law of morality could not be suspended for considerations of primogeniture, of passion, or of any thing which might weigh with an indulgent earthly parent; indeed, the interrogation—"if thou doest well, shalt thou not be accepted?"—carrying with it the force of a strong affirmation, implies that the Divine impartiality was already so amply illustrated and firmly established, that even the evil-doer Cain might be confidently appealed to on the subject. While the haunting remorse which went with him into exile disclosed that the sinner can not be exiled beyond the domains of justice; that besides the external Eden there is an Eden within, and that to lose that is to pluck up the tree of life by the roots, and leave the world one wide howling wilderness.

Death.

Viewed in the light of a penal infliction, from which man was at first conditionally exempt, Death must have originally come to him almost with the startling effect of an appalling revelation. The death of Abel would not, perhaps, on account of its violence, weigh much with the early generations of men, as an illustration of the original sentence against sin. But when the first natural death occurred—and, still more, when at length, after the event had been suspended century after century—when he had seen his descendants in the ninth generation—when he had reached his nine hundred and thirtieth year—the report went forth of Adam "he is dead; the father of the race has expired," what a deep shadow, as from the throne of justice brought near, must have fallen on the face of nature! And as, age after age, it had to be recorded of each individual of all these generations, "and he died," what an affecting proof was furnished of "the exceeding sinfulness of sin," what a demonstration of the fidelity of God to His word, and of the amplitude of *His* schemes who could defer its fulfillment either for a day or for a thousand years; and with what strained gaze, we may suppose, would the survivors labor to pierce the darkness which hung over the grave.

Examples of Faith and Piety, as Divine manifestations by Man.

Examples of eminent faith and piety formed a distinct method of revealing and enforcing the great principles by which they were originated and sustained; and thus contributed to the ends of moral government. They satisfactorily answered the question to which the Fall had imparted a profound interest—Is a life of holy obedience possible? As an indication of the Divine presence on earth, they were more conclusive than the radiance of the Shekinah itself—for they proved the presence of God in the human heart. Of such incarnations of piety, Enoch stood forth an illustrious example.* To what heights of excellence Abel might have attained, had not his life been so early terminated, we know not. Neither can we say how many were known and named, in their day, among "the sons of God," as proficients in spiritual excellence. But of Enoch it is briefly, yet significantly stated, that "he walked with God."† And, as if to intimate the singularity and eminence of the piety which, in his case, the language denotes, it is again repeated that "he walked with God."‡ He had come to place himself in entire harmony with the will of God. The autonomy or selfishness involved in the first sin, and which, in every separate sin, brings the human will into collision with the Divine—internally uniting all sins in one—was in him terminated. Although once disposed, like others, to alienate

* We have already adverted to the piety of Enoch as a Divine manifestation to *himself;* here we speak of it in its relation to others.

† Gen. v. 22. ‡ Verse 24.

himself from God, he had come to seek the perfection of freedom in the perfection of obedience—freedom, not merely from sin, but from all the outward and conscious restraints of law, because it is a law unto itself. His reconciliation with God resulted in a spirit of devotion: that devotion, in habits of practical obedience; and that sanctified law of habit, in the progressive attainment of holiness. His character was well-nigh normal. He had passed within the circle of the Divine attraction, and lived there. He walked on a mount of transfiguration. Every step took him nearer to the beatific vision. His translation is spoken of as the appropriate result:—"Enoch walked with God, and he was not, for God took him;"—as he thus walked, he approached so near to the central attraction that the earth suddenly saw him depart.

What a revelation, both of God and man, did this embodiment of piety, and its sublime result, exhibit! For, it is to be remembered that the whole was traceable—and by an Apostle it is traced, to a principle attainable by all—to *faith*. He walked with God, not by virtue of some undisclosed secret, not in consequence of any thing necessarily peculiar to himself, but by faith in the word and character of God. The faith which took Abel to the altar of sacrifice in early life, led Enoch to repair to it habitually for more than three hundred years. The faith which induced a comparative few barely to enter the way of life, induced him steadily to advance in it until he had attained to heights of holiness which, but for him, they might have been almost excused for deeming inaccessible—heights where he could freely expatiate over the sublime scenes of his future existence, and from which but little of earth remained visible, except what was calculated to repel by its depravity, or to alarm by its exposure to a gathering cloud. The faith which the irreligious around him were reposing in each other and in "the father of lies," he reposed in the infinitely blessed God. And thus he virtually rebuked all inferior piety; condemned the unbelief and practical atheism of the day; moved the world and overcame it, by standing on a position out of it and independent of it; and became so distinguished a witness for God, that God himself saw fit to signalize His approbation by the miraculous removal of His servant from the earth.

An invisible world.

The miracle of Enoch's *translation* was another event pregnant with Divine intimations, especially as pointing to *the existence of an invisible world.* "He was not, for God took him." "He was translated that he should not see death." Death had no doubt, by this time, come to be looked on by the skeptical world as a law of nature, from which man had never been even conditionally exempt. The solemn fact that, in his case, it is the penalty of transgression; or that he could, by possibility, have left the earth by any other mode of exit, only served to excite the general ridicule. But here was an event which re-proclaimed man's original condition; which affirmed that the law can never become superior to the Lawgiver; that the uniformity of nature for any given period simply proves that, during that period, such uniformity answers the Divine purpose better than the interruption of it would have done, but that it is nothing more than the expression of the Divine will for the time; for here, the miraculous became natural. The natural body was transformed into a spiritual body. Especially the visible and the earthly confessed their subordination to the invisible and the heavenly. There is ground to conclude that, as a public servant of God, the existence of an invisible world, and of many of its awful characteristics, had formed the subject of his warning addresses. "Knowing the terrors of the Lord, he persuaded men." But his message had excited derision. Here, however, the truth of his doctrine was Divinely attested, for that world had now absorbed him. The fact that "the spirits of the just made perfect" were all living unto God, could not now be rationally doubted; for there was ground to believe that he, a living saint, had gone to join them. The great doctrine of future rewards, and therefore of punishments, was now proclaimed by miracle; for here was one who, having walked with God till he had come to live in the very precincts of heaven, was now, as by a hand all but visible, suddenly drawn into the radiance of the Divine throne.

A future judgment.

The doctrine of *a future and final judgment* formed the subject of a distinct prophetic revelation. "Enoch, the seventh from Adam, prophesied of these [the irreligious of his day], saying, Behold, the Lord cometh with ten thousand of His saints, to execute judgment upon all, and to convince all that are ungodly among them of all their ungodly deeds which they have ungodly committed, and of all their hard speeches which ungodly sinners have spoken against Him."* Here

* Jude, 14, 15. Whence did the Apostle derive this language? There is no doubt of the existence of a very ancient book called "the Book of Enoch;" and that the Ethiopic version of it, which we now possess, was derived from an earlier Greek translation, and that again from the Chaldee or Hebrew original. The learned are about equally divided as to whether it was written in the first century of the Christian era or in the century preceding. Nor is it material to decide. For whether the Apostle was indebted to tradition or to this apocryphal book for the

we learn a part, at least, of "the burden of the Lord" which his messengers delivered. Even in that dawning of time, the eye of prophecy, piercing through all the intermediate ages, descried the pomp and solemnity of the final judgment with all the vividness of an impending event.

Doubtless that final scene was foreshadowed and foreseen in the threatened deluge. How impressively did the Divine prediction of the flood proclaim the calm, certain, and majestic movements of justice. The world probably then, as now, derided the idea of its destruction; scientifically demonstrated, in its way, the physical impossibility of a general deluge; proved historically that such an event never had taken place; and congratulated itself on the superior notions which it entertained of the Divine benevolence—notions which rendered it politely horrified at the bare mention of such a catastrophe. But on went the note of preparation, in the building of the Ark, without pause or relaxation. And many a sinner would see in the coming crisis, a prediction, by fact, of the last judgment. And the "preacher of righteousness" would solemnly point to it as an installment of the great doom predicted by Enoch; and which, from the moment of its first announcement, has

prophecy, the inspiration which guided his selection is a sufficient attestation of its truth. As, however, the writer of the book of Enoch, if he wrote before the Apostle, must have been indebted to tradition for the prophecy, there is no reason whatever why the Apostle might not have derived it from the same source. The probability is, that it is one of those winged sentences which came across the flood; and that it continued its flight from age to age, like a messenger from God, till the Spirit was pleased to give it a place in the record of his living oracles.

The Book of Enoch the Prophet, by Dr. Laurence. *Amer. Bib. Repos.* 1840. Silvestre de Sacy's *Notice du Livre d'Enoch* in the *Magazin Encyclopédique*, an. vi. tom. i. p. 382.

never ceased to loom and lower in the dark back-ground of time. And new and agitating thoughts of God, as the heart-searcher, the All-knowing Judge, would spring up, and forestall the doom of many a sinner.

The great moral division—the saved and the lost.

But the deluge was not to be an indiscriminate judgment; it was to present an epitome of the last great crisis in this respect also, that it would exhibit the salvation of some attended with the destruction of others, and that *the destruction was subordinate to the salvation, and in order to it.* The popular notion is, that the waters of the deluge sustained the same relation to Noah and his family which they did to the world at large; and that the only deliverance which he experienced, in connection with the flood, was deliverance from the death in which it wrapped all the other families of mankind. But no, the sense in which he was saved *from* it, is only a low, accidental, physical sense; as the champion of a people's liberties might be said to have been saved from the casualties of a conflict in which numbers had fallen, although, in the highest sense, and in reality, he, and liberty, and his people, were all saved *by* the conflict. So, says the Apostle Peter, Noah was "saved *by* water;" and hence he represents it as the emblem of baptismal water under the present economy. There was a moral deluge flooding the earth long before the physical deluge was predicted—"the floods of the ungodly;" and it was to save the Patriarch from these floods that the material deluge came. It was not sent to show how God could rescue His servant from its drowning waves; but in order that it might be, in conjunction with the Ark, the means of saving him from an already existing deluge of wickedness which had advanced and risen until piety was driven to its last refuge. The destruction of the world was not an end, but only the means to an end; and that end, the salvation of Noah, and of a principle to which even the Patriarch's deliverance was to be subordinated—that of the progress of the Divine manifestation in the history of humanity. And however unwelcome this interpretation of the predicted deluge may have been to the irreligious, and however vaguely it may have floated before their eyes, during the hundred and twenty years which elapsed before the prediction was fulfilled, the Patriarch doubtless beheld in it only a new and enlarged illustration of the great principle, characteristic of the Divine government from the beginning—that judgment is subordinated to mercy; that evil, whether permitted or inflicted, exists only for the sake of good, and in order to it.

Teaching by Names.

Another mode of Divine instruction and revelation was the bestowment on certain individuals of *names** commemorative or predictive of great truths and events. Names, at that time, were not arbitrary or numerical signs. They stood for primitive ideas; clothed great principles; reflected the vicissitudes of history; ranked with institutions. The human heart was then travailing with a great hope; and every new event, especially the birth of a child, became significant and kindled expectation. What a solemn disclosure was made in the *earthly* appellation given to the first man! What a flood of hope and joy gushed forth in the first utterance of the new name which Adam, just released from the expected doom of immediate death, bestowed on the mother of the species—*Chavah* (Eve) *Life*, "because she was [to be] the mother of all living." The names of Cain,

* See the *Onomasticon Sacrum*. Mathæi Hilleri.

Abel, and Seth, could never be intelligently pronounced without recalling, and virtually repeating, the leading events in the first family of man, and thus tending to familiarize the mind with all the principles of the Divine administration which those events illustrate. The Biblical idea of God was itself a sublime revelation, and of that idea His Name was significant. The earliest names by which the Divine being was pleased to make Himself known to His human worshipers appear to have been *El*,* *Eloah*, and *Elohim*—rendered in our common version, *God*—and denoting the *Supreme*, the *Adorable Power*. And though it would not be safe to infer the earliest conceptions of God from these primeval appellations, we may warrantably conclude that the minds of the faithful were constantly growing up to them, and more clearly reflecting them. In process of time, the Divine name, *El*, came to be compounded with human names, showing with what a power religion penetrated and possessed the mind. To say, *Mahlaleel*, was to summon to the *Praise of God*. Still more marked was the period when all the faithful came to be called collectively the *sons of God*—implying as it did the recognition of their profound relations to Him, their obedience to His will, and their faith in His word; and uttering, in

* One proof that this is the earliest name by which God was known to man is, that it is the *only* one which is found incorporated with antediluvian human names. The name *Jehovah*, therefore, as employed by the sacred historian in his account of antediluvian times, must not be supposed to imply that it was known dispensationally, if at all, during those times, but only that it was the Divine designation appropriately and generally employed at the time that Moses wrote, or at the time when the account which he adopts, under Divine guidance, was first made known by tradition or by writing. Ex. vi. 2, 3.

effect, a continuous prediction of the coming of the promised deliverance. At a later period, we come to names indicative of the mighty thoughts which were agitating the hearts of the sons of God, and pointing then to the pregnant future. Thus, to say *Noah*, was to repeat a prediction which looked on to the flood and beyond; while the names of his three sons dimly foreshadowed the history of three great branches of mankind.

Prophetic Teaching.

Prophecy, including preaching or public admonition, was an additional vehicle of Divine communication to sinful man. At first, the venerable Patriarch would address his instructions and rebukes only to the numerous members of his own family. But when, in the lapse of time, they who should have been united as teachers and taught, banded together in a league of irreligion, the mission of the "man of God" took a wider range and a more solemn character. Noah was a "preacher of righteousness." * That there was a succession of such messengers from God can not be doubted; for when the wickedness of man proved at length incorrigible, God said, "My spirit shall not always strive with man." The meaning of this language may perhaps be best explained by the parallel language in Nehemiah,† "Yet many years didst Thou forbear them, and testified against them by Thy Spirit in Thy prophets; yet would they not give ear." In a similar manner, the Spirit of God, in His prophets, struggled with the giant forms of antediluvian impiety.

Plurality of the Divine Name.

In justice to the greatness of the subject, I can not forbear pointing attention to the intimations of a plurality in the Divine essence contained in the opening pages of Revelation, and of which the language

* 2 Peter, ii. 5. † Neh. ix. 30.

quoted in the preceding paragraph is peculiarly striking. How remarkable, for example, that the *plural* term, Elohim, should be applied to the Divine Being; especially when there was not the least necessity for so doing arising from the Hebrew language itself. How much is this apparent anomaly increased by the fact that these plural names are construed with singular verbs, pronouns, and adjectives.* How awakening and suggestive the fact that Elohim, God, thus designated by a plural appellative, should also speak of Himself in plural forms: "And God said, Let us make man in *our* image, after *our* likeness!"† while in the declaration, "My Spirit shall not always strive with man," the idea of plurality combined with unity is still more fully developed. As I could not, however, open the discussion of this subject here, without forestalling proofs and illustrations belonging to a later stage of the Divine proceedings, and as I do not claim for it a distinct dogmatic form in antediluvian times, I will only add that, for us, and with our su-

* The attempt to account for this peculiarity by the Rabbinical rule of grammar called *plur. majestaticus*—made to meet this particular exigence—is now well-nigh exploded. Ewald affirms that "it is a great error to suppose that the Hebrew language, as we find it, has any feeling for a so-called *plur. majestaticus;* and that the word *Elohim* appears always to have remained in the *pl.* in prose from that (the earliest) time."—*Gram, of the Heb. Language of the Old Testament, transl. by Nicholson,* 1836. § 361.

† The attempt to explain this peculiarity by saying that it *is* the style of regal authority, assumes, without proof, both that it *was* the style of Hebrew rulers, and that it was the style of sovereigns at the early period of the Mosaic writings. In truth, it involves the solecism of attempting to resolve a suggestive peculiarity of the Divine language into an affectation of human language, which most probably remained unknown for centuries afterward.

perior light, the language appears to make an important disclosure, both of the internal economy of the Divine nature, and of some of the relations of that economy to the process of man's restoration. The Divine essence includes a subsistence designated the Spirit. The Spirit, already spoken of as transforming the material chaos, sustains the office of contending with the chaos of the moral world, rebuking and condemning the rebellion of the human heart; and the world is here at length warned that this contest of mercy draws to a close, and that Justice is about to unsheath his sword.

Sacrificial Animals and Covenants.

Other illustrations of the gradual development of primary truths and appointments might have been noticed. The distinction between beasts clean and unclean,* for example, denotes that an enlargement of the *sacrificial* ritual had already, at some time, taken place. And the manner in which the covenants made with Noah† are introduced, implies that the ideas which they embody were already familiar to his mind. But abundant evidence has been adduced that the development of the means of Divine manifestation, spoken of in our second and third chapters, had been constantly going on. Objects in nature had been consecrated to new and exalted ends. Man himself had become a new revelation. The voice of prophecy was no longer strange. Glimpses into the unseen world had been afforded. The fundamental principles of moral government had been republished, in effect, again and again. The family economy had shown its vast capabilities as a part of that government. The doctrine of mediation, embodied in Patriarchal intercession, had become familiar. Particular judgments were general-

* Gen. vii. 2.

† Gen. vi. 18; ix. 11.

ized into the prospect of a coming judgment all-comprehending and final. Pre-existing means of manifestation were not only brought forward, they were employed for higher purposes than before; and even the fundamental truths of the new economy were themselves constantly placed in new lights and received additional verifications. The mercy which had been promised had been also and often experienced. In the highest sense men had been saved.

CHAPTER V.

THE ACTIVITY WHICH THE LAW OF DEVELOPMENT PRE-SUPPOSES, AND WHICH THE FAMILY PUTS IN MOTION.

Law of activity.

In the preceding chapter we have exemplified the *fact* of man's development during the antediluvian period; in the present, we propose to specify some of those *principles* of man's nature which that development appealed to or pre-supposed. In other words, the law of activity justifies the expectation that man "will be found to manifest all that he is calculated to exhibit of the Divine nature, by developing or working out his own nature."* Even a material creation, if devoid of regulated activity, could be no manifestation of an ever-living and ever-acting God. Still more may activity be expected in that order of creatures whose distinction it is, that not only *to* them but *by* them the manifestation will be made. Such activity may be looked for in them, if only to help them to understand, by sympathy, the same property in the Divine nature. Accordingly, man has certain possibilities of active excellence stored up in him, by the voluntary employment of which he becomes an image, to himself and to others, of the Divine activity in creation and providence. These possibilities the family constitution tends to develop and to make actual.

* For the grounds of this law, see Pre-Adamite Earth, p. 61.

Pre-supposes Divine instructions.

Man's individual activity pre-supposes a world of objective conditions.* He came to find every part of his nature the center of innumerable appeals. But in addition to this pre-constituted harmony between man and nature, the very first movements of the first Patriarch pre-supposed the possession of a certain amount of material knowledge.† "That man could not have *made* himself is appealed to as a proof of the agency of a Divine *Creator;* and that mankind could not in the first instance have civilized themselves, is a proof, exactly of the same kind, and of equal strength, of the agency of a Divine *Instructor*." ‡ Men are apt to imagine that the advantages resulting from a course of conduct when it is completed were the motives which led to it; and therefore erroneously infer that every step of their civilization is the legitimate result of a previously-digested plan. But of all the truths developed by history, there are none more certain than these: first, that, with all man's freedom as an individual, yet in the great process of social civilization, "effects are generally produced before the causes are perceived; and that, with all man's talents for projects, his work is often accomplished before the plan is devised." § And, secondly, that not only has no savage family ever been known to emerge from barbarism by its own unaided exertion, but that the tendency of every tribe in such a condition is to grow worse instead of better.‖ The means of amelioration must come to it from without—from a people already civilized. Had the first man then been created

* Man Primeval, chap. vi. † *Ibid*, pp. 177, 178.

‡ Archbishop Whateley's Political Economy. Lect. v.

§ Dr. A. Ferguson's Essay on Civil Society, section 1.

‖ Dr. W. C. Taylor's *Natural History of Society*, vol. i. chap. xiv.

and left in perfect ignorance, in perfect ignorance he would have remained; or, rather, in that ignorance he would have speedily perished. Even if he could have imagined what is meant by civilization, the prospect of the complicated means necessary to attain it, and of his own utter helplessness in devising them, could have produced but one effect—that of annihilating hopelessness. But the very conception itself—even the consciousness of the want of improvement—pre-supposes an amount of acquired knowledge; for entire barbarism is unconscious of the want, and even resists the first attempts to impart it.

In harmony with these views, we have found the first father of the species Divinely put in possession, at the beginning, of a certain stock of civilizing knowledge. The great Parent himself gave man's activity the first impulse, and the right direction; indicating to him the fields in which his offspring might most profitably employ their energies. Doubtless, the knowledge imparted was of a kind not to supersede but to quicken the exercise of his own powers. It was a pound likely to "gain ten pounds more."

Family activity voluntary.

But in vain would man have possessed this knowledge as the means of self-development, unless the constitution of the family had been of a nature to leave his activity *voluntary*. Every one acquainted with human nature knows that the activity compelled by a force from without tends to cease the moment that force is removed; and this, notwithstanding many considerations of self-interest, may combine with that force to induce the continuance of the activity. Hence, it is always the wisdom of those in authority to encourage effort, to fan emulation, and to make activity voluntary. Here, in the first family, no external force existed even to compel it. Love was the mainspring of every movement; in love every effort was intended to find its ample reward.

Derives its voluntariness from love.

The family constitution secures the activity of its members by deriving this voluntariness from the powerful *motives of gratitude and love.* Love carries the mind beyond itself; and is the sense of its emotional relation to another as its proper object. That affection, which is the first great stimulus of the young of both sexes, is no sooner gratified in the attainment of its object than it turns its attention to the pleasant task of enhancing the happiness of that object. The new pursuit may often apparently involve the comparative disregard of the object beloved; but it is only because enlightened affection thinks of the future as well as of the present, and is prepared to sacrifice the pleasure of the passing moment, as the husbandman appears to cast away the precious seed, only that he may afterward reap a plentiful harvest. And most wisely and benevolently is it ordered, that the affection should operate with the greater force for encountering difficulties; that its ardor increases in proportion as it benefits and renders its object happy; and that the longer it continues, the mutual exercises of generosity which are brought to light, and the joint trials of fortitude which are involved, all tend to bring over the best passions of the mind upon its side. Now, from the moment the social constitution was founded, in the union of our first parents, this mighty spring of activity began to uncoil and expand, requiring an ever-enlarging sphere for its operation. Who can imagine them, as at first, alone in the world, without picturing their efforts for each other's happiness? How would a sense of their mutual dependence endear them to each other, and convert that labor into enjoyment which contributed in the least to the good of the object beloved! But what an accession to the strength of their mutual activity came with the birth of their first-born child! The new and powerful emotions awakened, as they gazed on his helplessness, loveliness, and new-born innocence, involved a new and sleepless principle of civilization, which asked an additional sphere of activity. For him a softer couch would be spread than had before been known. New words would be coined—words of tenderness and yearning love; to be uttered in tones new to the ear—tones of music to mingle with his dreams. Invention would be taxed in his service; and man be anew surprised at the discovery of his own resources. Every additional child would be a new bond of conjugal affection, and a fresh impulse to parental activity. And thus, while new demands continued to be made on their diligence, and the circle over which they had to extend their foresight and to exercise their superintendence went on enlarging, they were acquiring the habits necessary to fill that circle to its circumference with their industry.

Increased by emulation.

As the members of the family increased, they would be actuated by a spirit of affectionate *emulation*. This is seen even among young children. "The plays of natural lively children are the infancy of art. Children live in the world of imagination and feeling. They invest the most insignificant object with any form they please, and see in it whatever they wish to see."* While each, it may be added, strives to excel the other in the expression he gives to it; and thus to win the good opinion

* *Oehlenschläger*, in Mrs. Austin's Fragments from German Prose Writers, p. 162.

of those around him. As age advances, the same efforts are transferred to a wider sphere; and that which the child was believed to be, the youth strives to become. Here, opposite qualities, finding themselves side by side, are taxed to the utmost in a variety of ways, but all tending to the development of humanity. Strength puts forth its last efforts and seeks to become stronger, in the presence of weakness; and weakness repays it by admiration, reliance and the gentle ministry of its attentions and comforts. Wisdom itself is instructed, while sifting and simplifying its knowledge, and answering the keen inquiries of youthful curiosity; and youthful ignorance learns humility, industry, and habits of obedience, while in the act of acquiring the knowledge of other things. Each member, by living and moving under the eye of the whole, would feel himself constantly incited to vie with every other in his endeavors to minister to the general good. Every offering laid on the domestic altar is repaid with gratitude; every mite of pleasure added is an increase of the common fund of enjoyment; and idleness, if only for its unproductiveness, is treason to the domestic economy.

By division of labor.

Still further would this activity be secured by *the division of labor* of which the family constitution admits, and for which it provides. Labors which the isolated individual would never think of undertaking can here, by combination, be accomplished with ease; and a sphere which one alone would never dream of even entering can be filled with activity in every part. If Abel undertakes to herd the cattle, Cain can give his undivided attention to the cultivation of the ground, and so increase his knowledge, and improve his methods, of agriculture. Tubal Cain, by confining himself to metallurgy, can acquire a facility and a skill in his department which enables him to work up his material to the greatest perfection, and to produce it in the greatest abundance. And thus the history of the progress of civilization before the Flood, as since, would be found to be a history of the ever-increasing subdivision of the objects of human labor.

Paternal authority promotes and directs it.

The authority with which the father, as head of the family, is naturally invested, would enable him to turn the activity of its members to the best account by giving to it direction, unity, and strength. The knowledge and position of the parent give him the opportunity of discovering, as from a height, the peculiar aptitudes of his children in their earliest symptoms, and of furnishing the appropriate means for their development; so that a Jubal and a Jabal may not, by changing places, find their respective professions a drudgery, and leave them entirely unimproved. Every art, and every portion of every art, has a "mystery" which may engross the whole of a man's attention; but it is only when he gives himself to it *con amore* that he so masters it as to carry it to a state of greater perfection than that in which he found it. The parent, too, possessed the power of so directing the pursuits of his children as that the labors of one should enhance the value of the labors of all the rest; the husbandry of one subserving the pastoral employments of another, and the labors of both these contributing to give unity and value to the activity of the whole. And the authority which thus distributes to the children their several departments of activity is, of course, presumed to be the furthest removed from ignorance, caprice, arbitrariness, and selfishness; for it is not only the authority of age and experience, but also of a father, and therefore the authority of affection; while the obedience which hastens to fill those departments is presumed to be voluntary, grateful, and cheerful, for it is the obedience of youth, inexperience, and filial love.

Excited by the co-existence of other families.

The multiplication and co-existence of families which had branched off from the parent stock would still further excite to activity. The emulation which had existed within the single family would find a much wider sphere for friendly competition in endeavoring to surpass the efforts and the possessions of neighboring families. And if the division of labor among the members of the same family enabled them greatly to extend the range of their activity, how much more would that range be enlarged by the friendly co-operation of distinct families, even in the same district?

By the migration of families.

This activity would often be heightened to enterprise and daring when families migrated into remote districts teeming with new products, and furnishing new lines of industry, and new incitements to it. And if the physical geography of Western Asia resembled then what we know it to be now, almost every remove would exhibit the variety supposed. The families left behind, eager to share the attractive products of the new field, would have fresh inducements to labor in order to procure them; while the emigrants, accustomed to comforts they had left behind, and unable to create them in their new locality, would be furnished with powerful motives to enterprise in order to procure them in exchange. The corn and timber of the terrace-regions would be bartered for the products of the "land of Havilah, where there is gold, and bdellium, and the onyx-stone;" the rich fruits and balms of the lowlands, for the rock-salt of Anatolia; and "horses from the house of Togarmah"* (Armenia), for the herds fed on the table-lands of Iran.

By the family relationship of the whole.

And the relations of kindred in which they all stood to each other—to say nothing of the identity of their language—tended to the same advancement, by furnishing motives to constant and friendly intercourse. To the question of their numbers we shall presently allude; but whether they were comparatively great or small, they must all have appeared to each other, even to the last, in the light of one family, the latest-born of which was related, not remotely, to the parents of the whole.

Moral civilization; how promoted by marriage.

Ascending from material to *moral* civilization—which kinds, though distinct, are inseparable and mutually reactive—we have to speak first of the great law of *marriage*, as founded in the constitution of human nature. The Divine appointment, which limits the married state to individuals who are exclusively united to each other for life—as proclaimed in the creation and union of the first pair—was calculated to exercise an exalting influence on human character. It took the conjugal state out of the class of mere animal indulgences, and pointed to ennobling ends. It is essential to a Home.

The relations arising out of the conjugal state are calculated to touch every spring in man's nature. The parents themselves have been drawn to each other by a power which makes them one. Their children are parts of themselves. How powerfully adapted is the sight of an infant family to terminate improvidence, and to produce thoughtfulness and foresight—thus giving the future its due ascendency over the present. How softening and purifying

* Ezekiel, xxvii. 14.

—what a fountain of moral civilization in the bosom of a family—is the helpless little one, with its tears, its prattle, and the radiant innocence of its face! In communion with such freshness, how many a father has then first felt ashamed of his vice, and has hid it, if not even abandoned it! The relation of children to one another, especially that of brothers and sisters, operates to the same benign effect. Between these, love is seen in "sexual separation." The affections are cherished, while sentiments of chastity and delicacy are strengthened. And thus—as it has been beautifully expressed, "in giving us sisters, God gave us the best of earthly moral antiseptics."*

The family constitution provides a nursery for the benevolent affections. Not only is "sense consecrated in marriage," or its pleasures denied to the mere appetites that they may be ennobled and given to pure affection; not only does self-love, in the case of each of the parents, enlarge the sphere of its operation, forecasting and providing for each other and for their offspring, as parts of one whole; but in the family, the children, by being surrounded by objects of love, are detached from that selfishness which would otherwise place them in isolation from all around, and are trained

* Guesses at Truth, p. 306. *First Series.*

But must not the brothers and sisters of the first family have intermarried? Yes. But let the following facts be borne in mind:—First, that the same ground of necessity for such unions could never exist again to the end of time. Secondly, that the social and moral evils which such unions would certainly engender at any subsequent period, could have had no existence at a time when there were no other families in being. The natural necessity for the act ceased before its tendency could be felt. And, thirdly, the God of nature prohibits the repetitions of such unions by a law—the physiological law that the offspring of such unions tend more and more to degeneracy.

to regard themselves, not merely as units, of which society is the sum total, but as organic parts of which it is the vital whole.

By Longevity.

The longevity of Patriarchal life, too, afforded an extended opportunity for contrasting the effects arising from the violation of the laws of chastity and marriage with the consequences resulting from their observance. As to the *number* of offspring, for instance, ample time was then enjoyed for observing, on the largest scale, the fact, that while the laws of marriage tend to the steady multiplication of a people, polygamy, promiscuous intercourse, and licentiousness in all its forms, tend to reduce the fecundity of the species, and have, in some instances, led to the extinction of whole tribes. God would be seen signifying His will, on the same subject, in the *physical superiority* of the offspring of marriage as contrasted with the fruits of licentious intercourse. It would be apparent also in the quiet and comfort of a home, as contrasted with the bickerings, jealousies, and strifes of a harem; and especially in the training and education of the children of lawful marriage, as contrasted with the neglected condition of others.

By the laws of Reciprocity.

Another element of moral civilization which the family was calculated advantageously to develop, was that which relates to the laws of *Reciprocity*. The first family would present, in effect, a mimic rehearsal of all the tendencies to evil which society afterward came to exhibit on a gigantic scale; but most admirably adapted was the domestic economy to restrain them, and to develop the opposite virtues. As to the *sanctity of human life*, what constitution so adapted to waken and cherish the sentiment as one in which all were nearly related, and daily moved in the presence of their common parents? As to *Personal Liberty*—the first child was born with *rights* equal to those of its parents; for it brought into the world a constitution, or a separate and complete system, which rendered it capable of self-government, and separately answerable to God for the use of its powers. But, then, as its *condition* was not equal, how admirable was the arrangement which placed it in hands which, so far from invading its rights, would be ever ready to protect them, and which placed no limits to its *liberty* but such as led to its right application, and its full enjoyment! And when, as would naturally be the case, the superior strength of the first-born would be occasionally put forth, if only in innocent playfulness, to coerce the movements of the second, how well calculated was the parental voice which arrested the proceeding to call out the sentiment of justice implanted in the infant breast! As to the *right of property*, one of the earliest sentiments developed in childhood—how could the child be placed more advantageously for having it developed correctly? The too ready *meum* of the first child would come to be limited by the *tuum* of the second. And as the family increased, and little questions of childish property multiplied and required arbitration, what hand so likely to hold the balances impartially as that of parental love?

The same may be said of Justice, as it respects character, reputation, and veracity in general. What eye likely to be so quick in the detection of any thing calculated to weaken moral restraint, or to excite evil dispositions, as that of the affectionate parent? Who so loth as he to listen to any tale affecting the reputation of one of his children, even though told by the lips of another; or so prompt to examine into its truth, and to rebuke the slander? Or where could the child be placed in circumstances in which he would naturally be so likely to be trained to truth as under the parental roof? Here the first object is to train its senses to report truly; then to teach its tongue to express truly its own thoughts; and then to report no thought as truth, either of the past, the present, or the future, either of testimony or promise—but such as it believes to be true. And in no place could there be less interest to deceive, or stronger motives to speak the truth, than in the family.

In all these respects, too, the children of a family live under the influence of an example the most likely to affect them, and enjoy it during the most impressible season of life. For in the spirit and conduct of their parents toward each other, they behold justice administered by love; reciprocity, anxious only not to take more than it imparts; the voluntary denial of self, gaining its reward in a higher and a nobler whole.

By the multiplication of Families.

It is interesting to imagine the expansion and application of these sentiments as families branched off, multiplied, and subsequently co-operated in voluntary associations. As to personal Liberty, there would be ample room for its development and assertion, physically, intellectually, and religiously. And although as the family relations become more and more collateral and removed from the parent stock; and as other relations, such as those of master and servant, came into existence, human liberty would be increasingly endangered; yet the Patriarchal form of government would tend in that early age, more than any other form, to respect and preserve it. The sentiment which it was calculated to cherish was beautifully expressed by Job, when, centuries after, he said—

"If I denied justice to my male hireling,
Or to my female hireling, when they disputed with me,
What then should I do when God maketh inquest?
When he inquires, what answer should I give?
Did not He who formed me, form them?
Were we not fashioned alike in the womb?"

By the law of Property.

As to Property, there was scope for the development of the sentiment in all its various stages. There was the right arising from discovery; and the still higher arising from possession; and the highest arising from appropriation, or transformation, by labor and improvement. This right of subordinate creation—this feeling respecting a certain place or object, that it was *mine*, and that all which I can make of it will be mine also, is a most powerful stimulant to effort. At that period, too, human life, prolonged though it was, would be comparatively little less than a prolonged wonder. Every new movement would have all the uncertainty and excitement of an experiment. Every instance of success would be hailed as a discovery and a triumph. The raw material of the world was given into man's hand, and every new form which he gave to it, or new purpose to which he applied it, would call forth the applauses of his cotemporaries, and promise him immortality. But the rights of any one family, in respect to property, were the rights of all. As the families which had diverged in different directions multiplied into tribes, and as, by that multiplication, they approached each other again, it would become necessary to have these rights defined. And what parties so likely to prevent Judah and Ephraim from vexing each other, by establishing an equitable adjustment, as the Patriarchs of each, whose wisdom taught them their mutual dependence, and whose unforgotten relationship made them to love as brethren? *

Patriarchal rule strengthened by Morality.

As to Character, the Patriarch would continue to feel, even when his family had increased to a tribe, and every father in the tribe would feel with him, that whatever tended to impair its morality, tended in the same degree to impair parental authority. Hence, even when higher motives failed to influence, a reason for the maintenance of morality would be ever present and operative in the desire to conserve the necessary Patriarchal rule. And as the human family went on to multiply, the duties affecting reputation and veracity would increase in importance also. Greater reliance would have to be placed on unsupported testimony. Mutual confidence became more and more essential to mutual co-operation. And in such confidence and co-operation would be found the bond of a union, not solemnized, indeed, by formal treaties, but which yet invisibly cemented all the children of Adam in a family compact.

The Family eminently favorable to Religious Civilization.

Ascending, again, from moral to *religious* civilization, which kinds, like the material and the moral, though distinct are inseparable and mutually reactive—the three being parts of one whole—we find every thing in the family supposing it, and conducing to it. As to the *children*, what facilities the domestic constitution affords for their religious education! For here it may be commenced before their hearts become pre-occupied with conscious evil; while they are in a state of great susceptibility to impression; disposed readily to believe the parental word; and with the certainty that this impressible and improvable state will continue for a succes-

* Gen. xiii. 8, 9.

sion of months and even years. In an antediluvian family, indeed,

> "When still a hundred years beheld the boy
> Beneath his mother's roof, her infant joy;" *

and where the children were never entirely dismissed from parental authority and oversight during the parental life, these facilities and their salutary effects would be enjoyed for centuries.

As to the *Parents*, how inciting to holy diligence the *relations* they found themselves called to sustain! On becoming a parent, Adam would first know emphatically what a Father in Heaven meant, and feel more than ever his dependence upon Him. Respecting the *knowledge* they had to impart—what a tale had the first parent to tell! and during his long pilgrimage of nine hundred years, could it ever lose its affecting interest for his posterity? How many a question would he have to answer again and again respecting his paradisiacal state? And although the parents of later times would only be channels of many of those Divine communications of which he was the appointed *fountain*, the character of those truths, by awakening the curiosity, and exciting the imagination, of their children, would furnish their own minds with constant occasion for devout consideration. Such would be the case especially with the doctrines involved in the institution of sacrifice and the *family* character of the first promise. Respecting the *duties* they had to perform—especially the priestly duties of intercession and sacrifice—how affecting to the aged Patriarch himself to lead the devotions of a multitude of all ages who had sprung from his loins, and to remember that, in doing so, he was typifying a mysterious

* *Hesiod's* Works and Days. *Elton's* Translation, line 175.

arrangement on which he was not less dependent than his offspring!

As to the *family*, viewed collectively and in its successive generations. The manner in which the Divine revelations had been imparted—the proofs by which their authenticity could be established—the meaning of many of the figurative expressions employed (as; for example, in the first promise)—the period of the fulfillment of that promise—all this required more or less of induction, and would lead the devout inquirer to "search diligently what was the mind of the Spirit." Now the family was a constitution admirably adapted for repressing crude thoughts and dangerous theories, and for conducting such inquiries to a wise and successful issue. For, here, youth could sit at the feet of age, history correct and guide speculation, and authority and reason find the most advantageous point of union. Here, too, death came all the more solemnly for having delayed his stroke for long centuries, and, by leading the venerable Patriarch of generations down to his dark chambers, would impressively remind the survivors of their common relationship to each other, and of their near alliance to another state of being. But chiefly would the hallowing influence of religion be felt by the stated observance of the Sabbath. Then, reminded of their common origin, hopes, and destiny, they would be prepared for the activities of this world by being made to feel their relationship to God and to the world to come.

Here, then, in the family constitution, we find every thing presupposing the tendency of man to work out his own nature by activity, as well as conducive to such development. If this world was prepared for the coming of the first man, not less was the family economy designed, as an inner world, for the reception of the infant; whence, having received impressions from every object in the family, and having influenced them in return, he is to go forth to repeat the process in a family of his own, and to multiply and extend the relations of man to external nature. The milk which rushes to the mother's breast at the birth of her first-born, is but an emblem of the adaptations and activities of the domestic constitution. Here, by the sedulous affection which is ever developing the faculties of the child; marking every new trait in its character with wondering admiration; attracting its eye with colors; amusing it with sounds; by motions exciting its motions; guiding its random steps; teaching its first words; and thus preparing it to take part in the opening drama of life; new energies and resources are developed in the parents themselves. Here affection finds ample scope for denying itself, courage for daring, and industry for its manifold labors. Here is abundant room for patience to endure, authority to reward or to punish, fidelity to counsel and to warn, imagination to combine and originate, memory and hope to possess the past and the future, and piety to watch and pray and perform its thousand acts of holiness and love.

Man's history at the eve of the deluge, the history of his self-manifestation.

Now if, before the great process of human development began outside the garden of Eden, one could have been made acquainted with all the powerful springs inclosed in the human constitution, and about to press on every resistance they could encounter—if one could have foreseen that, from the first two a family was to spring, and from that family a multitude of others in successive generations, each member of which would bring with him the same principles of ceaseless activity; that every onward step would only prepare the way for a step further, and furnish the means for taking it, in the cultivation of a fallow world; and that even the day of rest was not to terminate on itself, but was, partly, to give to activity the character of devotion, and to constitute religion the great element of civilization—"man (we might have said) will require an extended area for the full play of his activity, and centuries of time to reap its higher, moral results, and a vast variety of unwrought material on which to exercise, and by which to develop his untried powers." Accordingly, we have seen that the area assigned him was the fertile and varied regions of Western Asia. Here, every thing awaited his coming favorable to the evolution of his powers, and a stock of knowledge was given him for the right commencement of his active career. And, here, for about two thousand years, the family constitution—so favorable to civilization in its highest sense—was laboring and enlarging, and constantly multiplying its external relations.

Every object, every event, and every trace, then, which that area was found to include at the close of that period, and which it would not have included but for his coming, is to be viewed as related in some way to the manifestation of man. In all this it might have been said to a spectator —in all this, you behold an exposition of humanity. True, you see not the whole field of results. Generation after generation has passed into the unseen world, and "their works have followed them." But the influence of their works remains and is active in the character of the existing generation. And true also, much of what you see is interesting in inferior respects; as, for example, the mutual relations and the capabilities of much of the *material* placed at man's disposal. But this is as nothing compared with the fact that he has discovered these relations, and taxed these capabilities, and that by so doing he has unfolded his own capabilities and relations. "Property is nothing else than the application of man's individuality to external things; or the realization and manifestation of man's individuality in the material world."* And, here, as civilization has advanced, he has laid his hand on object after object, ever seeking to multiply his image and enlarge his power. Those cultivated fields and numerous herds; those mechanical devices, and that substitution of brute strength, by which human labor is economized; those toys by which childhood is amused, and those symbols by which love is expressed; those lines drawn by the hand of justice around property, and those walls and fences which speak of insecurity; those clustering tents and more substantial houses, those tombs built by bereaved affection, and those altars reared by piety—what are they in relation to our present subject but a great hieroglyphic writing, in which man has inscribed his history on the surface of the globe, he himself being the great Hieroglyph. For by these means, each man, each family, each generation, has disclosed its own character, has influenced that of others, and by reaction molded its own.

In this scene of man's self-manifestation, we behold, *as far as it proceeded according to original law*, the scene and means of the Divine manifestation. This is its highest, its ultimate relation. Man was revealing his own nature in every movement of his activity, and in every impression which it produced. But God was revealing Himself in every spring and power inclosed in human nature. As far, therefore, as man's free nature was rightly evolved, it was a manifestation of the Divine Nature. Here, God manifested himself *by* man that he might be manifested *to* him.

* Lieber's Political Ethics, book ii. sec. 9.

CHAPTER VI.

THE CONTINUITY OF THIS DEVELOPMENT AND ACTIVITY IN THE MEANS OF DIVINE MANIFESTATION.

THE whole of the progress made in the unfolding scheme of Divine manifestation during the antediluvian period was continuous; so that, whatever the advance made by the eve of the deluge, it was either the growth and expansion of all the past, or else in perfect harmony with it. During each successive stage of that period, every department of art and science, of morals and religion, existed in this sense, in an all-related connection; and this, owing to the fact that the scheme of Providence consists, not of detached parts, but is one continuous and ever-evolving whole. Man himself, individually considered, is a continuous being, both as to his constitutional and his historical development;* and the history of the individual is only, in this respect, a foreshadowing of the continuous development of the family, and of the community or tribe.

Material civilization continuous.

This is true of the material civilization of that period. "Who then educated the first human pair? (asks the elder Fichte, in a burst of common sense too strong for the bonds of an infidel philosophy.) A spirit bestowed its care upon them, as is laid down in an

* Man Primeval, p. 190, etc.

ancient and venerable original record, which, taken altogether, contains the profoundest and the loftiest wisdom, and presents those results to which all philosophy must at last come." With the precise amount of the information directly imparted by the Divine parent to the first members of His human family, we have not now to do. For even if we could determine every thing which relates to it, the manner of its communication, the subjects to which it referred, and the advantages derivable from it, we should still be ready to assume that, for the most part, it would be only gradually applied and adopted. And then, having received its appropriate practical application, the skill which that application would impart, the hints and analogies which it would suggest, and the means it would supply, would ask for a wider sphere, and gradually lead to experiments and new discoveries.

Traces of progress from age to age.

Now, the fragmentary history of antediluvian improvements in the arts of life, as recorded in Scripture, harmonizes with this law. In the *second* generation we find a division of labor, and the recognition of the rights of personal property. "Abel was a keeper of sheep," and brings of "the firstlings of *his* flock." Cain, the husbandman, becomes *in course of time*, the builder of a city; or of a group of structures more permanent than the nomadic tent. Ancient tradition represents Seth, about a century later, as "possessed of a knowledge of astronomy."* The *third* generation is signalized by the statement, "Then began men to call upon the name of the Lord."† That the popular interpretation

* Jos. Ant. I. c. 2.

† This phrase may be rendered—"Then was a beginning made for calling *by* the name of Jehovah," that is, His name was in some way

of this language, that "now piety began to prevail," or that "public worship began to be general," is not the correct one is evident, from the fact that about this time the great religious apostacy began to develop itself in forms unusually monstrous and gigantic. Probably the correct interpretation is that which reconciles both extremes, by representing the two great parties, the Sethites and the Cainites, as drawing off more widely from each other; the irreligious more openly avowing their impiety, and the religious, more unitedly and definitely than before, "came out from among them," avowed themselves the "sons of God" (a Hebrew

adopted by his worshipers; or, "a beginning was made for calling *upon* the name of Jehovah," that is, in public worship; or, "a beginning was made for preaching *in* the name of Jehovah." The authority of great names can be adduced for each. I prefer the first chiefly because, if the clause be taken in connection with Genesis, vi. 1, as it should be (the fifth chapter which is interposed being a genealogical table), it immediately receives the explanation, that those spoken of were actually called *the sons of God.* In the text, however, I have united the three senses inasmuch as they who took the appellation *sons of God,* would also, if consistent, publicly call upon His name, and in His name call others to repentance. There is, indeed, a fourth interpretation of which the phrase is capable, directly opposed to what we have given, and sustained by Onkelos and the chief Jewish expositors, as well as by Selden and many other learned Christian interpreters. It is this, "then men began profanely to call themselves by the name of Jehovah;" applying the Divine name to themselves; just as the Selucidæ impiously took the name *Theos.* And it is not a little remarkable, though I have not seen the fact noticed in this connection, that in the fifth and sixth generations we find two Cainites, Mehaja*el* and Methusa*el*, in whose names one of the Divine names (not indeed *Jehovah*, but *El*, whence Elohim), is incorporated—the first name probably meaning according to Gesenius, *smitten of God*, and the second *man of God.* For the reason stated, however, I prefer the previous view, as harmonizing best with the context.

idiom for disciples), separated themselves to the worship and service of God, and began to "preach in the name of the Lord." In proportion as men ceased to worship God in their family capacity, it became necessary that the pious individuals and parts of families should associate, and form a separate community or Church. If we choose to have recourse to the Phœnician annals,* and to the Indian Puranas,† we might show how one discovery is supposed to have followed another, generation after generation. But the Scriptures, true to their high religious aim, occupy themselves for the next *three* generations in recording only Patriarchal names, and the growing dissoluteness of the times, leaving the *material* progress which that very dissoluteness implied, to be imagined or inferred. In the *seventh* generation we have a development of evil in the polygamy of Lamech, and of piety in the history of Enoch. During this generation, according to the Chaldean records copied by Berosus, reigned Alorus, the first of the antediluvian kings. And the Scriptural account of the period warrants the conclusion that the Patriarchal form of government was about this time invaded, and, in some localities displaced, by the "mighty men," and "men of renown," who then appeared. In the *eighth* generation, Jabal gave an impulse to a nomadic life; Jubal became famous for his improvements and inventions in music; and Tubal Cain, as a skilful artificer in metals. The cotemporaneousness of these latter advances reminds us how constantly an impulse given to improvement in one direction communicates itself in others; and as it arises partly from division of labor, so it tends to multiply such division.

* *Cory's* Ancient Fragments. † Asiatic Researches, vol. v. p. 241.

The *ninth* generation is remarkable only, in the Biblical account, for the predictive character of the name given by the Sethite Lamech to his son Noah. The building of the ark, however, in the *tenth* generation, implies the existence of arts which are not named; an indication that the few discoveries and improvements which are recorded, and which stand like lights along the pathway of that time, are only specimens of the progress made, and that the wide intervals were doubtless illuminated by other similar discoveries.

Vitruvius imagines that he finds the rudiments of architecture in the form of a Scythian cottage. The origin of instrumental music may have dated centuries before Jubal; and many an improvement would be made, after the time of Tubal Cain, by the artificers in iron and brass. For then, as now, the desires of men would require time to enlarge; and, being enlarged, would require time to be gratified. Then, as now, man would be unconsciously preparing himself for progress without proposing it; and would often find the means of improvement, without seeking them. And, in this way, new adaptations of means to ends, and new collocations of related objects, would be coming to light, the number of perceived resemblances would be multiplying, the linked chain of causes and effects would be lengthening, and the sphere of human thought and action be constantly enlarging.

Continuity of moral civilization.

As the numerical increase of antediluvian population would necessarily be gradual,*

* Any attempt to calculate the numbers of mankind at the epoch of the deluge must rest on mere conjecture. One arrays his statistics to show that they may have reached twelve hundred millions, a number immensely larger than that which subsists even at the present time. Another judges "the number to have been small; and that it was in a

the same character of progressiveness would mark the practical illustration of all the laws of *morality* which that increase tended to exemplify. New relations, offices, and duties were constantly coming into existence. Every additional family was an additional experiment of the domestic constitution, calculated to place it, in some respects, in a new light.

The will of God was clearly indicated, for example, respecting the number to be united in marriage, by the creation, at first, of one man and one woman. But the continued balance of the number of the sexes, age after age, notwithstanding their perpetual increase, was an ever-increasing confirmation of the same law. As time advanced, too, the evils resulting from polygamy would furnish still further and stronger corroboration of the law. And the same would be the case with the laws of reputation, character, property, and general justice. Laws would be acted on before they were adopted by any mutual agreement to that effect; perhaps they would not be formally adopted until they had been occasionally trans-

course of rapid progress toward extreme reduction, which would have issued in a not very distant extinction." One argues that the longevity of the Patriarchs was to compensate for the slowness of human multiplication. Another infers a rapid increase from the length of life, the infrequency of death, and the absence of every thing to prevent early marriages. One sees in the genealogical records a list of all that were born to the Patriarchs who are named; and another regards them only as units, compared with the multitudes born but not specified. In a word, the elements for a correct computation are wanting. The old world can not be measured by the standard of the new. One fact, however may be taken for granted, the certain effect of the tyranny and licentiousness which prevailed in diminishing the fecundity of the human species.

gressed. Every age would be adding to the mass of evidence in their favor; every district would, in effect, have its Sinai, where the voice of law "waxing louder and louder," would be heard enjoining, "thou shalt not kill; thou shalt not steal; thou shalt not covet!" And then would follow, in many instances, a perception and enforcement of the law from a regard, not merely to the personal and immediate consequences of its gross violation, but to the general social effects of the remotest departure from it. So that in addition to the sense of violence done to the moral nature of man by disobedience, there would be next the ever accumulating evils accruing to the individual and to society; and then the many motives arising from the will of God, and from the advantages of conformity to it. And thus, as mankind increased, morality was not merely extending her domains, but increasing her authority; she was at once objectively multiplying her laws, and giving stability to her throne.

And for this continuity of purpose, the longevity of the antediluvians was strikingly adapted. It gave them an opportunity of watching the operations of human conduct on a large scale. If they doubted respecting the morality of a certain line of conduct one century, they would perhaps witness its legitimate fruit in the next. Deviations from natural laws, well-meant, and for a century or two apparently answering well, would, during the life-time of the transgressor, and while the origin of the deviations were yet fresh in remembrance, begin to "bring forth fruit unto death." And thus the great laws of social life, subjectively written in the human heart, would come to be objectively written and increasingly verified in human history.

The continuity of the *religious* civilization of the period

Continuity of Religious Civilization.

appears, first, in the *serial* character of the Divine revelations. We have shown already that all the Divine communications made during the period were only, in effect, so many expansions of the great parent-truths disclosed in Paradise, and laid at the basis of the Patriarchal economy. All of them find their places under one or other of the two heads —that God is a moral governor—but that he is ready to exercise mercy to the guilty, and to save the penitent, through a medium of His own providing. These were the great truths illustrated alike in the first promise, and the institution of sacrifice, and in all the circumstances attending the preparation of the ark. While all the intervening communications were relative to the existing wants and circumstances of mankind; so that if these were continuous in their nature, those were also. Even the miracles belonging to the economy, were only the continued employment of an order of means in which the dispensation had commenced. If Noah prophesied, he was but the inspired medium of Divine communication, as Enoch and Adam had been before him. If Enoch was translated, it was an event which did but echo the faith, or corroborate the fears, of all who heard of it. And if a deluge was predicted, it was only in accordance with the deepening consciousness of human demerit; with the simple fact that the *laws* of nature were not *lawless*, but would be found to be as subservient to human punishment as they might have been to human happiness; in a word, that the moral government of God was more than a name, that it implied that He would continue to govern.

Secondly, the views of Divine revelation which the youth derived from his parents, would only form the basis for the additional views imparted by such new revelations as might be made in his own day, or as might be acquired in argument or in meditation as the result of his own independent reflection. This continuity is observable even in the changing errors of the period—for they appear to have advanced from the denial of a future judgment to the denial of a present providential government, and from that to the denial of the Divine existence. And if error, which is related only extrinsically, was thus continuous, the probability that the views of Divine truth entertained by the sincere believer would be continuous and ever-expanding is stronger; for truth is both self-consistent and all-related in itself; and the belief of it implies a mind in a self-consistent and all-related state with *itself*. So that every present view of truth would only prepare the way, both objectively and subjectively, for progressive enlargement. The wise anticipations of early life would often become the settled convictions of old age. Some of the conjectures of Adam would form a part of the creed of Enoch; and some of the opinions of the wise and the good in the time of Enoch would form part of the faith of the Patriarch Noah.

Continuity compatible with certain crises.

This continuity of the changes, material, moral, and religious, which formed the course of the antediluvian history is quite consistent with the following admissions: first, that it was not unmarked by striking crises and revolutions. Such "seasons of convulsion present the phenomena on which men dwell, and the eras by which they date, in the moral as well as in the physical world, where the silent process by which nature elaborates her productions, the slow moldering of mountains into new plains of inexhaustible fertility pass almost unobserved and unappreciated; but the attention is roused and compelled when the destructive powers of the hurricane and earthquake are let loose."* But great events are not to be viewed as isolated. They are the summation of long preceding trains of silent and unnoticed influences. Hence the folly of expecting sudden changes, whether great or small, in the progress of mankind. Nature never does any thing *per saltum;* and for this obvious reason, that every thing in her domain is all-related. A small change, therefore, or a change in any one relation, will avail little. Yet, doubtless, there were those at that time, as there are still, who in looking indulgently around on the evils with which society groaned, fancied that topical remedies alone were necessary; that if a particular change could be effected, all would henceforth be well; forgetting that all other relations must consent to it and be drawn along with it, and that in order to this, time is necessary; that for the benefit to be permanent, it must be universal in respect to the case to which it relates. Events, which have erroneously passed under the name of sudden and important revolutions, have often taken place with great and lasting advantage. But they were only the last term of a long series of changes which had been silently preparing the way for them—the launching of a vessel which had been long in building—and, as such, they were simply continuous.†

With inequalities of human development.

Secondly, all the departments of human development, material, moral, and religious, were never seen, probably, at the same point of progress, at any one moment, during the whole antediluvian period. To develop the entire man, without unduly

* Historical Parallels, p. 394.

† My Old House; or, the Doctrine of Changes, p. 44.

eliciting or depressing any one part of his constitution, is the great problem in the education of the individual. The same difficulty, with its attendant evils, appears in gigantic proportions in the history of every community. Material progress, belonging to the province of the senses and the understanding, may advance with the steadiness and certainty of a law of nature; but such progress, so far from securing any corresponding advance in the moral and religious sphere, may be the direct occasion of man's decline, and the exact measure of it. Here, will and motive come into play; and he may *choose* so to employ his material prosperity as shall make certain his moral degradation. In the primitive world, the Cainites devoted themselves almost exclusively to the advancement of a material civilization; and the degeneracy to which it led was the first of a series of lessons which Providence has ever since been giving to man on the utter inefficiency of mere knowledge, power, and æsthetic progress, to save him from ruin; or rather, on the certainty of their conducting him to it, apart from the supreme influence of religion. The Sethites maintained, for a time, a high religious standing; but, descending from their holy elevation, their morality vanished with their religion, and they sank through the successive stages of a refined but death-struck civilization.

With partial retrocession.

Thirdly, some branches of the antediluvian family of man exhibited signs even of retrocession. Such probably was the case with the family of the nomadic Jabal. He "was the father of such as dwell in tents;" a proof that this was not the primitive manner of life. Contrary to the pagan notion, that man commenced life on the earth as a savage, we here see that he has to retrogade in order to approach that condition. Nor, indeed, have we any trace of the strictly savage or hunting condition of life, until after the Deluge. In the conduct of Jabal, however, who introduced or promoted the change from a settled to a wandering life, we see the way in which a course of retrogradation might easily begin. And yet the change which led to this deterioration was probably advocated at first on the ground of its tendency to promote civilization; and its introduction hailed as promising a millennium—the last and best state of human society. In this way, an untried change often takes an unexpected direction, baffling all previous calculation and threatening to impede indefinitely the march of human progression. So far from the progress of mankind being the result of an inherent necessity or fate, all history shows that it is only the unfolding of a plan, which continues to unfold solely because it is never out of the hand of God. In proportion as man has been left to himself, he has ruined himself. He has laboriously constructed a palace of knowledge, wealth, and power; and has then converted it, morally, into a funeral pyre, in the flames of which he has expired. In virtue of the great plan of Providence alone it is that events which, when viewed in relation even to the long term of antediluvian life, appeared fraught with unmixed evil, might when contemplated in relation to the entire scheme of Providence, be found to be contributary of extensive good; as the stream which appears to be arrested by the mountain, flows round its base to receive fresh tributaries; or as the avalanche of snow which suddenly dams up the course of a river, gradually loses its own nature, and swells the stream.

And with miraculous interpositions. Nor, fourthly, were the miraculous interpositions which took place any breach of the law of continuity. For, first, such interpositions were necessary in order to prevent the termination of all progress; and, secondly, they were to be expected, as parts of a plan from which the Deity has never departed. The world itself originated in miracle; and contains in its bosom the memorials of having been, at distant intervals, the theater of successive creations. Man himself, originated in miracle, is preconfigured for the recognition of the supernatural as truly as he is for the belief of the natural. Hence, when it occurred, as in the translation of Enoch, it brought nothing new into human belief; the doctrine was there before. When an inspired communication was made, the Divine Being was but continuing the employment of a method for the impartation of *religious* knowledge, to which man had owed, at first, the elements of even *material* knowledge—the Parent was but once more speaking to His children on affairs of great urgency; and hence the revelation did but corroborate the pre-existing fears of the wicked and the hopes of the righteous. The seasons selected for such interpositions, too, would be such as to invite, or to excite, the expectation of them; and, when they did occur, so adapted would they be to the exigences of the time, as to stop nothing natural, and to set nothing unnatural in motion; their tendency being only to impair the force of the evils which threatened to destroy all human progress, and to give to that progress continuity and impulse.

The miracle of the deluge in this connection.

One part of the Divine procedure there is, however, which appears to deserve distinct remark—the prediction of a Deluge. In reference to that event, the antediluvian skeptic would probably object, as the scoffer of "the last days" will do, relative to another catastrophe, saying, "where is the promise of His coming? for, since the fathers fell asleep, all things continue as they were from the beginning of the creation?* All observation and experience are against such an event. Nature is uniform in her operations. The laws of the human mind compel my disbelief. I reject the prediction as unreasonable." Now, here the first error lay in confounding that inner circle called the course of nature, with that larger outer circle—the course of providence, which preceded nature and encompassed it; which originated it, employs it, and, at distant intervals, adds to it, or modifies it, at pleasure. That no similar event had taken place from the time of the Adamic creation might have been true. But, is that sufficient to prove that nothing like it ever will or can occur? Experience is, in this sense, against every thing till it occurs. Before the first family existed, the experience of Adam was against its existence. Indeed, during the first ages of the human dispensation, events were, and, from the nature of the case, must have been, constantly occurring for the first time. The existence of man himself was contrary to all that had previously taken place on the earth. If the proposition that nothing will take place but what has taken place is to be admitted, it must be because it is a principle of the Divine Being; and if it be such at present, it must ever have been such; and if it has ever been such, even before creation began, no creation could ever have taken place. There was no precedent for the creation of a world, any more than there is now said for its destruction.† Thus, the objection becomes an intellectual absurdity. The fact is, however, that the root of the error lay, as in the case of the scoffers of the last days, not in the intellect, but in the state of the affections. "For this they *willingly* are ignorant of"—that the exist-

* 2 Pet. iii. 4. † Binney's Discourses on the Power of Faith, p. 160.

ence of man himself, and of all those material laws on the stability of which they rely, were once unknown to the universe, and owe both the time and manner of their existence entirely to the will of God. It may suit the purpose of the skeptic, indeed, to reason from the analogy of a thousand years; but why, if he assume to be a man of enlarged and comprehensive views, why will he not rather reason from the analogy of ten thousand years? Of this he is *willingly* oblivious. It suits not his purpose.

Another error involved in such an objection consists in reasoning from experience acquired in one state of things to what is likely to take place in another state of things entirely different. That no deluge had taken place all the time the earth was not "filled with violence," was no rational ground for concluding that the event would not take place when the earth was so filled. If the new event was to occur when the earth had reached that new condition, and not till then, there was no contradiction of previous experience in the matter. There had been no experience whatever on the subject. All prior experience had related to a different state of things. But here was now a new state of things; "all flesh has corrupted his way;" and, if experience was to have any voice in relation to it, one would have expected to hear it suggest that this new condition of man would most likely call forth some new and correspondent movement on the part of his Maker. Inasmuch as such a moral crisis had never before been known in the history of man, for aught he knew to the contrary, the natural crisis which was in consequence threatened was its proper accompaniment. Events were constantly occurring, at that early period of the world, for the first time; and, for aught he knew, the natural crisis would recur as regularly as the moral crisis. Experience on this subject he had yet to acquire; and until, or rather unless, he had acquired it, to pretend to argue from it was to make the not unimportant mistake of arguing from his ignorance as if it had been knowledge.

But the principal error lay in testing the probability of the threatened event by evidence of which the nature of the case did not admit, and in rejecting that which was actually adduced. That God had spoken to them, "at sundry times and in divers manners," was susceptible of the clearest proofs. One of His servants attested that He had spoken to *him*, announcing the approaching punishment of the guilty world. The points for examination were, therefore, Was the prophet deceived, or was he deceiving others? Every objection which did not relate to the credibility of his testimony was irrelevant. If to this it were objected that human confidence, moral government, every thing essential to man's improvement, is made dependent on our faith in the constancy of nature, it might be sufficient to rejoin, that man was designed to tell the truth, and that his general observance of the laws of veracity is essential to the stability and progress of society. What, then, if, while pretending the greatest jealousy for the honor of nature and its laws—truth, justice, liberty—all the laws of the moral world were set at naught by him? What if, while protesting against the possibility of a deluge, as involving a doctrine subversive of all human progress, it should appear that his own subversion of moral law had actually arrested that progress, and made all further hope of it impossible; would not this appear to be a suitable occasion for God to interpose, with a view to a better state of things? Still more, if society had reached a state of ingrained depravity and moral disorganization, in which the last traces of a moral government were fast fading away; in which the bare idea of a moral Governor was derided, and the only thing deified was an abstraction called Nature—and this on account of the stability of her laws—would there be righteous retribution in the arrangement which should employ their idol as the instrument of their punishment?

But chiefly and conclusively, it might have been replied to such an objection, that, as to the threatened deluge interfering with the confidence and progress of the species, it was not a question of progress but of extinction; and of extinction on account of having violated all the conditions of progress: that the same authority which threatened the deluge, had suspended the sentence for a hundred and twenty years, evidently making its execution at all conditional on man's conduct in the interval: but that if the increasing guilt of that conduct should, after all, call for the infliction, the only parties whose confidence in the stability of nature would or could need to be renewed, would be the survivors of that catastrophe and their posterity; and that it was competent for the same authority which threatened the deluge, to promise, after its occurrence, that it should be repeated no more forever. He might even make a covenant with them, and engage that "while the earth remaineth, seed-time and harvest, and cold and heat, and summer and winter, and day and night, shall not fail."* And this, we know, He actually did. But as for the antediluvian sinner himself, whose disbelief of the threatening was a virtual daring of the Almighty to carry it into execution, it was an adequate answer to all his objections to remind him that the only kind or class of events with which

* Genesis, viii. 22.

he could properly compare his threatened removal from the earth, was that series of wonders which attended his introduction; and that so far from being out of harmony with that, on account of its preternatural character, nothing attending the destruction of the world could possibly surpass the wonders of its creation. And, it might have been added, that as at his creation, all the pre-existing laws of material nature had been summed up in his own constitution, and subordinated to his use for the highest purpose, so now some of them were to be temporarily employed in another manner, but still in entire subordination to the same ultimate end.

Indeed, the objection to the existence of miraculous phenomena, as calculated to affect the orderly course of human action, is the offspring of the merest puerility. It is enough to appeal, in reply, from speculation to fact. They never have produced this imaginary effect. Their existence has been confidently believed; and to those believing them they have had all the reality of fact; yet the results apprehended by the objects never ensued. True, had such phenomena been at the disposal of man, he might have employed them with an irrelevance and a frequency which might have produced the effects in question. But it is to be remembered that they are the interpositions of the Framer of the entire plan of providence; and that, as such, they form parts of His plan, and have their places in it, as much as the stars. All the miracles of Scripture, too, aim at high religious ends. And it is literally amazing how securely man can intrench himself from all sympathy with such, even though the assault be made direct from Heaven. "Men build over earthquakes." And if the repeated shock and ruin of an earthquake will not move him from a favorite spot, his earthly course is not likely to be materially disordered by a phenomenon the belief of which would involve the revolution of his moral life.

The state of the world, then, at the time of the Flood, exhibited the result of all the preceding states of the world. It was what it was relatively to all the past, and as such it was a manifestation of God. Even the progress which man had made in evil did but show the progress which he was capable of making in good; and occasion the ever-enlarging display of the Divine long-suffering. While the progress, and the continuity of that progress, which he made in religious knowledge, in moral excellence, and in happiness, showed that the plan in which he was comprehended, united all generations into one ever-increasing family and united them in a career of indefinite progression.

CHAPTER VII.

THE FAMILY RELATIONS WHICH THE PRECEDING LAWS BRING TO LIGHT.

A COMPLETE view of the relations involved in the Family requires us to notice the pre-existing relations belonging to each of the parties entering into the marriage state; the relations which that state itself supposes; and the relations consequent on it.

Pre-existing individual relations of man and woman.

As to the first; each of the parties contemplating marriage includes already a distinct system of internal relations, and is encircled by a corresponding system of external relations. These have been considered in "Man Primeval."* Under this head, therefore, it only remains for us to remark, as we proceed, how these pre-existing personal relations are affected by being brought into the new sphere of the married state.

"Man was created in a totally different manner from other creatures. God created one person, a man; but He created them wonderfully, both male and female in one, in His own image. In the sleep of the man He separated from him one woman, and He caused them to be man and wife, and He called their name Adam. The first man con-

* Chap. vii. On *man an all-related being.*

versing with his Maker in innocence, was the first prophet also whom God inspired with a knowledge of the future. He was not yet a father, and knew not, by any means of human judgment, how children would act toward their parents, or how the economy of families would be conducted in ages to come. Yet thus he sang: 'This is now bone of my bone and flesh of my flesh. She shall be called *Isha*, because she was taken out of man. Therefore [God said] shall a man leave his father and mother, and shall cleave unto his wife, and they shall be one flesh.' The circumstance alone upon which all marriage depends was one in which polygamy was *impossible;* and that is, a prohibition of nature. But the words of Adam are both a prediction and a law, and in them the inter-marriage of his posterity is declared to be a legal reunion of what in the first beginning were naturally one—the man and his one wife. They represent marriage and monogamy as simple synonymes. And so they are."*

Relations of husband and wife.

The most natural general division of the relations of the married state, like those of the individual man, is twofold—the internal and the external, each of these again being divisible into relations coexistent and successively existent. Beginning with the internal relations of the Family, we name first those between the sexes, as man and wife.

It might have been antecedently expected, that the laws of the universe would be found to have been established in prospective harmony with the designed constitution of the mind which is to expound and to profit by them. *That* mind has come; and we have found that it is so constituted as to touch those laws at all points. In other words, man,

* Nimrod, vol. iv. p. 468.

besides his own independent character, is connected with, and influenced by, all the objects and relations of the external universe. Similarly, it might have been expected that the constitution, physical, intellectual, and moral, of the first man, was prospective and anticipative of the creation of woman; and so also all that is specific in the constitution of woman is found to pre-suppose, and to form the completion of, that of man. The union of the sexes, then, in marriage, which is the root of all other social relations, is a Divine appointment, to which every thing specific in their respective constitutions, is pre-configured.

But more particularly; in saying that man's nature is a constitution or system of relations, of course, woman is included. No single characteristic of her constitution could be changed, without remodeling the whole The organic, animal, sentient, reflective, vocal, rational, voluntary, and moral parts of her nature, are mutually related and dependent. The last pre-supposes the first; the first is prospective of the last. And this fact may serve to determine all that can be meant by the "vexed" question, Whether or not the minds of the sexes differ. Whether or not they differ essentially, or, in themselves, abstractedly considered, is a question which may as well be left till we can witness such a thing as their abstract or disembodied manifestations. But, that their manifestations ever have and ever will continue to differ as long as they remain embodied, admits not of a doubt. To suppose the contrary, is to suppose the existence of a solecism in creation; of a creature in whom a specific difference in one part of its nature leaves unaffected the manifestations of the other parts of its nature; and, in so far, a creature of unrelated parts, or, without a constitution. But "His work is perfect."

If the constitution of woman be thus all-related in itself; and, consequently, characteristic in all its parts, it follows that her relations to man are just as numerous as are those characteristics. Whatever is found specific in the one may be expected to find its counterpart in the other. The *physical* difference of stature, size, and strength, in the one, is relative to the corresponding particulars in the other. The greater nervous sensibility of the one, points to the superior muscular development of the other. The consequent weakness and apprehensiveness of the former looked to the strength and courage of the latter for protection and support. As *social* beings, the peculiar sphere of activity belonging to each corresponds; for, while woman by her presence and gentler virtues, beautifies and blesses the domestic circle, the peculiar attributes and duties of man call him into a wider sphere beyond. As *intelligent*, the knowledge and habits which he acquires in that sphere deserve and secure the affectionate deference of home; and prepare him duly to appreciate the agency which fills that home with attractions. As *emotional*, the same objects affect them with the same relative difference; even the very love which they feel for each other, manifesting itself in acts modified by the same constitutional distinction. Remarkable is it, if not even antecedently inconceivable, that this relation should be found to obtain even in the *voluntary* part of their nature; that two distinct wills should in any respect so harmonize as to become practically one; that two personal beings of the same mature age, having certain distinct interests, and who, in the just pursuit of those interests, might have been expected to require spheres of activity so distinct as never to approach, should be found to attain even their personal ends best in one and the same sphere. And yet, so true is this, that marriage is actually a compact of wills; a union in which each receives a certain right in the person of the other, and is voluntarily brought under obligation to the other. How precious is that self-denial by which the parties are, to a certain degree, converted into each other: and each finds something "better than a mere self, by becoming part of a nobler whole;" by which the authority of the husband is subdued into a feeling of regard, as for his own flesh, and the obevience of the wife is raised into the dignity of an alliance with Law. And even as *moral* beings, the same relations of dependence and influence unite them. Neither sex alone is the standard of human nature. Each is to receive an impress from the distinctive excellences of the other, and to impart the spirit of its own. Each is to the other the image of distinct aspects of the Divine character; and, by being disentangled and drawn out from the inner circle of self, and made to find excellence and happiness in the love of the other, they are trained to look away together for their highest good to a union with that Objective Excellence, of which their own union is the sacred type and the mysterious pledge.

Conjugal love.

Still further illustrative of the Divine Goodness, would it be, *secondly*, if the man and woman should be made and moved to enter into the married state by the mutual perception of some excellence, real or supposed, in the persons sustaining it; thus determining each to a particular object. A vivid delight would thus be felt by each in the contemplation of the object selected; and, as a consequence, each would desire nothing but good for the other. Now, this is conjugal love; an affection which supposes the existence of some quality or qualities in the beloved object, which, by virtue of the constitution of the mind, are capable of yielding it pleasure. And, of this affection, marriage is the visible symbol or means of ratification.

Numerical proportion of the sexes.

Thirdly, and for the same reasons, it may be expected, that the sexes will be found to be *numerically* related. For it is only in this way that the social, intellectual, and moral claims of the sexes can be equally respected. Consequently, the peace, happiness, and well-being of the husband and wife can only thus be secured. Accordingly, not only were one man and one woman created at first for each other, but the same numerical proportion has been maintained substantially ever since. No science has yet traced the laws by which this result is attained. We can only perceive that untold myriads of particular incidents must have been placed and sustained in exquisite adjustment in order to produce it. This numerical relation of the sexes, then, is as much an indication of the Divine Will respecting the proportion in which they are to be united in marriage, as the distinct constitution of each is that they are to be united at all. If the one intimates his purpose that they should be united, the other denotes that the union is to be limited to individuals who are to be exclusively united to each other for life. And thus the appointment of nature coincides with the laws of social happiness and of morality; and all these arrangements and laws harmonize with the great end of creation—the Divine manifestation.

Relations of husband and wife successively existent.

Each of the relations between the sexes to which we have adverted, begins, from the time of marriage, to be drawn gradually closer. The existence of many of these may not at first have been thought of; or, if so, they may not have been felt. But if the union be what it ought to be, time develops and confirms them. Every day discovers something to increase admiration on the one hand, and to excite gratitude on the other. Their voluntary acts of affection speedily acquire the force of habit, until each, from being more constantly present to the mind of the other than any human being besides, becomes an ever-active element in the current of the other's thoughts and feelings. Every event, whether pleasant or painful, which their memory treasures, becomes a new bond of sympathy. Every present object engages their attention in common; while every event in the future excites them mutually to hope or to fear. Love impels them to look at every thing which occurs with each other's eyes; and to practice a kind of substitution, or mental metempsychosis, which tends to convert them, as far as the laws of humanity permit, into each other's nature. A process of assimilation this which only requires time in order to make the character, mental and moral, of the one the perfect counterpart of the other; and which, probably, in many an antediluvian family was actually completed.

Relations consequent on marriage; parents.

The great occasion which demonstrates and displays their relation is that by which they become *Parents*. Mysterious arrangement this, by which two human beings become the means of giving existence to a third; of producing by *means*, what God at first produced by *miracle*—itself a greater miracle; of producing out of themselves a creature in their own image, as the Creator at first made man "in His own image." Equally striking is the arrangement by which the birth of a child, while it necessarily gives a new object to their affections, and in so far divides their attention, should yet multiply, instead of diminish, their ties to, and double their interest in, each other. And yet from the moment they become parents, not only is every pre-existing relation modified, new ones are created. And, with every addition to their offspring, till they are encircled with new objects of affection, they go on becoming objects of increasing importance and interest to each other.

Internal family relations; parent and child.

In proceeding to speak of the connection between *Parent* and *Child*, we find ourselves involved in so fine and so complicated a web of relations, that no hand but His who wove them can minutely trace and analyze them. The law of propagation might have been, that the child should be related to its parents simply as one of the same race, or possessing the same human nature; though such a relation, besides having other disadvantages, would have been, perhaps, of too obviously artificial a kind. But, besides this general relation, every part of the constitution, physical, mental, and moral, of each of the parents, is found to be related to the constitution of the child—related, not separately, but blended in proportions, which are dependent on conditions, and determined by laws, of definite and exquisite operation.

Filial temperament derived.

That the physical constitution of the child is, to a great extent, a transmitted constitution, is too obvious to need remark. During its intra-uterine life, it is even a part of the maternal constitution itself. It consequently commences its extra-uterine, or independent, life with a derived temperament; and this physical temperament imparts a tinge to all its actions, and, within certain limits, a character to all its mental and moral manifestations. Its form and features are derived; often are they perpetuated in a family for ages; and sometimes they are reproduced after lying latent and disappearing for generations—while form and feature often react, and impart a character to the mind and a bias to the life which they could not otherwise have taken.

It does not follow from this, indeed, that "fortes creantur fortibus et bonis," * or that " ebrii gignunt ebrios." On the contrary, children are often found to differ mentally from their parents (even twins) under very great apparent similarities of organization; a fact which reminds us that " the Father of Spirits" imparts original differences of mind which are not traceable to organization as their cause, though their *manifestation* is affected both by moral and physical conditions.

Nor does it follow from the doctrine of a transmitted nature, that "the moral constitution essentially varies with the physical structure;" though the semblance of truth which the statement possesses, and the relaxation of moral obligation which seems to follow from it, have served to make it welcome and give it currency. That moral tendencies are transmitted, is a doctrine which has been receiving confirmation daily since the birth of the first transgression. " For by one man sin entered into the world." And equally beyond a doubt is it, that the *manifestation* of these tendencies will be affected both by the conditions of the physical structure and of the mind. Indeed, this is a fact which our subject leads us to affirm. But tendencies are not qualities, nor is the *manifestation* of moral qualities, the qualities themselves. These can be affected only by qualities of their own nature—by *moral* influences. And it is to be borne in mind that whatever moral tendencies may in this way be derived, man's moral nature, considered

* Hor. 1, iv. Od. 4.

as a constitution, is as substantially unaltered and unalterable as that of his body; and even more fixed, because based on unchangeable laws, and appealing to immutable principles.

It will be seen, then, that the constitution of the child is, as far as we can understand by its *manifestations*, a transmitted nature. And it is found that the influences transmitted depend on the kind and degree of health enjoyed by the parents, individually and unitedly considered; or their respective ages, relative to each other, and to the average term of human life; on their intellectual and moral states, absolutely considered and as compared with each other; and on an incalculable number of the modifications of which these various states are susceptible.

From the time the independent existence of the child commences, these relations, or their effects, begin to operate in a new manner; and innumerable others are added to them. At first, the child is almost as dependent on the mother for sustenance as it was prior to its birth; while every strong emotion of the mother affects the condition of the child, through the medium of its natural nourishment, much more deeply than it does the mother herself. Her bosom is its first paradise. Her face the first object on which its wandering eye learns complacently to settle. Her tones lull it to repose, and mingle with its dreams—with its being. Her eye discourses with its infant mind, while yet words are, to it, mere inarticulate sounds. Her every movement gives to it a new sensation. And thus at the moment of its birth its education begins; and, from that moment, never knows a pause.

Parental influence. Whether or not the child shall be subjected to certain influences depends on the will of the parent; but, if it be subjected to them, it no longer depends on his will whether it shall be affected by them or not. By the appointment of God, the laws of dependence and influence operate uniformly. As soon as the mind of the child begins to open, it is susceptible of impressions from every object and event within its little horizon. The looks, the tones, the most indifferent acts of the father, are its laws. His authority is an ordinance superior to every other; and on which the child is prepared to believe every thing—even the most casual remark—which is often treasured up as an oracle. His example is copied, even to its least actions and gestures; and his every movement, like a living seed in fertile soil, reproduces itself in corresponding fruit. Owing to the love of his child, he may be regarded as ever working in fire.

Modified by circumstances.

The kind of influence shed on the child by his parents differs, indeed, as his age advances, or as his susceptibilities of impression change with time. Thus he is influenced by the *amount* of knowledge imparted by them, and by its *kind;* by the *time* of its impartation; by the *order* in which it is communicated; and by the *manner* in which it is conveyed. But from day to day, and from hour to hour, he is handed on from one class of influences to another; or, rather, he is never out of the plastic and molding hand of parental influence. "Some parents talk of *beginning* the education of their children: the moment they were capable of forming an idea, their education was already begun—the education of circumstances—insensible education, which, like insensible perspiration, is of more constant and powerful effect, and of far more consequence to the habit, than that which is direct and apparent. This education goes on at every instant of time; it goes on like time—you can neither stop it, nor turn its course. . . . . Here, then, is one school from which there are no truants, and in which there are no holidays." *

Increased with increase of children.

On the birth of every additional child a new element of influence is introduced into the family, by which the parents are placed in new relations to the children already existing. Not more important is the addition of a province to an empire, than is the addition of such a member to the domestic circle. Every movement of the parents in relation to it has a relation, in a different manner, to all the rest. In their conduct toward that one, the parents are moving and influencing all. And in proportion to the increase of the well-regulated family is the increase of authority and power which the parents acquire over all its members.

Relations successively existent.

Supposing the family constitution to be complete, and, as such, to be adapted for action, we have next to regard it in relation to time. The first moments of its existence shed an influence on every succeeding moment. The parents are constantly writing their own history, physical, intellectual, and moral, on the characters of their children and domestics; and, on the former especially, the transcript is deep and ineffaceable. If, indeed, the impressions which are thus daily imparted were obliterated every night, and the character restored to a *tabula rasa*, the consideration would lose much of its solemnity; although, even then, the fact that, during so large a portion of their active existence the characters of all within the domestic circle had taken their hue principally from parental and other domestic influences, might

* Anderson on the Domestic Constitution, p. 380.

well awaken an anxious sense of responsibility. But these relations of influence, so far from intermitting, are ever widening and deepening in their onward course. Yesterday lives again in to-day. Impulses become principles; wishes pass into purposes; actions into habits—habits of imitation, obedience, and enduring resemblance. And thus "the child is father of the man." The character of the family at the close of every month, and of every year, includes the sum-total of all the influences of the past multiplied into each other. How mighty the sum of influences involved in the completed character of an antediluvian family!

Children and parents.

The relations of influence existing between *children* and *parents* are mutual, though by no means equal. After the principle of conjugal love, the birth of a child is the next great element or spring of civilization. Even before the child can consciously receive impressions, it begins to occasion them. "What though man *is* born the most helpless and dependent of all living! In the first hours of his existence, when a few indistinct or unmeaning cries are his only language, he exercises an authority irresistible over hearts, of the very existence of which he is ignorant and unconscious; nor will the infant wait long before he advances in his claims and in his influence. A few weeks only will pass away, when the smile and the tear, signs of emotion peculiar to his species, will bind the two parties together by ties of peculiar strength. And if the infant be of a determined character, it may soon be seen to rule a weak parent, and even to exercise an influence over a whole family."

And this hold on the parental affection goes on increasing with time. "A fact worthy of remark," says Aimè Martin, "is, that maternal (or parental) love only lasts in each animal the time necessary for the preservation of the species. . . . . In the morning the parent would have waged furious war for those young ones whom in the evening she can not recognize. And this indifference awakens no regret, leaves no remembrance, enters the mind at the very time when gratitude, and habits long formed, seemed to render it impossible." Now, the love of man for his offspring, as distinguished from mere instinctive impulse, begins where that of the animal terminates. Their presence acts on his whole nature, as the influence of a constant and strong appeal. His every act of self-denial for them only serves to endear them to him the more. In many most important respects he regards them as parts of himself. They soften his heart, and develop and dignify his character. He cultivates his own mind in the very act of teaching them, as well as in order that he may "feed them with knowledge and with understanding." And fain would he "impart to them even his own soul also."

Child and child.

By the same increase of family, the *children* are placed in new relations *to each other*, and brought under a new influence. A new object of affection is introduced among them, whose tender helplessness operates on them like a softening element, cherishing and strengthening their natural susceptibilities, and thus prolonging the period during which they themselves are easily impressible. This influence, again, is varied, according to the *sex* of the children. That love which forms the domestic bond is capable of unlimited diversity, according to the diversity of its objects. However delicate and difficult the analysis may be, the love of the brother and sister differs from the love of sister and sister, and of brother and brother. In a subsequent page we shall see the wisdom and goodness of this Divine arrangement. This influence also varies according to the *age* of the children. Each, of course, stands related to the others in the relation of elder or younger; and consequently of weaker or stronger, teacher or taught, imitator or imitated, superior or inferior.

Servants and child.

The presence of *servants* in a family creates other relations between parents and children, as well as between the servant and children themselves. The authority which the parents, as master and mistress, are seen to possess over the servants, operates as so much influence on the minds of the children. In addition to which there is the parental authority which is delegated to the servants over the children; and the involuntary influence which they naturally possess over them as their superiors in age, and knowledge, and power; and the subtle influence which arises from the perception, that, with all this superiority, yet, *in rank*, they are inferior.

External relations; of the individual to nature.

Passing on to man's *external* relations, we have to notice, first, the relations of the individual man to *nature*, including in that term, the climate of the district in which he lived, its soil, external features, and scenery, its botany and zoology, its relative situation and extent. Each of these particulars, indeed, would operate as a distinct element of influence; but as they are themselves mutually related, and as any one or more of them, by affecting any single part of the human constitution, would indirectly affect the whole, we can speak of their relations to it only in a general manner.

As a being *physical*, *organic*, and *animal*, the natural geography of his locality would be found related to his physical development, his instinctive propensities, and to the period of their reaching maturity; to the character of his diseases; and to the quality, if not also to the quantity of his food—determining, at least, what they should *not* be, and thus affecting his occupation, by inducing him to scour the country as a hunter, to remove from district to district as a shepherd, or to become stationary as an agriculturist or an artizan.

As a being *sensient* and *perceptive*, the flavors, odors, and colors of its vegetable productions, the forms of its animal life, the beauty or boldness of its landscapes, the brightness of its atmosphere, the length of its days and its seasons—would be all found related to his sensibility and taste, and disposing him to be more or less objective. The ἄσπετος αἰθὴρ of Greek literature partly accounts for the surpassing excellence of Greece in every artistic representation of beauty, and for its objective character and life. In the case of the antediluvian, these causes, and others combined with them—such as the attainableness of minerals, metals, and colors, would partly decide in what particular branch of art his perception of the beautiful or sublime should chiefly express itself; just as the marble quarries of Pentelicus and of the snow-white Megarian, invited, by their splendor, the chisel of Phidias and Praxiteles. The same influences would affect the character of his architecture. From these causes, too, his dress would take much of its character; being more or less durable, according to his materials; more or less warm and changeful, according to the seasons; and more or less gay, according to the atmosphere—for "under a perfectly clear and blue sky, nothing is gaudy." And the same causes would be found related to his amusements. In the "Paradise Lost," Raphael, "the affable Archangel," shows to the father of mankind his degenerate antediluvian posterity, dancing and carousing, late at night, on the open plains: and the character of the climate would determine the point.

The physical geography of his residence would be found related to him as a *reflective* being—by the length of its day, and the nature of its seasons, inviting him to sensitive objective pleasures, or shutting him up to his subjective resources—by the number and variety of its natural phenomena—especially, at first, of its meteorology—being so few and unvarying as hardly to need arrangement, or so numerous, changeful, and distracting, as to discourage and defer the hope of classification. By its productiveness—its extreme fertility and resources, rendering labor for food comparatively unnecessary, and thus tempting him to retrograde in civilization rather than inciting him to advance; its extreme poverty, by consuming all his time in labor, leaving him little opportunity for improvement; or its medium character, exercising alike his body and his mind. By its climate allowing him to lay up a store of food, so as to secure him seasons of leisure; or requiring him to prepare and procure it from day to day; dissolving him to a state of indolent lassitude which disposes him to seek no answers even to his own inquiries, to be content that effects should have no causes, or bracing him to an ever-inquiring activity, which finds many causes for a single effect. By its atmosphere, inviting, for example, to the contemplation of the midnight heavens, as in Italy, where "the sky is so clear you seem to see beyond the moon;" or on the plains of Chaldea, where the stars appearing larger and brighter than they do to us, and as if let down from the firmament, invited to astronomical studies. And by its zoology—the prevalence of the lion or of any beast of prey tending to retard civilization; the presence of a domesticable animal, such as the ox or the horse, the ass or the camel, tending to promote it.

As endowed with the higher gift of *reason*, it would be found related to him variously. For its facts, according to their number and character, would, more or less, call for theories to unite and account for them. In proportion as its phenomena, either by their connected, their sublime, or their startling nature, favored inquiry, it would lead him to ask for the *noumenon*—even the "eternal power and Godhead." In certain states of mind, the sight of a vast landscape, or of "the great and wide sea," would awaken an idea of the illimitable. While his leisure, and the climate, would be more or less friendly to the exercise and development of his subjective tendency.

As a being capable of *language;* besides calling for names for all its objects, its phenomena would furnish him with numerous epithets, and suggest idioms and comparisons. While his voice would insensibly harmonize with the prevailing sounds of nature around him, and his pronunciation more or less accord with its general voice.

Its relations to his *emotional* nature need hardly be pointed out. It is obvious how its mere meteorological changes may, at times, keep his hopes and fears in play; how its produce may affect his gratitude; its scenery conduce to his cheerfulness or otherwise; its climate elate or depress him; and its every familiar sight and sound be to him an occasion of aversion or of desire. The very fact that what he beholds is *his own*, endears it to him, and implants in him a wish to retain it, enlarge it, or improve it.

As a *voluntary* being, its climate would affect him; by

its tendency to enervate and relax the frame, until every obstacle to action becomes "a lion in the way;" or by so tensely bracing it for activity, that motion itself becomes a pleasure; by its soil, botany and zoology, as they were more or less calculated to invite and reward industry and enterprise. The original grant of the different kingdoms of nature for man's dominion is, in effect, repeated in every instance in which he goes to take possession of a new district. He then receives investiture to govern a province of creation; and, as he looks on his new domain, that domain, with all its thousand voices, may be regarded as asking him, "Have you the necessary strength of will to subdue me, and have dominion?" The process of subjugation is a perpetual exercise of the will, which strengthens by exercise. Every cultivated field, and every domesticated animal around him, is a triumph of his will. By its scenery—the voice of the mountains, and the voice of the sea, each shouting, though in different accents, "Be active, energetic, bold, and you shall be our king; be otherwise, and you must be our slave."

On all these accounts it would be necessarily related to him as a being capable of *moral distinctions*. By favoring the undue development of any one part of his nature, it indicates to him the class of moral distinctions most endangered. Its general tendency would be toward the extreme of self-indulgence or of asceticism, Stoicism or Epicureanism, Polytheism or Pantheism. The aspect of nature, whether stern or cheerful, would tend to become his own aspect. But this again would materially depend on his occupation—with what part of nature it brought him mostly into contact, and what leisure it left him to hold communion with it. Who can conceive of the stern majesty of the Mosaic

Law speaking from any throne but that of a thunder-riven Sinai? The flower, the gloomy forest, the quiet nook, the burning sun, the objectless plain, the midnight sky, the cataract, the mountain, the ocean—each has a voice of its own in which it speaks to him of the future or the invisible, as containing the sanctions of right or wrong, and to which, in corresponding tones, the voice of conscience within him replies, "Deep calleth unto deep." It whispers a fable, or sings in poetry, or thunders in prohibition; but always with *a moral*, which says "thou shalt," or "thou shalt not." It is ever renewing its imagery on his imagination, so that its brightest scenes will mingle with his visions of future happiness, and its most repulsive with his ideas of future misery; rendering virtue proportionally attractive and vice odious. His visible will be ever tending to embody for him the invisible.

The same relations successively existent.

Man is to be viewed also as a being *successively* existent. In infancy, the relations in question are of the most despotic kind; and parental tenderness and skill are busied in mitigating and adjusting them to its passive helplessness. Objects engage attention; not merely a succession of objects, but a succession of properties in the same objects—motion, color, form. "Hence it is that our life in childhood is so inconceivably significant. At that age, every thing is of importance to us; we hear every thing, see every thing, and all our impressions are vivid; whereas, at a later age, we do every thing with design, and we lose in depth what we gain in extension of impressions."* At that early age external nature imprints itself photographically on the

* Heinrich Heine, in Mrs. Austin's Fragments from German Writers, p. 62.

mind, without the formality of preparation for the process From objects and events, the child comes to notice their internal changes, and to find an interest in their connection. He consciously theorizes on their causes, efficient and final, and moots inquiries which exercise his rational powers. Thus is erected a demand for words and forms of speech which enlarge and enrich his faculty of communication, and still further exercise and develop his mind. In this way external nature erects itself into a vast theater, in which every thing appeals to one or other of his emotions. In proportion to the energy of his will, however, he imprints on surrounding nature his own character, molding its objects, and linking its events, to suit his own purposes; and thus comes to control that which, at first, threatened to vanquish him. While every step of his course is calculated more deeply to convince him that the hand of law is on every thing; on himself in relation to every thing, on every part of his nature; and that, in the eye of the Lawgiver, his every act bears the impress of right or wrong. Thus his relations successively multiply and change. He who at first appeared to be almost at the mercy of external nature, comes to subordinate it to his own purposes. And though it is true, to a certain extent, in this, as in other respects, that "the child is father to the man," it is also true that "when he becomes a man he puts away childish things," rises above nature in this most important respect, that he ascends by it, and then from it, to the supernatural.

Of man to man.

Man himself is a part of the objective universe to his fellow-man. As such, he sustains relations specifically different from those which connect him with the inferior parts of creation—a system of co-relations arising from identity of constitution and of destiny.

As a physical, organic, and animal being, inhabiting the same earth, dependent on its material means of subsistence, and susceptible of being similarly affected by its physical geography, he is related to him by space or neighborhood, as well as by activity and strength. By these he is physically able to displace and dispossess his fellow, or to aid and protect him; to co-operate with or to molest him.

His fellow-man is related to him as a *sentient* being, by personal appearance; by the frequency of seeing him; by the voice, and every thing by which he could appeal to his senses; and by the identity of the impressions derived by both from the same objects. He is *reflective;* and here is a being who has surrounded himself with the manifestations of his own mind; and who, besides thus acting on him suggestively, like nature, can directly impart his own knowledge, and who will influence him according to the particular direction of his knowledge. As capable of *speech*, his fellow-man is related to him according to his greater or less command of the right language; his oath-like veracity or otherwise; and according to the degree in which he employs respectively, the persuasive or the didactic, the argumentative or the dogmatic, form of communication. He is *emotional;* and here is a being who can not merely, like natural objects, excite his emotions, but can also return them. He is *voluntary;* and here is another voluntary being; each conscious, from his own self-knowledge, that he can not force the will of the other, but that he can not fail to affect it, by his patience, perseverance, and by the degree of his ascendency over the inferior parts of his own nature, and over outward objects. And as a being capable of *moral* distinctions, his fellow-man stands related to him by the degree in which these distinctions are embodied in action, and in which he thus becomes a living manifestation of God. Each of these relations admits of being graduated by a scale of innumerable points. Nor is the individual related to any two of the race in precisely the same manner.

Successively existent.

Viewed as *successively* existent, he may be said to be born into an artificial man-made world; such, at least, is the circle immediately around him. Custom has pre-arranged the manner of his reception. His first toys come from the hand of man. His impressions of yesterday are displaced or deepened by his impressions of to-day; and as his horizon enlarges, and new objects come into view, they do but increase his acquaintance with man. Every man around him is, more or less, a representative of the age in which he lives, and, therefore, of all his cotemporaries; so that by being brought into contact with any given individual, he is brought into contact with the age, and is increasingly molded and influenced by it. His physical inferiority renders him dependent on the use which others make of their superior strength, even as to the amount of personal liberty which he shall enjoy; and his very consciousness of this fact can not fail to influence him. Even the scenery of nature acquires a character from the presence and activity of man; the Acropolis with the Parthenon and without it, for example, would affect a Greek very differently. An object which he would otherwise have passed by unnoticed, might burn itself into his memory on learning that it was, or had been, deeply interesting to others. Little of his knowledge is derived from his own observation, but is conveyed to him as the fruit of the experience of others. The first maxim or proverb he received, contained, probably, in a condensed form, the generalized experience of thousands. Custom after custom would leave its impress on him. Law after law would impose its obligations on him. One object of friendship after another would engage his affections; and one opinion be modified or succeeded by another, until, had he written memoirs of himself, after living through centuries, he might have fancied himself at times to have transmigrated, or to be writing the biography of distinct individuals. And, in looking back over so long a tract of time, how difficult, not to say impossible, would it be for him to determine the occasion or the manner of his adopting this or the other view, which yet, in the course of time, came to exercise no inconsiderable influence over his entire character. And if the influences which acted on him directly on all sides, as he passed through life, defied calculation, how much more so would the complicated and far-reaching relations of which these influences were the results.

His relations to God.

Equally obvious are the relations in which man stood to all those *Divine remedial* means glanced at in a preceding chapter. Thus, the return of the Sabbath invited him to rest from the fatigues of *bodily* labor. In harmony with his *sentient* nature, there was the cherubic glory, distinguishable from every other spectacle in creation. Or, supposing that to have been withdrawn, there was the place of sacrifice, and the solemn symbolic rites; the prophetic ark; the venerable preacher of righteousness; and the ever-speaking place of burial. For death, then, considering the comparative recency of the doom, and the great length of human life, must have had a preternatural voice.

The appointment of a certain time and place for religious instruction and worship, recognized man's *reflective* nature —his power of attention, the force of habit, and the law of association; while the subjects of the Divine communication were of a nature to answer every inquiry of a practical importance likely to interest an intelligent being situated as man was. They explained him to himself; his origin and moral history; the nature of his own inward conflicts, and the source of the prevailing depravity around him—tracing it to that apostacy from God by which both the laws of self-government and of the Divine government were violated, and man, as an all-related being, put himself out of harmony alike with God and with himself. They announced to him the promise of a deliverer, and placed within his reach the means of present interest in his deliverance. They told him that life, both for himself and for his race, was disciplinary and probationary. While, by the preaching and the translation of Enoch, they hinted of other worlds, and pointed to a time of judgment, and to a state of future rewards and punishments.

In harmony with man's power of *communications by signs*, God speaks to him either in the oral exposition of the Divine revelations, or in the tables which record them. On the one hand, thoughts which have dwelt from eternity in the Divine mind, are thus committed to the vehicle of language that they may be revolved for the coming eternity in the mind of man. On the other hand, man could not utter a word in prayer which was not heard by God; nor express a thought which did not blend, so to speak, with the Divine thoughts—which did not detain the Divine Being in communion. In harmony with his *emotional* nature, every part of Divine revelation was a manifestation of one or other aspect of the Divine character; each aspect appealing to a corresponding emotion in man, and calculated to keep his entire nature in sympathy with God.

One truth said, "Hope in Him with all thy heart;" another, "Be filled with sorrow;" another, "Rejoice;" another, "Admire;" all were summed up in the command, "Thou shalt love the Lord thy God with all thy heart." And what must the Divine excellence be, when all creation is but a counterpoise to its attracting power; when, even as it came fresh from the Divine hand, all the visible glories of creation did but furnish the centrifugal balance to His centripetal power!

As man is a *voluntary* being, God signifies to him his own will. Obedience or subordination to that is the only condition of the liberty of man's will. Insubordination is derangement, lawlessness, and slavery to some other part of his own nature. Still, no force must be employed to induce obedience. Motives to subordination are presented sufficiently strong to render man inexcusable if he does not comply; but not such as to frighten or force him into submission. Indeed, forced obedience is a self-contradiction. So that, although the Supreme will announces itself in the imperative form, and declares, "Thou shalt," or "Thou shalt not," man is still at physical liberty to disobey; and although the evidence that God hath so spoken is sufficient, it is not, therefore, efficient, but may, if man pleases, be denied. It must not be irresistible. And although the Holy Spirit reclaims the disobedient will, it is simply by, not forcing it, but setting it at liberty. Regeneration is self-restoration; so that truth is no longer treated as falsehood. In harmony with man's *moral* nature, he found his relations to God increased; each new relation giving rise to a new obligation, and all his obligations enforced by corresponding motives. Every part of the new dispensation of mercy might be regarded by him as "a tree of knowledge of good and evil," placing him on a higher probation than at first; but making every thing to depend, as then, on "the obedience of faith."

Successively existent.

As one of a race originated by creation, but whose members come into being consecutively and by means, he stood related to God as his *mediate* Creator. Every step through life, too, by unfolding the adaptations of nature and of man to meet his wants, to develop his constitution, and to influence his character, placed him in new relations to that *Providence* which had included the whole in its plan.

The idea of God, however early and gradually it may have taken its place in his mind, was the admission of an ever-active and transforming power. As the great pre-existing facts of Divine revelation were brought within his view, opening successively new aspects of the character of God, his relations to God went on increasing. And as other facts were added for the first time in his own day, these relations multiplied still further. The preparation of the ark, for example, converted the earth, in effect, into the judgment-hall for the awful proceedings of the descending judge.

If the individual sustain these external relations, every antediluvian *Family*, as composed of individuals, would necessarily sustain them also.

Co-existent relations of the family to nature.

Physical geography would partly determine the *marriageable age;* the occupations of husband and wife; the time which each would have at disposal for the company of the other, and their fitness for such companionship; and would thus exercise a powerful influence on the whole domestic constitution. As *parents*, it would be found related to the average number of children in a family; to the consequent amount of labor necessary to provide for them; to the time they could bestow on their education, separately and jointly; to their fitness for educating them, and to the length of time the children would remain unmarried. Nature would be found related, through the parents, to every part of the constitution of the *children;* to their early amusements, tastes, and habits; and to the choice of their subsequent pursuits. And, similarly, it would affect the relation of *master* and *servant;* as to the number of the servants wanted, the nature of their occupation and consequent influence on each other, the trust reposed in them, the closeness of their intercourse with the family, and the nature of their servitude.

Successively existent.

The family sustains relations *successively* existent. In contemplating *man* as successively existent, we saw that the last moment of his life was, to a certain extent, influenced by his first; here, we see one age linked to another in a similar manner.

"The empire of climate (says Montesquieu) is the first, the most powerful of all empires." Without admitting this statement in its unqualified force, climate must doubtless be allowed to exercise a powerful influence. But the climate of one region is much more despotic than that of another. The same climate is much more despotic over the same people in the early stages of their civilization than it is subsequently. Civilization may even considerably modify the climate itself. Besides which, man becomes progressively powerful in his influence on man, and at length the chief agent in his civilization. In the early stages of human improvement, the sea appears to be, what the Roman poet calls it, *dissociabilis;* but, in proportion as the art of navigation advances, it changes its character, and becomes *sociabilis*—"the great highway of the nations." The antediluvian world, probably owing to their central situation, knew little of navigation. Still the extent of region occupied would naturally include great geographical variety. And the effects of this variety, accumulating for more than two thousand years, would be summed up—modified, of course, by circumstances—in the character of the latest generation. The necessary occupation of one region might tend to develop a spirit of enterprise and create "men of renown;" the character and climate of another would be favorable to the growth of "giants in those days;"* while that of another might go

* Almost every record of antiquity hands down the tradition of a family or race of giants. Nor does their existence appear to be any more enigmatical than the amazing strength, magnitude, and duration of many of the structures of the ancients—the pyramids, for example, and the hundred-gated Thebes. And yet if we had only the tradition that such structures once existed, it would be regarded, by those who sapiently measure every thing ancient by a modern standard, as simply mythical. Such, too, would be the certain fate of any mere records of the departed giants of the vegetable and animal kingdoms. Geology points us to past worlds of gigantic ferns, tree-grasses, and lofty mosses; and to reptiles tall and bulky as the elephant, rhinoceros, or hippopotamus. "There were animal-giants in those days;" and why not human giants in later days? Representatives of the fossil monster-growths of the coal-measures and of the reptile dynasty, indeed, still exist. But the existing giants, of the reptile class, for example, "the crocodiles and boas, hardly equal in bulk the third-rate reptiles of the ages of the Oolite of the Wealden." The size of the body oscillates between certain extreme limits. During the early period of man's history, the extreme development of his bulk and strength took place to a much greater extent than at present; though the instances of gigantic stature which still occur are more frequent than is commonly supposed.

It is erroneously inferred by many that these antediluvian giants sprang to account for the fact respecting its women "that they were fair." Each region, according to its peculiarities, would tend to develop corresponding characteristics in its inhabitants; while that part of the constitution so developed, whether physical, intellectual, or moral, would tend to modify all the rest. In one Patriarchal family, stationary residence and hereditary occupations would gradually develop qualities which it might yet require centuries to mature; while, in another, similar qualities would be gradually obliterated by removal and change, and be replaced by their opposites. And thus the history of one family, as compared with that of another, might exhibit a prolonged struggle with the influences of external nature, ending in mastery, or in a gradual adjustment and consenting to them; or else in a general compromise with them.

To cotemporaneous families.

Every *cotemporaneous* family would sustain, to every other, relations of distance or neighborhood, of number, sex, and personal attractions, determining, partly, the nature and amount of its intercourse with them, and the degree of its influence over them. The family or tribe most advanced in *civilization* would be found giving law to opinion as to what constitutes competence and wealth; as well as on all subjects of fashion and usage, and of laws regulating family inter-

from the union spoken of in the context between the sons of God and the daughters of men. Whereas the statement seems constructed expressly to guard against such an inference: "In those days were the (well-known) *Nephilim* in the earth. Also *after that* the sons of God," etc. Two periods are spoken of. Giants existed prior to the period of the unions in question, and continued to exist afterward. The ungodly mixture of the two races and their offspring denoted the licentiousness of the period, and the insolent conduct of the giant race marked the violence of the times.

course. In this connection, too, *language* would make slander possible; in other words, we advance from speech respecting things to speech concerning persons. Intercourse between family and family would multiply the objects of *emotion*, and quicken its activity. Nor could the sphere of its operation be thus enlarged without robbing or enriching the immediate circle of home, and benefiting or injuring other circles.

By these means, the *voluntary* power, as developed in the family government, would be affected; for, in proportion as the emotions are excited, the difficulty of carrying them out into appropriate action increases, while their demand for excitement goes on increasing also. In proportion as they are allowed to terminate on themselves, the will is enfeebled; the consequence of this is, that hopes and fears are not so easily excited—rewards do not so easily secure obedience, nor correction restrain from evil. And in this important respect, each family, by its example, influences others.

And thus each family would be found sustaining to the others *moral* relations; multiplying them by multiplying the objects of thought, desire, and pursuit; tending to confound them by calling good evil, and evil good; or virtually defeating them by making convenience, custom, or expedience, the motive for attending to them instead of the will of God.

Successively existent.

As the first human pair had multiplied into a family; giving rise, for the first time, to the endearing relations of parent and child, brother and sister, so that family again had branched off into a new generation of *other families*, giving rise to the additional relations of uncles and aunts, nephews and nieces, and cousins; and these again into remoter affinities, until the connection of kindred became so attenuated as no longer to receive specific names; while relations arising from neighborhood, or country, or physiological similarity, or identity of temporal interests, would begin to grow into importance. Still, however great the number of families living at the time of the flood, and however marked their physical differences may have been, the identity of the whole as the progeny of the same stock, would, owing to man's longevity, be of such easy verification as to remain entirely unquestioned. If, as we have remarked, the physical and mental development of the members of one family would be influenced to some degree by the peculiarities of its relations to external nature, the corresponding developments in the members of another would be influenced by that family; while the characteristics of each, acting and re-acting, would be carried on to the next generation. Social intercourse, marriage, exchange of produce, the commerce of mind, would ever be tending to multiply, and to cast wider and wider over society the ties which should have kept them bound into one brotherhood. Each generation, as it rose, would enter into the possession of all the accumulations of the past. Laws awaited the coming of its members, and were ready to bind them. Customs were ready to mold them. Ideas and proverbs were current to inform them.* Language, in which to express

* I may suggest that some of these, in the form of moral maxims, are, not improbably, to be found in that book of (I believe) co-Mosaic antiquity, the Book of Job, chap. viii. 8, etc. "Ask now of the former generations, and attend to the search of their fathers; for we are of yesterday, and know nothing; because our days are a shadow upon the earth. They will speak unto thee, and give thee instruction; and will

those ideas. Paths had been worn for them. "Great names had been among them," which historically influenced them. Family sepulchers, before they were born, awaited their decease. Many an altar, gray with antiquity, told of past generations of worshipers, and was invested with such precious associations that "they favored the dust thereof, and took pleasure in its stones." As time advanced, the year became a calendar of great events.

Each generation, too, would be influenced by anticipations of the future. "Coming events," casting "their shadows before," would appeal to its hopes or its fears. Those, for instance, who were both after the building of the ark was commenced, would, doubtless, be affected differently from all who had gone before. Great changes then, as now, would be always considered to be impending; and, according to their character, would work like leaven in the general mind. And thus each generation receiving from the past, added to it something of its own, and devolved it on the future. So that the generation living at

teach thee from their observations." The proposed inquiry is to be made, not merely of older men, but of former generations; and the reason assigned is, that we are both a *recent* race, and are *short-lived*, compared with those from whom the maxims had come. These begin at the 11th verse, and are characterized by most antique simplicity. Similarly, the so-called "statutes of Adam," or "precepts of Noah," no doubt date from antediluvian times. Their form and number, as found in Maimonides and Selden, may have been different; but who can suppose that no moral and religious maxims whatever were floated across the flood? And if some such traditions may be expected, what more rational than that they should have expressed the simple and fundamental elements of all religion and morality: to abstain from idolatry—To worship the true God—To commit no murder—To abstain from licentiousness—To administer justice, etc.?

the time of the flood became the heir, and was found in possession, of the results of all the relations of dependence and influence which had originated in the first man.

Co-existent relations of the family to God.

The family is *divinely* related in its parts and as a whole. The *husband*, as such, is the subordinate representative of God to the wife; and the father, as such, to the children; but in a different respect to the two parties, answering to the different relation in which he stands respectively to each. So also the *wife*, as such, is related to God mediately in the representative character of her husband; while she herself sustains a representative relation for her children. The *children*, as such, are related to God mediately through their parents; while each child, and every part of each, enters into direct relations of its own, answering to the progressive development of its constitution. The *servants*, by placing a part of their nature at the disposal of another, sustain new and additional relations to God.

The family constitution is an organic whole; having, like the individual, ends of its own to answer, and a similar ultimate relation to the great end—the former harmonizing with the latter. As such, it brings to light new views of the various attributes of God already revealed, for the family is placed in new relations to each. It is a government, representative of the Divine government. As the head of the constitution, the parent is to teach, intercede, and rule, as prophet, priest, and king, and to do every thing for God.

In speaking of the relation of the family *to God*, we have to recall the distinction, before referred to, between the truths which introduced the dispensation and formed its basis, and those Divine communications made subsequently, from time to time, as the state of the antediluvian human family made them necessary.

The same successively existent. The remarkable manner in which *the primary truths* of the dispensation—the promise of a Deliverer, and the institute of Sacrifice—harmonized with the domestic constitution, is obvious. To name only the following respects: the promised Deliverer was to be of the seed of the woman; was to come through the family constitution. Every child born, therefore, was a new and a living memorial of the great promise. Every prayer offered in faith, for offspring given, bore a relation to the "seed" yet to come. Sacrifice would be offered by the parent for the family before the children were in a capacity to present it for themselves. Both the promise and the institution would be received on parental testimony. While the stationary symbol of the Divine presence would invite them to sacrifice and worship in their collective or family capacity.

Especially is it instructive to remark in what various ways the *second* class of the Divine communications recognized and corroborated the domestic constitution. Thus the principal agents employed by God as "preachers of righteousness" were heads of families; such were Adam and Seth, Enoch and Noah. In harmony with the weight naturally due to parental testimony, it does not appear that miracles were performed to substantiate it. The translation of Enoch, indeed, was God's own testimony to the truth of His servant's message; but neither Enoch nor Noah appear to have been empowered to perform miracles. Had such been the case, their claim to be believed even by their own children, when they testified for God, would have rested, not on their parental relation, but on the supernatural evidence they adduced. The parental office, too, would be greatly enhanced by the longevity of the Patriarchs. For nine hundred and thirty years the father of mankind continued in the midst of his multiplying offspring. And as their lives were of corresponding length, the chain of testimony by which Divine communications were transmitted from him to the cotemporaries of Noah consisted at most only of a few links. The necessary effect of this arrangement would be to increase the importance of the paternal relation. The same effect would be produced by the method adopted, doubtless by Divine direction, for perpetuating the remembrance of certain informations, whether historical or prophetic, by giving significant names to children. This was calculated to make Divine communications as enduring as the family constitution itself, by making them a part of it. By the *times* most probably selected by God for the employment of the paternal agency to impart Divine revelation. If there be one season more than another in which the heart is prepared to receive lasting impressions, it is surely when listening to the closing accents of a dying parent. This is emphatically the *mollia tempora fandi.* Yet this was the season when the postdiluvian Patriarchs were led, by a Divine impulse, to gather their children around them, and to tell them of things to come."* The probability is, therefore, that this method characterized the Patriarchal dispensation from first to last. And in proportion to the greater length of antediluvian life, must have been the greater solemnity of the scene in which lips, which had been revered as almost oracular, for centuries, uttered their last accents. Nor did the Divine procedure ever cease to

* Gen. xxvii. xlviii. l. 24, 25.

harmonize with the family character of the dispensation; for those eventually saved from the general wreck were Noah and *his family.* It is not improbable that there were some antediluvians whose character might have sustained a favorable comparison with that, for example, of Ham. But the Divine conduct, true to the last, to the *Patriarchal* character of the economy, selected, not the individual members of different families, but one family.* Noah is represented in Scripture as a prevailing intercessor with God. It is not improbable that owing to his earnest entreaties, either the deluge was delayed as it was, or else that some mitigation of the world's doom took place. And very likely it is, that as the preservation of his family would naturally form the frequent subject of prayer to God, it was accorded, partly at least, as an answer to prayer. And thus God himself sustained, from first to last, the relation of Pater-familias to the antediluvian; while in an especial manner he was "the God of all the families" that called upon His name.

Here was a great system of relations, touching in *space*, every part of every human being, and of the world which he inhabited, and reaching to the throne of God; while, *in time*, it reached from the first moment of creation to an indefinite futurity—a mighty web-work of dependence and influence.

* The fact that Noah was five hundred years old when he became the father of Shem, Ham, and Japhet, is no ground, indeed, for inferring that he had no children previously. The average age at which the other antediluvian Patriarchs became fathers would lead to a contrary conclusion. But these three were born to him after the Flood had been threatened: and the probability is that they were selected or sent by God to furnish a parentage for the new world as little as possible saturated with the corruptions of the old world.

CHAPTER VIII.

LAWS WHICH THE RELATIONS OF THE FAMILY CONSTITUTION PRESUPPOSE.

The family presupposes laws.

THE family is not a system of mere vague relations; it is a constitution pervaded by definite laws. Supposing it to have originated in the Divine purpose, it is only to be expected that it would be pursued on a plan; and a plan supposes the orderly arrangement and concurrent operation of certain sequences of events for the attainment of certain ends.

We have seen that each preceding economy—mineral, vegetable, and animal—was respectively impressed with the regularity of law. The constitution and history of individual man form a nobler illustration of the same fact. If the family be only the further development of the individual, we are justified in expecting it to report a further development of law. Accordingly, we find that nothing belonging to the family is indifferent in its effects.

If, as we have seen, the natural laws of the preceding dispensation are brought on into the family, its welfare requires that the family should fall in with and obey them. Even in those respects in which the Creator deemed it necessary, at first, to initiate and instruct men, He was but practically enforcing His own laws. Had He taught man any thing else, it would have been unavailing, because incapable of application. Apart from the stability of nature, the discoveries and improvements made by Jubal and Tubal Cain, and other antediluvians, in agriculture and the mechanical arts, would have been impossible; and so also would have been the training of others in these arts, for the laws of one day could not have been relied on the day after. Discoveries were made, then as now, just in proportion as men were content to learn the laws of God in the material world from Himself. The moment they looked away and began to speculate what these laws might be, or ought to be, the progress of discovery stopped, and it stopped just because they were then virtually legislating in a sphere which God had legislated already.

Union of the sexes in marriage, a law. Celibacy.

If the view which we have taken of marriage be correct, every thing relating to it must be either an act of obedience to a law of nature, or a violation of it. If, for example, the sexual desire be a part of the human constitution, it can not be immaterial whether or not it be gratified. The Roman Church may plead that it is a carnal affection, and that, in the instance of men set apart for the service of God, it ought to be repressed. But woman is not to be thus branded as "a pollution" with impunity. Never has this violence been done to a natural law, even on a small scale, without recoiling in some form of, at least, secret evil; and where practiced on a large scale, and for a length of time, it has uniformly drawn after it a train of festering social evils. That many have passed their lives in consistent celibacy "for the kingdom of heaven's sake," is not to be questioned. But as little is it to be doubted that it unfitted them for sympathies and duties which properly belonged to their sacred office; for marriage is not less deeply written in man's soul than in his body. In vain is it for Church or Council to attempt to elevate celibacy into a virtue; a deep-seated law of human nature cries out against it.* A large proportion of those who take the vow, come to regard it as a restriction against which nature rebels, or as involving an abstinence from one form of gratification which may seek compensation in other forms, deeply polluting to themselves and to society.†

Violations of this law.

If the sexual desire be a part of the human constitution, the manner and the degree in which it is gratified can not be immaterial; for, as the constitution of man includes a variety of other laws, the desire can be rightly indulged only in harmony with those other laws.

Licentiousness.

Then it can not be indifferent whether or not the desire be gratified *indiscriminately*, or to any excess. This would be to abolish the very name of HOME, to reduce the parental relation to the bestial, and the social to the gregarious; so that man would be distinguished from the mere animal only by his excessive sensuality. It is as evidently the will of the Creator that the desire should be yielded to only within certain limits as that it should be gratified at all, and for the same ultimate reason.

The intercourse of the sexes, *apart from marriage*, has been pleaded for, permitted, and even legally sanctioned, on the plea of preventing greater enormities. Man was

* In M. Souvestre's *Minstrelsy of the Bretons*, an account is given of a distinct kind of poetry called the *sone*, which has almost entirely grown out of this kind of feeling.

† See Quart. Rev. vol. xciv. p. 157, etc.

thus striving to improve on the Divine legislation. But, in the obvious tendency of such an expedient to diminish marriages, in the disease propagated, the *habits* of lewdness produced, the contempt poured by society on the parties chiefly concerned, and in the injuries inflicted on social morality, the laws of nature proclaim their violation, and loudly call for redress. To see the evils of such a departure from the law of chastity in their proper light, however, we must wait until we can find a country in which marriage, and every thing answering to it, are, and long have been, abrogated; and where the sexes live in common. Nay, a country in which nothing like marriage *ever* existed; for, if it have once existed there, the posterity of such unions can never be certain how much they continue to be indebted to that former state of things. But the unnatural experiment of sexual intercourse without marriage has never been avowedly made in civilized society, except in countries where the law of marriage prevailed; that is to say, in a country where marriage was the *rule*, a very small party, pretending to a new discovery in social law, has sometimes been suffered to form the *exception;* and has escaped, owing to the very fact that it was the exception, the worst consequences of its guilt. Sometimes, indeed, these consequences have become so threatening that other parts of the community (though by no means of fastidions morals) have sternly demanded the abatement of the nuisance. The law of marriage, however, is so obviously fundamental to society, that it has formed the rule of communities, even in their worst condition. Hence, in that monstrous state of mankind which called for a deluge, we are told that "they married and were given in marriage, till the day that Noah entered into the ark."

It may, perhaps, be objected that occasional aberrations, and individual instances of licentious indulgence need not be followed by all the evil consequences we have described. To this it is sufficient to reply, that by every such act a law of God is violated; and that, as the least evil which can result, two minds are polluted; habits of evil are confirmed; and a member of society already lost to it, perhaps, in the highest sense, receives the renewal of her sentence of degradation.

Polygamy.

Polygamy is only an ill-concealed compromise between lust and law; between the law of marriage and the indulgence of sensuality—the former being bribed to throw a vail over the latter. And, doubtless, in a corrupt state of society, where unbridled sensuality was threatening social disorganization, a plurality of wives would be deemed an almost virtuous expedient. And probably, not a few specious arguments would be advanced in its defense. But it was an infraction of a natural appointment; and the injured law proved too strong for the sophistry. The inequality which it produced in the distribution of the sex, and which, by leaving many men single, would lead to prostitution; the distraction of affection; the domestic jealousies; the degradation of the woman, who, by ceasing to be the equal and the companion of man, becomes his timid slave, or the mere instrument of his sensual gratification; the prison-like surveillance of her movements thus made necessary; the diminished number of healthy children resulting from such concubinage; and their necessary want of parental education*—all proclaimed that polygamy is a violation of the domestic constitution. Perhaps, the most favorable circumstances in which such

* Cuvier's Animal Kingdom, vol. i. pp. 76, 77.

an experiment could be made, was in Patriarchal times. But those are the very times which denote that in no case can the Divine arrangement on the subject be departed from with impunity. Indeed, the first reference to the evil, in the fragmentary allusion to antediluvian Lamech,* is of a kind ominous of a train of alarming results.

Physical conditions of marriage. If, as we have seen, animal propagation takes place according to definite laws, and if these laws have been brought on into the human economy, it follows that the ages, health, and other physical conditions of the married pair, can not be matters of indifference. Accordingly, these natural laws are found to hold on their way without any respect to the character or purposes of those concerned. Lycurgus might well ridicule the indifference of men to the *physique* of their own race, contrasted with their attention to natural laws in cultivating the breed of their horses and dogs. And, though his aim was low, and most of his methods barbarous and immoral, and therefore unnecessary, the men of Sparta was the result. Nature was justified of her children. Statistics undeniably prove that marriages too premature bring on sterility; that they produce children more subject to mortality than others; that precocious marriages generally produce a greater number of daughters than of sons; that the period of the greatest fecundity is before the age of thirty-three of the man, and twenty-six of the woman; that all things being equal, the marriages most productive are those in which the man is, at least, as old as the woman, or older, yet not much exceeding her time of life; and that the products of marriage are subject to the in-

* Gen. iv. 19, 23, 24.

fluence of city and country, freedom and slavery, want, and plenty, climate and occupation.*

Interest, policy, and expediency may make it desirable that health and disease should be united; or youth and age; or that marriage should take place independently of affection, and of all the physical facts we have specified. But these laws are no respecters of persons nor expedients. However virtuous the parties may be, natural laws require their appointed condition of fulfillment; or, however vicious, they ask but the same; and having obtained them, they know no partiality, keep no sabbath, but run their appointed course. Morality is highly favorable to their accomplishment, because temperance, health and social propriety are promoted by it, and these are in harmony with the laws of offspring. Both the natural and the moral form, in different degrees, parts of the same great whole. And wherever this proximate end of marriage—the production of healthy offspring, is not attained, it is just because the laws relating to marriage have been, in some respects, disregarded.

The respective spheres of husband and wife determined by nature.

That the respective spheres of the husband and wife should correspond to the respective differences of their constitution, is another law of the married state. This difference, indeed, has been, in almost all ages and countries, unduly magnified by the husband, to the consequent depression of the condition of the wife below her proper social rank. It was a saying of Cleobulus, one of the seven sages of Greece, "Let your daughters, when you give them in marriage, though girls in age, be women in understanding;" "by

* Sur l'Homme, et le Développement de ses Facultés, par M. A. Quetelet, t. i. c. ii.

which (says his biographer, with obvious astonishment) he implied that *even* girls should be instructed."* With the Athenians, woman was merely the household drudge, incapable of rational intercourse and friendship. The fact that a large proportion of the female children are destroyed in China tells its own revolting tale.† "Here, wolf, take thy lamb," is said to have been the old Russian formula of marriage. "As the prophet has not assigned any place for women in his paradise (says Ali-Bey-Badra), the Mohammedans give them no place in the mosques;"‡ and hence the Mussulman idea that women have no souls. Because they do not belong to man the *sex*, they have been too generally treated as not belonging to man the species. But women can not suffer alone. Every other part of the family organization suffers the loss of her just influence, and shares, by re-action, in her degradation.

"Chivalry (said Rahel) was a poetical lie, necessary to restore the equality of the sexes." But if much of man's politeness betrays an uneasy sense of his injustice, we must not be surprised if woman herself, in calling for redress, should be occasionally found asking for something more; something either unattainable or destructive of the family economy. If she is not permitted to paint even her own ideal of "an interior," she may be expected to attempt a Rubens, a Michael Angelo, or a Fuseli.§ Withhold from her the power of being the vestal priestess of home, which

* Diog. Laert, Lib. i. § 91.

† Gutzlaff's Journal of a Voyage, etc., pp. 174, 188.

‡ Travels, vol. i. p. 69.

§ "You must change the physical organization of the race of women before we can produce a Rubens or a Michael Angelo. I wish to combat that oft-repeated, but most false compliment, that genius is of no sex.

she was meant to be, and it will not be strange if she aims to assume some character grotesque and unnatural. Deny her that equality of rights to which she is entitled, and we can not be justly surprised if she aim at an absolute equality of condition. Such is ever the retributive reaction of unrighteousness.

But as long as woman retains her distinctive constitution, and continues to be, by that very fact, unfitted for certain extra-domestic spheres, no human arrangement could place her in them, without immediately beginning to develop a train of social, and therefore of personal, evils. That she has a power treasured up in her nature—a reserved power beyond that which the domestic function requires, and which has never yet been developed and applied, I fully believe. But let that energy take a direction which should, even indirectly, ignore or disparage home, and, if the misapplication were to begin to-morrow, nature would begin to reassert its injured claims the day after, and would continue to do so till things had reverted to their natural state.

Home education a law.

If the infant human being is introduced by a Divine ordination into the bosom of the family, it is implied that all the requisites for the development of his constitution exist there; and they exist there for the express purpose of his receiving the gradual and orderly development necessary to his well-being; and no part of this Divine arrangement, delicate and complicated as it is, can be tampered with without incurring proportional evil.

There may be equality of power; but in its quality and application, there will and must be, difference and distinction."—*Mrs. Jameson's Sketches*, vol. ii. p. 120.

Then "home education" is a law of nature; and to send the child forth from the circle into which the hand of God hath led it must be a violation of that law. Plausible reasons may be assigned for such a step—and for what can they not? "Cosmopolitism, in particular, has endeavored to substitute a sort of universal citizenship, in place of the family affections—regarding these as so many disturbing forces."* Lycurgus may take the new-born infant from its parents, with a view of propagating a sound and superior race.† Plato may abolish the family, in his *Republic*, on the plea of reducing multiplicity to unity, and of drying up one of the sources of division among men. And Aristotle may advocate the same procedure, in order to escape the difficulty of placing women on a footing with free men, as if they were "by nature capable of the same virtues."‡ Or society itself may come to be in a state which may render it difficult to pursue any other course; and the evils resulting from it to the individual may be of subtle operation; and those resulting to the family and the community may ask a considerable time and an extended scale for their development, and may even be partially disguised and neutralized by counteracting agencies; but if domestic education be a duty devolved on the parents by God, it is untransferable by man.

"From motives of high-toned though mistaken benevolence, persons have sometimes tried to devise a substitute in a case for which no substitute or scheme can be found—the negligence or indisposition of parents." Rules, too, may be devised for rendering the evils attendant on such a departure from the course prescribed by nature, as innocu-

* Chalmers' Bridgewater Treatise, vol. i. p. 233.

† Plutarch's Lives. ‡ Polit. Lib. i. c. 8.

ous as possible; but the tones of the mother's voice can not be imitated, and the house in which they are never heard, has nothing but hollow echoes for the heart of the child. Nothing can compensate for the want of the paternal smile and frown. The Being who has made the parents the instruments of the child's existence has placed in their hands exclusively the key to the recesses of its heart; and, if they fail to employ it, those depths remain closed to every other agent. In a word, no extra-domestic tuition, however well administered, can make up for the absence of that instructive sympathy and parental influence which tuition and discipline pre-suppose.*

The very fact, we have said, that the child is introduced by the Divine ordination into the bosom of the family, distinctly intimates that there, and there only, all the requisites for his education were intended to be found. The child is naturally loving and sympathetic, admiring and imitative; and where should parties be found more likely to return its love, and more interested in setting it an example worthy of imitation, than the parents? The child is naturally inquiring, believing, and confiding; and where can parties be supposed to exist more interested in feeding it with knowledge, telling it the truth, and winning its confidence, than the parents? The child is naturally disposed to follow the guidance and to obey the dictates of another; and whose government is more likely to be exercised without abuse, and solely for the good of the child, than that of its own parents? Every thing good and great which man accomplishes is effected, more or less, by a division of labor. The education of the human being pre-eminetly requires such division; but where can that "labor of love"

* Isaac Taylor on Home Education, c. i.

be found more minutely and wisely divided than between the father and the mother, between patience and power, tenderness and authority, the instinctive love of offspring and the moral regard for the excellence and well-being of that offspring? The welfare of the child depends on the acquisition of good habits; but habits are formed only by the frequent and long-continued repetition of the same measures; and where can the patience and perseverance which such repetition requires be looked for so confidently as in the steady affection of married parents? The child is disposed to look up with reverence to that which is in any sense above him; and who are so likely to pray for him, and with him, and to point his attention and affections to God, in order that he may attain the high end of his being, as they who have been the means of giving him being?

Whatever tends, then, to invade this Divine constitution of things, or even to weaken the ties between parent and child, can not fail, sooner or later, to be productive of evil. The pretexts for such a violation may, as we have seen, be strikingly plausible, and the facilities for falling in with it may be greatly multiplied; but if there are such things as self-executing laws of nature, it will infallibly bring its own punishment with it.*

* Let me not be misunderstood:—In the actual state of society, public schools are indispensable for some classes. My remarks apply to the state of things which has not only made them necessary as the supplement of home education, but which regards them as an ample substitute for it, and to the evils which must necessarily result. "So true is what Pestalozzi says—'There are no better teachers than the house, or the father's and mother's love, and the labor at home, and all the wants and necessities of life.' It is this *domestic* education, which, of all others, is most wanting in all classes under our present system. Without it *public* education may be good in an *intellectual* point of view (though even that

Laws which education itself supposes.

Their education supposes laws. "Every power exerts its agency under some laws." Here is a being full of powers; powers awaiting development, and capable of endless and unlimited application. How important to examine the constitution of this being, and reverentially to study it, in order to ascertain the laws under which its capabilities are to be developed, and its agencies exerted! For as, from its very nature, its education must be simply the gradual utterance and orderly assertion of all its latent susceptibilities and powers, the forcing or the repression of one part must lead to the detriment of the whole; so that the best and only proper process must be that which develops not any one part alone—even the highest—but every part in the greatest unity. "It is not a soul, it is not a body that we are training up (remarks Montaigne), but a man, and we ought not to divide him. As Plato says, we are not to fashion one without the other, but make them draw together like two horses harnessed to a chariot." *—"The exercise of one faculty will only improve that faculty, and is not adapted to improve any other.† Nothing has more retarded education than ignorance and disregard of this great principle."‡ Pestalozzi represents the preservation of harmony and equilibrium between all our powers, as the first law of education.

is difficult); in a *moral*, it must be defective, if not worse. The tendency of modern institutions—fond of masses, and co-operation, and broad effects, and sudden display—is to weaken and limit these home-bred influences."—Education Reform; by T. Wyse, Esq., M.P., vol. i. p. 81.

* Montaigne's Essays, xxv.

† This remark, though substantially true, requires limitation.

‡ Simpson's Philosophy of Education, p. 93.

What, then, shall we think of the fatal error—an error which one might laugh at, so egregious is its folly, did not its universality and its pernicious effects call rather for tears—which trains a section of the human being; taking a faculty here, and a member there; virtually turning the entire being into a magnified limb; practicing the foot of one as in dancing; the hand of another as in writing and music; the memory of another; or the bodily movements of another; and which miscalls the one-sided process *education?* What shall we say to the destructive mistake which confines its training to any one part of the human constitution, and leaves all the other parts undeveloped and without direction; which under the notion of preparing it for some one relation in life, incurs the hazard of not merely leaving it unfitted, but of actually disqualifying it for every other relation; and which, by disturbing the internal relations and destroying the constitutional balance of the youthful being, commences a conflict within him between his various powers, which more or less embitters his existence, if it does not destroy his character. The multiplied evils resulting from what generally passes under the name of education, proclaims in accents loud enough, one would think, to startle stupefaction itself, that nature has been outraged in this most important respect among others—the derangement of the physical harmony and interdependence of the different parts of the human constitution.

Other laws might be named, pre-eminently instructive and fruitful of obligation. Such are the following: That education begins with life. Nature does not study, in this particular, parental convenience; knows nothing of accommodating delays nor of formal beginnings. The child is born into her school, and receives its first lessons with its first breath; a school in which every thing teaches, and where every moment brings its lesson. That teaching, to be useful, must be accurate. Nature's teachers are laws; and her instructions, truths—the knowledge of things as they are. Her pupils, indeed, may graduate in blunders if they will; but this is not her fault. She sets no false lessons; and never has to recall her words or to correct her statements. That habits of correctness can be acquired only by a process of repetition and revision. The power of seeing and of walking is the result of ten thousand corrected actions of the eye and the foot. "Line upon line, and precept upon precept," is the Divine rule in nature as well as in providence. That nature, while thus profuse and untiring in her lessons, invites the independent efforts of the child, and does nothing for him which he can do for himself. She neither grows crutches nor makes machines. Stumbles and falls without number, are permitted, rather than that we should be kept too long in leading-strings. And if (like the Greek physician with the king of Persia) she puts a spice-filled mallet into our hands, the medicine on which she relies is the muscular effort of using it. That nature, while thus full of incitements to independent effort, knows nothing of an "intellectual forcing house." Nothing is done for mere effect, or to gain a medal. Buds are not opened with a needle, nor fruit "brought forward" by an oven. Winds, frosts, and a whole magazine of checks are employed in order to secure late seasons rather than early. The mind is assumed to bring with it a principle of spontaneous activity; and nature shows itself expert, not indeed in retarding the growth of the child as a whole, but in delaying the development of any one part or faculty to the prejudice of the rest, and in thus training and regulating the easy and orderly expansion of the entire compound being. That in this natural training and development of the human being, no power is entirely repressed, nor even met with a directly opposing force. Nature destroys neither her poisons, nor our appetite, lest we should eat them; but hides them among a vast number of wholesome edibles. She does not deprive a child of sight because his tendency may be to become all eye, but makes a counteracting appeal to all his other senses. She quietly permits our errors to-day; foreseeing that to-morrow we shall be in a situation to see and to correct them. That nature associates pleasure with right, and pain only with wrong. All her commands are pleasant as "apples of gold in baskets of silver;" thou shalt eat, thou shalt observe, and run, and rest. Duty is not made hateful, in her school, by being assigned as a punishment. Her pupils are never made to read *her* Bible as an infliction for misbehavior. Her rebukes are always well-timed, exactly proportioned to the offense, strictly consequential on it, and never administered in anger, but as the remonstrances of a friend. So far from ruling by fear, she, like Montaigne's father, would have all her children awake to the sound of music, and render obedience another name for enjoyment. That nature not only provides for, but pre-supposes the happiness of the child. Indulgences, stimulants, and officious interference may kill its enjoyment, but rags, dirt, and houselessness can not. It does not need to be made happy, but asks you only to allow it to be happy; to "stand out of its sunshine." The simple air is its "laughing gas;" a stick and a stone its crown and scepter. It finds happiness without seeking it. It enters on life, a sealed fountain of joy; all that nature does is to break the seal, and to dig channels for the gay and dancing waters as they flash and glide away in the sun.

But if these are facts and laws of nature, one thing is clear, that we are bound to act in harmony with them. And yet how generally parents act as if being at cross-purposes with nature were the same thing as being at one with it. Rather they ignore it altogether, as if the family were an excepted territory, and nature lived only out of doors—in the fields. They set the house-clock, without once thinking of the place of the sun; forgetting that as the child will look only at the former, so much the more is it their duty to regard the latter. Walk as fast as they may from east to west, the earth will carry them still faster from west to east.

Object of education in relation to society.

Not only is it the object of a true education to develop the human being in the greatest unity with himself and with nature; but, as we have seen that he is one of a society, its further design must be to place him in harmonious relation with that society, as a member of the organized whole. He can not live to himself. As a social being, his existence is, and must be, relative. Of all the multitudinous objects the earth contains, his fellow-men are to him the most important; so completely are their interests bound up with his, that his social welfare and theirs are one. *His* natural rights are the exact measure of their natural rights. The justice, veracity, and compassion which they owe to him, is the standard of his duties toward them. Whatsoever he would that they should do to him, he is to do also to them.

Then all sectional or denominational education, by being exclusive of some part of the human family, is a violation of a general law. It erects a barrier where, if such a thing had previously existed, education should have been employed to break it down. Instead of developing the mind, it develops a prejudice; it "gives up to party what was meant for mankind;" and, by so doing, defrauds the man of much of the happiness for which he was intended, and the community of much of his usefulness. For awhile, the evils of a party education may not be apparent; it may even promise advantages and success. But while these are partial and temporary, those are universal and permanent. Truth, justice, and benevolence have been violated; and the fragmentary man is seen in a fragmentary and disordered society, which is wasting its powers in fruitless contentions with itself, when it might have been presenting the glorious spectacle of one harmonious family, in which each cared for all, and all for every one.*

In relation to God.

But even supposing an education to be inclusive of all the human family, so that each was taught to live as a portion of the whole, would this exhaust all its legitimate objects? Is there no part or being in the universe besides to be included? Or is the glorious ORIGINATOR AND SUSTAINER OF THE WHOLE so very irrelevant and unimportant to His own system, that He may be omitted, and yet the education be sufficient and complete? Or is all that part of the human being which

* The writer must not be here supposed to be speaking of a professional as distinguished from a general education. This was the chief difference between the systems of Pestalozzi and De Fellenberg. The former aimed only to *develop*, the latter was designed to *fit* for the particular *social* position of the pupil. A good education should aim at both, making the general *development* the basis and starting-point for the special *adaptation*.

relates to Him, so very insignificant, or so loosely, if at all, connected with the other parts of the human constitution, that it may be left either to languish, or to take care of itself, with perfect impunity? His appointment of a Sabbath would seem to imply that He attaches *some* importance to religious instruction and worship. And the office of the Patriarch to sacrifice for his family and to lead their devotions would seem to intimate that the place which the Divine Father has assigned to Himself in the arrangements of the family is not of a secondary nature. But notwithstanding all such considerations, and whatever may have been the habits of the antediluvians, we could tell of times in which religion commonly formed no part of education; in which to say that a youth was educated by no means implied that he had received even a first lesson in religion; and in which, if he had received any religious instruction, it was necessary, at the peril of being misunderstood, to prefix a specific term, and to say that he was *religiously* educated. And is it to be supposed that this contravention of a primary law could take place with impunity? It has come to be a somewhat familiar method of intimating to the public the perfect absurdity of certain proceedings, to compare them with the senseless blunder of a party advertising the drama of "Hamlet," with the part of Hamlet omitted. Here, however—if the ludicrous and the lamentable may be compared—is a blunder of a similar kind; but of a magnitude so surpassing as to overwhelm one with consternation at its possibility. Here is the grand spectacle of creation exhibited for years before eager and inquiring eyes, with the part of the Creator omitted; and, it might be added, with the connivance, if not by the special desire, of the parents. Here is a succession of human beings, professedly instructed in the laws and duties of society—with the character and even the existence of the Lawgiver omitted. Here are a number of parents, supposed to be intelligent beings, professing to teach their children a multitude of important things, but with the grave omission of adverting to any intelligible end as the design of the whole. "We learn (said a heathen who saw something of the enormous blunder*) to play on musical instruments, and to dance and to read, to farm and to ride . . . . we are taught to do all those things which, without some instruction, we can not do well. But the object for which all this is done—to live a good and happy life—remains untaught; is without the direction of reason and art, and is left altogether to chance." And is it to be supposed, we repeat, that this contravention of a primary law can take place with impunity? One of the first evils naturally resulting is, that the importance of education itself comes to be undervalued, for its most vital part is omitted; then something else is substituted in its place; then the supreme influence of God being lost to the family, the subordinate influence of His representatives, the parents, follows; as the consequence of this follows a more general spirit of social insubordination and license; then, as it begins to be felt that "something must be done" to remedy the evils, and as the parties feeling this still misunderstand the nature and end of education, their expedient is of a kind to aggravate the evil. In the antediluvian period, these evils were allowed to work themselves out fully, and to reach a crisis.

Education to be harmonized with the Divine plan.

If the family constitution be thus pervaded by general laws, it follows that its end can be attained only in proportion as the heads of

* Plutarch.

families harmonize their proceedings with the Divine plan which the whole pre-supposes. Each parent is, to the child, a personification of law; the only law which it knows. The example of one, therefore, must accord with that of the other, not merely in acts but in habits. Their habitual example must agree with the precepts of each, and enforce them. Nothing in the customs or by-laws of the family must counteract their precept and example. The variety of daily occurrences must only furnish varied illustration of the self-consistency of the family system. "It was the care which Lycurgus took to harmonize the discipline of the school with the laws of the state (says Plutarch) which infused his laws into the manners of the children, and made them suck in a zeal for his political instructions with their very milk; otherwise his zeal would have signified but little. So that, for above five hundred years together, his institution continued in force, as if it had taken a deep and strong dye, which could not easily be washed out." So also, one element of contradiction in the family may vitiate the whole economy. Every part must be in harmony with every other part, and the whole with the will of God as expressed in His laws. These, like so many straight lines, must pervade and symmetrize the whole, and render it true to His own government. This is expressly why He has organized the family constitution. Surely if He has deemed such a plan necessary, it can not be safe to omit any part of it; still less to run counter to any part of it; and less still to live and act in neglect of the whole. What shall we say, then, to the astounding fact, that society, taken as a whole, never thinks of this Divine arrangement; and that any serious and detailed proposal to square the general education of youth with these laws of education, would be scouted as fanaticism? They can not, any more than mere physical laws, be infringed with impunity; they never have been; and hence the Patriarchs themselves justly suffered the consequences of their violation.

But perhaps it may be said that as the family constitution was meant to attain more ends than one—ends in subordination to each other—though it should fail to attain the highest, it may yet attain the inferior ones. And true it is that the animal and social ends may be partially gained while the great ultimate one is lost—but only partially gained. One law is never broken alone; nor is the breach ever followed by only a solitary effect. The violation of one part of the domestic economy contravenes the spirit of the whole, and vitiates all its designs. What then, we ask, can be thought of the family in which the whole is ignored; and in which the same ignorance and the same random proceedings prevail generation after generation?

Instances occur in which the evils attendant on such disregard of natural and moral laws become so apparent and startling, that the most unreflecting parents are, at times, alarmed by them. They admit to each other that "something must be done." But "what to do" is the question. If a *wish* could but effect the desired change, it would be effected at once. If resolutions for the future; or if an occasional, and perhaps a passionate passing effort would avail, every thing would be rectified. But more than this would suppose principle and plan; and of that they have never dreamed. And, as less than system will not avail, nothing, in effect, is done. Life is spent in miserable expedients, not so much for removing the evil, as for keeping it in abeyance a generation longer, leaving the next generation to do the same. A political government which manages to survive from month to month, only by resorting to temporary stratagems and by the dislike of the people for a change, is justly chargeable with a want of sound statesmanlike views. Yet, here is a constitution meant to run parallel in its happy results with the moral government of God, by being based on the same principles; but, through losing sight of those principles, the subjects of this constitution, so far from embracing the happiness of the eternal future in their plan, are compelled to resort to every kind of subterfuge and device for warding off the pressing evils of the present.

And that which renders this view of education or family government disheartening, even to depression, is—not the insensibility of parents to its unsound condition; though that is ominous enough—but the fact, that of those who are in some measure alive to the disease, comparatively few are aware of the nature of the remedy. According to the Divine appointment, the formation of the youthful character takes place agreeably to laws, and the family government must be harmonized with a predetermined plan; but these persons, however well-meaning, are quite content with expedients. With them, every change promises a cure; and a succession of devices is the only remedy.

There is, indeed, one stage deeper in evil, of which this state of things admits, before it reaches a crisis; and that is when, even supposing the nature and necessity of the remedy have come to be generally seen, its application proves morally impracticable. That men should come to be generally impressed with the idea that a recurrence to first principles is necessary, is, we admit, in the highest degree improbable; and improbable just because it presupposes their knowledge and appreciation of those principles which their education did not include. But surmounting this improbability, and supposing them to have arrived at the conclusion that, as every thing else has failed, there might possibly be something worth trying in a return to the first principles of the family constitution ; how conceivable is it that such a conclusion would find them in a state of moral inability for making the attempt. Now, such a state we deem it morally certain the families of the antediluvian Patriarchs had reached.

During the whole of that period, the domestic economy was pervaded by general laws—organic and intellectual, social and moral. In the absence of these, the training and even the existence of the family would have been impossible. Parents would have been not only exempted from responsibility, but would have had ground for more than complaint. But these laws were ever present and available. So that on the eve of the deluge, after generations of families had passed away, and after every law, perhaps, natural and moral, had been variously perverted, not one had been repealed. Man's nature was more than ever developed for evil, and all the laws of the family were daily experimented on, and subjected to some fresh form of perversion. But even their violations only illustrated by the fearful results, how definite, permanent, and universal was their obligation.

CHAPTER IX.

OBLIGATIONS CONSEQUENT ON THE RELATIONS AND LAWS OF THE DOMESTIC CONSTITUTION

Law of obligation.

EVERY human being exists under an obligation to promote the great end of existence commensurate with his means and relations. For as every thing necessarily expresses something of that Divine Being whose manifestation is the end of creation; and has received existence in order to manifest that resemblance, and so to contribute toward that end; and is placed in a system of relations in order that such manifestation might be possible, it follows that there are as many obligations as there are relations, and every change and increase of the relations is attended with a change and increase of the obligations.

Pursuing the same order here as in the chapter on the *relations* of the domestic constitution, we begin with the obligations of the family, internal and co-existent.

The marriage union obligatory.

For reasons already specified, it is obviously the will of the Creator that, as a general rule, every man and woman should be united in marriage. For, as at the first, it was "not good for man to be alone," so at any subsequent period, celibacy, in proportion to its extent, would tend to defeat the Divine designs.

Mutual adaptation of husband and wife.

For the same reasons that this union should exist at all, it should exist between parties adapted to each other; the union, that is, should be as perfect as possible. It is evident that the elements of union between the married pair, may be as numerous as are the distinctive parts of the human constitution. Was the first man, for example, a being organic, animal, social, intellectual, emotional, voluntary, and religious; then, the first woman, if the union between them was to be complete, must have sustained a relation to him in each of these respects. To make this apparent, it is only necessary to imagine what that union would have been, had either the man or the woman been entirely destitute of any one of these distinctive parts of human nature. If, then, the entire absence of any one of these elements from either of the parties—say, of the intellectual, involving idiocy; or the emotional, involving utter insensibility—would have been fatal to the happiness and design of the union, any *defect* of either of these parts would, in the proportion of such deficiency, affect the happiness and the design of the union also. That is to say, if no part of the human constitution be a matter of entire indifference, it can not be indifferent what the particular state of any part is; since there must be some one state which, for the well-being of the parties united, would be better than any other.

In order to the perfection of the union, then, each party must be, in all respects, the counterpart of the other. This, however, by no means implies that any of their qualities, physical, mental, or moral, should be precisely equal. On the contrary, the perfection of their union may require a slight diversity in all the respective parts of their constitution.

And then, as all these parts are not of equal importance, it follows that, could we graduate the scale, we should be able to estimate the exact degree of the closeness and perfection of the marriage union in any given instance. We could determine for example whether or not the union cemented by their animal sympathies was equally strong as the union arising from the sympathy of their intellectual or their moral nature.

Now, when the number of the faculties and susceptibilities of the human constitution are remembered, and then the innumerable combinations of which they are capable, it may be inferred that there are no two persons of either sex equally eligible in all respects for union with any individual of the other sex. In other words, there is always some one person more eligible for union with any given individual of the other sex, than any other in the world.

It may be objected that this fact can never be of much practical value, since life might be spent in vain in discovering the most eligible party, in any given instance, for the marriage union, and that omniscience alone could in any case attest the truth of the discovery. To which it may be replied that at the first the difficulty could not have been great; that had the principle of uniting the most eligible always been acted on, the difficulty would never have been insurmountable—and that even now, however difficult and hopeless the selection of the one right individual may be, the selection of an individual from the one right *class of character* is easy enough, if judgment be allowed a voice in the proceeding. At all events, it will be admitted by all that the principle of adaptation never should be, and never is, entirely lost sight of. Every approach to an utter disregard of it is denounced or derided by the voice of public

11

opinion. But, if the *entire* neglect of it would be wrong, then every degree in which it is neglected is proportionally wrong. In other words, the marriage union ought to be formed between such parties only as are in every respect, if possible, adapted to each other.

This adaptation would relate, as we have already remarked, to every constituent part of the human constitution. But, besides these, it would relate to the age, and health, and strength of the parties; as well as to their tastes, habits, and acquirements. And, then, as population increased, and property distributed men into classes, those points of adaptation would be further multiplied; extending to wealth and social rank. It can hardly need to be repeated, however, that those points of adaptation are of immensely different value. Generally speaking, those of the highest value are the least considered. And "what (asks Johnson), can be expected but disappointment and repentance from a choice made in the immaturity of youth, or in the ardor of desire, without judgment, without foresight, without inquiry after conformity of opinions, similarity of manners, rectitude of judgment, or purity of sentiment? Such is the common process of marriage. A youth and a maiden meeting by chance, or brought together by artifice, exchange glances, reciprocate civilities, go home, and dream of one another. Having little to divert attention, or diversify thought, they find themselves uneasy when they are apart, and therefore conclude that they shall be happy together. They marry, and discover what nothing but voluntary blindness before had concealed; they wear out life in altercations, and charge nature with cruelty." * Whereas, it is just because "nature"

* Rasselas, c. 29.

is not consulted in the affair; because they thoughtlessly act as if nature had given them a dispensation from all attention to her laws, that the evil arises. The probability is, that the amount of domestic misery springing from all the conjugal violations of chastity, added together, is as nothing compared with the concealed wretchedness origin ated by ill-assorted unions.

The union based in affection.

The marriage union is based in an affectionate preference for each other of the parties united. Not only should they be conscious of a mutual regard, but of an affection stronger than that which they feel for any others. The act of seeking this union implies such preference; nor can there be any rational prospect of happiness without it. This preference is quite distinct from the mutual adaptations of which we have been speaking; commonly springing from the real or imagined perception of some of these very adaptations; and not unfrequently (such is the compensating power of love), supplying the absence of others; or even calling them into existence.

Subordination of the wife.

This union recognizes and implies the partial subordination of the woman to the man. Subordination there must be, as between the right hand and the left. The only condition on which this or any society can exist, is, that each member surrenders something to the other, or that there be some things enjoyed by them in common. The extent of the surrender involved in the married state is clearly indicated by the social nature of the union; for it must include every thing necessary to attain the ends of this union. But as it was antecedently possible that the husband and the wife would entertain a diversity of opinion respecting many of those things, it was necessary that the right of decision should rest with one or the other. For sufficient reasons, this right belongs to the husband. But as his authority is only official, implying no inherent mental or moral superiority, so her submission, not only implies no inherent inferiority, but contains an element of excellence to which mere authority can make no pretense. But this subordination is *partial;* and the social nature of the marriage union indicates its limits. The woman is as much an individual, an integer, a personal being with rights and responsibilities, as the man. Their marriage is a compact of persons, of two normal human beings, having certain distinct and independent interests. Prior obligations to others, such as those to parents and to society, though modified, remain unrepealed. Responsibilities, also arising from the moral part of our nature, and which respect our relations to God, can not be overruled by marriage.

Union of one to one for life.

The same relations which give rise to these obligations, denote also that the marriage union be of one to one for life. This law may be violated by polygamy, licentiousness, and divorce. From which it follows that every thing leading to such results should be scrupulously shunned. All lascivious representations and obscene books; all unchaste conversation, looks, and gestures, and the indulgence of all impure thoughts; every thing, in short, is to be avoided which tends to the only evil that justifies the dissolution of the marriage bond, because it defeats the great end of existence—practical licentiousness. The resolution obligatory on each is, "I will walk within my house with a perfect heart; I will set no wicked thing before mine eyes."*

* Psalm ci. 2, 3.

Conjugal obligations internal and successive.

As the preceding duties arise out of the different parts of the human constitution, considered in its conjugal relations, those which we are about to specify respect the period during which these relations continue.

As *sexual*, the primary object of the marriage union is to be remembered, in order to the avoidance of every thing likely to defeat it, and the observance of whatever tends to attain it.* This is quite consistent with the apostolic view of marriage, as a discipline in purity.† "The body is not the prison of the soul, but its holy organ, which, like the soul itself, must be preserved pure and undefiled. And marriage is that state in which the soul is to master the body as its true instrument, instead of abandoning it to the fierce violence of the passions." ‡

As partakers of *animal life*, the health and sentient well-being of husband and wife are, to a considerable extent, given into each other's hands. This, therefore, they are bound mutually to watch over and preserve. As *social* and mutually dependent, each has an appropriate sphere to fill from day to day with the "labors of love." On him it devolves to provide for the necessary support of his wife; and to her it belongs to turn the provision which he makes to the best account. But while their respective duties are properly distinctive, circumstances may arise to devolve some of the duties which belong to the one upon the other. Their lines of duty may intersect. They are to know no rival interests. Their well-being is undivided, one.

They enjoy, as *intellectual* beings, the best opportunity for acquiring an intimate knowledge of each other's character. Such opportunity they are bound to improve

* 1 Peter, iii. 7. † 1 Thess. iv. 3, 6. ‡ Olshausen *in loc.*

in every possible way. By the kind correction of each other's errors, as they come to light, and by the enlargement of each other's knowledge, they are to aim at such a course of mental improvement as shall fit them to become the teachers of their children, and as shall render them the cheerful and useful companions of each other's declining years.

As *emotional*, each is to aim to be worthy of the love of the other. Not by mere verbal professions of regard; nor by the slender attractions of external accomplishments; nor by capricious acts of kindness; but by the habitual avoidance, on the part of each, of every thing calculated to give pain to, or to diminish the love of, the other; by each, whenever individual gratification is concerned, preferring the pleasure of the other to his own; and by each evincing a constant desire for the happiness of the other as essential to his own enjoyment. In this way each becomes to the other "the desire of the eyes."

They are *voluntary* beings, and as such they enjoy the best means of mutual endearment and improvement, by making every service required of each other a reasonable service. By explaining, as far as possible, the grounds of his wishes; and, where that is impossible, by showing that his will is swayed by love, the husband is to transform his authority into affection. While the wife, by

"Those graceful acts,
Those thousand decencies that daily flow
From all her words and actions, mixed with love
And sweet compliance, which declare unfeigned
Union of mind," *

* Milton.

is to show that, by following his will, she is obeying her own.

As *moral* and *accountable* beings they are, by respecting the decisions of each other's conscience, to strengthen its authority. By the exercise of forbearance, where forbearance is necessary; by the mutual admiration of every thing estimable; and by prayer for each other's highest welfare, they are constantly to improve each other's character, to convert marriage into a discipline of virtue, and thus to be ever finding in each other new cause for affection, and for gratitude to Him who has given them to each other. Although perfection, in the highest sense, is unattainable, they are, in this way, to be ever advancing toward it. And for this they are responsible, increasingly responsible. Obligation accumulates with opportunity. And at every onward stage of their course—say, at the return of every anniversary of their union—they are held responsible for all the excellence and consequent happiness which they might have possessed on that day, had they discharged their respective duties toward each other during every hour of every preceding day.

Obligations as, and of, parents.

As *parents*, the relation of the husband and the wife gives rise to additional obligations. Each becomes an object of augmented interest and importance to the other. All the duties, which we have already specified, are now bound on them by an additional tie. And every child born to them does but increase their claims on each other, and give them a new interest in each other's health, and affection, and virtue, and qualification for domestic usefulness.

The parental relation involves obligations extending to every part of the constitution of the child, and reaching from its birth, and even before, to the moment of separation by death. Next to the personal, the parental relation is the most sacred and momentous which man can sustain. If the creation of the first man was an event of universal and unending interest, the birth of every infant human being partakes largely of the same interest; and the parent can properly apprehend his responsible position only as far as he regards himself as standing to his offspring in the relation of a subordinate creator. The birth of his child intimates that the great end for which the first man was made is yet unattained; that means continue to be employed for its attainment; and that, in the final summing up of those means, he will be held responsible for having made the most of the young human being for the attainment of that ultimate end.

Prospective parental obligations.

If the healthiness of children depends partly, as we have seen, on the healthiness of their parents, it most obviously follows that unhealthy and ill-assorted unions should be conscientiously avoided, since they can only be the means of propagating deformity, wretchedness, and disease. Within certain limits, parents frequently live again in their children. "Yet we every day see very sensible people, who are anxiously attentive to preserve or improve the breed of their horses, tainting the blood of their children, and entailing on them not only the most loathsome diseases of the body, but madness, folly, and the most unworthy dispositions, and this too when they can not plead being stimulated by necessity, or impelled by passion."* And may we not add that we every day see, not merely sensible, but some religious peo-

* Prof. J. Gregory's Comparative View of the State and Faculties of Man, etc., pp. 18, 19. Dr. Pritchard's Researches, vol. ii. pp. 536–551.

ple, who ignore all such considerations, if they do not even deem their religious sensibility shocked at having their attention called to them. They would not be at all surprised at an insurance company requiring a regular list of searching questions respecting habits and health to be answered, before undertaking the risk of a small sum of money; but when they are about to marry, though they "have, in the generality of cases, the health and happiness of five or more human beings depending on their attention to similar considerations," * they either do not give the subject a thought, or else dismiss it as belonging to the domain of providence.† They should remember, however, that the Bible is not insensible to a fine physical organization,‡ and therefore the professed reverer of the Bible ought not to treat lightly the laws which secure it. If the *mens sena* seldom exists apart from the *corpore sano*, still more rarely is a healthy piety found in such isolation. That tree of righteousness is likely to yield the fairest fruit, and to reach the nearest heaven, all other things being equal, whose roots strike the deepest in the earth of our nature. The very command that "children should honor their parents," looks back with a most inquiring and significant aspect to the entire life of the parties to be honored. That "the sins of the fathers shall be visited on the children to the third and fourth generation," is not an arbi-

* Combe's Constitution of Man, seventh edit., p. 163.

† If thou knowest that every black thought of thine, or every glorious independent one, separated itself from thy soul, and took root outside of thee, and for half a century pushed and bore its poisonous flavors or healing roots, O, how piously wouldst thou choose and think! And dost thou, then, so certainly know that such is not the case?—*Richter's Levana, or the Doctrine of Education*, p. 34.

‡ Ex. ii. 2; 1 Sam. xvi. 12.

trary threatening, but a law of nature; and no parents lend themselves to its fearful operation so directly as they who ignore the conditions of a healthy progeny.

Prospective maternal duty.

If the infant, before it is born, is liable to be affected by the physical condition and mental impressions of the mother, she is bound to act, during that period, conformably with its well-being. Like a lens, collecting and transmitting beams of fire, while itself is dark and cold, she may be the medium of effects to her child more deep and lasting than any of which she herself is conscious. This, too, is a law recognized by Scripture. For if Sampson is to be a Nazarite from the womb, his mother, in the prospect of giving birth to him, is strictly forbidden to drink wine or strong drink. As to the manner in which both parents should provide for the comfort of the infant at birth, the conduct of the Divine Parent toward his first children is to be received as a pattern in this respect, which every human parent should copy.

When does education begin?

If the education of the child begins with the moment of its birth, it follows that with that moment begins also a series of sacred parental duties. Its education can be no more suspended than its life. Prior to its birth, the mother may be regarded as living in the soul of the child; at that moment the child begins to live for a time in the soul of the mother. While the father is yet marking the moment of its birth, its first pulse has already dated its training for eternity.

The number.

That moment introduces it into a circle in which every motion and tone, every color and form is a symbol for its sense, and sheds an influence on its awakening emotions. Solitary and unrelated as it may look, cascades of influence stream on it from all sides round. Every object soon becomes a book; every place a school-house; and every event plows in some winged seeds which will be bearing their appropriate fruit ten thousand ages hence.

Rapidity.

Besides the *number* of the influences rained on the youthful human being, the *rapidity* with which he absorbs them is to be considered. As he never grows so rapidly in after life, in proportion to his nourishment, as he does during his earliest infancy, so it is the period of his greatest mental and moral assimilation.

Power.

After that, the power of absorption gradually diminishes. "Life has first a flight, then a leap, then a step, then a halt." If, during the first six years of life, children learned only as much as we could teach them, they would continue to be children all their lives long. But these six years form their creation-week, during which chaos subsides, elements separate, continents upheave, forms of life and power take their appointed places, and toward the close of which the future man appears. While we have been teaching him to walk, he has been mentally running and flying in a thousand directions. While we are filling his little hands with flowers, the garden and the field are pouring all their botany and zoology into his mind. We think we have done much in drawing a little finger-furrow, and carefully depositing therein two or three selected seeds; but nature meantime has been shedding her spores by millions over the whole surface.

And permanence of first impressions.

And a third consideration, which renders this early period of transcendent importance, is—that the impressions then received are seldom, if ever, entirely effaced. "Every first thing continues forever with the child; the first color, the first music, the first flower, paint the foreground of life. Every new educator effects less than his predecessor; until, at last, if we regard all life as an educational institution, a circumnavigator of the world is less influenced by all the nations he has seen than by his nurse." * Fable tells us that the cat, transformed into a lady, on seeing a mouse, forgot the decorum required by her new form, and sprang from the table at which she was sitting, to seize on her prey. For the vessel will long retain the scent of the liquor first put into it: † a fact happily employed by Horace to illustrate the necessity of early imbuing the minds of the young with principles of virtue. Words and looks fall on the little one with greater force than the laws and deeds of after years. Much of its formal education consists in correcting the impressions and disentangling the associations of its first years. The crooked limb has to be loaded with iron in order that it may be straightened. Yet, no sooner is the constraint removed, than the previous tendency to distortion proclaims itself again. In the great majority of instances, the hand of artificial cultivation is no sooner withheld than the underlying strata begin again to "crop out." If formal education is dyeing in the piece, the spontaneous education of early childhood is dyeing in the wool. And even beyond this, the thread so dyed is then, if ever, held by the fates of ancient fable to be tangled for life with good or evil.

Obviously, then, the parent should keep the fact distinctly in view, that, from the earliest childhood every thing is

* Richter's Levana, pp. 16, 87.

† Quo semel est imbuta recens, servabit odorem
Testa diu.

calculated to affect the formation of character, and that nothing relating to character is absolutely indifferent; but that every thing viewed in this connection is right, and ought to be; or is wrong, and ought not to be. At first, indeed, parents can do little more than protect it from ungenial influences, and give it the southern aspect of a cheerful home. Let there be no thorn in its soft lap-nest, and no cloud in the maternal heaven that hangs over it. Save it from uttering the cry of impatience and passion, and surround it with the clear, quiet atmosphere of a happy spirit, and it will spontaneously evolve all that is sparkling within, and meet, like an opening bud, all that is joyous without.

The world into which the little sojourner of earth comes, is, in every respect, preconfigured to his constitution. The maternal womb in which he has been silently preparing for birth, was not more exquisitely adapted to every part of his bodily frame, than the larger sphere into which he comes at birth is related to his bodily, mental, and moral nature. And the nice adaptation of the lungs, which had previously lain motionless, to the surrounding air which they forthwith begin to breathe, is only a specimen of the hidden adaptations and slumbering relations which he brings with him to the different parts and aspects of the great system into which he comes. Now education is simply the gradual awakening and development of those latent adaptations and susceptibilities, by the measured adjustment and orderly application of the different parts of that great surrounding system into which he has come. When the Father of spirits provided for the creation and education of the human race, He wisely determined the nature of our impressions, the extent of our knowledge, and the subjects of our ideas, by determining the extent and character of the objects which should compose the system into which we were to be introduced, and the laws by which they should excite and affect our minds. And, in a similar manner—although much of the scene into which the infant comes is wisely pre-arranged by a Hand above parental control—that same Hand has strewn unnumbered objects around the infant, leaving it to the parent to select those which are appropriate, and requiring him so to place and to employ them as to elicit and direct the tendencies of his child, and to form his character.

Obligations arising from the child's bodily wants.

The *bodily* appetites and wants of the child claim the first care of the parent. This obligation is violated in various ways; by inattention to those primary conditions of health—air and exercise—for the child is both plant and animal; by indulgence of the appetites; by enfeebling effeminacy of treatment; and by a hot-house forcing of the intellect. Seeds of sickness are sown at the very period which should be devoted to the cultivation of health. And a diseased body is the greatest despot upon earth, tyrannizing over the mind and soul, and holding the man in life-long slavery.* The parent should remember that the child is not an angel but a human being; and its physical demands must be met and gratified by objects appropriate to their nature. If the shaft of a column is to be firm, and the sculptured capital to point to the skies, the base resting on the earth must not be neglected. The higher faculties can not say to the lower "we have no need of you." The

* Plus le corps est faible plus il commande; plus il fort plus il obéit. Toute les passions sensuelles logent dans des corps efféminés; ils s'en irritent d'autant plus qu'ils peuvent moins les satisfarie.—*Emile*, Liv. I.

robust and joyous gymnastics which nature dictates to children—girls as well as boys—proclaim the vital truth that a healthy mind presupposes a healthy body.

From its social,

As a *social* being, the child comes into the world with instincts which prepare it to seek and cleave at once to the maternal bosom, as to its proper home. But the physical nourishment which it there imbibes is by no means all that it derives—though nothing more may meet the eye. In the quiet and holy communion which there ensues, every part of its social nature is solaced and nourished also. Though it is for a time unconscious as the flower of the falling dew, its affections find their first impulse in the element of love which there encompasses it. If its birth is the reproduction of the mother's physical life, its love and trust are the reproduction of her emotional life. All its early looks, tones, and movements are one prayer and thanksgiving to maternal affection, predictive of the wider range the same emotions will take at a later period. When first it throws its little arms around her in gratitude and love it is foreshadowing its wider embrace of society. Hence the sacred duty of the mother to nurse her child herself, if possible. By transferring it to "a cold hired bosom," she is depriving herself of a rich natural enjoyment, and depriving her child of an aliment more important to its welfare than even her milk.

And sensational nature.

The education of the *senses* is the basis of all education. The objects of sense lie around the child, range beyond range, from those of touch to those of sight, immeasurably remote; and to the distinctive characters of all these classes, it is the duty of the parent to direct the attention of his child. Such was the method adopted by the Divine Creator for the percipient discipline of the first human being. Having formed the various objects of animate creation, He "brought them to Adam to see what he would call them."* And this, we may suppose, was only a specimen of the "Lessons on Objects"—only a part of an extensive system of easy illustrative instruction which the Maker of the mind adopted, as that which was best suited to awaken and direct its activity. And still the book of nature has inexpressible charms for the opening eye of the infant mind. The country is God's school-house, play-ground, story-book, and picture-book, all in one. Nothing tends more directly to cultivate and delight the young percipient being than the sounds and colors, the forms and motions of natural objects, and the varied sensations occasioned by them. They are "the georgics of the mind," nourishing it and filling it with pleasure, while they engage it to look beyond themselves. But here, as was obviously implied in the Divine training of the first man, *accuracy* is every thing. Vagueness of idea, and language, inconsecutive reasoning, and a mental and moral life of cloudiness, are the natural fruits of ill-educated senses.

From its power of speech.

As soon as infantine gestures begin to pass into *speech*, parents incur a new responsibility. Language has well been called the gate of the soul. With every new word the mind of the little one emerges a step further. Every object which it names is mentally taken possession of, and a fresh bond is established with the world without. In proportion to the rapidity with which it learns to speak, is likely to be its want of accuracy. But parents should remember that language is not the utterance of words, but the art of using them as the signs of ideas. "It

* Gen. ii. 19.

is a matter of infinite importance to acquire this distinctness at an early period. The *idea* should be kept *clear* and *precise*. The *word* should be kept *steady to the idea.* These are the two great rules."* Half the vices of society owe much of their currency to an indolence of thought, content to live in a haze of ambiguous words, which shades their deformity. A crystal perspicuity of diction tends, especially in youth, to secure clear and truthful distinctions and definite moral judgments.

Of reflection.

As the relations of things within and around the child are calculated to awaken and exercise *reflection*, it is the parental duty to point his attention to them. The relations of resemblance and difference early attract his notice; and on the strength of these relations, the young philosopher forms many a mental classification which he has subsequently to re-arrange. His ever-recurring *why?* and *what?* are the true germs of the inductive method of tracing effects to their causes. Hence the importance of the parents being able to aid the opening effort of the mind, instead of hurtfully repressing or ignorantly misdirecting it. How much may depend on their calling his attention to the relations of his own constitution; for how often, owing to their neglect of this great duty, has he rued their guilty omission in the loss of health, of intellectual vigor, or of moral character! The great system of relations around him is the natural ordinance of God for perpetually proclaiming "His own eternal power and Godhead." But the parent who neglects to call the attention of his child to it, leaves him, in effect, in the midst of a fragmentary, unrelated, disordered world; and liable to complain of the want of that very wisdom and

* Wise, on Education Reform, vol. i. p. 116.

goodness of which the world is full. And yet, how few the schools in which there is as much care taken to illustrate the "power of God as to teach the power of the Greek particle!"

Reasoning.

The child early evinces a capacity for *reasoning.* But how much skepticism and misery would many a man have escaped, had the child or youth been taught the laws of thought, and been shown how all reasoning reposes, finally, on instinctive beliefs and ultimate facts. At first, indeed, the ultimate fact in which all infantine excursions of thought terminate, is the testimony or authority of its parents. And though, as its power of intellect increases, the field of its excursion widens, the same creative wisdom which predisposed it to rest at first on the parental word has provided that it shall repose, at last (if at all) on the perfections and purposes of the Great Parent. And to that ultimatum it should be trained to lift its eye as soon as it begins to look away from the circle of sense. Nearly all the reasonings of our natural theology in later life are merely an attempt to retrace our steps through early misconceptions to that *idea* of God which was meant to be seen by its own light.

Imagination.

The *imagination* is as much a part and power of the human constitution as the appetite, and equally requiring to be regulated and fed. "Children are little Orientals," each with an Aladdin's lamp and Arabian Nights of his own. Nor should the former be extinguished nor the latter shortened, except by the slow dawning and progress of knowledge. Children personify every thing. Every scene is dramatized, and they will address and reply to themselves, rather than that the drama should be incomplete. While their elders are only listening to a tale, they are acting in it. A good story or picture-book, is more to an imaginative child than the discovery of America to Columbus. On turning over every page, he stands looking "from a peak in Darien." Nature makes them free of the region of romance; but, according to our utilitarian notions, nature is wrong, and one of the first offices of education is to lay this whole region under interdict. The child's head, forsooth, must take precedence of his heart. The rainbow must be explained. No sooner is he caught enjoying than he is required to reflect. He must stop eating that his bread may be analyzed and expounded. Nature has designedly cast a film over his eyes, by which every thing is clothed with a poetic halo; but he must needs be led, as early as possible, to the tree of knowledge—his parents often the serpents on the tree—that he may *know* that he is naked. If religion holds the *sanctum sanctorum* of the human temple, imagination in childhood occupies its outer courts; but it seems to be thought, judging from prevailing usages, the sooner the altars are overturned, or turned into "the tables of the money-changers," the better.

A wise parent will follow the Divine method of education; according to which the child is placed from the first in a circle of wonders, and finds, in the opening pages of Scripture, scenes of enchantment never to be surpassed. He will remember that it is the books which the child reads out of school which leave the deepest impression, and, therefore, require the most careful selection. Let him distinguish between children's books and childish books. Let him not fall into the mistake that every thing must be written *down* to the comprehension of children. Their sense of interest runs ahead of their understanding, and helps it on. He should know that manhood is not distinguished from childhood by the *growth* of all the powers, so much as by the simple *exchange* of some—not so much by *superiority* as by *difference* of capacity—and that no book suited for the child's department can be too *old* for it. Genius is requisite in order to cater for the imagination of children. They will cast aside many a book through which an adult is plodding, not because they do not understand it, but because it is not true to nature. Let a child's book correspond to his keen and fresh perceptions, and then, the richer it is in interest, and the more exquisite in art, the more intensely will it be relished. An imagination wholesomely fed in early life, prolongs our youth, invests even the common-places of life with interest, erects an ideal in the mind which is always drawing it upward, and which may be rendered auxiliary to that religion in whose department alone it can be realized.

Emotions. The *emotions* and dispositions of which the infant being is susceptible open a wide field of parental duty. As each of the innumerable objects included in the family circle is of different value in the great system of things, its degree of emotion should be different also. Then the parents should early begin to arrange them before the eye of his mind, rank above rank; always aiming to place the most important in the most attractive light. Some of these—whether they appeal to his animal, social, intellectual, or moral nature—it may, for a time, be improper that he should desire or even know; and such should, if possible, be removed from the eye of his mind. If fire be brought near to inflammable gases, even the safety-lamp is no infallible guarantee against ignition. Other objects which can not or need not be kept out of sight, may be made the occasion of an early exercise of *self-denial.* Others, though desired at the moment, may be properly withheld for a time; and may thus become the means of both exercising and rewarding *patience.* Others, not improper in themselves, may be best at distant intervals, and in regulated proportions; and may thus be made to inculcate lessons of *moderation*, *economy*, and *foresight.* Toward other objects it may be necessary to stimulate him; aiming, however, to inspire him with the *emulation* which consists in the love of excellence, rather than with the desire of excelling; and with the wish of acquiring it himself, rather than with a feeling of displacency that it is possessed by others—which is *envy.*

In the circle of visible domestic objects, the most important are the child's kindred and fellow-men; and to these his relations must be pointed out, in order to the cultivation of his social and virtuous dispositions. As they are *sentient* beings, capable of pleasure and pain, they should be made the occasion of exercising his *humanity.* And the same disposition should be exercised universally—to the mere animal as well as man. Shriek at the sight of any creature, and the sound will echo through the whole of the child's life, begetting that *fear* which is as nearly allied to *hatred* as hatred is to *cruelty.* On the other hand, caress a dog, or any animal, in the presence of a child, and you are giving it the best lesson on benevolence, and nourishing its kindliest feelings. Teach the sacredness of life. Let not pity be wasted on the occasion of a fall, or on his suffering some trivial pain, for the dangerous luxury of self-commiseration, to which it will lead, tends to produce a sense of exacting self-importance.

As those around him are *intelligent* beings, and he is

constituted to impart his mind to theirs, and the converse, he should be taught the value of *truth* and *sincerity*, without which he himself could know and believe next to nothing, and the whole system of things would go into confusion. Teach him to abhor a falsehood; let him see, that is, that you yourself abhor it. Nothing is so self-punishing and irreparable as a lie. Correct the first and least deviations from accuracy. "If a thing happened at one window (says Dr. Johnson), and a child, when relating it, says that it happened at another, do not let it pass, but instantly check him; you do not know where deviation from truth will end." Occasionally refuse to take a hasty answer, that he may learn to reflect. Belief is natural to a child. He has to *learn* not to believe, and often it is a painful effort. Do not ask him to conceal a thing; this itself is enough to bring a cloud into his clear sky. Sacredly fulfill every promise you make to him, or satisfactorily explain your reason for not keeping it. In this respect, be what you desire the child to be.

Surrounded by beings equal to himself, he is to be taught that his rights are only equal to their rights; and consequently, that in all his intercourse with them there is to be *justice*, or right feelings and right actions. There could be no sphere so favorable as the family for teaching him that every individual is as deserving of his love as he is himself; and that, therefore, he should do to each of them as he would that they should do to him. This would tend to inspire him with *generosity* toward the needy, and *compassion* for the suffering, and *gratitude* when he himself is the object of the kindness of others.

This brings us into the region of moral æsthetics, where the noble and the pure, the beautiful and the good reside.

The feeling of shame artificially taught by modern civilization tends to hasten the evil it pretends to retard. Mystification stimulates curiosity; warnings alarm rather than prevent; and instruction robs the child of its innocent want of shame, before the time for conscious modesty arrives. In this way, the sculptor stains his own marble, though its value depended on its perfect whiteness. If girls especially, "like the priestesses of antiquity, should be educated only in holy places," what sanctuary so sacred from all that is rude or immoral as home! And if "nothing so roughly brushes the tender auricula dust, or flower-pollen, off the minds of girls," as prudish alarms, where can such alarms be less called for than in the hallowed inclosure of the family?

Children love the *beautiful;* and nature looks to the parent to unfold to them her ten thousand attractions. Examples of constancy, self-devotion, and heroic aims, awaken their *admiration* and high-souled *enthusiasm*, and make them conscious of a greatness which belongs not to the present nor the visible. On this account, they should be taken as much as possible into the presence of ennobling objects; and be encouraged to linger often and late in the silent temple of the mighty past.

Love is social holiness; and the family was meant to be the home of love, and its chief occupation to train the affections. In the presence of conjugal love, the children begin life in an atmosphere of affection which prepares them unconsciously to breathe love to each other. They do not wait for parental caresses, or for self-sacrificing proofs of affection, before they begin to love; the enjoyment of affectionate words and looks suffice. It is much more difficult to make one's self disliked by them than to be loved.

And the best way to nourish their love is to let them understand it by action, to encourage them to taste the pleasure of loving by serving the object loved.

In developing the right emotions and dispositions, the less *said* didactically on the subject the better; *example* is every thing. The parent who does not exemplify the qualities he inculcates, can not be surprised if his words produce nothing better than words. On the principle that like propagates like, deeds alone beget deeds, and only life kindles life. "Sidney and Hampden will make patriots, though the wisest *maxim* that ever fell from their lips should fail." And the parent who would successfully teach, must himself *be* the great lesson and the spirit of all lessons. He can teach love only by loving. His example, filling up all the intervals of formal instruction, acts with the silence, constancy, and power of a law of nature. *Je ne suis pas la rose, mais j'ai vecu avec elle.* His children will imbibe excellence by living in its atmosphere.

The emotional nature of little children is never stimulated without injury. All they ask is play-room, and the removal of every thing painful. Before they begin to play with the external world, the world plays with them; or, rather, it plays on them a perpetual stream of impressions of which they are little more than the delighted recipients. And even when they begin to select and employ objects, they are embarrassed with their riches. Yet, it is at this moment, when their little hands are already full of flowers, that the inconsiderate parent attempts to fill their arms also. Nature dilutes her oxygen, but he would fain administer it to them pure, and even "above proof." More activity surrounds them with a heaven of sunny cheerfulness, in which the affections quietly unfold and grow; but he must needs employ a burning-glass. Few children are more to be pitied than those who are exposed to the jading influence of a constant succession of sights and toys. Pleasures force and forestall their nature; and by irritating and exhausting their emotions, shorten the season of youth. The *Nil admirari* is the natural result. And yet, as if this were not inflicting a sufficient evil on their moral nature, the same parent would not unlikely guard them against the least religious emotion as alarmingly dangerous. The tendency of his treatment is to render them insensible to every thing which is not artificial and unnaturally exciting, and yet to repress the finest part of their nature, and the best preservative against all that is low and evil.

Will.

The *will* determines the amount of a man's *power*. According as it is influenced by right motives or wrong, it determines his *character*. In this complex sense, the will is the *man*. In the early discipline of the will, the object is to restrain the child alike from the extreme of obstinacy and of too great pliancy. In the latter instance, the child must be led to see that he is in danger of becoming the slave of circumstances, of being dragged at the wheel of every folly, written on by every finger, and of willing only with the will of others. Gradually he must be shown that in allowing his emotions to terminate in themselves, he is wasting the very impulse which was meant to carry him out into appropriate action; that even good wishes are valuable only as they harden into purposes; and that purposes require for their accomplishment a reiteration of acts which strengthens into confirmed habits. Another child may be self-willed; requiring to be frequently shown the errors of his obstinacy; to be left at times to suffer its effects; and to have it inculcated in various ways that he only is fit for the society of voluntary agents who is prepared to yield as well as to exact submission. Now, the only way in which the will can be trained to govern is by being, from the first, wisely governed. And one of the most difficult problems of education is, to form the child to obedience without impairing his freedom. Indeed, the solution of the same difficulty in relation to their subjects forms the chief occupation of every human government.

No original quality of the mind, even though existing in dangerous excess, should be opposed directly or crushed. Brought within proper limits, it will have its value; and this is best effected by cherishing, appealing to, and developing a counterbalancing disposition. In other words, attention should be given, not so much to the weakening of any one quality, as to the strengthening of its opposite. The mother who saw her little one running unconsciously to the edge of a precipice, did not attempt to save him by a shriek or a scold; but kneeling down, and baring her bosom, the child ran back to it.

The parent should *never despair* of bringing harmony into the character of a child by thus counteracting the excess of one quality by the compensative influence of another. The evil deplored may prove to be only a fit—the idiosyncrasy of childhood. At all events, the child himself should never be led to imagine that the disease is deemed incurable. An unpromising spring not unfrequently issues in an abundant summer; and an intractable childhood (as Bacon remarks), like a crooked piece of oak which makes the knee-timbers of a ship, may be qualified to occupy an important post in the vessel of society.

The apparent incapacity or intractableness of some children is only the early indication of *individuality of character*. An unreflecting educator strives to force every mind into the same press, and to force it in the same mold; resenting the least obstacle offered by the child as treason against his machinery. Like the Red Indian's squaw, who fastens every child from birth to the same board, he would reduce his pupils to the condition of mental mummies. But the wise parent, instead of laboring merely to reproduce himself, aims to produce the ideal child. Michael Angelo saw, in the unhewn mass of marble, the future statue; and in each mass a different statue. And the parent will aim to liberate, not roughly, but with care, the spiritual individuality which every child unfolds. Unpromising as it may at first appear, it may only await the coming of the proper object or occasion, in order to explain its anomalies, and to run a successful career. Home education affords peculiar facilities for such discrimination of treatment. And how many a youth might it have rescued from the mortification of having his mind misunderstood and dwarfed by an unsuitable training, as well as of making the subsequent discovery of having chosen an unsuitable profession.*

Independence of character.

Independence of character, without which man, meant to be a cause, becomes only an effect, is not unfrequently prevented or destroyed by over-help. In the present day even the teacher is in danger of being bewildered by the endless Guides, Translations, Aids, Helps, and Explanations of every thing by which he is beset. So much the greater is his danger of forgetting

* Newnham's Principles of Physical, Intellectual, Moral, and Religious Education, pp. 228–230, and 380, 381.

that, in teaching, the nicest art consists in knowing when to leave the pupil to teach himself. While the watch is being wound up it does not go; and many a child is not only subjected to this process continually, but the consequence is that his *going* is prevented forever after. The bad effect can never be rectified. Instead of being shown the way to the living streams, that he might slake his thirst at pleasure, they have been brought to him and decanted into him. Knowledge has been given to him instead of the power of observing, judging, and acquiring knowledge. He does not even know that he knows. Ideas have been taught; not the power of using or of adding to them. In effect, the mind has been impaired by the very process which should have given it power; and the child might adapt and adopt Hadrian's epitaph, "The multitude of physicians killed Cæsar." *

Attention.

In the education of the will, the first aim should be to interest the *attention*. Judging, indeed, from the representations of some parents, one might be led to suppose that the unwillingness of their children to attend, or a propensity to flit from object to object, without settling on any, was a proof of cleverness. And even their mode of teaching, instead of tending to collect, concentrate, and fix the too-easily dissipated and weak, is calculated to dissipate and enfeeble the strong. But this is to prolong the mind's infancy. At first the child simply perceives; its mind is passive, and *observes* nothing. It does not see for looking. Gradually it becomes active; directs itself to certain objects in preference to others; attends to them. When it becomes capable of this *tension*, the duty of directing it begins. To occupy it

* "Turba medicorum perdidit Cæsarem."

fully, without exhausting it, should now be the twofold rule. Accuracy, promptitude, and extent of range, are the qualities to be aimed at; and books, subjects, and methods are to be valued according to their tendency to develop them.

Importance of rules. Will alone can train and govern will; in other words, *there must be laws.* Parental rules are to children what the laws of nature are to us; forming habits of instinctive compliance, giving unity to the conduct, and imparting confidence in the future. Care should be taken, however, that they be not too numerous. Here the rule *pas trop gouverner* should be observed. Children are easily bewildered by the multiplicity and variety of commands; so that law itself becomes an impediment to obedience,* and tempts to resistance.

The law of laws is, *never to give a command which is not obeyed.* Once authority is established, obedience becomes a habit. In order to its establishment, the edicts of the parental monarch should, at first, be unaccompanied by explanation or reason. *Voluntas stet pro ratione*, otherwise the child-subject is likely to occupy himself with the preamble of the bill when he should be obeying its requirements. And even when the time comes for explanations, reasons for assertions should not be given so early as reasons for requests; the former may lead to doubt and questioning, for the understanding does not move so promptly as the heart; the latter appeal to the affections and call for action. Every appearance of *indecision* is to be avoided. *Never lay traps* to catch a child in his fault, nor wait for its full development; but remove, if possible, the least incite-

* Obest plurumque iis qui discere volunt, auctoritas eorum quidocent. Cic. de Nat. Deor. L. I.

ment to it, and repress its earliest indication. No must. not be weakly changed into Yes. Rules and refusals must not be sugared over and concealed; this, besides betraying weakness and practicing delusion, begets self-will while seeming to cultivate a sense of duty. Equally to be deprecated is that *uncertainty of mood* which is ever oscillating between the extremes of relaxation and rigor; and which seeks to recover the lost authority of one hour by the severity of the next. Obedience should be inculcated neither in *a doubting* nor in *a defiant* manner. The will speaks only in the imperative mood; and the calm and quiet tone of its utterance should denote the determination of a mind conscious of strength. Never threaten, only state. Do not mistake scoldings for lessons or injunctions. A child easily distinguishes a decided from an angry tone, and the tendency of anger is to awaken resistance. On this account a thing should never be suddenly snatched from the hands of a child; its earnest request should not be met by a passionate refusal; violence should not be opposed by violence; it is an attempt to extinguish fire with oil.

Punishments.

Laws imply *sanctions*. As far as an appeal to fear is concerned, the following rules are of principal importance: Let every culpable omission be followed by that which should be shown to be its just *consequence*, rather than by a so-called punishment. Thus, if the lesson be neglected during the hour of study, it should be prepared during the hour of recreation; by which means the deprivation is connected not so much with the teacher as with the child's own negligence. Except in the case of very young children, *a short delay* between the fault and the punishment may be tranquilizing and useful to the parent, and even more salutary to the child than the punishment itself. At first, forbid as gently and *punish as lightly* as possible—by word or look; that you may have resources left. He who begins with a twig will soon come to a stick; for the skin hardens under the lash (this is, of course, only a metaphorical illustration). *Certainty* of punishment is of vital importance. Why is it that "the burned child dreads the fire" more than the cut child dreads the knife, even though the cut may be worse than the burn? Partly because the fire will certainly burn, but the knife will not certainly wound. *Never punish by lessons*, making that distasteful which should be always welcome. It is better that the *severity* of the punishment should fall below, than that it should exceed the fault. Exaggerated reproof and rigor are likely to make the child think more of the injustice he suffers than of the evil he has done, to lead to equivocation and concealment, and to harden instead of correcting him. Still less should punishment be accompanied with *taunts or derision*. "Making a public example" of a child is the way to paralyze a delicate mind, and to render a high-spirited one defiant. The correction which is administered seriously and *sorrowfully* is likely to purify the sorrow of the child; and the perception that you respect its feelings will tend to render it's feelings more tender. Peculiarly precious is the moment when, as the excitement of correction subsides, and its young heart yearns for a look of forgiveness and love, its whole nature is softened and open to receive "the word in season." Quietly and apart, the child may then, if ever, be won to salutary self-inspection. Gradually this may be made to lead to a habit of daily self-inquest, somewhat after the tabular plan suggested by Franklin. Meantime, probably, the parent could not occupy himself much more profitably than in seeking for the faults of his children in himself.

Improper mode of rewards.

Perhaps there is no department in which the art of miseducation has more nearly approached to perfection than in that of incitements and rewards. In how many families is the heart indulged and spoiled as a reward for a little exercise of the head; and the child is allowed to be self-willed and capricious as a reward for being clever. A little bit of finery is made the adequate reward of morality; and a small intellectual feat is taught to find its goal in something extra to eat and drink. A little violet-like virtue no sooner modestly peeps above-ground than it is proclaimed, bepraised, magnified, and killed; or turned, by being made ever present to the consciousness of the child, into a poison-plant. Show-children are got up and exhibited, as if they were as insensible to flattery as prize poultry. Emulation is provoked in a manner which calls into activity some of the worst qualities of the heart.

Now, instead of pursuing this thoughtless and ruinous course, the aim should be so to stimulate and reward lower degrees and kinds of excellence as to lead to the attainment of the higher. If the child must have rivals, let him compete with himself; the boy or girl of to-day emulating the same child of yesterday. Let not success be praised so much as the effort to succeed. Let it be seen that a higher value is attached to diligence, perseverance, and good conduct, than to any external accomplishment to which they may lead. The will to obey and the desire to please, may often be present and active, even where the form is defective; in which case, the former should receive more of commendation than the latter of blame. Both praise and blame should be distributed in such degrees as will produce the desired effect, and in no greater. Rewards bestowed lavishly wear themselves out, creating an appetite not to be appeased. While in a well regulated family, pervaded by a sentiment in favor of order and excellence, a smile, an approving word, the gentle pressure of the hand, fills the whole house with sunshine. In the former instance, the craving is after the sensuous result; in the latter the preference is given to the excellence which rises above it. The wise parent will seldom have to seek obedience; he finds himself in the enjoyment of a love out of which all obedience grows, and which finds its richest reward in his approving smile.

Religion.

There is nothing deserving the name of education apart from religion. In addition to the properties which place the child in relation to the visible and the social, there is that which makes him consciously akin to the unseen and the eternal. And a religious education is that which surrounds him with a sense of the Omnipresent, and builds up within him an altar to it; which rears his conscience into a higher tribunal than any earthly, and pointing away to the highest; which meets his vague dreams of Infinity, by spreading a clear heaven over his head, with a guiding pole-star in it; and his deep yearnings to be loved, with the knowledge of Him in the thoughts of whom the young spirit shall delight to sun itself, and the love of whom shall be in the stead of the Ten Commandments. Heaven is nearer to us in infancy than ever after. Surely that alone is education which causes it to pass into us.

At first the mother stands to the child for a religion. His earliest piety is mother-love. He sees every thing by her light. His dependence and her support symbolize, and prepare him for all that can follow. Gradually his love radiates around and above. Extending his regard from her to her injunctions, he can not become aware that they bind his parents also, without feeling dimly conscious that there is something greater even than they. And as one dreamy presentiment after another wakes up in the depths of his soul, he is prepared to look up, as the maternal finger points to heaven, and to find in God that which he had previously found in her.

The love of God is the earliest form of adoration. Fear must not be allowed to create the god of infancy. Reverence will not fail to temper its affection; but its first piety should be eminently the love of the heart. Neither is argument or discussion in place at first. Proofs presuppose doubt, and may tend to awaken them. Whereas the child knows no logic but that of the heart. It climbs not laboriously by a ladder, but mounts on wings. Parental assertion and example are its only evidence; emotion its best proof. Here, therefore, example is every thing. In proportion as the *spirit* of piety educates, the *means* become unimportant. It finds them without seeking. Newton reverently uncovering his head at the great name of God—what an affecting exposition of the third command! But imagine him to have immediately after taken that name in vain! No one can teach religion who is himself without it. Mere catechizing is not religion. A chapter in the Bible is no amulet against evil habits. Loose general precepts and theological prate may deaden sensibility and engender hypocrisy, but are little likely to kindle or foster piety.

Motives are of different classes; and the child is to be taught the supremacy of those which recognize the spiritual and the infinite. If he is not to be unduly sensuous, let him not be led to regard the pleasures of sense as the appropriate reward and end of good conduct. If he is not to be selfish, let him not encroach on the rights or comforts of others, especially of dependents. If his affections are not to be limited to his parents, let them not resent his waywardness as directed against their authority alone, nor allow him to look on *their* forgiveness as all in all. While his heart is yet sore at having wounded their feelings, he should be led to ask the forgiveness of his Father in Heaven. Every thing happy, beautiful, and sublime should be made, by some grave and passing remark, to point his mind in the same direction. And especially should he be trained, by short and simple prayers, to give utterance to those sentiments slumbering within him which no other language can express.

Apart from religion, our teaching may only serve to illustrate the vast distinction between knowledge and wisdom; for it may only prove its efficacy as a means of perversion. And the necessity for religious training increases with the increase of intellectual acquisition. Instead of vulgarly computing the value of knowledge by the number of the things known, let it be seen that the parent estimates it by its influence on the child's character; that it belongs to religion to give tenfold value to every part of his nature; that it is infusible into every duty, and gives dignity to every station; and that it does this by placing him in harmony with the will of God. As he lives for many ends, he is to be impressed chiefly with the supremacy of the great end. And as he approaches the period for becoming himself the head of a family, he is to be shown that even the domestic constitution itself is only a means to that end; and that its own immediate ends are attained best by the constant subordination of them to that ultimate end. In a word, the whole of his training should tend to prepare him for the time when he will be given into his own hands, and for the remoter time when he will have to govern a family of his own, as part of the great community of families designed to carry on the process of Divine manifestation.

The responsibility of the parent is greatly enhanced by the fact, not only that these properties of the human being are all-related, and that each has its proper value differing from all the rest, but that they come into operation *successively*, and accordingly as they are each, in turn, placed and regulated, they project an influence for evil or for good on all his subsequent history. Even if they were all developed at the same time, and were of equal importance, so that like the parts of a machine, they could be put together, and set a-going at once and forever, the parental office would be the most responsible on earth. But owing to their differing values and successive development, that responsibility is raised to the highest point; for not until the child is capable of self-government is he out of the parental hand; the relative adjustment of all these parts and properties alone can impart this capacity, and this capacity, moreover, relates to a being who, after training others, is himself to live forever.

The child regarded as successively existent. Precocity.

In this connection, parents need especially to be reminded that the *premature development* of any one part (say of the intellectual) is sure to involve the injury of the whole. Nature offers no prize for the best answer to the question—How may the mind of the child be most early and rapidly developed? On the contrary, it reserves pains and penalties for the outrage. Intellectual precocity is commonly only "another name for cerebral disease." In some instances it leads, by a physiological necessity, to precocity in vice. Rousseau affirmed it to be one of the arts of education to know "how to lose time."* And in proportion as the stimulating influences supplied by material civilization multiply, the art of "postponed excitement"† becomes at once more difficult and more important. Let the heart be occupied and the emotions trained; but care should be exercised, lest by taxing and expending the mental forces too early in life, the whole remainder should be a history of sterility and exhaustion.

Memory.

Memory, too, taken in its wide, popular acceptation, as not merely a faculty of reception, but of reproduction, demands more thoughtful cultivation than it ordinarily receives. Were it merely, as it is generally thought to be, "the storehouse of the brain," it should surely command the most anxious parental attention; but by being so much, it becomes more, namely, a basis of character. A verbal memory may be of little account, but a memory for things, for sequences, analogies, and impressions, is vital. What the child spontaneously remembers with the greatest frequency and facility, furnishes the parent with a clew to its natural character, and may aid him in the formation of its voluntary memory. The very order in which things are deposited in the mind reacts beneficially on the moral character. The laws of the ancient lawgivers were promulgated in verse; both because order and harmony are the best *mnemonics*, and because, by being easily and pleasantly recalled, they were the more likely to be observed. Pythagoras wisely

* Emile, l. 2.

† I. Taylor's Home Education, pp. 14–17.

advised his pupils to recall at night the events of the day, aiming alike at the exercise of their recollection and the improvement of their character. In addition to this, the child may be advantageously requested, as a voluntary exercise to relate what it remembers of a favorite book, the parent always taking care that the book be of a useful kind. Meanwhile, it would be a valuable moral discipline for the parent to bear in mind that impressions left by his own example are likely to be remembered, even when his precepts are forgotten.

Habits.

That which renders the age of childhood so responsible to the parents is, that it is the period during which *habits* are formed.

> "The clay is moist and soft, now, now make haste
> And form the pitcher, for the wheel turns fast."*

And the pitcher, once formed, may be more easily broken than altered. Habits of intellectual accuracy can be formed only by the frequent repetition and revision of subjects. Hence, one of the chief rules of Jacotot, *Repetez sans cesse;* and the still older proverb, *Repetitio est mater studiorum.* Thus, in childhood, each word has to be learned, each syllable to be acquired, and correct articulation is the result of hourly repetition; but once the habit has been formed—and it is formed without the least consciousness of labor—the syllables ever after arrange themselves without any attention from the speaker. Something more, however, than mere oral repetition is necessary to form the character to virtue. Admirably has Butler said, "Going over the theory of virtue in one's thoughts; talking well,

* "Udum, et molle lutum est, nunc, nunc properandus, et acri
Fingendus sine fine rota."—*Pers. Sat.* 3.

and drawing fine pictures of it, this is so far from necessarily or certainly conducing to form a habit of it in him who thus employs himself, that it may harden the mind in a contrary course, and render it gradually more insensible; that is, form a habit of insensibility to all moral considerations."* Here practice alone makes perfect. Lycurgus would not allow his laws to be written, lest the youth should be reading them when they ought to be practicing them; knowing, says Plutarch, that principles interwoven with the manners and breeding of the people, become habits; and that "habits would answer in each the purpose of a lawgiver."† And hence, that alone is deserving the name of education in which, however small the amount of knowledge imparted, that knowledge is sought to be *applied;* in which the great aim is to reach the heart of the child, and to impress it with a sacred regard for truth and duty, and a deep reverence for the will of God; in which the character is sought to be built up into habits of order, attention, and filial obedience, based on that piety which is the beginning of wisdom.

Harmony of constitution.

From first to last the education of the child is to be conducted with a view to the harmony and unity of its constitution. In a former chapter we saw that the world into which the little human sojourner comes is in every respect preconfigured to its constitution; that the adaptation is so complete that there is not a susceptibility or power slumbering within it which has not its corresponding object in the universe without; nor an object or event, physical, intellectual, or moral, in the external universe which has not a responsive counterpart within the outline of that infant being; and further, that

* Analogy, part i. c. 5. † Life of Lycurgus.

his well-being depends on the gradual awakening of those latent adaptations by the measured adjustment and orderly application of the different parts of the great surrounding system into which it has come. What can result, then, from the plan which confines its operation to the development of any one part of the human constitution—say of the intellectual, or of some one faculty of the intellect—while it abandons the physical to weakness and early disease, and leaves the social and moral to the dwarfed and shriveled condition of a paralyzed limb; what but a community of human monsters, who live to proclaim that every thing intellectually absurd is both physically and morally wrong? Or what can we say of a process which, instead of training the human being for the duties and enjoyments of the physical, intellectual, and moral life, bends all its energies to train him for "a fashionable life"—an artificial state of existence; which, by rendering him as independent, and as incapable as possible, of all the means of God's providing, and which awaited his coming into being, contravenes, at every step, some natural laws—what, but that when the evil has filled society with its proper fruits—pride, impatience, discontent, insubordination—and when society is at its wit's end for remedies, it should yet prove blind to the natural connection of those fruits with such a process, and should persevere in it to its ruin?

Parental authority transitional.

If there be a time when the authority of the parent over the child be absolute—in infancy—and if there be a period when the child is to enter on the duties of self-government, it follows that from the first of these periods to the last the authority of the parent should be ever in a transition state. From simply commanding, he should proceed to explain the reasons of his commands; from these again, to the expression of desires and the manifestation of a generous confidence; and from these to the frequent option and discretion of the child, preparatory to the moment of giving him entirely into his own hands.

And increases with the increase of the family.

With the increase of the family, the parental duty is further increased. Wisely, indeed, is it ordered that the experience acquired in the training of the first, should tend to give the parents a proficiency for the training of the second, and so onward. And still more that both the example of one child should assist the parent in his training of another, and that his own treatment of one should be felt beneficially by another, as if it had been directed to himself. But in order to this, the conduct of the parent must be characterized by strict impartiality; every apparent deviation from it should be accompanied by the reasons for such deviation; and no opportunity should be lost of inculcating their duties to each other, of endearing them to each other, and of praying for each other, giving them the enjoyment of ministering to each other's happiness. Not only should great respect to the welfare of the children be had in the choice of servants, but in every part of their conduct toward their servants also, parents should remember that they are indirectly giving an influential lesson to their children, likely to bias their conduct toward the same parties.

Filial obligation.

Every obligation is correlative; so that if it be the right and duty of the parent to seek the welfare of the child, it is the duty of the child to respond in every respect essential to the attainment of that object, or resulting from it. Thus if it be the duty of the parents to maintain the child, it is his duty *gratefully* to recognize his dependence on them. If it devolves on them to teach and to educate him, on him it devolves to believe, and to submit to the necessary discipline, whether administered by them directly, or by an agent of their appointment. If they are under obligation to love him, and to let their every outward act be an expression of well-regulated love, he is under obligation to live in the constant exercise of filial affection toward them. If it is their duty to command, it his duty to obey because they have commanded. And if it is their duty to cultivate his moral nature, by teaching him the will of God, and by becoming his intercessors at the throne of mercy, it is his duty to regard them with reference as "the ministers of God to him for good." In a word, if it be their duty to instruct, to pray for, and to govern him, it is his duty to believe, to reverence, and to obey them.

If the obligation of the parent changes, however, from that of exercising absolute authority to that of friendly advice or parental regard, the duty of the child passes through all the intermediate stages, from implicit obedience to self-government.

And if the time arrives when the parent requires the maintenance and tender care of the child, it is the sacred and delightful duty of the child to provide for and consult his comfort. And, be it remarked, that just in proportion as it ceases to be the duty of the child implicitly to *obey* his parents, his obligation to respect and love them increases. For the longer he enjoys their parental care, the greater his debt of gratitude becomes; and the longer he lives, the greater is his opportunity of estimating the full value of parental care, and the more capable he becomes of repaying it in acts of disinterested affection.

Obligation of child to child.

If the relations existing *between the children* of the same family be such as we have stated in a preceding chapter, it follows that every child, on reaching a state of responsibility, is under various obligations toward every other child of the family. The striking manner in which one child is the object of imitation to another, especially the elder to the younger—even to a greater degree, for obvious reasons, than the parents themselves—renders the position of the elder children highly responsible. Still further is this responsibility increased where a portion of the parental authority is delegated to them from time to time, and for specific purposes. The character of one child is often impressed, for evil or for good, on all his brothers and sisters.

External obligations; local and material.

Passing from the internal obligations of the family, the first object, *external* to it, claiming attention, is its *place*. It must be somewhere. If our first parents must quit the garden of Eden, Adam must begin to "till the ground from whence he was taken," in some locality without. If Cain is exiled from that locality, he is soon found dwelling "in the land of Nod, on the east of Eden." From that moment a series of duties commenced in relation to his knowledge of the dangers, products, capabilities, and laws of health peculiar to the region. This is only saying that he was to put himself in harmony with nature, obeying its laws, and availing himself to the utmost of its properties and powers; and that he was to do this as the only means of his attaining the great end of his existence in that or in any other part of the world. And all his knowledge of nature was, of course, to enter into his training of his children.

The duties of every family, say cotemporaneous with

Noah, were relative, not only to the nature of the district it inhabited, but also to the manner in which its predecessors had fulfilled their obligations in this respect. Had the principal natural phenomena been noted, and the right practical application of them been made? Each family had inherited much useful knowledge of this description from those who had gone before, was bound to add to it something of its own, and to transmit the whole to its successors. So also in relation to the laws and government of the family; many of them were doubtless the result of experience and observation, arising out of the nature and circumstances of the country inhabited. But the point to be noted is, that at any given era from the creation to the flood, in any given family, there was a certain amount of the knowledge of nature and of practical conformity to physical laws, which could not be wanting without implicating some party or parties in the guilt of such deficiency. If, for instance, the tendency of the climate was to enervate, to induce indolence, or excessively to develop the passions, domestic laws and discipline should be framed to remedy such tendencies. Food, amusements, the kind and amount of labor—nothing was entirely indifferent—and if not, it was the duty of the members of the first family to make every thing in this department a matter of conscience; and if it was the duty of the first family, it was the duty of the second, and so on of each in succession. Nor could any one family fail to take its bearings, in relation to the local and physical duties of its own day, without sharing in the guilt of all the families which had preceded it.

But all this is only saying that the history and characteristics of a region should form part of the education of those inhabiting it. The proposition seems so obvious as to render a formal statement almost ridiculous; yet the practical adoption of it exposes to still greater ridicule. Even the laws of health are only beginning to be considered. Sanitary laws require to be enforced by severe penalties. When Zeno consulted the oracle as to the manner in which he should live, the answer was, that he should "inquire of the dead." In the midst of a pestilence we sleepily propose the same question, and receive the same answer, remanding us to "the thousand fallen at our side, and to the ten thousand at our right hand." But the evil no sooner slightly abates than we resume our slumber at the edge of the cess-pool, or amid the fevers of an undrained Campania.

Moral obligation.

Next to nature stands *Man*. If the first human family had a right to exist, and therefore to the means of life, and was held responsible to God for preserving the one and for employing the other, the coming of another family could not dispossess it of its rights, nor release it from its obligation; nor could it dispossess nor release that other, except on grounds which would repeal and destroy its own claims and duties. The relations existing between the two, and which arose from the identity of their constitution and design, gave rise to a system of equal and reciprocal obligations. Nor could the inequalities of their *condition*, which, to them, were mere accidents of existence, affect the equality of their *rights* and obligations, unless they could be shown to affect the identity of their nature.

Justice.

Justice requires, therefore that it should form a part of the education of every man to leave every other man in the unmolested enjoyment of *liberty*, of physical liberty—to go, stay where, and do with himself what he pleases, provided the exercise of that liberty interfere with the liberty of no other party: of intellectual liberty—to investigate what subject he pleases, and to arrive at whatever conclusions they seem to him to warrant; providing, again, that his doing so do not interfere with the happiness of any other man: of liberty of speech—to communicate whatever he may deem to be truth; but always on the condition before stated: of emotional liberty—to love or hate, desire or loathe, whatever object he pleases; still, however, on the same condition: of voluntary liberty—to follow the bias of his will, and to seek the accomplishment of his purposes, in any way not inimical to the happiness of others; and, above all, of liberty of conscience—to worship God or not, and to worship Him in any manner that he deems best; always providing that his liberty infringes on the liberty of no other person.

If to the enjoyment of this liberty it be objected that a man may so employ it as to ruin himself, the answer is obvious—that to abridge his liberty would not remedy the evil; that, as to moral liberty, such abridgment would be rendering him incapable of virtue; but that the means to be employed are moral, suited to his nature as a moral agent.

Property.

Justice requires that he should recognize the right of *property;* the right, that is, which a man possesses to use something as he chooses, provided he does not, by so doing, interfere with the right of any other man. This is the only right by which he himself can employ the personal pronouns concerning any thing which he possesses, and call it "*his* own," or say "it is *mine.*" This property may be originally acquired by the gift of God, or by personal labor; or by exchange, gift, or inheritance; but however acquired, if it be the rightful property of another, he can not molest him in the possession of it, whether it be a toy in the hand of a play-fellow, or the muscular labor of a fellow-man, without infringing the law which alone protects himself from becoming the prey of the strongest, and without which society could never have begun to exist.

Reputation.

Reputation is a kind of property also; for, as he who owns a piece of land and cultivates it is entitled to the fruits which it produces, so, if the manner in which he cultivates it gives him a reputation for skill in that department, he is entitled to the advantages of that reputation; and those advantages may be of greater value to him than the fruits which his skill has produced—he, at least, may value them more. By the cultivation of his land he became entitled to those fruits resulting from the operation of the laws of cause and effect which govern the materials on which he operated; and by his *manner* of doing it he becomes entitled to that esteem resulting from the laws of cause and effect which govern the opinions of men toward each other. Now, justice requires that he should be left in the enjoyment of his reputation, if, by so doing, no other and higher law be infringed. The same principle forbids us to publish the bad actions of a man without an adequate reason; to draw general conclusions respecting his character from a single action; to suspect and causelessly assign bad motives to the actions of men; and to lower them in the estimation of others by means tending to bring them into contempt.

Confidence.

Confidence, also, is another species of property. It is that precious property with which man barters with his fellow for the equally precious element of truth. Truth and trust form the staple commodity by which the commerce of mind is maintained. By laws of cause and effect, as certain in their operations as those which govern labor and its fruits, and skill and its reputation, truth and confidence are linked together. Annihilate truth, and there could be no confidence; annihilate all confidence, and the voice of truth would gradually become silent. Now, every man who makes a communication or a promise, calculates on this confidence in his fellow-man; hence he is said to "draw on his faith," and he "expects credit" for truth. The moral constitution which predisposes the one to tell the truth, is met by a corresponding constitution which predisposes the other to believe what he is told. Justice requires, therefore, that confidence should receive its equivalent, truth. To give it falsehood instead, is to give it base coin in exchange for its gold; is to defraud it of more than what would have been the value of the particular truth, in the stead of which it has received a falsehood; it is to lessen its confidence in that principle of veracity on which alone it has to depend in all its intercourse with man, and thus to threaten the very existence of society. The law of veracity, then, forbids the utterance, as truth, of what we know to be false; of what we do not know to be true; of what may be true in fact, yet so as to convey a false impression to the hearer, whether by exaggeration, by extenuation, or by the misleading accompaniment of tones, look, or gestures. These remarks relate to veracity as to the past. The same law, in the case of promises, binds the promiser to the sense in which he meant and supposed the promisee to receive them. Only thus can we project our plans, so as to embrace the distant and connect the past with the future; for only thus can we make our knowledge of what has been available for all subsequent time.

Character.

Character is property also, and property of the highest value. It is the only enduring possession properly his own, derived from all the past, and the only imperishable capital with which he can hope to purchase the "goodly pearl" of happiness for eternity. Justice forbids, therefore, that we willingly vitiate the character of another in any manner or on any ground whatever. We are prohibited from weakening the moral restraints of men alike by our conversation and by our example; and from exciting to action their evil dispositions, by viciously stimulating their imaginations; by pandering to the appetites of others; by using others to minister to our vicious desires; or by cherishing in any way the evil passions of men.

Sympathy.

All this would have been due from man to man, and from family to family, even if man had retained his first and normal condition. But he became a *sufferer*, and as such he is entitled to *sympathy*. His suffering, whatever it may be, incapacitates him, to a certain extent, for that happiness which is the proximate end of his being, as well as for actively answering the ultimate end of existence. We owe him sympathy, therefore, both as he is our fellow-man, and we may be his fellow-sufferers; and as he is the creature of God, and under His Divine protection.

Forbearance.

But man is a sufferer by becoming a *sinner*. As a man, justice is his due; as a suffering man, sympathy; as a sinful man, *forbearance and forgiveness*. In rendering him all three, we are but doing to him as we would that he should do unto us. In the first, the man is supposed to be just—in harmony with all the laws which respect his relative conduct; and we are bound, *in the sight of God and man*, to be just toward him in return. But, in the second, this same man is supposed to be a sufferer—out of harmony with the laws of his own being, and, as such, fallen on the great highway to happiness and unable to reach its end; and we are bound, *in the sight of God*, to help him, but to do it in a way compatible with his well-being on the whole. In the third, we contemplate the same man as a sinner, a transgressor, it may be, against God, society, and himself. But in exercising mercy toward the offender—provided it can be done without defeating the ends of justice—we should remember that we are manifesting a disposition on the Divine exercise of which our own happiness and the continuance of the world are suspended, and by which a fellow-man is aided to answer the end of his being, after his hope of so doing had perhaps been justly forfeited.

Education should embrace all this. The duty of the individual, in these respects, is the duty of the family; and that education is chargeable with radical deficiency which omits its inculcation. Each family, while it forms an organic whole, complete in itself for its own temporary and internal purposes, is not only a living branch of the great genealogical tree of the race, but is dependent on other living branches for its own continuance and well-being, and for answering the great end of the domestic constitution. If, then, it be an essential part of education to take the child from his appetites, in the gratification of which he may be content to circumscribe himself and settle down, and to show him that there are other parts of his nature to which his appetites are to be held subsidiary—parts of a wider range and a nobler destiny, and which ally him to the past, the future, and the invisible; and if it be important to take him from this center of himself, commanding as the view may be which he there attains of his own interests, and to show him that he is only a single member of the family into which he has been born, and to point out his dependence, relations, and obligations to every member included in his family circle, and during every moment he remains in that circle; equally important is it that he should be duly taken to the verge of that circle to be shown the family circles beyond; to have it impressed on him that they all touch or intersect each other; that there is a line which circumscribes the whole; and that the well-being of each is made dependent on the well-being of all the rest. "The laws of education are the first impressions we receive (says Montesquieu*), and as they prepare us for civil life, every private family ought to be governed by the plan of that great household which comprehends them all."

Each generation has its duties.

Obligations devolve on the individual and the family as *successively* existent. Every man ought to compare what has come to be the laws, the maxims, and even the language of his fellow-men with the obvious will of the Creator. He is to protest against every other standard than the will of God. Every deviation from it he is to resist. Whoever may call sweet bitter, and bitter sweet, he is to call things by their proper names. However long the boundary line between good and evil may have been removed from the place in which God fixed it, he is to spend life in an endeavor to replace it; or he must expect to be dealt with as a partaker of other men's sins.

In the entire series of families, from the creation to the

* Esprit des Lois, tome iv. c. 2.

flood, each stood in the relation of a middle term between the past and the future. But as the social character of no two generations was precisely alike, it followed that the duties of every family were of a kind peculiar to the age, and formed the work of its generation ; a work which could not have been forstalled without neglecting the duties of the day, nor delayed without allowing evils to accumulate to a disheartening amount for all that came after. It was the duty of each family, then, to inform itself of its real position in relation to the past and the future ; to estimate the social derelictions of all the past, observing what led to them, and what they had led to ; to compare the state of the family *de facto* with the family *de jure*, or with its normal character in the Divine mind, in order that the duties of its generation might become apparent. In the whole range of the Patriarchal dispensation there never was a period when the great Pater-Familias was not entitled to look for a certain amount of social excellence and perfection in the families of men—namely, the precise amount which would have resulted from the perfect discharge of every family obligation during all the past—and an amount, therefore, increasing with every succeeding generation. If, then, no one generation exhibited the amount of excellence, no one family belonging to it could accept that state of family apostacy from God, contenting itself to neglect the reforming work of its day, and thus perpetuating and aggravating the apostacy, without sharing in and consenting to all the guilt of the past. This is obviously the meaning of such startling declarations as, "that the blood of all the prophets, shed from the foundation of the world, shall be required of this generation." The apostacy which, having begun with the first man, so speedily "brought forth fruit unto death" in the first family, in the murder of Abel, was perpetuated in every succeeding generation. Just in proportion as each generation allowed the tide of evil to roll on, did nothing to arrest its progress or diminish its force, but contributed to swell the evil by its own additions, it stood chargeable with the guilt of all the past. The last generation, therefore, of any given period, standing, as it would, amid the comparative wreck of all that depended on the human will in the family constitution; surrounded by the most monstrous forms of evil, the growth of centuries; ever and anon startled by Divine indications of a coming judgment; and yet evincing no disposition to retrace its steps, but rather to advance in evil, deterred by nothing but the dread of consequences; that generation justly inherits the guilt of all the past.

To God; or religious obligations.

If it be important to show the child that his appetites are not the central and supreme part of himself, that he is not the center of his family, nor his family the center around which other families are to revolve, how important that his views should be directed to that *glorious Being* who has organized the domestic constitution, and who is at once its center and circumference. Every new view which he receives in childhood of the Divine character brings with it a corresponding duty. The motive which would lead him to trace with interest his derivation from some distinguished human ancestor, should receive an indefinite accession of strength, as often as he refers his origin to the Father of Spirits. And the gratitude with which he refers his daily comforts to his earthly parents, should be heightened immeasurably as he comes to understand the great system of Providence which originates and includes all his daily mercies, and all the channels through which they come to him. As life advances and opportunities offer, he is bound to examine and to verify for himself all the religious truths which he had previously received on parental testimony, and to see that no portion of Divine revelation had been omitted. As other intimations of the Divine will presented themselves during the antediluvian period, whether directly by the inspiration of holy men of God, or inductively by the advancing course of nature, he was bound to add them to his previous store of sacred knowledge, as full of practical applications. As he rose from the dominion of sensible objects, it was his duty to look at the character and will of God through the more ethereal medium of faith; and, from being satisfied with the intercession of others, and with stated times and places of devotion, to advance to hold personal intercourse with God; and, like Enoch, habitually to "walk with God." Thus from the first moment in which he lisped the awful name of God, till the hour when he was waiting to ascend into His immediate presence, he was to grow in grace and in the knowledge of God.

Each generation had its own religious duties.

Similarly, it devolved on each generation to transmit from the past to the future every particle of Divine revelation; all its religious advantages of Divine appointment; the evidences of that revelation and those appointments; the supposed meaning of that revelation, and all the providential illustrations of the spirit and value of those advantages. The generation cotemporary with Noah, for example, were bound to perpetuate the memory of the first promise, and the celebration of the great institute of sacrifice, and the evidence on which they both rested. They were bound to show that the revelations afterward made from time to time were in perfect agreement with each other, with the character and wants of the times when each was given, with the spirit and design of the first promise and of sacrifice, with the law of Paradise, and with the prior truths involved in external nature; and they were bound to accompany all this with the abundant evidence which they had at command. And, further, it was their duty to notice and point out all the admirable illustrations of the dispensation to the family constitution. Every family was bound to exhibit the enlightened, useful, and united character of a church or society protesting against prevailing error; worshiping God collectively in spirit and in truth; interceding for the religious well-being of every family; ready in every way consistent with the time to promote that well-being; and thus aiming to arrest the flow of evil from the past to the future, and to acquire such fitness for usefulness, that, through it, all the families of the earth should be blessed.

Obligations of the parent to prepare for his religious duties.

Every parent, therefore, was to be the *prepared* religious instructor of his family. In order to this, it devolved on him to acquaint himself with the origin, history, and evils of prevailing errors; with the evidence and claims of every antagonist truth; and with the peculiar moral wants and "signs of the times." Whatever time was necessary for the efficient discharge of this obligation, it was his duty to secure. The occupation of the parents was not to be such as to leave the child an orphan. Neither was their object to be their own quiet rather than his well-being. And whatever means it may have been necessary to employ in order to secure that well-being, they were bound to employ them. This is the great lesson deducible from the whole: that if the branches are to bear, we must begin with watering the roots; that education alone produces education; the teachers themselves must be taught. No amount of genius exempts an artist from the necessity of study and practice; and shall education, the noblest of all the arts, be the only one not studied? At present, the family, in which every thing should be sacred to law and duty, is pre-eminently the sphere abandoned, as by common consent, to chance. Let the period of parental education arrive—especially of female education to qualify for maternal duty—and a family millennium would begin.

CHAPTER X.

THE WELL-BEING OF THE DOMESTIC CONSTITUTION MEASURED BY THE DISCHARGE OF ITS OBLIGATIONS.

Law of well-being.

IT is a law of the family, as well as of the individual, that each shall "enjoy an amount of good or of well-being proportioned to the discharge of its obligations." For to fulfill the law of its being, or to find its own highest end, is to answer the great end. Nor could it be supposed to be in any way deprived of its right, while thus fulfilling the law of its being, without the great end itself being, in so far, defeated.

Every thing in the family is under law.

The more important of the *conditions* of the well-being of the family are considered in the chapters on its relations, its laws, and its consequent obligations. From these, it appears that every thing relating to it is, and must be, in contravention of, or in obedience to, a law. And to suppose that the same effects would follow from the contravention as from the obedience, is to confound together things inherently different; and to imply that there is no end to be answered by the domestic economy, no well-being to be aimed at, or no appropriate means for its attainment. Yet, judging from its history, such would appear to have been the prevailing practical creed on the subject in all ages. That, in order to promote its well-being, it should be necessary to know any thing of its being or constitution; that this constitution should literally consist of things so stable and unbending as real laws; that not attending to these laws should be followed by effects essentially different from those which ensue from attending to them—real disadvantages—penalties; these are facts which few have even thought of; and, of those who have been reminded of them, the great majority turn from them as mere airy speculations, too remote and refined for daily life; while they find it most congenial to their self-love to treat their domestic troubles, not as retributive, but as the mysterious and arbitrary appointments of God. A glance at the nature of the domestic constitution, and at its historical working during the antediluvian period, is all that is necessary in order to rebuke such willing error, and to illustrate the validity of the present law.

Its well-being regulated by the social condition of woman.

The estimation in which women are held in a country, supplies a just criterion of the degree of its civilization. The degraded condition in which Solon found and left them—viewing the wife as a mere household drudge, with whom rational intercourse and friendship were impossible—gradually led to a depravation of manners, not in Athens merely, but in the states of Greece generally, which could not but sow the seeds of social dissolution. "The family can not exist without marriage, nor can it develop its highest importance without monogamy. Civilization, in its highest state, requires it, as well as the natural organization and wants of man."* And from the moment in which man concedes to woman the rights which he claims himself, and honors the

* Lieber's Polit. Ethics, part. i. b. ii. § 24.

powers of the mind and heart more than mere physical prowess, the sex begins to assume its proper position in society, and civilization advances.

By the degree in which the laws of marriage are observed.

In proportion as the laws of marriage are complied with—in the union of parties corresponding to each other in age, healthiness, affection, character, and aim—healthy and affectionate offspring, conjugal happiness, and a consequent power of general usefulness is likely to be the result. This fact was recognized and involuntarily honored by imperial Rome during the period of its greatest degeneracy. For even then, at the height of its licentiousness, its laws implied that marriage is of the greatest importance, viewed as a mere political advantage. But the fact admits of the most minute verification. Modern statistics illustrate the graduated manner in which the laws in question stand related to the number, the mortality, the physical and mental enervation of offspring.* Every instance of departure from these laws is found to be attended by a corresponding deduction from the well-being of the family.

Inferior ends attained best by aiming at the highest.

But that on which it may be more important to insist here is, that the subordinate ends of the domestic constitution are likely to be attained only in proportion as the great end is aimed at intelligently and supremely. True, laws, as far as they are separable, operate independently of each other. So that if a man obey the laws of health, he will enjoy health, even to the moment of his being executed for violating the laws of society. If he observe the latter he will be honored even though, and perhaps partly because, he was oblivious of the former. If he observe both sets of laws, physical and

* Quételet sur les Hommes, etc. b. i. c. 1, 2, 3.

social, he will enjoy the advantages, even though at heart an infidel toward God. So, also, compliance with the physical condition of marriage is likely to secure the greatest number of healthy offspring, whatever may be the intellectual and moral character of the parents. But who does not see that, apart from moral, apart even from intellectual restraints, such compliance would form the exception, and unbridled sensuality the rule? in which case, even the physical advantages of the institution, together with the institution itself, would soon come to be lost. We freely admit, on the other hand, that the higher end is occasionally aimed at to the neglect of the lower, and to the consequent detriment of both. But the proposition now before us is, that a regard for the great end of the family economy is the only security that its subordinate laws will be obeyed, and its inferior ends be attained; and that in proportion as that end is answered these are answered also.

Evils of lax discipline.

Thus, a regard for the Divine Will, by supplying motives for parental chastity and temperance, tends to secure the physical welfare of the children. Supreme regard for the Divine approbation, by tending to exempt the parents from self-reproach, and inducing self-respect, tends also to inspire the children with filial reverence, and to render the government of the family comparatively easy. "The notion, indeed, that a family is a society, and that a society must be governed, and that the right and the duty of governing this society rest with the parent, seems to be rapidly vanishing from the minds of men. In the place of it, it seems to be the prevalent opinion that children may grow up as they please; and that the exertion of parental restraint is an infringement upon the personal liberty of the child. But all this will not abrogate the law of God, nor will it avert the punishment which He has connected, indissolubly, with disobedience. The parent who neglects his duty to his children, is sowing thickly, for himself and for them, the seeds of his future misery. He who is suffering the evil dispositions of his children to grow up uncorrected, will find that he his cherishing a viper by which he himself will first be stung. The parent who is accustoming his children to habits of thoughtless caprice and reckless expenditure, and who stupidly smiles at the ebullitions of youthful passion and the indulgence in fashionable vice, as indications of a manly spirit, needs no prophet to foretell that, unless the dissoluteness of his family leave him entirely childless, his gray hairs will be brought down with sorrow to the grave."*

Benefits of religious training.

The parent can not place himself in the soul of the child in order to educate him, without recovering much of the simplicity of his own childhood, nor labor to form his character without, at the same time, building himself up to a higher point of excellence. By training his children to love God supremely, he is securing their love for himself more effectually than as if he sought it directly. The earlier he begins this moral inculcation the more successful he is likely to be; and the sooner they become consciously amenable to the laws of the Divine government the sooner they are capable of that self-government which leaves little more to the parent than occasion for gratitude and joy. While, by leading them to God in worship, he is deepening his own interest in their welfare, consecrating their attachment to himself, and binding them closer to each other. The parent who complains

* Dr. Wayland's Moral Science, p. 333.

of "want of time" for thus training his children, needs to be reminded that the laws of the family, like those of health, "punish so severely, when neglected, that they cause the offender to lose *tenfold more time*" in suffering the consequences, than would be requisite to obey them; to say nothing of the heritage of evil entailed on his children. On the other hand, every moment consecrated to the formation of their characters is sure to be paid in hours and days of spontaneous obedience, and in the sunshine of a happy home, the mellow light of which will be thrown forward on all their subsequent course. And this affection of the children, secured chiefly on moral grounds, is the strongest guarantee the parent can have (though it has, probably, never occurred to his mind as a motive) that they will tenderly provide hereafter, if necessary, for his temporal comfort. "On the blue mountains of our dim childhood, toward which we ever turn and look, stand the parents who marked out to us from thence our life; the most blessed age must be forgotten ere we can forget the warmest hearts."* And the child, in obeying the voice which saith, "Honor thy father and thy mother," though forgetting that it "is the first commandment with promise," is, in various ways, laying a foundation for his own temporal prosperity.

The Divine promise to such training.

The law which we are now illustrating comprises the Divine affirmation, that "a child trained in the way he should go shall not depart from it when he is old." This is not to be viewed as the language of a promise so much as the statement of a grand principle of the domestic constitution. Some, indeed, may be ready to object, that they know many a painful excep-

* Richter's *Levana.*

tion to its truth in the circle of their own acquaintance. Now, when failure ensues in any other department of duty, we do not rashly conclude that the connection between means and ends has at length come to an end; we infer rather that there has been something faulty in the employment of the means. The failure of parental training, indeed, in certain instances, may not furnish a looker-on with any ground for concluding that but little has been done for the child's welfare. Comparatively much may have been done; more than many an instance attended with success. No human eye might be keen enough to detect a fault in it; no human being be justified in pronouncing censure. Still, we must believe that the training was not commenced early enough; or that it was not continued long enough; or that it suffered interruptions; that there was too much reliance on other means, to the neglect of prayer; or that prayer was not combined with the adequate employment of other means; that certain parts of the training were not pursued in the right spirit—appeal being made to fear, vanity, or the appetites, or that parental example did not in some particular enforce parental precept; that the influence of one parent neutralized that of the other, or that the example of some other party did; that some specious or prolific evil was winked at or undetected; that indulgence and severity so alternated as to destroy parental authority; or that there was a want of adaptation in the training to the peculiar character of the child; or else a want of holy earnestness pervading the whole: something must be wanting, or we must impeach the faithfulness and grace of God. Where nothing is wanting in the means employed, nothing is ever wanting, on the part of God, in the end obtained.

We do not forget the native tendency of the heart to evil; and have no sympathy, therefore, with the theory which represents the human mind as being at first pure and spotless as a sheet of unwritten paper, and as being stained only by subsequent impressions. Rather it resembles the paper which is covered with the secret writing of an invisible ink, and which has only to be placed near the fire in order to bring out and make visible all the characters. But then it comes to the parents before whom it has been so placed, and in order that they may keep it from the exciting element. It comes to them free from the blots and stains of *actual* transgression, to be preoccupied as quickly and fully as possible with the writing and signature of Heaven. And so absolute is the law which impels the child to believe their every word; to imitate their every tone, gesture, and action; to receive the ineffaceable impressions of their character, that their every movement drops a seed into the virgin soil of its heart, to germinate there for eternity.

Neither do we forget that the child himself is a free agent; and that much depends on his own dispositions. It is this which renders the training of a child an art, a science the most sacred; and, next to that of his own salvation, the most momentous occupation in which a parent can be engaged. On the other hand, however—unless we are prepared to accept the alternative that here there is no connection between means and ends; that causes may be put into operation without any corresponding effects being produced; that though, in every other department of human agency, God has graciously arranged that if certain things be done certain results shall follow, yet that in this particular sphere the rule is departed from—we must believe that in the day of final account it will appear, that the right means rightly employed in the training of childhood uniformly produced corresponding fruits. However diversified these results may be, and though falling short in numerous instances of the desired end, they never fall below the just and full operation of the law in question. The sovereignty of God may rise above the law, and exceed the just expectation of the parent; His faithfulness guarantees that the end shall never fall short of the measure and quality of the means employed. This is the parent's encouragement to aim at the highest results, and to expect the most blessed consequences.

Tends to the well-being of the community.

The constitution of the family was designed, not for the well-being of the children merely, but of each member of the household, of the entire family, of the whole community of families. By creating at first one common father of the species, the Creator designed that each individual should stand related to all the rest, and feel himself pledged to promote their happiness. By rendering us necessary to each other's welfare, He sought to train us up to a humble imitation of His own goodness; to make every hand and heart a consecrated channel for His love to flow in; and thus to find a large proportion of our happiness in the happiness of others. Every good action tended, by a law, to benefit even the doer; and to do this, not merely by purifying and refreshing his spirit, and by strengthening the principle which produced it, but, such is the harmonious constitution both of the physical and social systems, by more or less favoring his health, security, confidence, and honor. While, besides the direct advantage of every good action to the immediate object of it, the fountains of gratitude and joy would be unsealed, a motive would be supplied to repeat a similar action in his own conduct, and a useful influence be thus projected into the future. In such a state, he who approached nearest to the pattern of the Divine excellence would be the object of the greatest admiration; and as admiration leads, by a law of our nature, to imitation, men would be perpetually advancing toward higher and higher degrees of perfection. Inferior excellence being drawn upward by the strong moral attraction of that which was above it, a process of assimilation to the blessed God would have been constantly going on, from family to family, and from age to age, which would have rendered earth a copy of heaven.

Ideal family.

Well might the mind be haunted, age after age, with a social ideal never yet realized! Life a sacred thing. Every child a Divine promise. Every family beginning the race anew from a higher point. Brothers and sisters ministering angels to each other's purity and beneficence. Every addition a new element of happiness. Education the rearing of a living temple. Conjugal love a central fountain in warm, fragrant, perpetual play. The father the representative of God; feeding them, as a prophet, with more than angels' food; as a priest, standing at the portico of the temple, to guard it from pollution, or ministering at its holy altar, and finding his spirit purified and refreshed by the service; swaying, like a king, a divine scepter, and tasting the Godlike blessedness of seeing his subjects find happiness and freedom in obedience. The mother, the earliest to enter the infant heart, and to take possession in the name of God; radiating on her children the light and life of her own intense affection, and invested in addition with the delegated and solemn reverence of paternal authority. Home, the home of the affections; where law is superseded by love; where the lowliest act is consecrated and ennobled by the highest motive; and where separate individual interests are forgotten in the aim of each for the good of all. The family, sending forth its youthful members—each with a heritage of happy recollections and holy habits, impressed with the sanctity and high responsibilities of the domestic constitution, studiously trained and qualified to enter on them, and determined to raise still higher, if possible, in his own new circle, the standard of his own early home. The aged patriarch, happy in the consciousness of having linked his mind for good with all his own immediate offspring, and cheered by the prospect of transmitting, through them, the happiest influence to others through an ever-enlarging circle. The generation, conscious of rising, and aspiring to rise still higher; recognizing in its present blessedness the proof that God is its *Pater-familias;* and valuing the future chiefly as the means of perpetual approximation to the only perfect home in the bosom of God. Such are the capabilities of the family, and the sunny visions at which it hints.

Its possible good, made equal evil possible.

But the domestic constitution, by thus preparing a sanctuary for goodness, inviting its practice in the purest form, and providing for its diffusion and perpetuation, unavoidably opened a door for the possible entrance and diffusion of evil. The well-being of the economy depended entirely on man's voluntary conformity to the laws of its constitution. Involuntary defects might arise, and partial derangements of the system might consequently ensue; but these would only afford the family occasions for new displays of concern for each other, and new incentives to holy obedience. But every voluntary transgression, besides involving its own immediate punishment in the bosom of the transgressor, by exhibiting and diffusing a spirit of insubordination to the great Lawgiver, struck at the happiness of the race. This had been one of the effects of the first sin; and every subsequent transgression had but repeated and aggravated, in this respect, the effect of that sin. Indeed, the family constitution was a moral government. It presupposed, and was pervaded by, general laws. These laws were based on, and sanctioned by, equity. So that the reward of obedience, and the punishment of disobedience, were alike secured; and the well-being of the family depended entirely on its conformity to the laws of the domestic constitution.

Antediluvian history, brief and fragmentary as it is, supplies a practical illustration and confirmation of the law now under consideration. The first sin, as we have just observed, however numerous the respects in which it was unique and stood alone, had this, in common with every other subsequent transgression—that, by resisting the supremacy of law, it set an example of insubordination, and invited or dared the infliction of the threatened penalty. To have withheld that infliction, therefore, would have been to trifle with the sanction of the law, as the sinner had trifled with the law itself.

Illustrated from antediluvian history.

When, after the lapse of years, that seed of sin had brought forth fruit unto death in the first family, the Lord said to the murderer, "Why art thou wroth, and why is thou countenance fallen? If thou doest well, shalt thou not *be accepted?* and if thou doest not well, sin lieth at thy door."* This, evidently was not addressed to Him as a new revelation. The interrogatory form in which it was put to him, intimates

* Gen. iv. 6, 7.

that the principles involved in it were familiarly known and admitted. From which we are to infer that man had never found himself otherwise than under law; that obedience had been uniformly followed by happiness, disobedience by punishment. So that Cain, if he complained at all, could only complain that he was not allowed to form an exception, that the moral government of the individual and the family was not repealed, and repealed for no other reason than because he had chosen to rebel against it. On the other hand, his victim had "obtained witness that he was righteous, God testifying of his gifts."* Obedience to parental direction, and "faith" in Divine appointments, had led Abel to the altar of sacrifice in the exercise of penitence and holy trust. The spirit of the family constitution in its highest aim, had been honored, and the worshiper accepted; and now, though he had died a violent death, he had ascended to another domain of the Divine government, where obedience and happiness are one; while the fratricide was left to groan under the consciousness of his guilt, and, by presenting to the eyes of his own descendants a living monument of the Divine displeasure, to remind them that they were the subjects, too, of moral government. The inspired narrative now becomes deeply interesting. An account is given of the posterity of Cain, ending with Lamech. Of him it is stated that he was a polygamist; and it is implied that his polygamy was, in some way, associated with violence and bloodshed. From these hints it may be inferred that the family economy was no longer answering its moral design in the line of Cain, but was subverted and disorganized in some of its most important laws. The narrative then introduces an account

* Heb. xi. 5.

of the posterity of Seth, whose name is supposed to denote that he was regarded as the substitute for the martyred Abel, and who probably copied his pious example. Up to a certain point in this line, the domestic institution appears to have answered, in some degree, its important end. But "it came to pass, when men began to multiply on the face of the earth, and daughters were born unto them, that the sons of God* saw the daughters of men that they were fair, and they took them wives of all which they chose."† At this period, and in this manner, the family disorganization and open apostacy from God, which had hitherto been confined to the descendants of Cain, began to gain ground among the posterity of Seth. Family after family was founded in filial insubordination and disregard of the law of God. What could be expected to result from connections which were thus based in self-will and revolt, but a

* The phrase "sons of God" has received three very different interpretations: a *mythologic*, denoting super-terrestial beings; a *metaphoric*, denoting men of distinguished power; and a *moral*, denoting religious charactèr and affinity. The first comes from the Alexandrian Gnostics and Cabbalistic Rabbins, and is acceptable to those only who are eager to throw suspicion on Scripture, or who find a pleasure in writing or reading of "the loves of the angels." Our text contains no trace of such an idea. The second interpretation would not be incompatible with the context, but the article before the name of God denotes that the Being intended is κατ ἐξοχήν, God, the one true God, leaving it to be inferred that those also who are here called his sons are truly, that is morally, such. So that we are shut up to the third or moral interpretation of the phrase. And this, in addition to the reason last assigned, is in accordance with the *usus loquendi* of Scripture, and best suits the strain of the context. The progeny of Seth, the great religious party, by intermarrying with the irreligious, brought on a moral crisis of the most depraving nature, by confirming and extending the general apostacy.

† Gen. vi. 1, 2.

progeny of evil? The offspring of such marriages, might, indeed, be physically vigorous and strong. For, true to the constitution of nature, the physical laws would hold on their way, irrespective of character and motives, till the absence of moral restraint proclaimed itself in the degenerating effects of a self-destroying profligacy. Accordingly, "when the sons of God came in unto the daughters of men, and they bare children to them, the same became mighty men who were of old, men of renown"*—notorious for deeds of prowess, oppression, and blood. The constitution which had been calculated to produce "a godly seed," became the occasion of generating "a seed of evil-doers." For when once the highest authority is cast off, there is no resting-place short of the lowest resource—the iron hand of physical force.

Even to the last, however, one family remained in which there prevailed a regard for the laws and objects of the domestic constitution. "Noah was a just man, and perfect in his generations, and Noah walked with God."† That all his sons were not strictly virtuous, the conduct of one of them subsequent to the deluge, sufficiently proved. Still, the Patriarch had set them an example of reverence for God and obedience to His will, which brought with it a rich reward. For example: when it is said of the self-willed and irreligious, that "they took them wives of all which they chose," we are, probably, to infer, not only that they made their choice in obedience to their sensual desires, but also that they disdained the limitation of one woman to one man. Noah had been governed by this divine limitation; and he enjoyed the gratification of seeing each of his three sons act in obedience to the same law.

* Gen. vi. 4. † Gen. vi. 9.

"Moved with fear," he had obeyed the Divine command to build an ark; and though his obedience exposed him probably to the taunts of the ungodly, the event proved that his family had sympathized with his reverence for the word of God. And "Noah found grace in the eyes of the Lord." And the effect of the grace which he found was shared by his children. And often, may we suppose, when the dreadful catastrophe had taken place, and the spared family was floating solitarily and securely in the ark, would they gratefully recall their family obligations, and trace their well-being to the grace which had led them to regard it as a Divine institution.

CHAPTER XI.

THE ORDER OF THE LAWS OF THE FAMILY CONSTITUTION IMPLIED IN ITS WELL-BEING.

The law of order; We have seen that man, as a member of that peculiar constitution, a family, is an all-related being in an all-related system. According to another principle, we expect to find that every law and obligation of the domestic constitution comes into operation on the individual subjected to it, according to its priority of date in the great scheme of creation and providence.

In the conjugal union; The order prescribed by nature in the formation of a family is that of puberty or sexual maturity, love, marriage; an order never reversed with impunity.

In the formation of the family; The welfare of the wedded pair requires that provision be made first for their *physical* well-being. Although the ultimate end of the institution is of a moral nature, yet a tent must be provided before an altar, and in order to it. In other words, physical laws must be first satisfied, with a view to the observance of other and higher laws.

And in its physical well-being. The husband and wife may be eminently virtuous, and desirous of rearing a virtuous offspring; but their character and desires do not exempt them from the *orderly* operation of law. A succession of physical laws must first be satisfied, in order that children may be born to them; and other laws, in order that the children born may live; and others, that if they live they may be free from deformity and disease, so as to be capable of parental training; and others still, that they may not be deficient in those intellectual and moral qualities the absence of which would tend to frustrate the best parental endeavors.

However earnest the parents may be to honor the Divine appointments in every event dependent on their will, the involuntary laws of nature proclaim their distinctness from the voluntary laws, and their independence of them, by the constancy of their operation. They know no Sabbath. Even the day after the Adamic creation was completed, the first Sabbath exhibited no pause nor abatement of their universal activity. And, doubtless, on the last Sabbath prior to the deluge, the laws of birth made many a parent "rejoice for joy that a man-child was born into the world."

Parental love begins in instinct.

The virtuous parent loves and provides for his children from high moral considerations; he is bound to do so. But parental love is, in its origin, only an instinct belonging to the animal as well as to the man, and is quite irrespective of moral considerations. As distinguished from this mere impulse, parental affection begins where that of the animal terminates. It is a graft on it; a growth of slow and steady progress, the result of numerous influences and motives of a subsequent date. And as the instinctive impulse is the first to appear, so it is the last to expire. For even when every moral consideration has ceased to operate, this natural instinct will still inhere and evince its inextinguishable strength. But how it can be regarded in such a case, as it often is, as a redeeming quality of human nature, it is difficult to see. Its presence merely indicates that the man has not sunk *below* the brute.

Conjugal precedence.

According to the arrangement of the Divine Creator, the man was not made for the woman, but the woman for the man. As persons, their rights are equal; but in the constitution of the family "the head of the woman is the man." * He is the fountain of domestic authority. Whatever the governing influence exercised by the mother may be, it presupposes the prior authority of the husband, is derived from it, and should be supported by it.

The parts of the human constitution appear successively.

Anxious as the parents may be to complete the education of the child at an early period, the Creator has prescribed the order of development of the several parts of its constitution; nor can this order be ever violated without incurring corresponding penalties. Physical nourishment and vigor lie at the basis of the whole. However early the pruning and training of the young tree may begin, it is supposed to be already well set in the soil. If the "seeds have not much earth, they may forthwith spring up, *because* they have no deepness of earth; but when the sun is up, having no root, they will wither away."

It appears to be a misconstruction of this order which leads some to contend that, in seeking to reclaim the savage, he must invariably be civilized before he is Christianized; reclaimed physically before, and in order to, his being reclaimed morally. The mistake arises from confounding to-

* 1 Cor. xi. 3.

gether the different parts of the human constitution considered as co-existent and as successively existent. In the child they can be cultivated only as they begin physically and successively to exist. In the adult savage, they are all potentially present. If, indeed, he were hungry, food must be given him before he could be expected to profit by any moral appeals. But difficulty of obtaining food is no more a question of barbarism than it is of civilization. He is supposed to be simply insensible to his degraded condition, bodily, social and moral. And experience has shown that, as his moral condition is the worst, so in the ordinary degrees of barbarism, it is that part in which he is most accessible to appeals;* and that when once his attention is aroused to that, he awakens to the perception of his bodily and social degradation.

Which part to be first trained.

But nourishment is not training; and though the bodily wants of the infant are the first to be supplied, the *affections* are the first to be cultivated. But this primary training of the heart may, and should be, commenced, by the very manner in which its physical wants are attended to. "In the very exercise of the superior faculties, the inferior are indirectly acquiring a habit of restraint and regulation." This moral culture is the loosening and fertilizing of the soil in prospect of the intellectual sowing. Good habits prepare the way for good reasoning. Such habits, all rooted in love, are the child's ethics; and "I could almost say that *ethics* is the best logic." Now, for such moral training there is but one period; and that begins with the earliest infancy. Then, the child's love of its mother is religion; and its reverence for the looks and tones of its father, morality.

* Simpson's Philosophy of Education, pp. 3, 97.

Order in which the mind unfolds. Education, then, does not begin with instruction. And with what should instruction itself begin? This question can be answered only by determining another—what are the susceptibilities or powers of the child which present themselves first for guidance? Nature herself has an order, and her order must be adhered to. The child at first simply *perceives;* the faculty is passive. But though it is little more than a ready recipient of impressions from without, each impression evolves much more from within than it communicates. And all that can be done, at first, is to protect this process of happy and spontaneous evolution from disturbance, and to regulate it by the presence of objects few, simple, and of a nature to delight. Perception is followed by *observation*, which includes a degree of attention. The young mind directs itself to one object in preference to another. It derives more than mere impressions from external objects; spontaneously it compares and combines them. Then follows the power of *reflection*, by which the mind, revisited by thoughts of absent objects, recognizes and revolves them. A sense of *analogy* now begins to evolve; things are classed and placed according to certain relations; and *memory* comes into play, whose first and last want is order. The *reasoning* faculty, involving the power of *abstraction*, follows; and *imagination*, employing, consecrating, and towering above them all.*

It is not to be supposed that these faculties make their appearance in regular succession, as children may be required to enter a parlor according to their ages. In this respect, nature is no martinet. Powers and susceptibilities,

* Hints on the cultivation of these powers are given in the Chapter on Obligation.

in early life, are of very unequal growth in different minds. Education, according to the faculties, once almost entirely neglected, has, in some modern systems, been pushed to excess. That things should, to a certain extent, precede words; and the pronunciation precede the spelling; that learning by heart before the child understands is not so sensible a plan as helping it to understand first; that the knowing faculties precede the reflective; and that sentiment anticipates reason;—these are rough facts to be generally acted on. But the Pestalozzian system, with many advantages, appears to me to call for an order too rigorous and refined for general use. The great thing for the parent or teacher to do is, to know distinctly the end he aims at in education; to lay down a plan for its attainment; and to be careful that his plan observes the order of nature; neither inverting nor forestalling her laws.

Filial affection rises to the love of God.

The order in which the love of the child graduates is from the stage of instinctive love to moral affection, and from this to the love of its heavenly Parent. Desirous as the parents may be to lead its affections up at once to the Creator, the previous stages of the path must first be passed through. For awhile, the maternal care is the only Providence it knows; and the father's experience a world of grand enterprise, and of power unlimited. In vain it strives to climb the height of his knowledge—his virtual omniscience; nor can it conceive of a Diviner guarantee than his promise. To see its parents bend in worship, and to hear them speak with holy awe of their Father in heaven, is itself solemn and suggestive as a ladder set up from earth to heaven. The wise discipline too which leads the parent kindly to repress its selfish desires, and constantly to aim at its moral welfare, invariably begets in return the highest order of filial love and confidence; evincing the power of the child to discriminate between instinctive and moral affection, and preparing it to embrace that Heavenly Parent of whom the earthly is but an imperfect representative. And let the parents remark that, from the moment they begin to point their child to God as an object of reverence and love, they are pursuing the certain course for augmenting its moral affection for themselves; while its intelligent love for them is a valuable means and a pledge for its ascending to the love of God.

Means of education and their order.

The means of education are threefold; example, authority, and reason. The first begins to produce its appropriate effect before the second is understood, and the exercise of the second prepares the way for the third. Not that there is a definite point of time at which the first terminates, and at which the second makes way for the third; but there is an order observed for the commencement of each, though the first co-exists with the second and the second with the third. And this order of the means by which the parent influences the child only corresponds with the threefold capability of the child to be influenced. Thus, answering to the involuntary effect of parental *example*, is the instinctive power of infantine *imitation*. The *authority* of the parent is met on the part of the child by a disposition to believe and obey *because* it is the parent who *testifies* and *commands*. And the *reasoning* of the parent is responded to by the *intelligence* of the child, enabling it to appreciate the grounds which recommend and enforce the claims of truth and of virtue, independently of parental example and authority. Similarly, in the means of teaching, pictures precede lessons, and lessons, logic. And, on the part of the taught, the involuntary admiration of the first, is followed by voluntary attention to the second; and this again, by the comprehension and approval of the third. The process becomes, at each step, increasingly subjective.

Order of social development.

Regarding man as a social being, it will be found that his desires precede his dispositions; his inclination to appropriate, that is, exists before his readiness to distribute. Even when he comes to distribute that which he had previously appropriated, increasing his enjoyment by participation, present gratification precedes all regard for the future. Improvidence is one of the last evils which disappears as social man ascends the scale of improvement. The disposition to appropriate for the family precedes the readiness to distribute more generally; in other words, the proprietary or possessory feelings precede that sense of justice which prompts a man to treat others as he expects to be treated by them. Indeed, in every respect, the laws of relation between different families suppose the prior relations of each distinct family, just as those again presuppose the laws of relation in the *individual* constitution. From which it is to be inferred that any scheme designed to affect and improve the character of families must depend for success on its affecting each member of which the little community is composed; the change and improvement must begin with the individual.

Importance of observing that order itself is a law.

Order, then, is itself a law. So that if the well-being of an individual, or of a family, depends on obedience to laws, this law of order must be obeyed also. Indeed, it will be found that when men have at length come to attempt something for the improvement of themselves or others, the failure which often ensues commonly arises from their disregard of the order in which it should be done. They seem to imagine, first, that provided something be done having a tendency to improve, it matters little what it is; or, secondly, that if it be important to select the right thing, the order and the manner of doing it are quite immaterial. A discussion on this point is, in their view, mere trifling, and argues a want of heartiness and earnestness in the object. When the derangement in a piece of machinery is to be remedied, they would deem the mechanist mad who did not feel that every thing depended on the proportion, the disposition of parts, the relative arrangement of the whole; but when man's disorders are to be remedied—man's, whose constitution includes all laws, physical, intellectual, social, and moral, they are ready to deem him mad who thinks any thing respecting the orderly application of the remedy. They wonder, indeed, afterward at the failure. In the case of the machinery they would deem failure, from a corresponding cause, inevitable; would patiently show that a single error in an early part of the process becomes ten by the close. And they forget that man is meant to be no exception to the law of order, but its grand exemplification.

CHAPTER XII.

THE SUBORDINATION IMPLIED IN THE ORDER AND WELL-BEING OF THE DOMESTIC CONSTITUTION.

The law stated.

"EVERY law subordinate in rank, though it may have been prior in its origin, is subject to each higher object or law of creation." This is only saying, in effect, that in no case are the means put in the place of the end.

Of this law we found numerous illustrations in our consideration of individual man. We saw it, for example, in the subordination of the kingdoms of nature to man's authority; in the subjection of his appetites to self-love; of self-love to his affections; and of these three to his sense of duty: while each of these were found to have its own class of objects ranking according to its importance.

The filial yields to the conjugal.

In the formation of the family, the relation of parent and child yields to the subsequent relation of husband and wife. Tender and absorbing as the connection of mother and daughter may have been, a period arrives in which it must hold a secondary place. Not that filial ties and duties cease in consequence of the new relation. They remain in some respects unchanged; nor should the marriage contract ever be so interpreted as to violate them.* But the new relation becomes para-

* Wayland's Moral Science, p. 308.

mount, and the prior relation subordinate.* "Therefore shall a man leave his father and his mother, and shall cleave unto his wife, and they shall be one flesh."† The two relations, the filial and the conjugal, are intended to exist in the harmony of subordination.

The instinctive subordinated to the moral.

All the prior instincts and affections which man shares with the animal world are brought into the family circle to be subordinated to a high moral end. The laws of the domestic constitution do not exist as a mob, but as a well-ordered hierarchy. And as in the individual man conscience is sovereign *de jure*, so in the family a religious power is to sway the whole. It is an institution for the service of God. Every thing in it exists as a means to this end. In fact and practice, indeed, it may exist for a time, at least, for almost any end but this —for mere sensuous and temporal purposes. But in proof of its supreme religious design, it is only necessary to remember that even all the subordinate ends attainable by the family are best secured by placing the whole in homage to the throne of religion.

Family based on subordination.

The constitution of the family is based on the principle of subordination. The little

When first she wears her orange-flower . . . .

And doubtful joys the father move,
And tears are on the mother's face,
As parting with a long embrace
She enters other realms of love;

Her office there to rear, to teach,
Becoming as is meet and fit
A link among the days, to knit
The generations each with each.

Tennyson's *In Memoriam*, xxxix.

† Genesis, ii. 24.

society could not exist without it. The man, as husband and father, holds all under God, and represents Him. The woman, as wife and mother, holds all under her husband, and represents him. By standing in a line with his authority, she presents to the eyes of the children the image of his power invested with the light of her own love. The children, again, hold all from their parents, to whom, for a time, they look up to as the only objects of reverent affection they know. Obedience—the affectionate subordination of the filial will to the parental—is as essential to the harmony and development of the child's own internal being as to the harmony and well-being of the family; and, for a time, it is the only image which can be given of obedience to God. The children themselves stand in a line of subordination. It is this which makes the family a school of self-discipline. Here the first sacrifice of self is made to others on the altar of love. Here restraint is first imposed, and accepted as guidance. Here the will finds its highest freedom in obedience, because it chooses to obey. A family thus regulated is simply attaining its own immediate ends by subordination to the great end.

Nature subordinated to the supernatural.

The ancient material economy has been shown to be subservient to the Divine end of the dispensation. This law received illustration in every supernatural event of that period, but preeminently in the deluge. Having already shown, in the chapter on Continuity, that such an event was not antecedently incredible, I shall here limit myself to two remarks. First, that the subordination in question is only in harmony with a general law. Inorganic nature had been taken up into organic life, and mere organic life had been given up to the uses of animal life. Man himself, made of the dust of the earth, is the standing miracle of nature. Invested with universal dominion, he is constantly occupied in subjecting every thing around him to his free-will. The subjection, indeed, can take place only in harmony with the nature of the things acted upon; but the ends proposed, and the directness of his action for their attainment, are preternatural. And every instance in which man controlled and employed the elements and forces of nature to his own free ends, was a foreshadowing of the occurrence of a deluge, or of any other subordination of nature which the Creator might deem conducive to the attainment of His ends.

Secondly, the belief in the uniformity of the course of nature yields to the appropriate evidence of Divine intervention. That nature has a course or constitution is presupposed; for, apart from such uniformity, no evidence could prove such a departure from regularity as comes under the denomination of a miracle. When, therefore, the Divine intimation was made, by Noah, that the destruction of the world impended, the truth of the prophecy was simply and properly a question of evidence. The objection that "all things continue as they were from the beginning of the creation"—the objection which will be alleged, according to St. Peter, against the prediction of another destruction, "in the last days"—was perfectly irrelevant. It was, indeed, perfectly illogical, also untrue. It was *illogical;* for what, if the laws of the system had never been interrupted during the whole range of human experience, was that a demonstration that they never would be?* But the objection is *untrue;* for while, on the small scale of two or three thousand years, no grand

* See page 172.

interference with the course of nature had taken place; subsequent discoveries demonstrate that on the vaster scale of thousands of cycles, many such an interference had been repeated—that periodic change is a law of nature circumscribing the other law of intervals of regularity and apparent repose. But the point to be here considered is, we repeat, that the objection is *irrelevant*—the truth of the prophecy requiring to be tried, not by analogical presumptions, but by the laws of evidence. Was it adequately supported by proof? That it could be so substantiated is only saying that the law of testimony is itself one of the laws of nature; and that, like any other law, it is capable of verification; and that, if it be so verified, man is made to believe it, whatever the subject of the evidence may be, is only saying that the law of testimony and the law of belief correspond with each other, both being parts of the great system. Indeed, it is only saying that man is related to the universe; that he has the power of believing beyond his experience, for the same reason that he has the power of believing at all; and, therefore, that the evidence of the ordinary course of nature yields to the superior evidence of the intervention of a new cause. "By faith, Noah, being warned of God, of things not seen as yet, moved with fear, prepared an ark to the saving of his house; by the which he condemned the world, and became heir of the righteousness which is by faith." His prior experience of the regularity of nature yielded to a higher law of his own mind, and of the Divine procedure.

The past subserves the present.

Every past period of the family economy was meant to be subservient to every successive generation. Then, as now, every present age was of greater importance than any past, not only numerically, but also as inheriting its knowledge, as occupying an advanced post in the march of humanity, and as enjoying enlarged relations and means of influence on all the future. Accordingly, the Law of Paradise yielded in importance to the Promise and Sacrifice of the new economy. The first dispensation stood as a frontispiece to the second. Each age as it arrived and passed away became the end of the one preceding, and a means in relation to the next. In this sense it is that the antiquity of the world is its childhood. The relations and obligations of each succeeding family and generation surpassed in number and importance those of every previous period. So that the age cotemporary with Noah ought to have inherited more of every element of progress from the age immediately prior than from any other, as well as to have communicated more to posterity.

CHAPTER XIII.

THE LAW OF INFLUENCE IMPLIED IN THE ORDER, WELL-BEING, AND DESIGN OF THE FAMILY CONSTITUTION.

Law of influence.

THE law of influence may be thus expressed: every thing in the family sustains a relation, and possesses a right, in the great system of means, according to its power of subserving the end; or every thing brings in and with it, in its own capability of subserving the end, a reason why all other things should be influenced by it, the degree in which they should be influenced, and the degree in which it, in its turn, should be influenced by every thing else. For if every created thing necessarily expresses some property of the Divine nature; if it possesses that resemblance on the condition of manifesting it in subserviency to the great end, and is placed in a system of relations in order that it might be able to make the manifestation, then every thing in the family will sustain an active and a passive relation, or will have a right to influence every thing of inferior, and a susceptibility of being influenced by every thing of superior, subserviency to the great end.

In the conjugal union.

In the pre-existing kingdoms of nature, and in the human constitution, this law universally prevails.* The family may be expected, on the

* Man Primeval, c. ix. pp. 242, 243.

ground stated, to illustrate it still further. Accordingly—beginning with its internal relations—"marriage is a contract between a man and a woman by which each receives a right in the person of the other, which right is conferred for their mutual happiness, and for the production and education of children,"* in subserviency to the ultimate end of creation. Every violation of the law of chastity, on the part of the husband, is an infringement of the right of the wife, and *vice versâ*.

Supremacy of the husband.

On the ground of this law it is that the husband is made the head of the wife, and of the domestic society. It is a Divine arrangement which recognizes, not, indeed, any abstract superiority of nature, but the fact that he possesses certain qualities and facilities for his office which the wife does not possess. He has a right, therefore, to expect her affectionate submission and obedience as a wife. On the other hand, she has a right to expect that he will not use his authority unjustly or unkindly, but purely for the good of the family constitution; that her yielding shall be rewarded with love, and with the recognition of that element of superior virtue which it includes, and which the exercise of authority does not include; and that it be not expected to extend to the sacrifice of any of those moral relations and obligations which render her a person, and which give her the rights of a person. In a word, she has a right to all the influence necessary to the well-being of the domestic constitution; and this is second only to that of the husband. How wise and benevolent is that arrangement by which his exercise of authority, and her subordination, become an occasion for the love, the improvement, and the happiness of each;

* Lectures on Paley, for the Use of Students in the University, § 4.

and by which her weakness and exposure find protection and respect in the very law which might have been made the means of her oppression and degradation. Her affectionate subordination alone can secure her rights; and these alone can secure her from degradation and wrong.

The rights of parents.

The rights of the parent;—these, of course, are commensurate with his obligations. If he be under obligation to train up his children in such a manner as to secure their own happiness, the good of society, and the end of existence, he has a right to employ all the means requisite for the attainment of this end. Nor is any individual or society entitled to interfere with his rights, provided he restrict himself to these limits.

When speaking of the parent's obligations, we saw that he is bound to discharge his duties in a manner suited to the advancing character of his child. He has a right, therefore, to vary his method of training the child, for the same reason that he is invested with any parental rights at all. During its infancy, his authority over it is absolute. As it advances in knowledge, and reason, and in moral qualities, he has a right to relax the reins of authority, and to commit it more and more to its own self-government. And in proportion as he discharges his duty from a regard to the will of God, he has a right to expect the love, obedience, and reverence of his child. Indeed, if the parent were to train up his child, in every respect, in the way that he should go, he would have a right to expect that when he became old he would not depart from it. Accordingly, the declaration of Scripture to this effect is not a temporary promise, but a statement of one of the great laws of the family constitution. And thus it admirably comes to pass, that the very point of time at which the ever-diminishing rights of the parent to *control* his child has reached its minimum is the moment when the child passes over into the hands of God, and becomes, by the habits of virtue in which he has been trained, a free and an obedient subject of the Divine Government.

In the power of the various kinds of parental influence.

Further, it may be expected that if the various means which the parents employ are not of precisely equal value, each will bring in it, and with it, in its own capability of subserving the end, a reason why and in what degree it shall influence, and be influenced in return. Accordingly, if the means by which youthful character is influenced and formed be authority, reason, example, and prayer, it will be found that mere *authority* exercises the lowest degree of influence in this respect—that *reason*, as it comes from a deeper source in human nature, being the addition of the intellect to the will, so it goes deeper into the nature of the child, carrying along with it his judgment or rational powers—that *example* penetrates deeper still,* for besides the will and the intellect, it includes the practice, implying that the authority of conscience is superadded, and thus enlisting on his side the moral affection, admiration, and sympathy, of the child; while *prayer*—besides presupposing that the will, the intellect, and the conscience are already engaged, and are manifesting themselves in authority, reason, and example—evinces his high and holy determination to call in a power beyond his own, to enlist on his side an agency which has access to all the springs and principles of human nature, and thus to engage the youthful character to seek its formation in the hand of God. Now, all this the parent has a right to expect;—for it is only saying, that if he

* Hence the Latin proverb, *Precepta ducunt, at exempla trahunt.*

is held responsible for the attainment of a certain end, he is entitled to expect that the means with which he is intrusted will prove successful in proportion as he employs them.

The inferior influences the superior.

As every thing brings in it, and with it, in its own capability of subserving the end, a reason why all other things should be influenced by it, and the degree in which they should be influenced, so it may be expected that the right reception of parental influence on the part of the children would react beneficially on the character of the parent. For as "there is nothing so little which in its kind is not endowed with some reality which the beings of a more exalted constitution do not possess so precisely, or in the same manner, and upon the same account, therefore, the least things strive to imprint upon the greatest their realities and signature; because, little as they are, they still represent God as good and communicative." * And nowhere is the law more strongly illustrated than in the reaction of children on the character of their parents. The cedar-wood sheds its fragrance on the hand which carves it. True, the child may act involuntarily on the parent, while the influence of the parent is, to a considerable extent, exercised intelligently and with design. But not the less true is it that the parent is benefited; the helplessness of the child appealing to his tenderness, its obedience tending to prevent an abuse of the authority obeyed, its implied faith operating as a salutary check on his testimony, its efforts to understand improving his own powers of reasoning, its imitation of his example rendering him at once more affectionate and more circumspect, and its opening piety proving both the reward and incentive of his piety.

* Pierre Poiret's Economie Divine, ou Système Universel, vol. i. c. 7.

The family a school of excellence.

So that, by the operation of this law, the family is constituted a school of excellence in which, by the constant action and reaction of each upon all, every member is constantly making progress. The child, indeed, is the party chiefly benefited. "The process is in itself most useful; it is a good thing to doubt our own wisdom, it is a good thing to believe, it is a good thing to admire. By continually looking upward, our minds themselves grow upward; and as a man by indulging in habits of scorn and contempt for others, is sure to descend to the level of what he despises, so the opposite habits of admiration and enthusiastic reverence for excellence impart to ourselves a portion of the qualities which we admire."* And in this way the child is constantly drawn upward by the strong attraction of superior excellence. But by the operation of the same law, the parent is benefited, and thus reaps the fruit of which he himself had sown the seed; and by the attainment of greater excellence, becomes fitted for still greater usefulness.

What the child has a right to, educationally.

The rights of *children* are commensurate with the nature and obligation of children. To say that they relate to maintenance and to the just exercise of parental authority, seems inadequate to the subject. For if every person brings with him a right according to his power of subserving the great end of existence, it follows that the child has a right to all the means possessed by the parent for the full development of every part of his nature, physical, social, intellectual, and moral; inasmuch as he possesses naturally the same power for subserving the great end which his parent, or any other human being, does, and is under obligation to that effect.

* From a Preface by Dr. Arnold, to the "Poetry of Common Life."

If he has a right to the means, it follows of course that he has a right to the time necessary for their due employment; and a right to expect, therefore, that his parents will not give that time to other objects, innocent in themselves, which is necessary for his education and well-being. On the same ground, the child has a right to follow the dictates of conscience as soon as it becomes capable of deliberate decision. To develop this capability is the very end of parental training, for it is only in proportion as he attains it that he can answer the end of his own existence, or that of the family constitution; to interfere with it, therefore, in any other way than by aiming to supply him with further instruction, is to defeat the very end of education and of existence. Now, all these rights are essential to the well-being of the family, and to the end of its existence.

Rights external to the family.

If every one sustains a relation, and possesses a right, in the great system of means, according to his power of subserving the end, it follows that the rights of every man are equal, for every man possesses the same constitution for the very purpose of answering that end. Inequality of *condition* is not the point at issue. The question is, whether one man has not the same right to use his inferior strength, if he can use it justly, which another man has to employ his superior strength. If he have not, it can be owing only to its inferiority, and then the question of universal right becomes one of physical might, and earth a scene of muscular conflict. From the mere absurdity of the converse, then, it follows that the relation of every man to every other is that of an equality of right, and this alone can place him on a common basis of responsibility in reference to the great end.

According to the operation of this law, therefore, every

man has a right to enter into the marriage relation, provided he contracts it in a manner which does not interfere with the right of any other man. For as the great process of individual happiness, social well-being, and Divine manifestation, is made dependent on the family constitution, he, as a member of the human family, has an equal right with every other member on the condition supposed, to enter into the relations of the family, in order to the attainment of these ends.

Family rights.

If every man has a right, in relation to his fellows, to live for the same end as every other man, he has an equal right with them to the means. And for the same reason that every individual man possesses this right, every family possesses it also. Whatever means its members can acquire by labor, or purchase by wealth, or attain by superior knowledge or virtue, without any infringement of the rights of others, belong to them for the same reason that existence belongs to them; for it is only by the recognition of this right that the end of existence can be answered. For the same reason, they have a right to do all the good they can to the members of other families, provided they seek their advantage without any violation of their rights, or of the rights of any other parties; for it is only in this way that, besides answering the end of their own existence, they can enable others to do the same, and thus carry on the great process.

The best family the most influential.

It is easy to see how, by the operation of this law, the best family would come to exercise the greatest amount of moral influence over other well-ordered families. By strictly observing the law of reciprocity—or respecting the rights of others—it would come to be honored by others for its high sense of justice. And if to these duties of perfect obligation, it added those of imperfect obligation, or lived in the exercise of true benevolence—regarding itself only as a channel of good to others—it would be honored still more. Even the irreligious, while hating it with one part of their nature, would tacitly approve and applaud it with another. The approach which it would make to the character and conduct of the Divine Being would invest it with a measure of Divine influence. By the very superiority of its excellence, it would contain within itself a reason why all other families should be influenced by it, and assimilated to it. And then it would evince its high subserviency to answer the great end of the domestic constitution, by drawing other families within the attraction of its influence, and rendering them capable of subserving it also. The unobstructed operation of this law is essential, then, in order that God may not be defrauded of His right, or may behold the manifestation of his all-sufficiency to the utmost degree to which the domestic economy is capable of exhibiting it.

The great distinction of antediluvian times.

Accordingly, it was in harmony with this law that the Divine distinctions of the antediluvian Patriarchy were awarded. The rejection of Cain and the acceptance of Abel was a rehearsal, in the morning of time, of the final judgment. "This (says F. von Schlegel) is the leading subject of primitive history—the struggle between two races—the first great event in universal history. This original contest and opposition among men, according to the twofold direction of the will—a will conformable to that of God, and a will carnal, ambitious, and enslaved to nature—often recurs, though on a lesser scale, in later history; or at least we can perceive something like a feeble reflection, or a distant echo of this primal discord."* It commenced the grand classification of mankind; and implied that all other distinctions are to be merged in the two great classes of the obedient and the disobedient. In passing by all inferior piety, and assigning to Enoch the new honor of translation, it was implied that piety itself admits of distribution, or forms a hierarchy; and that its highest awards are reserved for the highest order. While, in the person of Noah, distinguished excellence was crowned by the Divine hand for all after time. Character calculated to exercise the greatest influence on earth, was proved to exercise it in heaven, by the signal manner in which it was reinforced from thence. To him that hath shall be given. The owner of the ten talents is he who is made the ruler of ten cities.

* The Philosophy of History, vol. i. § 2.

CHAPTER XIV.

DEPENDENCE OF THE FAMILY CONSTITUTION, AND OF THE REMEDIAL SYSTEM WHICH UNDERLIES IT, ON THE GOOD PLEASURE OF GOD.

Law of dependence.

In a preceding chapter we have glanced at certain respects in which family well-being was dependent on man himself—on his obedience to law; in this, we shall specify certain facts in which the constitution of the family was entirely dependent on the will of God. Corresponding facts, already considered in the Treatises on nature and on individual man, are of course brought on into the family economy. Here, others are added to them; thus enlarging the domain of contingent truth—truth ascertainable only by observation and experience, and multiplying our illustrations of the Divine sovereignty. By this sovereignty we understand *choice* in opposition to caprice. For, doubtless, the Divine decision is regulated by reasons worthy of his infinite wisdom; and, as such, it is equally removed from caprice on the one hand, and from a blind necessity on the other.

In the relation of the sexes.

One of the first facts to strike us, as evidence of design, in looking at the family constitution, is those relative characteristics of the sexes, by which two beings—each a distinct, complete, and independent person—become the complement of each other, and mutually necessary to social progress. The diversity of relations observable between the sexes of the other species, shows that the Divine Creator has resorted to no one plan from necessity; that he has chosen a special plan for each of his special purposes; and when but a few only of the social and moral advantages arising from His human arrangements are thought of, we can not but feel that "He is wonderful in counsel, and excellent in working."*

In the mode of continuing the species.

How shall the human race be perpetuated? The first three human beings were each produced in a different manner. In the fable of Deucalion and Pyrrha,† it is suggested that each sex might have evolved a descendant like itself, and by means little dependent on its own resources. In the vegetable and animal world, the modes of reproduction are diversified without end. The human method (though common to all the species of its own class) is obviously of Divine selection and appointment. Antecedently, no method could have been imagined, which was not attended with disadvantages apparently insurmountable. In the existing arrangement, no human science can explain how it is that both sexes can proceed from the same maternal parent. One thing is certain, that the arrangement chosen secures effects the most precious to human welfare; many of which must have been lost by the adoption of any other method.

In the numerical proportion of the sexes.

Equally remarkable is the numerical proportion of the sexes. The highest interests are dependent on the preservation of this proportion; myriads of incidents are necessary to this preservation; these incidents have gone on multiplying

* Isaiah, xxviii. 29.

† Apoll. l. i. p. 23.

with every age; but still the proportion remains. As if to make its preservation still more difficult, the structure and offices of the sexes differ, and death removes each, at every various period of their earthly course; and yet the proportion continues. It is found, even, that the mortality of males exceeds that of females; but the average equality is maintained unaltered, for the difference of births is in favor of the male sex. In this constant maintenance of a particular proportion, amid fluctuations untraceable by human science, we hear Providence reporting its appointments and presence.

The possible progress of the race provided for.

The present arrangement provides for the progress of the race from age to age. The instincts, and habits, and capabilities of all the inferior animals are stationary within certain limits. The readiness of men to complain of the law by which children inherit parental deficiencies and their consequences, denotes the antecedent likelihood that they would have preferred a constitution analogous, in this respect, to that of higher animals. But, supposing the law of hereditary transmission abrogated, the improvement of the race, by human means, would be arrested. The improvement of any given generation would be limited to itself, and must die with it. But by arranging that the parent who has obeyed physical, intellectual, and moral laws, shall transmit certain qualities to his child, favorable to its development in the same respects, provision is made for the progress of the human family, not merely by the transmission of ever-accumulating stores of knowledge, but by the constitutional improvement of the individual.

Striking and unique is that arrangement by which the human offspring are retained for so long a period in a

The long retention of the child in the parental hand.

state of susceptibility and of dependence on parental care. The poet of ancient skepticism sang of this long period of infantine dependence as a state of supposed inferiority to the young of the brute creation. The Theban fable pictured men as starting full-formed from the dragon's teeth which Cadmus had sown. Our first parents actually commenced life with this fullness of power. The animal speedily attains maturity, and becomes independent of parental care. There was, then, no inherent necessity why the young of the human parent should remain so many years a babe, a child, and immature. Had the period of its dependence, however, been only as long as the brood remains with the parent bird, the endearing names of father and mother would have been empty sounds; little opportunity would have been afforded to them for the formation of its character; and one of the most pleasing illustrations of providential appointments would have been lost.

Choice of the region for antediluvian man.

Equally dependent on the sovereign will of God were the *external* relations of the family. In the preceding treatise, we saw that the earth was a specific place for a specific race; so that a very slight change in our constitution would render us unfit for it, and a slender change in its laws would make it unsuitable for us. But, besides this general adaptation, the Divine will must have selected the particular region of the earth to be occupied by antediluvian man.. Indeed, the choice of the locality of Eden determined, in a general manner, the district which would come to be gradually occupied; for Eden would be, most likely, its center. And the character of this entire region, as to the distribution of its land and water, its hills, valleys, and plains, and every thing included in its physical geography would be selected with a direct reference to the right development of the family constitution; just as the books, and exercise, and toys of the child are selected by a wise father with a studied reference to its education. At the moment when our first parents came forth to take possession of that first theater of human development, all its physical susceptibilities and influences, when brought into contact with the human mind, were divinely foreseen and determined; as well as all the changes of which they would admit from age to age. For example; if, as is probable, the vine was one of its fruit-trees, it was there by the Divine planting, as truly as the tree of the knowledge of good and evil was in Eden, or as the timber-trees of which the ark was built. And equally was it the will of God that, if the vine was cultivated, its fruit should be pleasant to the taste; and that, if taken to excess, it should intoxicate. While, the very fact that intemperance was attended with inebriety, was the mode by which the Creator indicated His will that it should not be so employed; leaving it contingent on the will of man, however, whether it should be thus abused or not. Equally dependent on the will of God was it to determine both the susceptibilities of man to external influences, and the character of the scenery, climate, and fertility of the regions destined to act on man's susceptibilities; but, at the same time, it was equally dependent on the will of man, as long as there was room for him to change his locality, in what particular district he should reside. So also the kind and the limit of the knowledge which it was possible for the antediluvians to acquire, as far as it depended on external nature, was regulated by the Divine predetermination. True it is that, even within those limits, the means of human knowledge was inexhaustible. But, still, the restriction was special; and, evidently, an object of Divine choice.

Instinctive co-operation of families.

Still more dependent on the will of God would antediluvian man perceive his condition to be, if it should appear at any given period that, without any foresight of his, all the cotemporaneous families were in a state of mutual dependence and co-operation. He could hardly practice on himself the self-deception of man in later times, and suppose that society, such as he found it, was the result of human sagacity and design. He lived too near the origin of society to indulge in such dreams. Besides which, the earth was gradually "filling with violence;" threatening to burst the natural bonds of society; so that the strength of the family instincts was the last hope of the community. It was impossible, therefore, to remark, not only that those natural ties held out against all the disorganizing forces which essayed to burst them asunder, but that, even in the worst times, they continued to produce much social enjoyment, and that they only needed to be revered in order to convert the entire population into a happy family, without feeling that it was a provision resolvable into the Divine choice.

Families united in generations.

Nor was the chain of dependence which linked the families of one generation to the generations following less obviously in the hand of God. There was a sense in which the number of families forming each generation, and the number of members in each family, as well as the amount of responsibility and influence transmitted from age to age, were subject to the Divine appointment; for they could be neither more nor less than were consistent with the attainment of the end for which the dispensation was continued. But while the maximum and minimum of these conditions were thus subject to the will of God, within these limits there was ample scope for the free agency of man to move at large and unrestrained; so that the last generation would feel as conscious of freedom as the first.

Man's recovery direct from God.

If man, having virtually denied his dependence on God, and having incurred the penalty of this breach of the primary law of his nature, should yet receive the offer of deliverance from that penalty, this, one might suppose, would render the sense of his dependence perpetual. Now such was actually his position. When, as a transgressor, he had nothing to look for from the equity of the moral governor, the rich mercy of the sovereign interposed, in a manner consistent with that equity, the means of his recovery. As his sin had consisted in the self-willed assertion of his own sufficiency, the new duties prescribed to him were specially adapted to impress him with a sense of his dependence. At the altar of sacrifice, every thing he had alienated from God was symbolically brought back. He was there reminded that he was indebted to God not only for the animal he sacrificed, but also for the continuance of his own life, which he then virtually surrendered. The promise of a Deliverer, by appealing to his voluntary belief, respected his freedom as a moral being; while, by referring its fulfillment to a future period, it kept him in a state of disciplinary dependence. Both the promise and the sacrifice proclaimed that henceforth he would be as dependent on God for well-being as he was at first for the gift of being itself. Drawing near to God, as the priest of his family, the very act memorialized him that he was indebted to benevolence both for the existence of his family relations and for the possibility of their happy existence. The worshiping family of a late period could not look back along the line of its pious ancestry without marking its dependence on the Sovereign Author of the family constitution, through which had been transmitted, from generation to generation, that sacred knowledge and influence of which it was then reaping the advantage. How marked, too, was the dependence of the faithful on the will of God, for the unexpected additions which were made from time to time to their inspired knowledge, by direct Divine communications; as well as by his seasonable interpositions for their security and well-being! And how emphatically was the dependence of the ungodly world on the long-suffering of God proclaimed, by that closing intimation that it was reprieved for a hundred and twenty years! During the hours and moments of that period, it depended, not merely from the throne of God, but over the gulf of perdition

And of a nature to teach dependence.

In these several respects, the Patriarchal constitution, viewed in its multiplied relations, internal and external, presented at any given period an aspect of dependence on God. Every thing around it bore marks of "the good pleasure of His will." Nothing was left indifferent and at large. Within the domestic circle, the wife and husband were dependent, in unnumbered respects, on each other; and the children were dependent on both, in a manner meant to serve as a perpetual memorial of the dependence of the whole upon God. They could not go forth without encountering memorials that God had written command or prohibition on every object of nature. Sights and sounds, tastes and places, were but so many tests of obedience. The rights of every other family taught them that their own rights had limits; that an adjustment even of human wills was essential to the general well-being; much more the harmony of the whole with the Supreme will. But at the altar of sacrifice the supremacy of the Divine will was recognized in the most intimate and affecting manner. Move wherever else they might, every thing was constructed to remind them that they were in the midst of a God-willed system; but, there, they came not merely to acknowledge this sovereignty, but to entreat that by the exercise of it He would, in a manner consistent with equity, forgive them for having violated His will, and would restore them to harmony with Himself again.

Primogeniture.

Now, first, the law of primogeniture—so often afterward set aside by the Divine choice of a younger son—was disparaged in the rejection of the first-born, Cain. The adoption of Abel and of Seth in his stead was the Divine inauguration of character to the highest distinctions in the kingdom of God.

Longevity.

The change in the duration of human life which took place after the flood, shows that antediluvian longevity was, directly or indirectly, determined by Divine appointment.

Period of the deluge.

The same "good pleasure," too, which selected the period for the commencement of the economy, was heard announcing the moment of its close. And as often as the patriarch appointed to build the ark looked around on his ungodly cotemporaries, how deeply would he feel their obligation to the Divine forbearance, as well as that his own sublime vocation was simply because he had "found grace in the eyes of the Lord."*

* Gen. vi. 8.

CHAPTER XV.

ULTIMATE FACTS AND NECESSARY TRUTH INVOLVED IN DEPENDENCE OF THE DOMESTIC CONSTITUTION.

Evil of disregarding the ultimate character of facts.

THE contingent points to the ultimate and the necessary. If the family be so directly dependent on the will of God, as we have shown it to be, we may expect to find that its constitution discloses certain points at which it merges in that will. Partial explanations of some of its phenomena may be possible; but, having ascended two or three steps in our genenralization, we come to a fact which contains no explanation of itself, and of which we can conceive nothing anterior, except a Divine appointment to that effect. A torpid disregard to the ultimate character of such facts, and of the originating and upholding Hand which lay behind, will account for much of the ungodliness of antediluvian times. A disposition to look only at the facts themselves, and to ascribe them to inherent forces, or to view them as self-contained and self-sufficient, characterizes much of the so-called philosophy of the present day.*

Love, the ultimate fact of the family.

The great nltimate fact of the family constitution is love. This is at once the centripetal and the centrifugal force by which all the

* Man Primeval, c. xv. pp. 312–315.

bodies of the domestic heaven are both held together in a system, and yet kept in activity and diffusion. But what is love? It beat in the first bosom, and was the earliest inspiration of poetry; the subtlest philosophy has analyzed it; age after age has celebrated it with ardor ever fresh; all apprehend it; but none can explain it. We may be told that love is an affection of the mind, excited by the perception of qualities, real or imaginary, calculated to delight. But this only and vaguely describes the nature of the occasion which awakens it. Advancing a step further, love may be represented as a compound emotion, including a vivid delight in its objeet, and a desire of good to that object. But the latter of these two elements is the result of the former; and the former is, not love itself, but only its concomitant. It is happiness to love; but in the order of nature, the act of loving must precede the pleasure we experience as flowing from it. We may be told, moreover, that love is modified according to the objects which it embraces. But who would think of describing the difference between the scent of the rose and the violet to one who had no sense of smell? and the fact that the modifications of love are distinguishable, not by any description of the variety of the feelings themselves, but by such distinctive phrases as conjugal love, parental love, and filial love, shows that the emotion of love is an original property of the mind, and as such, admits of no formal definition. The meaning of love must spontaneously arise in the mind, and the emotion itself be consciously felt, or no definition can ever originate it. Hence, he is the most popular and instructive writer on the subject, who, instead of attempting to define the indefinable, assumes the presence of the susceptibility in the general human heart, and proceeds to paint its manifestations. These are always and every where. The great genealogical tree of humanity, blossoming and bearing fruit in every age, has its root in love; but that love itself has its root in Heaven.

The family a collection of ultimate facts.

The idea of the family itself embodies and expounds itself in a number of ultimate facts. The relation of the sexes in the human kind has much in it that is special and unique. The conditions by which its social and moral improvement is secured are selected and distinctive.* The relations, conjugal, parental, and filial, which bind the family together, are of Divine institution. The advantages flowing from these relations—division of labor, reciprocal aid, and mutual sympathy—were all chosen and foreseen by a higher providence than man's. It is a common error, indeed, to ascribe to human forecast that which can have arisen only from Divine appointment. When certain social phenomena are developed, men are apt to conclude that, because they can trace them to certain principles, they have fully accounted for them. But whence the principles? Marriage, the root-principle of the family life, is implanted in humanity. Its advantages, intellectual, social, and religious, must have been seen before they could be calculated on. Man was moving toward the final ends of marriage, long before he could have been fully aware of them. When he found himself surrounded by them, reflection began to enumerate, classify, admire, and calculate on them. But as far as he has experimented on the family life, he has impaired its value, and even vainly threatened it with dissolution.

Ultimate facts of the mind.

In the corresponding chapter of the preceding treatise, we replied to the question,

* See the preceding chapter.

What is mind? And we saw that matter is only the condition and means of its manifestation. With the family these mental manifestations began to exhibit an ever-enlarging variety and diversity. And the same train of remark which led us to the conclusion that mind is a distinct entity, warrants the conviction that peculiar mental differences are original; distinct from all properties of a physiological character. Every separate mind is an ultimate fact, distinct from all similar facts, however much it may be dependent on them and influenced by them. This *influence* also of mind on mind, is itself a profound mystery. How shall a mind inclosed in matter gain access to another mind similarly inclosed, so as to mold and form it? Antecedently to experience, this might have been propounded as an insoluble problem. But even experience supplies only a practical solution. We know, as a fact, that mind affects mind, and can specify many of the means and results; but the *modus* of such spiritual action, as well as of the coalescence of one will with another without any loss of freedom, is known to the Father of Spirits alone.

Man's knowledge of God special and dependent.

The kind and degree of man's knowledge of the Divine character and will could be resolved only into "the good pleasure of God." Man's knowledge of every kind, indeed, was thus special and dependent.* The number and function of the senses and organs by which he should reach the external world; what they should find there when they had reached it; together with the laws of thought and feeling by which he, the subject, should interpret such external objects; all that should enter into his constitution, and all that should be present in nature to meet it, were things which fell

* Man Primeval, c. iv. p. 300, etc.

within the Creative choice. But when man, endowed with a corresponding power of choice, in order that, in this highest respect, he might resemble and move in a line with his Maker, chose to exercise that power for the very opposite end, his continuance and recovery were facts resolvable only into the sovereign will of God. Why was he spared? Why did he call upon God in prayer? Why was he found at the altar of sacrifice? Why did he cherish the hope of a Deliverer? He could only reply that God had so willed. From the moment of man's transgression, the Divine Being might, hypothetically speaking, have so withdrawn as to leave man's heart empty of hope, and the universe empty of every spiritual object calculated to enkindle hope. But his hope, his prayer, and his sacrifice, were only the human exponents and reflections of certain Divine facts—that he had heard God's voice in tones of compassion, had caught a glimpse of His throne as a throne of mercy, and had seen His face looking for reconciliation. These, for him, were ultimate facts. At the altar the human will coalesced with the Divine will. In prayer he left all media behind, allowed nothing to come between him and God, placed himself in intimate contact and communication with Him. While, by reposing on the great promise, he passed over, with all his most precious interests, into the Divine purpose, identifying himself with it for all the future.

Faith; the family favorable to its development.

Reminding us of that principle of faith which is an ultimate fact of the human constitution, and for the development of which the family is peculiarly favorable. When the human infant comes into the world, it resembles a temple on the day of its opening. Ten thousand objects are waiting and eager to enter, but the doors must first be thrown open. One after another they unfold, and in crowd the throngs. Day after day they repeat their visit, with multitudes of new faces added to them. At first, all are admitted without question, pass-word, or hinderance. In full faith, the soul is laid open, and the streams flow through it. After awhile, a higher order of applicants press for admission; and the young human being begins to look around for *authority*. Proof is, as yet, out of the question; the highest proof is authority, and the highest authority the parental. The example of his parents guarantees alike his belief and his conduct. His trust in them becomes obedience to their injunctions; and a sense of duty takes root. And as he perceives the same sense influencing their own conduct, and that of all around; and as he feels it blend mysteriously with certain vague and solemn intimations within him, he is gradually prepared to hear of a higher and a holier authority than that of his parents—One in whom they themselves are already confiding. With increase of age, comes the exercise of his own judgment and the demand for *evidence* to warrant his faith. He does not so much doubt as discriminate. He withholds his confidence from the wrong object, only that he may give it without reserve to the right. Every thing coming from God—when once ascertained to have come from Him—is welcomed as an angel, and trusted as an oracle. "Faith, then, overcometh the world." By faith Abel sacrifices as if no Cain stood by to disparage his offering. By faith Enoch walks with God, and is translated, as if all the world kept him company. By faith Noah, being warned of God, prepares an ark, as confidently as if all heaven had been present to aid him.

But what is faith? An analysis of its nature belongs to

a subsequent place in this series. At present, we have only to do with the fact that, whether its nature be regarded as intellectual, as emotional, or as both combined, it is a constituent and ultimate function of the human mind. Authority, evidence, trustworthiness, excellence of the highest order—these only *appeal* to our confidence. Instead of creating faith, they presuppose and seek to awaken and engage it. In the family it is elicited, cherished, and trained by a thousand selected objects; clasping each like the infant arms thrown around the maternal neck. Society is based on it, and cemented by it; so that the same antediluvian population which discredited the coming deluge on the alleged ground of insufficient evidence, were yet lavishing their confidence, in secular matters, on the slenderest testimony. The human character can not rise to its true altitude, nor bear its noblest fruits, except as its faith embraces God. This consecrates the entire temple, and fills it with worship. Faith, in its highest form, is the repose alike of the intellect and of the affections.

Necessary truths.

From these ultimate facts we ascend to the necessary truths on which they repose, and in which they have their ground; from the contingent expressions of the Divine will to the Infinite nature of which that will itself is the expression. Considered as mere phenomena, the existence of all the objects and events in the created universe is entirely contingent on the sovereign will of God. Those of them which must be regarded as ultimate facts are contingently necessary; necessary on the supposition of the phenomena being called into existence, but only on that supposition—while these ultimate facts themselves presuppose truths, or principles, which are purely and absolutely necessary.*

* Man Primeval, c. xvi.

Essential distinction between love and hatred.

We have spoken of love as the ultimate fact of the family constitution; a fact which presupposes not merely the inherent excellence of love, but the necessary and eternal distinction between it and hatred. The two can not be commuted. But the existence of the distinction depends not on the ability of any created being to conceive of it. From eternity it had existed, in the only mode in which a truth can be said to be eternal, in the Eternal Mind; and, like the Supreme Intelligence, it is indestructible and unchangeable. Accordingly, it may be remarked, in passing, that in the economy of the family was seen the first beaming of a truth which went on receiving illustration, and filling our horizon with light, till it was announced in the sublime aphorism, "God is Love."

Obligations arising from relations necessary.

The obligations of the family economy rest on the same background of necessary truth. The relations which bind the family together—conjugal, parental, and filial—are contingent on the good pleasure of him who made us. But having constituted the relations, he could not but require the conduct appropriate to them. He was under no obligation to set up the family constitution; but, having done so, it was no longer optional whether or not he should enjoin the resulting duties. "He can not deny himself." * "Children obey your parents in the Lord, for this is right;" † right, whether verbally enjoined or not, inherently and essentially right. There is a harmony between the relations and the duties, not depending on our perception of it—that would make our perceptions the rule if not the ground of obligation—but perceived by the perfect intellect of God himself, a harmony

* 2 Tim. ii. 13. † Eph. vi. 1.

not depending on any outward realization, but having an *à priori* existence of its own. Having been pleased, however, to constitute the relations, He can not but call for the dispositions and conduct which harmonize with them.

Man acts on beliefs before he accounts for them.

There is no branch of human knowledge or activity, which, if generalized to the utmost, does not bring us into the presence of some fundamental and necessary truth. The laws of forces, as exhibited in the material universe, rest on the conception of causation or power. The subject of government leads directly to the primary idea of right or justice. All æsthetic creations presuppose an archetype of order, harmony, fitness, and beauty; point to the idea of perfection. As we know not, however, how far such ideas had worked themselves clear in the human mind prior to the flood; and as we know little even of man's conduct in relation to them at that time, compared with what history records of after-times, we, for the present, reserve the subject. Doubtless, they were all vaguely present to him, as occasion arose, from the first. Even the family obligations, just referred to, involved conceptions of duty and destiny, in which he confided, quite irrespective of any reasoning on the subject. Man acts on certain shadowy beliefs and ideas, long before he can verify them by any philosophical deduction. They lie like the unfolded flower beneath the lake; or like the man's thoughts, dimly and darkly, in the infant's brain. It was not till the dialogue of the mind with itself had commenced, that man began consciously to recognize their presence. "The Greek tongue was for a long period destitute of any word to denote *consciousness;* and it was only after both the philosophy and language of Greece had passed their prime, that the terms συναισθάνομαι and συναίσθησις were applied not merely to denote the apperception of sense, but the primary condition of knowledge in general."* These are subjects which constitute the mountain-tops of truth—the last to be free from mist.

Man's redemption the expression of an eternal attribute.

Similarly, the grand aspect of the Divine character which throws forward its first outline in the promise of deliverance and the institution of sacrifice, long remained in comparative shadow. It was not till "the fullness of the times was come," that even the pen of inspiration announced clearly that the real victim had been "verily foreordained before the foundation of the world."† Not that the recovery of man was an absolute necessity for God any more than his creation; but the attribute of holy love in the Divine character which led to his recovery (but which might have adopted other forms of manifestation), was necessary. And now first the Perfection which chose to illustrate itself in our recovery, and which, having so chose, could not but adopt the method most worthy of itself, began to loom from the eternal past, and to make itself dimly present. And, doubtless, the faith of many a holy Patriarch "saw it afar off, and was persuaded of it, and embraced it."

* Sir W. Hamilton's Reid, p. 757.

† 1 Peter, i. 20.

CHAPTER XVI.

THE CONSTITUTION OF THE FAMILY AND OF THE MEANS OF MERCY IN ANALOGY WITH EVERY PRECEDING PART OF THE DIVINE CONDUCT.

In the evolution of a system of Divine manifestation it may be expected that every part will be in harmony with every other part. For if the whole is to be, in some respect, an analogue of the Divine Being, every separate portion of it must be similarly related to every other part, otherwise the whole will not resemble Him.

The family economy arranged on a plan.

Now that the family economy is arranged on a plan is apparent from such considerations as the following, some of which have been discussed already: From the numerical proportion of the sexes. From the fact that the characteristic difference of the sexes are relative to each other. From that principle of love by which the characters of the husband and the wife become assimilated, and their happiness doubled by participation; while the authority of the one becomes an occasion for the increased affection of both. From the relative character of their respective spheres; each supposing and completing the other. From the fact that the children are, in a substantial sense, multiplications of the parents; begotten in their own image. From the fact that the new cares and duties attendant on the infant family bring to light a succession of new resources and virtues in the parents; so that the very event which seemed to threaten the happiness and strength of their union, proves to be the only thing which was wanting to complete the development of their character, and to render their love indissoluble and entire.

Brought adaptations to light.

Through each successive stage of the family growth, every part of the organization proves to be foreseen and provided for; and is constantly bringing to light new adaptations as integral parts of the whole. Prior to the birth of the first infant, the question might have been asked, How will its wants and feebleness be suitably met? The reply was instinctively given by the arms which opened to receive it; by the maternal nourishment which literally rushed to meet its opening lips; by the voice instinctively modulated to tones of tenderness, unknown before, which saluted its ear; by the looks of love which spoke to its eye; and by the thousand caresses which showed that its coming had been looked for, and its wants calculated on by One who had formed the entire process as part of a plan. Then, again, as it emerges from infancy, its propensity to imitate pre-supposes an example worthy of imitation; its instinctive readiness to believe, implies and looks for parental testimony and instruction; and its disposition to yield and obey, seems listening for the parental authority which shall guide and command. Either of these series of qualities, without the other, would exist in vain. Their correspondence forms the means of mutual endearment and improvement. Meanwhile, circumstances only are wanting to bring other adaptations to light. The addition of each brother and sister is, to the child, like the fulfillment of a prior expectation. Its social nature has tendrils ready to embrace it. And as the family multiplies and advances in years; and its various members, of both sexes and of different ages, are seen living under one roof; moving harmoniously under the direction of one will; combining their separate lives of industry for the good of all; and showing that if one member suffer or rejoice, the same feeling pervades the community; who can hesitate to recognize the development of a plan?

Community of families.

But the fact that any given family forms a constitution in itself, prepares us to look for the larger constitution which encircles it. As it was not good for individual man to be isolated, so it is not good for a family to be alone. The rearing of each family is prospective; and supposes the co-existence of other families, by union with which other families still will come into existence. The affinities of kindred thus spread and multiply; and the holy charities nurtured in the family circle prepare its members, when they go forth, to diffuse their benevolence to the circumference of society. But there are acts and aspects of the family which look even beyond this. There is One who is the Father of all its members; of whom the earthly parent, when acting in his highest and most sacred capacity, is only a representative; and by whose conduct of domestic worship they are reminded, not only of the sacredness of their relationship to each other, but of that better world where all the scattered members of His family shall be forever united in one.

Successive communities.

And not only does the domestic constitution embrace a number of co-existent families, it includes them also considered as successively existent. Whatever there was of knowledge, and excellence, and happiness, among the members of the human families living at the time of the flood was found among them as the survivors of all the families which had sprung from Adam. If every thing could have been taken from them which they inherited from the past—all the instruments of art and means of social enjoyment, owing to the division of labor which had been gradually obtaining, and to the subsequent combination of those labors; all the classifications of things; and all the secular knowledge which had resulted from the inductive experience of generations, and which had gradually taken the form of proverbs and familiar sayings; all the transmitted knowledge of God, and the silent but ever-active influence of the great departed; how slender would have been the stock which remained to them, and how sensible would they have been made that they were only portions of a connected whole.

The family a Divine conception.

That the entire constitution is a Divine conception appears from the fact that while each succeeding part supposes the part preceding, the entire series exists quite independently of human forethought or design. Thus, the existence and training of the child presuppose the parental instincts; these again presuppose the sexual; and these again the special moral affection of shame. Without the last, by which the decencies of life are preserved, the world would be destitute of homes and of family ties—one wide scene of bestiality; without the second, the race would not be continued, for no children would be born; and without the first, no children would be reared, for they would be abandoned as soon as born. The absence of either of these principles, or even their existence in different proportions from that assigned to them, would derange and destroy the framework of society.

Independently of all human design.

Now, it by no means follows, as some have foolishly imagined, that because on retrospection we see the well-working of this social arrangement, therefore it was prospectively sketched out by man, and deliberately prosecuted, antecedent to all experience. We do not act with a view to produce it; our conduct assumes its existence. "The state existed before the individual," says Aristotle. And, in the same sense, the family may be said to have existed before the individual. That is to say, the family is not a constitution set up by man as the result of mature reflection. The perception of its advantages did not lead to its existence; its existence was at first necessary, in order to exhibit its advantages. The only mind in which, with all its complicated arrangements and far-reaching advantages, it was preconceived, was the mind of Him who seeth the end from the beginning; and who, in order to the family, created the individual. Like the coral-animals, laboring for ages at the bottom of the Pacific, each one in his own cell, and each family in its own branch, but ignorant of the same wide-spread activity which is constantly going on all around, and which is destined to emerge in an island group, or in a continent, the model of which is in the hand of the Creator, each family of man, from the fall to the flood, was, unconsciously, living and laboring for all, as far as its involuntary movements were concerned; while, as free agents, the well-being of each was perfectly coincident with the good of all, and essential to it. The constitution of the family, as we have now described it, so obviously implies its analogy with the other portions of the great plan to which it belongs, that we shall simply indicate a few illustrations.

The family in analogy with the great plan.

No fact or principle of importance can be pointed to in the constitution and history of the first man, which was not analogically repeated in the constitution and history of the first, and of every subsequent family.

The analogy of the human parent.

In the paradisiacal economy, for example, we saw the Divine Creator, after providing a place suitable for the reception of his offspring, "make man in his own image: in the image of God created He him, male and female created He them." He was their Father, their only parent—a name by which, subsequently, He was often pleased to designate Himself—and, as such, He provided for, instructed, and governed them, or they would have perished; and all this He made subservient to training them for self-government, as the subjects of his moral government. Now, although there were numerous conceivable methods by which a succession of men might have come into being, the method which God was pleased to appoint is one by which man, having prepared a home for their reception, is made the subordinate producer of offspring "in his own image." He is their father, and they are dependent on him for protection, provision, and instruction, as the first man himself was on God.

Of his authority.

In that primary economy there was but one authority which the new-made creature was to obey, and that was the authority of the Being to whom he owed his existence. Similarly, the family is a monarchy; the supreme authority and only head is the father. "The husband is the head of the wife." His will is the law of the children, and during their infancy, it is, as far as it is exercised for their good, absolute. This is essential to the well-being of the domestic government.

And teaching.

In imparting the rudiments of knowledge to his new-made children, the Great Father taught them speech, and selected and employed external objects about which to exercise it. All the natural objects around them had been made and placed there, as the signs of ideas and truths in the Divine mind, and as intimations of the Divine character; their value, therefore, depended entirely on their awakening the same ideas in the human mind, and enabling it rightly to interpret His character. The human parent pursues a parallel course. He places objects before his children—many of them made by himself on purpose—as the signs of thoughts in his own mind, and as indications of his character and his relationship to them. And the value of the signs depends entirely on their awakening thoughts and feelings in the filial bosom responsive to those in his own. The application which the Divine Parent made of the rudimentary knowledge imparted to his new offspring was a moral one. The easy command which he laid on them was, to them, a revelation of their own character as well as of His; for in teaching them their amenableness to His authority, He was at once laying open to their consciousness the great distinctive principle of their new nature—the power of voluntary obedience; and giving them to feel in that very perception, that they were the subjects of moral government. And their conscious guilt and happiness, immediately on their fall, showed that, though the Governor himself was invisible, His laws were taking effect and executing themselves.

The moral use made of knowledge.

As soon as the opening intellect of his children renders them capable of moral distinctions, the first authoritative command or prohibition of the parent awakens within them the consciousness of responsibility. That simple consciousness takes them at once from under the involuntary government appropriate to the mere animal creation, and places them under moral government; indeed, their own animal appetites are among the first subjects of that government. And as certainly as they indulge those appetites in known violation of parental authority, they become sensible of guilt and self-dissatisfaction. Even if they only intend or attempt such violation, and though the parent himself be absent, their inward struggles, and their consciousness that the constitution of the family is against them—that the moral sense of each of its members condemns them by anticipation, combine to show that, even in their own views, they are under moral government.

The family a sphere of probation.

The form of government under which our first parents were placed was that of probation; a state in which their subsequent well-being was made dependent on their present conduct, and in which they were open to inducements to obedience and disobedience. The family constitutes a similar state of probation. Even the form of its opening stage is remarkably analogous to that of the paradisiacal state. For, by taking one object out of the hand of a child, by removing another beyond its reach, or by addressing it in the tones of prohibition, the language of the parent is, "thou shalt not." Not unfrequently has he to complete the sentence, and to say, in the language of the Divine Parent, "thou shalt not eat of it." Nor is the immediate object of the prohibition less similar in the two instances; namely, to teach the parties that, for the present, at least, they must be guided by the will of another, with a view to their personal improvement; in other words, to teach them the self-government, which in its laws, is identical with the laws of the Divine Government. So that, in the family, the child is literally on probation for mature age. Nothing which he does terminates in itself. According to what we have seen to be a law of human nature, active habits are strengthened, and passive impressions weakened, by repetition. The objects and events of the family keep this law in perpetual operation. Every day is a state of trial. Every hour bears a probationary aspect for all the future; and "the former part of life is an opportunity put into our hands, which if lost can not be recovered."*

Obedience dependent on faith. The obedience of the first human beings, and their probationary success, depended ultimately on their faith in the declaration of their Divine Parent. And this dependence, be it remarked, was owing to no arbitrary appointment limited to the occasion; but rested on a fundamental law of the human constitution, and a law, therefore, of universal application. Hence, in the family the same dependence obtains. If the parent says to his child, concerning any thing likely to injure him, "Thou shalt not do it," or "Thou shalt not have it on pain of such or such results," it is obvious that if the child believes the parent he will refrain; if he does not believe him, he will do or take the thing forbidden. Whether it be inherently pernicious or not, is not here the question; for even if it were a deadly poison, the child would still have to rely on the word of his parent that it was fatal; and he would but have to do the same if there were nothing inherently injurious in it.

Consequences of disobedience. The analogy holds also between the consequences of the first act of disobedience and those flowing from signal filial transgression. Whether any thing more than the external consequences of the first sin passed over to the descendants of the sinner is not here

* Butler's Analogy, part i. chap. 5

the question. That these did, and that they were effects of terrible import is evident. But fearful as they were, and unique as the entire transaction must, from the very nature of the case, ever continue to be, it is not so entirely separated from all subsequent events as to be without analogy. By a single act of transgression the child may incur the forfeiture of the parental roof, and entail worse than disgrace on those who descend from him. The poverty of the prodigal is the poverty of his children. The intemperate and licentious, sometimes by a single act, entails disease on his offspring, and renders his descendants loathsome for some generations to come. An evil once incurred, on travel its effects in unbroken series to a distant futurity. The family constitution is so compacted, and society so organized, that actions never terminate in themselves, and their influence propagates itself for evil or for good forever. That the influence and effects of the good should be thus perpetuated, is seldom, perhaps never, objected to; and yet, as it takes place in virtue of the same general laws which account for the similar diffusion of evil, the one can not be consistently objected to without objecting to the other also.

The principle of mediation.

And this brings us to another most important point of analogy between one of the aspects of the moral government of God in its opening stage, and the family government—we refer to the principle of mediation. In the first promise, and in the institution of sacrifice, the Divine Being was saying, in effect, that the consequences of man's transgression should, in some way, be remedied by means of the conflict and sufferings of another. Now, all pre-existing nature was already in analogy with such an arrangement. All its processes and operations in the family, as far as they came under man's observation, were to be conducted *by means.* The child comes to the enjoyment of life through the pain and travail of another. From early perils and death he is saved by the self-sacrificing watchfulness of the mother. The patient toil of the father is the price paid to save him from ignorance and want; but the evil from which man was to be saved was the consequence of transgression. From similar evil the child is saved, in the family, *by means of others.* He may, indeed, do much himself toward remedying certain kinds of evil. But the evil may be of a nature to incapacitate him for helping himself; and, to be parallel with the evil in question, it is of such an evil only that we are supposed to speak. Now, the occurrence of such an event brings to light an antecedent remedial provision. The tears of the mother, or the efforts of the father, save him from the effects of his voluntary misconduct. Or, it may be, that the tender and earnest intercessions of the mother save him from the just infliction of the paternal displeasure; and, still further, it may be that the maternal intercession is both the means of bringing the son to repentance, and is the ground on which the father sees reason to extend that forgiveness which he would not otherwise have conceded even to that repentance itself. Be that as it may, the child is pardoned and improved, and that by means of the self-denial and suffering of others; for even the compassion which prompted the remedial effort, includes in itself an element of suffering. We do not say that this is all that mediation includes.

Self-will remedied by self-sacrifice.

Further, the very act which rendered the promised mediation necessary is itself in analogy with the doctrine. For, as by the self-will and self-indulgence of one man evil was entailed on others, by the self-denial and self-sacrifice of another, the evil was to be remedied. Here is seen the operation of a general law, in virtue of which every thing we do, whether good or evil, entails consequences, or sheds an influence upon others. We do not say, indeed, that the mediation contemplated in the first promise intended no more than that we have described. We only affirm, that as far as the doctrine of mediation was taught in the first promise, and under the Patriarchal economy, it was based on a general law, and found its analogies in the family constitution. As if to call attention to the coincidence between the two, the Deliverer was to be born of "the seed of the woman;" a law of the family was to be made subservient to the law of moral mediation in its highest form. And as faith in parental character and testimony is essential to filial obedience and well-being, so the belief of this promise was indispensable to a participation of the blessings flowing from its fulfillment. The degree in which the child confides in his parent is the degree or measure in which he is likely to be benefited by him; just as the degree in which our first parents confided in the Divine promise was the index and measure of the advantage they would derive from it.

Divine revelation and parental instruction.

This brings us to another important point of analogy—the fact that the first promise, on the belief of which man's well-being was suspended, was a direct revelation from God. Now, not only was there nothing, at that time, in the family organization to contradict the probability of such a method of communication, but much that was analogous to support it. God had taught his new-made creatures many other things which were essential to their welfare directly and personally, and had, so far, made this the natural method of disclosing certain facts; and their direct disclosure of facts to their children was but in harmony with this method of Divine teaching. The one was not, at that time, more remarkable than the other; for, as far as man was concerned, they both were new; nor had he an established course of nature by which to judge of the probability of the continuance or discontinuance of the one any more than of the other. Not only do many of the parental disclosures come to the children with all the directness of a revelation, but, at the time they are made, and for years afterward, the children do not know whether such disclosures are made in harmony with a course of nature or not. All that they feel is, that the being making them is their father; and, in their fullness of their confidence, they are prepared to believe alike a human discovery and a Divine revelation. As the Creator had directly imparted to our first parents knowledge relating both to their temporal and eternal welfare, their parental relation devolved on them the duty of teaching their children the same truths in the same manner.

The relation of will to will.

But how did such direct divine communications consist with the free agency of the creature receiving them? In the preceding volume, we saw that the introduction and co-existence of a second will was at once the problem and glory of the universe. Here, we see that will beginning to find itself surrounded by the indications of a plan. These indications, indeed, have since been constantly multiplying; indications that man is in the midst of a progressive and all-related scheme. Even the first promise, containing, as it did, the germ or primary outline of Divine revelation, bears, in this respect, a striking analogy to the first outlines of either of the kingdoms of nature as geologically brought to light. But even at the beginning, man found himself within the limits of an all-encompassing plan. The same Being who had chosen the dimensions of the world he should inhabit, and the number and variety of the objects it should contain, and who had thus set a limit to the materials of his knowledge, now intimated that, as a moral being, he was the subject of government; and a government supposes order, subordination, and the operation of laws. The promise of a Deliverer, too, implied foresight, providence, and the existence of a forelaid scheme of mercy, of which his future acts will be the filling up. Now, if man is thus placed within the sphere of the activity of another will, how, it might be asked, can he assert the liberty of his own will? With the discussion of this question we have not now to do, but only with its analogy. The family constitution is strikingly parallel. The mystery is repeated in the coincidence of the wills of the husband and wife. For while their individuality forbids and prevents the loss of the personality of either—and that personality lies in the voluntary part of their nature—their happiness depends on the harmony of their separate wills, and is in proportion to it. The mystery is repeated in the freedom yet coincidence of the parent and child. The parental plan or purpose related to the child before it came into the world; and, as such, continues to influence its movements, directly or indirectly, from infancy to old age. But who thinks of questioning its accountability on that ground? Conscious of moral freedom, the child never ceases to assume that he enjoys it, and to act accordingly; while, at the same time, he finds that freedom in the very act of conforming himself to wise parental law. Thus, the very mysteries of the Divine government are analogically repeated in the mysteries of the family government.

The family a part of God's moral government.

Reminding us, in conclusion, that the family constitution is in analogy with the moral government of God, as being a part of it and in subserviency to it. "Framed for this brief and transitory, yet all-important, state of existence, and to expire with the last generation of human beings, still it points to what is permanent and unchangeable. In its constitution, as far as we can penetrate, it displays the nearest approach to the Divine government, and, unquestionably, it bears this resemblance, with an immediate view to the best interests of that government. As man himself was originally created in the image of God, so it would seem, in the depth of his condescension, He intended to place him at the head of a government, the shade or similitude of His own." * And as, in the Divine government, the glory of God is coincident with the well-being of the creature, so in the family, the honor of the parent and the welfare of the child are coincident. So that the highest interest of the child, the highest honor of the parent, and the highest glory of God are coincident.

* Anderson on the Genius and Design of the Domestic Constitution, etc.; Part i. § 8.

SECOND PART.

CHAPTER XVII.

THE LAW OF CHANGE; OR, HISTORY OF THE PROBATION OF THE FAMILY.

Grounds for expecting the end of the family probation.

NUMEROUS grounds existed for expecting that, sooner or later, the family dispensation would be succeeded by another. If, for example, the attainment of the great end of the Divine manifestation be in its very nature progressive, this is only saying that the process must ever be kept open to receive the addition of new effects or of extended revelations. Accordingly, this patriarchal stage itself is a superinduction on preceding stages. And as we could not have contemplated the display of the Divine power without being prepared by it for the coming illustrations of wisdom; nor of wisdom without feeling that we were as yet standing only on the threshold of the great process; so now, in the moral department, we could not have comprehended the constitution and condition of man in Paradise, as illustrative of the holy character and government of God; nor the new dispensation of mercy which succeeded his fall, and which continued to be administered age after age, notwithstanding his perseverance in transgression, without being prepared to witness some new exercise of judgment or mercy suited to the depraved condition of mankind.

And besides these two grounds of expectation—the first derived from the purpose of God, and the second from the analogy of his procedure in accomplishing that purpose—several special grounds for such an expectation had occurred since the introduction, and during the continuance, of the family economy. Every prophetic warning, the translation of Enoch, and every Divine reference to the future, were so many solemn intimations that displays of the character of God were yet in reserve, such as eye had not seen. Among these intimations, the affecting command received by Noah to prepare the ark was prominent and decisive; for, while it foreboded judgment, it was a special provision for the continuance of the race, and therefore for the continuance of the Divine manifestation.

Besides which, and chiefly, the primary promise of the dispensation was yet unfulfilled. "The seed of the woman" had not yet bruised the serpent's head—the moral deliverance of sinful man had yet to be effected. Every thing was still looking forward. Here there was an additional reason for the expectation of further displays of the Divine character, based on the most valid of all grounds—the faithfulness of God. And then there was the special one arising from the alarming pitch to which the depravity of man had attained. Even had the family constitution answered its design in rearing "a godly seed," and in securing the general prevalence of virtue, new displays of the Divine perfections were to be looked for in fulfillment of the designs of mercy. But a state of things had obtained in the domestic constitution analogous to that which obtained in relation to individual man in Paradise. The family had been on probation; not, indeed, in a sense identical with the probation of Adam; but on probation in a sense in which it has never been since. That was the only dispensation during which nothing existed *ab extra* to interfere with it, and consequently the experiment respecting it was comparatively complete. Here, then, in the family had been a new theater for the development of all the capabilities of man. The head of the family was officially the image of God; his children were the subjects of his moral government; his will was, until they became capable of self-government, and in order to it—their reason. The welfare of this new Paradise depended on the character of the governor, and on the obedience of the filial to the paternal will, just as the welfare of man in Paradise depended on the obedience of his will to the will of God. But the family had fallen. Its subservience to the ultimate end of its existence had long been the rare exception. For ages it had been prolific only of an ungodly race. The domestic hearth had become the center of an evil power which penetrated and polluted the remotest parts of the patriarchal constitution. Laws and influences which were meant to be "unto life," were perverted and productive only of moral death. And the evil, so far from abating, increased in virulence and enormity with each successive generation. All the partial checks which had been administered by Divine warnings and rebukes, had failed to arrest the onward tide of personal and social depravity. A twofold reason then existed why God should "arise out of His place;"—some solemn judicial infliction was necessary to vindicate the rectitude of His government, as well as to prepare the way for those ulterior revelations of mercy which the existing generations had, by their enormous depravity, incapacitated themselves for receiving.

The law or conditions of change.

Granted, then, that a change was to be expected, let us look for the law of the change, or for the fact that the time and manner of each successive change is itself regulated by a law. The time (as we have said) for the change in any given department of the Divine manifestation, will of course be determined in a manner, and for a reason, differing with the particular nature and design of the department: either by each existing stage passing through all the combinations and changes of which it admits before another begins; or, by its existing long enough to show that it involves all the possibilities necessary for answering such and such ends, were its continuance permitted; or else until it has sufficiently taught the specific truth, or answered the particular end, for which it was originated. But whatever the particular reason for determining the period of change may be, it is evident that the law of time for every change, and of the manner of the change, must harmonize with the great end of the whole—the manifestation of the Divine all-sufficiency. For, were a stage of the manifestation to be recalled or replaced a moment before it had, in an adequate manner, demonstrated the Divine all-sufficiency for that particular stage, the great purpose would not be answered. From which it follows that no such change or interposition takes place arbitrarily or capriciously, but as the law of progression, and of the end, require it.

Now, that the period of the deluge was not capriciously selected is evident, from the language of God respecting the maturity of human guilt, and from His "waiting" one hundred and twenty years during the preparation of the ark. For, while the latter implies that the infliction of the deserved punishment at an earlier period would not have been agreeable to the forbearance of God, the former intimates that it would not have accorded with His justice to delay the infliction to a later period.

The specific design of the economy.

But what had been the specific design of the antediluvian dispensation which was now about to be closed? What made the time selected the appropriate time for its termination? And how did the time of its continuance, and the manner of its termination, subserve and illustrate the great and ultimate end?

Its great lesson of dependence ignored.

In answer to the first inquiry, we think it is clear from a survey of the ground we have gone over, that the design of the patriarchal economy before the flood was, proximately, to illustrate the great truth that the well-being of the family, or of social man, no less than of individual man, depends on the coincidence of his will with the will of God; or, on the recognition of a fact, namely, his social dependence on God, involving, of course, the consequent insufficiency of nature, at its best, to render him independent of God; while, ultimately its end was to illustrate the all-sufficiency of that long-suffering which waited while this great truth was fully wrought out and established.

In the paradisiacal economy man had been taught the same truth in his individual capacity. Endowed with a will, he was in danger of exercising it in opposition to his Maker; of saying, in effect: "If I may but exercise my own will irrespectively of the Divine will—if I may but have this Paradise entirely, and use it for my own ends—I shall be happy." The object of the primal prohibition was to forbid and prevent this fatal experiment; but, failing in this, man learned by painful experience, the truth which he had refused to learn by teaching. And now the great lesson was to be inculcated again in another form; for still every thing depends on his loving conformity to this necessary law of his being. A dispensation of mercy has received him; providing a twofold remedy for the twofold effect of his sin—restoration for both his character and his condition. Possessed of these remedial means, he also finds himself, as the founder of a family, in a situation presenting the most powerful motives, both to return to obedience himself, and to train his children to obedience also. Here again, then, is danger; only now that danger is twofold:—first, lest man should not avail himself of the proffered remedy, and be restored to obedience; and, secondly, lest he should take occasion, from his new domestic relations, as he did before from his paradisiacal resources, to spend life in a vain endeavor to render himself practically independent of his Father in heaven. He is now in danger of saying, in effect: "If I may but employ this new social power as I will—multiplying its relations, cultivating its capabilities, directing its activities, and molding the whole to my own purposes without restraint—I heed not the promise of a Deliverer, but shall be sufficient for my own happiness."

Now, that the special design of the family economy, and that the consequent danger of man, were such as we have described, is determined by the language of inspiration on the subject. The evident object of the sacred writer, in Gen. vi. 1, 2, is to lay his finger on the origin of that apostasy which opened the last flood-gate of evil on antediluvian man; implying that for the religious to unite themselves with the irreligious, was to detach themselves from God; and that this perversion of the family constitution frustrated the design of its antediluvian existence, and rendered its dispensational or probationary continuance morally abortive. And *therefore*, "God said, my Spirit shall not always strive with man." And equally evident is it that man's consequent social danger was such as we have stated; for he practically employed the very language which we have put into his lips. "The sons of God saw the daughters of men that they were fair;" just as Eve saw the tree that it was pleasant to the eye. Here was the closing stage—the last turning-point of importance of the family probation. Social man was about to repeat the act of individual man, and to take the forbidden fruit. "And they took them wives of all which they chose." The sensual triumphed over the rational and the moral. The sons of God, in their social capacity, apostatized from God. Their self-will came into direct collision with His authority. The family had fallen from its high object of constituting the Church of God.

What made the proper time for ending the economy.

We are now prepared to answer the second inquiry—What made the time selected the appropriate time for the termination of the antediluvian economy? We reply, that we conceive it had then existed long enough, and had passed through all the combinations and changes requisite, to teach the specific truth, and to answer the special end of the economy; or, that it had then completed the cycle during which it had passed through all the conditions necessary for answering that special end; and that, as to the ultimate end, it had thus demonstrated the all-sufficiency of the Divine forbearance for that particular stage of the great process.

The apostasy of the Sethites.

Now, if the special design of the economy was, as we have represented it to be—to establish the great principle, that the well-being of the family, or of *social* no less than of *individual* man, depends on the practical coincidence of his will with the will of God; and if man chooses to incur the danger to which we have adverted, of practically contesting this fundamental principle, what are the conditions necessary to demonstrate his utter inability to succeed, and thus to establish the fact of his dependence? The whole of these conditions, we most reverently admit, can be known only to "Him who seeth the end from the beginning," and who will ultimately show, to the conviction of the universe, that not one condition essential to the demonstration was wanting. And we freely concede, also, that many of those conditions which we may conceive to have been necessary, and which we may warrantably presume to have been actually present, we can not *prove* to have been so, owing to our extremely limited knowledge of antediluvian history. But, remembering the multiplied relations and obligations of the domestic constitution, we may state generally, that if the time should arrive in its history, when, after a long and diversified exemplification of the happiness flowing from individual and social obedience, and of the growing evils resulting from self-willed disobedience, the great majority of the families still in professed allegiance to God, should yield to the growing power of evil, and go over to increase that power still further—this would be ominous of the experiment hastening to a close. For, in taking that step, it would be evident that experience had been reading her lessons to them in vain; and having taken it they would have made themselves incapable of afterward profiting by her lessons. Now, on inspired testimony, such appears to have been actually the case. For "it came to pass, when men began to multiply on the face of the earth, and daughters were born to them, that the sons of God saw the daughters of men, that they were fair; and they took them wives of all which they chose. And God said, My Spirit shall not always strive with man, for that he also is flesh." At what particular period of antediluvian history this social apostasy from God began is uncertain; but as it was not till the human race had greatly multiplied, and as it is closely associated with the ominous declaration, "My Spirit shall not *always* strive with man," the probability is that it was at a somewhat advanced stage of that history. Up to that period, however, whether early or late in the economy, the practical issue of the family constitution had, humanly speaking, been uncertain. If there had been a party against God, there had also been a party for Him—those who were called after Him and who called upon Him. The gradual diminution of the numbers of "the sons of God," indeed, and the proportionate increase of irreligious families, boded ill for the result of the contest. Still, as long as the families who worshiped God formed a party, a community, a Church, the contest was, to all human appearance, between the principles of the religious party and those of the irreligious party, rather than between the latter and God. And who could say whether the superior moral condition, and order, and well-being of God's party, might not, sooner or later, begin to win over some of the irreligious, and so induce the prospect of a hopeful change? Time must be given to determine the result. If, when this great social experiment is over, "every mouth is to be stopped," as to the way in which it has been conducted, opportunity must now be afforded for ascertaining which party will vanquish, and which will yield. Evidently much, if not every thing, depends on the families of God not receiving into their bosoms members of the alienated party. Every thing depends on their converting their families into fortresses for God, in order to secure themselves from the invasion of the enemy. Distinctness, separation, is their only safeguard. If this ceases, the last barrier to the incursion of evil is gone. And if the religious capitulate, the triumph of evil will be complete. The contest will be no longer between community and community, nor between man and man, but between man and God. And such was the actual result of the trial. Promiscuous alliances between the families of the righteous and the wicked took place in considerable numbers; and from that time the contest was as good as ended. The very salt of the earth had lost its savor; "thenceforth it was good for nothing, but to be cast out, and to be trodden under foot of men." The process of social corruption hastened on, with ever-accelerating rapidity. Wickedness was propagated faster than human beings. The last rational hope for the family dispensation, was, under such circumstances, extinct.

All conjugal obligations violated.

In our chapters on the relations and obligations of the family economy, we saw that the parties united in marriage were brought under as many conditions as there are parts in the human constitution. If the time should arrive, then, when those relations generally come to be disregarded, and the consequent obligations violated, man could not complain that he has not had the opportunity as a social being of placing his own will in the stead of God's, and of reaping the fruits. Now there is ground to believe that this actually took place. The sexes were numerically related; but, from the time of Lamech onward, polygamy had been practiced. The union was designed to be restricted to individuals who should be exclusively united to each other for life. But, from the intense sensuality of the period, there is ground to conclude that this Divine appointment was not unfrequently subjected to every kind of violation of which it was susceptible; not to that of polygamy merely, but also of divorce, incest, fornication, and adultery. For the same reasons that the marriage union should exist at all, it should be formed between parties suited to each other. But as on the only admissible principle of classification, the greatest difference existed between those who professed to obey the will of God and those who disregarded His will, for the former to choose the latter in marriage, was to confound all distinctions, and to oppose the design of the economy. This was exchanging law for lust; and proclaiming that, henceforth, marriage should be made the occasion of placing the creature in the stead of the Creator, and of rendering it independent of Him for enjoyment.

All parental and filial relations disregarded.

As to the mutual relations and obligations of parents and children, if the time should come when the family, in this respect, after passing through successive stages of degeneration, should sink and settle into a state of conflict and corruption, its self-destructive condition would surely show that nothing but evil could henceforth be expected from it. Now, that such became its actual condition is evident from the giants in evil which it propagated. Doubtless there were, even to the eve of the deluge, many expressions of the family affections extant. These affections were the last to quit the depraved heart; and, accordingly, many a parent looked proudly on his first-born, and fondly on his youngest child; and many a child prized above all things the parental embrace. But these affections, though capable of the highest and holiest application, are, in themselves, only instincts. Man shares the love of offspring with the animals. And the complaint is that, in the course of the antediluvian economy, they came to be applied generally to worse than animal purposes. The self-willed parent found himself surrounded by self-willed offspring. Having himself ceased to be the representative of God, he could not be surprised to find that his children were "in his own image." Their education consisted in the development only of their inferior powers. Parental authority, example, and teaching, became so many ordinances of impiety. Servitude alternated between slavery and resistance. The family, in relation to God, was no longer an orderly government conducted in subordination to His supreme government, but a confederacy against Him; while, in relation to its own members, it became perverted into a mass of social self-corruption.

Natural objects perverted.

If the time should arrive when the vast variety of natural objects belonging to the regions inhabited by the antediluvian families, and their artistic capabilities, have come to be perverted to evil purposes, so as to be turned, in effect, into weapons against the Being who had appointed them, as well as to be destructive of man himself, it is evident that no useful purpose could be answered by permitting man any longer to abuse them. Accordingly, the probability is, that during the lapse of that long period, the robust health, the strength, and the extreme longevity of the antediluvians came to beget a proud self-reliance, which set death and the invisible world at defiance. The mineral kingdom, probably, instead of supplying him with the means of erecting an altar to God, only afforded him the materials for erecting strongholds, or with the symbols of idolized wealth; thus serving to shut out from his view his dependence on God. The virgin fertility and tropical luxuriance of the vegetable kingdom, instead of supplying any thing that should ascend in incense to its Maker, was made to minister to his self-indulgence and intemperance.* And the animals in whose domestication and use he might have learned valuable lessons of self-government, and have shown himself the humble representative of Him who had, at first, invested him with dominion over them, became the victims of his passions, or were pressed into the service of harassing and destroying his fellows. Every thing was misapplied and out of place. Instead of serving as emblems of spiritual truths, symbols of invisible objects, and occasions for grateful reference to the Giver, they were made to divert the eye from God, were taxed in every way to serve in His stead, became the exponents and instruments of man's depravity, and the means by which he conducted a perpetual service in which he himself was at once priest and idol. Having revolted from God himself, man had carried away with him all that God had given into his hands. But, as might have been expected, just in propor-

* The popular notion that Noah planted the first vineyard has no countenance whatever in the Biblical statement on the subject. "And Noah began to be a husbandman, and he planted a vineyard." This does not imply that others had not planted vineyards before the flood; nor even that he himself had not. He may even have been a husbandman before. The original for *begin* is often redundant (as in Gen. vi. 1), and the probability is that he was only resuming his antediluvian occupation.

tion as he perverted them, they reacted and perverted him; tending at once to conceal his dependence and to multiply his wants.

Families unite for evil.

If the time should come when the relations of family to family, and of one community of families to another, shall be employed only to answer sensual, unjust, and impious purposes, every principle of moral government will warrant and call for Divine interference. Now, as we have already seen, from the moment when "the sons of God saw the daughters of men that they were fair, and took them wives of all which they chose," the higher design of the conjugal state was defeated; it was prostituted to sensual purposes; and the doom of the family constitution itself, as a distinct economy, was sealed. Hence, the reason assigned by God for terminating the probationary contest with man is, "for that he also is flesh." In other words, His own professed worshipers, by joining the sensual for sensual ends had merged the last hope of recovery in profligacy. And being thus perverted into an evil to the individual, the family became also an organization of social oppression and wrong. "There were giants in the earth in those days;" and even after it was so that "the sons of God came in unto the daughters of men, and they bare children to them, the same became mighty men which were of old, men of renown."* Brute force bore down law and right. Families banded together for the perpetration of more extensive wrong. Men became renowned in proportion to their deeds of rapine and bloodshed. And "the earth was filled with violence through them."†

The apostasy universal.

But all the relations of the individual and the family center ultimately in God. If the

* Gen. vi. 4. † Gen. vi. 13.

time should come, then, when, instead of leading to Him, they became perverted into occasions of impiety and of deeper apostasy from him, the continuance of the family constitution, in such a state, can answer no useful purpose. "The earth also was corrupt before God; and the earth was filled with violence.* Here the close connection is marked between impiety and social depravity. Having cast off the authority of God, men were embroiled in a contest as to whose human will should prevail. There was only one point in which they were all agreed—that the will of God should not obtain. The fires of one true worshiper after another had been extinguished, till now, perhaps, only one solitary altar remained. The name of God was uttered only in the imprecations of blasphemy. And, although no idols of wood and stone might have been actually set up, it was only because living hero-worship supplied their place, and a disbelief of a superintending Providence made a gross polytheism less acceptable than practical atheism or material pantheism.

The stages passed through.

Let it be supposed, then, that the antediluvian population had reached the revolting state of depravity we have described. Still the question would arise—through what process have they reached it? Is it the result of all but a sudden plunge into evil, the smart of which might react and induce them to return to obedience—or is it the last stage of a long transitionary descent from bad to worse, in the course of which they have passed through the intermediate states of sin and error? For, unless it be the latter, who shall say but that if the trial were prolonged and diversified still further, they might not yet be recovered to God? Now, although owing to

* Gen. vi. 11.

the absence of historical data, we can not enumerate the various stages and forms of evil they had actually run through (as we shall be able to do when treating of the post-diluvian population), we are able to show that they had passed through all the conditions necessary for demonstrating the dependence of the family on God; as well as their own fixed determination not to yield to Him; to convert every social relation into the means of doing without Him; and to be miserable rather than obey Him.

The ultimate design of the family lost sight of.

We have seen that, by the institution of marriage, God proclaimed His will that a high and holy purpose should be aimed at; that all other ends, however proper and important in themselves, should be subordinated to that purpose; and that the attainment of it presupposed the religious character of the parties united. Now, we can easily suppose, from what we know of society generally, not only that the ultimate object of the conjugal state came gradually to be wholly lost sight of, and that the institution which was meant to elevate the sensuous into the sacred actually drew down the so-called sons of God themselves into the depths of sensuality, but that, in the course of that period, unions took place between parties in every stage of unfitness, for every improper end, and with every suitable inducement to refrain of which the circumstances of the times admitted. We can conceive, for example, that at any one period, a certain number of marriages were possible, each differing in some respects from all the rest, but all unsuitable in the *highest* respect, and likely to be productive of sin and misery. In the age following, we can conceive the number of such possible combinations to be greater; and in the age following, greater still. Suppose, then, that after this state of things had lasted a certain time, attention had been called to it; and that, as the evil increased, a feeling had come over the patriarchal communities, that if the evils arising from such immoral combinations went on increasing for a certain time longer, it would then be evident that the experiment of substituting man's will for the will of God on the subject had failed; and even that the inferior ends of marriage could best be secured by aiming supremely at the higher end. Now the probability is, that "the preachers of righteousness" often enlarged on this subject, showed that as nothing but evil had ever resulted from man's self-will in this respect, so to persist in it longer would only aggravate the evil. Heedless of the warning, however, the experiment went on; every new combination promising a new result; every succeeding age swelling the evil, and rendering a return to first principles more difficult, until those principles themselves were forgotten, derided, or impeached; and it had actually become necessary to arrest the entire process of corruption, if only in order to save the inferior ends of marriage, and to prevent the loss of civilization.

Family sins became customs.

The laws of the marriage relation made a certain number of sins possible, as well as a certain number of immoral theories on each relation. Was each of those sins committed and persisted in—polygamy, divorce, incest, fornication, adultery? and were such theories broached and practically maintained? Did we know the history of the period, we have no question whatever that we should find that most of the modern theories on the subject existed, in the germ, among the antediluvians. Though such views might not have been formally propounded, no doubt many a St. Simonian and Communist contended, in his own little circle, that social ties were not binding; and that nothing more was wanting to render men happy than to root up the domestic affections, and to augment the amount of sensual enjoyment. And no doubt many a willing disciple made the experiment on a small scale, and diversified it to the utmost. At all events, polygamy became prevalent; the necessary results of which would be the animalizing of the man, the social degradation of the woman, the consequent cheapening of her as mere food for ordinary licentiousness; and, when the ordinary forms of sensual indulgence palled, the origination of unnatural forms of pollution.* So that however many theories the marriage relation may since have given rise to, we have no doubt that all those of which the patriarchal state admitted were practically resorted to, not merely in solitary instances, but each of them by different parties, in successive ages, and under ever-changing circumstances; until the original type of marriage had been virtually lost, and man had incapacitated himself for returning to it.

Education misunderstood, and parental restraint lost.

In preceding chapters we have seen that the nature of the human constitution predetermines the nature of the education necessary to develop and train it; and that the mutual relations of parent and child give rise to mutuul obligations. Now, the very nature of the cause which, on scriptural authority, added the last great impulse to the growing depravity of the race—namely, promiscuous unions between the religious and the irreligious—demonstrates that parental restraint was gone, and therefore that education had been disre-

* The early reappearance of some of these enormities in the post-diluvian world is to be inferred from certain Mosaic prohibitions, and from the Hebrew of Job, xxxvi. 14.

garded; and hence the retributive reaction of filial lawlessness. Doubtless then, as now, every thing that tended to develop any one or two parts or faculties of the human being was misnamed *education*. Every indulgence was allowed calculated to strengthen the passions and encourage self-will; and yet parents wondered how soon they lost all command over their children. Every part of the human being was more or less developed except his moral nature; and yet parents lamented that their children evinced so little power of self-government. Wealth, power, idleness, every thing hazardous to the moral health and enjoyment of man was entailed on children; and yet parents complained that their children were not so useful and happy as industry and self-control would have made them. Having surrendered their children to the influence of circumstances, by neglecting to cultivate the resisting and controlling power within, parents, no doubt, readily adopted the modern theories, that character is determined entirely by organization, or by external influences; and regarded it as a discharge from all obligation. Yet each generation, though pursuing the same course as its predecessors, hoped that its own history would prove an exception to all that had gone before; till it would come to be satisfied at its not being much worse than those of preceding times; and finally settle down in the conviction that to attempt improvement would be to struggle with an ordination of nature.

Material civilization aggravates moral evil.

But did the antediluvian enjoy the so-called "ameliorating influences of material civilization?" The excitement of hope with which every physical discovery is still hailed, as if the panacea for man's multiplied ills were just coming to light, notwithstanding the uniform failure of all such hopes, might well excuse the antediluvians for indulging similar visions. The discovery of new fruits and articles of food would promise abundance and enjoyment; improvements in the arts, by facilitating labor, would afford leisure for intellectual cultivation; and the discovery and occupation of new and fertile regions would give scope for enterprise, industry, and the accumulation of wealth. Poets would sing and philosophers would prophesy of the good time coming. The age would be congratulated on the advent of a poet in the person of Lamech; and the fact of his being a polygamist and a homicide would be charitably overlooked, if it did not even add to his popularity. And when his son Jubal came with "the harp and organ," the idolaters of æsthetics would rhapsodize on genius and social regeneration, and the near approach—if the saints would but let the world alone—of a millennium of earth-made pleasure. But how disappointed would they be—unless, indeed, they were as insensible to the lessons of experience as mankind has ever been since—at finding that every step in material civilization was a step onward in evil. Not, indeed, that this was a necessary result; but just because that *material* progress, instead of being put under moral control, was placed in atagonism to it. The "fruit of the vine" became the means of intemperance. The fine arts, as far as they were practiced, pandered to the passions; and even if they refined them, procured for their indulgence softer names than before, under which they might be followed with greater impunity. The products of a new territory ministered to luxury, and led to wars for its possession. Wealth became equivalent to vice; and power to oppression. And thus, after ages of growing degeneracy, the antediluvians illustrated the truth, so often exemplified since, that, in the absence of moral principle, it is not only possible, but certain, that people will reach the highest point of material civilization, and the lowest point of social demoralization at the same time.

The number of man's social duties the number of his sins.

In a preceding chapter we saw that the relations between family and family gave rise to numerous corresponding obligations and correlative rights. The number of these obligations and rights were the number of man's social vices and crimes. Not that it was ever possible for these obligations to be all disregarded at the same time; probably there was no period when many of the social virtues were not practiced within certain limits. But the evil was that they came to be practiced for the basest purposes. Hospitality came to be little more than the mutual pledge of confederation in the commission of acts of violence. Patriotism, or clanship, meant, not so much attachment to a particular tribe, as hatred to the families of another community. The rights of property could be maintained only by physical force; personal liberty would next be violated as a matter of course; and this would be followed by a reduced estimate of human life. But this would be to sacrifice three of the primary elements of civilization; and, consequently, to commence a retrogression to a state of barbarism. Accordingly, there is ground to conclude that some of the antediluvian families had actually retrograded from the pastoral and agricultural life with which the first families commenced their course, and had betaken themselves to the more wild and wandering habits of the hunter. And such a change would naturally tend to the dissolution of the patriarchal form of government; for not only would the large family or tribe break up into small companies, in order the better to range the wilderness, but the lead would be given to the most daring, which would often be the most youthful. Parental restraint would become increasingly distasteful: and paternal decrepitude a growing burden. So that, in such cases, both the family form of government and civilization were alike endangered.

All the means of recovery perverted.

But especially did the conduct of the antediluvians present the aspect of a persevering endeavor to defeat, step after step, all the means provided to impress them with a sense of their dependence, and to secure their obedience; and a determination to leave no means untried in order to exist and be happy apart from God. The religious basis of the dispensation was laid in the promise of a Deliverer, and in the appointment of the symbolical right of sacrifice; and we have had occasion to admire the Divine adaptation of each to the purpose of man's recovery to obedience. But the sacrificial institute had come to be disregarded; and the promise was probably perverted, as it came to be under a subsequent dispensation, into a ground of hope for the appearance of a hero of gigantic or martial attributes. And such a character, no doubt, became the standard of ideal excellence, to which their "men of renown" aspired and conformed. We have seen also that this religious basis of the dispensation, and the nature of the family constitution, were admirably adjusted and fitted in to each other; so that the family government was, in all its leading features, remarkably analogous to the moral government of God. But its laws and sanction had now lost their force for all moral purposes, and had come to be replaced by the dictates of a sensual self-will.

Every stage of error passed through.

Now, there is ground to conclude that in the progress of this monstrous perversion, the antediluvians passed through all the descending stages of error, speculative and practical, to which their simple creed could innocently give rise. Three of these stages are distinctly marked in their history, and in the order in which we might have expected to find them. To deny the doctrine of future retribution appears less revolting than to question the present providential government of God; while this, again, is less revolting than to question the Divine existence. Accordingly, the first of these doctrines appears to have been the first impugned. Hence the burden of Enoch's prophecies was the coming of the Lord as the Judge of the ungodly. Still the judgment was delayed; and "because judgment was not speedily executed, the hearts of the sons of men were set in them to do evil." Next, therefore, they advanced to the practical denial even of His superintending providence, and to persecute and "utter hard speeches" against all who believed it. Death itself, probably, was affirmed to include nothing judicial, but to be purely natural. The translation of Enoch was the Divine rebuke of that skepticism; and, probably, it was only one of several important events directed to the same object. Then came the third stage of the world's infidelity—the practical denial of the Divine Existence. As if there were no future judgment, no present providence, no living God, "they ate, they drank, they married, and were given in marriage, till the day that Noah entered into the ark, and the flood came, and destroyed them all."

In extenuation of this ever-advancing guilt, it could not be pleaded that the means of prevention were too abstract and intangible for the sensuous state of the comparatively uneducated mind of primitive man. The Sabbath, the Shekinah, and Sacrifice, appealed to the senses. Great truths were embodied in acts, and illustrated by examples. Every thing spiritual had a symbolical and objective form. Nor could it be pleaded that life was not prolonged enough to enable the antediluvian, who had much of his knowledge of the evils of disobedience to acquire, to profit by his experience and retrace his steps. His longevity of many centuries gave him ample opportunity for proving that no law of God can be violated with impunity, and for forming his own character and that of his children accordingly. But so far from profiting by experience, he first became insensible to its lessons, and then spent the large remainder of life in accumulating the moral difficulties, and the means of depravity, for all who should come after him. Mercy spared him; but he relented not. Justice threatened him; but he quailed not. A solitary witness for God, such as Noah, convicted him of unbelief, and called him to repentance; but the faith in God which such a change required, and the sense of humble dependence which it expressed, revolted his pride and self-confidence; and the only effect was that he gave more faith than ever to objects which deceived him, and took more closely to his heart the things which were piercing and polluting it.

The whole an attempt at independence of God.

And all this took place, be it remarked, in a practical attempt to achieve independence of God; to wrest God's world from Him as a means of doing without Him. Not, indeed, that the antediluvian is to be supposed to have always consciously and formally placed this object before his mind. He came to think of it only at intervals; and these intervals would go on enlarging, until it would come to be a feeling rather than a thought. The habit of impiety gathered strength, and acquired an impetus of its own, after the originating impulse had ceased. "And God saw that the wickedness of man was great on the earth." Had his sin only paused in its progress; had his guilt stood at a certain height, however mountainous; had it left certain possibilities of evil unrealized, he might yet have been spared, reclaimed, and forgiven. But God saw that "every imagination of the thoughts of his heart was only evil continually." Social virtue had slowly retired from one family relation to another; and piety from one faculty of the man to another, like a protesting and retreating friend, till now the last point was vacated to evil. The sophistic defense of evil was the chief occupation of the intellect. The emotions sought their objects amid the excitements of lust, and rapine, and gigantic schemes of self-aggrandisement. Memory rioted in the recollection of past atrocities. And imagination feasted on visions of evil, possible and impossible. Had the evil been local only, the bad might have been spared for the sake of the good; but "all flesh had corrupted his way." Every addition to man's numbers had been an additional element of hostility to God. Generation had followed generation, only to take up the original quarrel and to widen the breach, until now it had reached its limits. "The earth was filled with violence." The great caldron was full to overflowing. Still, upward of a century was added to the term of antediluvian probation. "The long-suffering of God waited;" but it waited only to be despised, and to behold the last shades added to the dark picture of human depravity.

Time of punishment determined by guilt.

"And God said unto Noah, The end of all flesh is come before me:" that is, both the consummation of antediluvian guilt and the termination of the reprieve. The time sustained a relation to the guilt, and was measured by it. And, now, both had reached a crisis. During the lapse of that eventful period, then, as many families, and as many members of families, had existed, as were necessary to give the family constitution an impartial trial. That number of families and individuals had included every variety of character, placed in every variety of local situation, under every description of influence, and amid every kind of circumstance, necessary for demonstrating that the well-being of social, no less than of individual, man depends on the practical coincidence of his will with the will of God. Of that immense multitude, no two had been precisely, and in every respect, alike; and yet they had "turned every one unto his own way." While each circumstantially differed from all the rest, the whole had united in the guilty experiment of finding happiness apart from God. In the prosecution of that unnatural endeavor, they had exalted every thing, in turn, into the place of God; and the result had uniformly left them more deeply immersed in depravity and guilt. How could it possibly be otherwise? For what, in the wide range of universal nature, could supply the place of infinite excellence? Man's all-related nature—the noblest part of it—had been constituted expressly to harmonize and unite with it. In his willful self-divorce from God, therefore, he was arresting the development of his whole nature, and adding wretchedness to his guilt. And in the vain attempt to replace his loss, or in oblivion of it, he had wrought up every form of Divine goodness into evil, and had run through every stage of guilt, necessary to show that his condition was as hopeless as his character was godless. Nothing remained "but a certain looking for of judgment."

How it subserved the Divine manifestation.

How, then, did the time of its continuance, and the manner of its termination, subserve the great and *ultimate* end—the Divine manifestation? Its continuance illustrated the all-sufficiency of the long-suffering of God, inasmuch as he did not terminate it until man had completed his guilty experiment. From the moment he attempted to be happy without availing himself of the Divine method of restoration, his doom was virtually sealed; for the longer he persisted in his course, the more effectually was he denaturalizing himself. The violence which came to fill the earth, was but an outward picture of the violated state of his own constitution. Still, though "He who seeth the end from the beginning" foresaw this, unless man himself had been allowed to make experimental proof of his own insufficiency; unless he had been suffered to exhaust his last device; he would never have *known*, in the only sense in which knowledge avails him, that he was "without strength." True, the minute particulars of that prolonged effort are unknown to the post-diluvian world; for, owing to the material difference of our situation—if only in relation to longevity—the knowledge could have been only of very slender advantage to us. Accordingly, we know only that which immediately concerns us—that the family dispensation enjoyed, during the antediluvian period, peculiar advantages for answering the great end of its existence; but that, in oblivion of that end, and in the assertion of its own self-sufficiency, it never ceased to wrestle with the laws of its constitution, though every struggle diminished its strength, until it had reached the last stage of moral debility, and even of social disorganization.

Now, if man could have foreseen that so long a period would have elapsed before that stage would be reached, his natural inquiry would have been—Can it be possible that God will wait for its arrival? The event proved that it was possible. Divine long-suffering was sufficient for it. Under each subsequent economy, God himself has referred to his patience with the antediluvians as an illustration of his forbearance. And, in eternity, when the history of the Divine procedure will be seen and studied in all its minuteness and fullness, it will doubtless appear that long-suffering waited till the last unit was added to the sum of human guilt; that it went even beyond, and illustrated the sovereignty of the Divine patience.

But if this extension of the period of antediluvian probation illustrated the sovereignty of God, it may be added that its termination at a certain point exemplified the Divine equity. Strict equity would have admitted of an earlier termination of that economy; but, in consequence of that compensative and remedial arrangement contemplated in the first promise and in the institute of sacrifice, it did not *require* that termination till the family constitution had passed through all the conditions necessary to convict it of its inveterate self-will, and of its hopeless insufficiency for itself. Till then, the sovereignty of God had reigned, and had availed itself even of the last moment. But when that moment had come, sovereignty itself, being based on equity, gave place to the requirements of justice. The "fullness of time" had come for man's deserved punishment. "And the Lord said unto Noah, come thou and all thy house into the ark." And Noah went into the ark.

"And the fountains of the great deep were broken up, and the flood-gates of heaven were opened." That signal illustration of the moral government of God left no part of the universe with which man had to do in the same state in which it was before. It changed the moral relations of the whole. All the multitudes who had lived and died in self-willed disobedience it convicted of the deepest guilt, and ratified their condemnation.* All who, like Abel, Enoch, and Noah, exercising faith in the promise of God, had obeyed His will, and suffered persecution for obeying it, were now justified in what they had done; for here God himself was "making bare his arm" and responding to their confidence. That holy will itself, so long resisted and despised, was now taken out of the dust in which it had been trampled, and vindicated in a manner which brought the world to the bar of judgment. While the Divine manifestation, so long obstructed in intention, by that self-willed race, beheld, in their removal, an open path for another stage in its onward course.

* Heb. xi. 7.

THIRD PART.

THE REASON OF THE METHOD AND OF THE HISTORY.

CHAPTER XVIII.

SECTION I.—THE REASON WHICH BELONGS TO MAN'S CONSTITUTION AND INVOLVES HIS WELL-BEING.

The law stated.

All the preceding laws respect the *method* of the Divine procedure, in connection with the new remedial and family constitution. The *reason* for this method is now to be considered; or the law which leads us to expect that the beings to whom, and by whom, the Divine manifestation is to be made, must be constituted in harmony with the laws of the objective universe, or that these laws will be found to have been established in prospective harmony with the designed constitution and the destiny of the being who is to expound and reflect them, to profit by and advance them. According to our theory of the Divine manifestation, then, the reason is twofold; the first part being founded in the constitution of the creature by whom the method is to be embodied and illustrated, and involves his well-being; and the second part relating to his destiny, as the means of Divine manifestation by and to himself, and so involving, in addition, the glory of the Creator.*

* Chapter i.

Art and science made possible.

In my illustrations of this part, in the Preadamite Earth, it was shown that while laws of some kind, and therefore method, are indispensable to a creation, quite irrespective of man's relation to it, yet that, in prospect of man's coming, the Creator, in appointing the actual laws of uniformities of the inorganic world, was only saying, in effect: Let the objective conditions of astronomy, physics, and chemistry exist. In appointing the plan of organized bodies, He was providing the objective conditions of botany and of the cultivation of the earth, in its various branches. And in designing the laws and method of sentient being, the external conditions of animal physiology, domestication, classification, and the different branches of scientific zoology, were provided. In other words, the Divine Creator was practically saying: Let all the objective conditions of the various arts and sciences be ready, that when man, the destined minister and interpreter of nature, shall come, the arts and sciences themselves may be possible. All beyond these objective conditions, man was to bring in his own constitution. So that, in giving to the human mind its actual constitution (as we saw, next, in the Treatise on Man Primeval), the Creator was but saying, in effect: Let the *subjective* conditions of art and science be added to the already existing objective conditions. We saw also that, in adding these subjective conditions, he was adding the materials of a science fundamental to all the rest—the science of anthropology—of man in the union of his animal and spiritual nature or pneumatology and physiology. To the question, therefore, Why man is constituted as he is; Why he reaches the external world through a body, and reacts upon it and upon himself by a mind; and Why he

Anthropology.

is conscious of both? the first reply is—That art, and science, and self-development, might be possible to him and for him. Further, we saw that other laws of the method made *philosophy* possible; the philosophy which ascends from an account of things to account for them; from signs to the things signified; from laws to the knowledge of the Lawgiver. So that if asked, Why man is made to recognize the dependent, the ultimate, and the necessary? the only reply is—In order that he might have a *natural theology;* that he might find himself in a temple in which every object is symbolic of the Divine presence, and is ever inviting him to acts of grateful self-improving worship. And then we found that other parts of the method made *moral government* possible; that man, as a moral being, found every property and power of his nature on probation, and every part of the system into which he had come arranged in relation to it. And thus it appeared that there was not one of the laws of the method which was not indispensable as a condition either of his individual well-being, or to the attainment of his destiny as a means of the Divine manifestation. Even the special character given to the probation of the first man, we found to be only a true and direct illustration of these laws.*

Philosophy.

Natural theology.

Moral government.

The momentous event of that probation has now landed us in a new stage of inquiry. We have found the family constitution in process of development, and a basis of mercy underlying the whole. Why this constitution and this basis? This question, like all the preceding, admits of a twofold reply. In its relation to God, the answer belongs to the section following.

Why?

* Chapter ii.

In respect to man, our reply is, that they make the highest well-being of the race possible.*

That the family might be possible.

Now, that this is true of the family constition is evident from the facts that the family is only the unfolding of the individual—the natural and harmonious development of social man; and that to tamper with its laws, is to derange the individual and to tend to arrest the progress of the race. The basis of the family-life is marriage; and the essence of marriage consists in the permanency and exclusiveness of union between individuals of different sexes. So that in making the desire for such a union a part of human nature, the Creator was but issuing the fiat: Let the FAMILY be possible.† By arranging that the authority, instruction, and example of the parent should be responded to by the obedience, belief, and imitation of the child; and by prolonging the plastic period of childhood and youth through many years, the Creator was saying: Let EDUCATION be possible. Division of labor, in loving co-operation, began between man and wife, and appeared in the play of their infant children; and the parental affection which prompted them to provide, if only a day onward, for the wants of their children, involved the idea of PROPERTY, and led to its acquisition. The same affection, by investing the life of its objects with sacredness; by imparting to them all the stores of parental information; and by aiming to benefit them by exchange, barter, and intercourse with other families, made CIVILIZATION possible, and contained its germinating seeds. The government of such a community of young responsible natures as the family

Education.

Property.

Civilization.

* Chapter iii.

† Chapters iv. and v.

includes, in which questions of *meum* and *tuum* had to be daily decided, right to be protected against might, the welfare of each to be treated as the interest of all, and in which the whole was administered by impartial affection—

Social ethics.

contained the conditions of social ETHICS, and was a sphere eminently favorable to their development. While the Divine arrangement by which effects become causes and propagate themselves in linked and endless succession; by which the knowledge which is thus made attainable is also transmissible from generation to generation; and by which the race is not only united in generations, but is renovated and started anew with each generation, was always inviting the present to improve on the past and to inspire and enrich the future: in other words, it was the Divine mode of saying:

History and progress.

Let HISTORY and PROGRESS be possible.*

All the laws of the method present in the family.

Now, there is not one of the laws of the method which is not present in each of these possibilities. They are older than the family, and form the very conditions of its existence. The repeal of any one of them would have converted each of the possibilities we have named into an impossibility. The law of continuity, for example—itself linked on to other laws—is essential to the history and progress of the race. The laws of order and subordination, of influence and obligation, lie at the foundation of social ethics. The same laws, combined with those of activity and development, are essential to property and civilization. Laws of relation, uniformity, and obligation, are among the conditions of education. Marriage itself is only the law of relation taking a unique form. The entire family constitution is but a Divine con-

* Chapters v. to xiii.

ception employed to embody these laws in a new form, in order to carry forward the process of the Divine manifestation by man and to him. They form the subjective conditions of the family, and make it possible; just as the family itself conditionates the well-being of the race, and makes it possible.

Why the well-being of the family is only possible.

But why should the family and the laws which it embodies make the well-being of humanity only *possible* and *practicable?* Because its Divine Originator is a Moral Governor and not a Fate, and because man is a free responsible agent and not a machine. This is the very soul of the Divine method. Constituted as man is, he would be justified in complaining were it otherwise; for how could he know either his powers or their limits in a sphere which left him no option and encouraged no effort. Or how could he answer his high end, either of exemplifying the Divine excellence, or of voluntarily subserving the Divine design, in a circle in which freedom was only a name and necessity the only reality? Accordingly, it is a vital characteristic of the Divine method that in each of its laws, and in all its procedure, it should be in strict harmony with man's free nature; contemplating him as a being meant to understand, appreciate, voluntarily subserve, and enjoy the Divine manifestation. And this peculiarity and prerogative of man's position account for much which is commonly deemed mysterious in the Divine arrangements, both of the human constitution and of the universe at large.

Virtues and vices made possible by marriage.

The single distinction of sex, for example, coming up, as it does, from the depths of the pre-existing organic and animal worlds, and forming the earth-root of humanity, makes possible, in the case of a free being such as man, a greater number of virtues and vices than all his other bodily endowments together; for it underlies his entire nature. Marriage is at once the complement and reduplication of his social nature. But the very fact that the points of union may be as numerous as are the distinctive parts of human nature, leaves it possible that they may be all points of repulsion and collision. The love which should form the basis of the union may be simulated by lust, vanity, or interest. The subordination which it involves may be perverted into oppression. Its life-long exclusiveness may be violated by polygamy, divorce, and the various forms of licentiousness. And the purity of which it might have been the discipline and the sacrament, lifting sense into the region of the supersensual, leaves open a door through which sensuality may drag down and animalize man's whole nature to a depth to which the mere animal can not descend. Yet no voice from Heaven can be expected to "forbid the banns," in order to avoid this liability. Such an intervention would shut out all the virtuous and hallowing possibilities of the union. All that man, as a free being, could either ask for, or admit of, is, that the obligations which belong to the union do not exceed his means of compliance.

By offspring, and their education.

By offspring and their education man is invested with the power of not merely completing and enlarging his social nature, but of multiplying himself—raising up other human beings in his own image. He has it in his power, however, to poison their existence before they see the light; to destroy them by anticipation.*

* La passion la plus effrénée et la plus chère à la nature humaine . . . . . . verse seule plus de maux sur la terre que tous les autres vices ensemble. Nous avons horreur meurtre; mais que sont tous les meurtres

He is not merely the means of giving them physical life; like the prophet extending himself on the dead body of the child; he underlies and overlies the entire nature of his children, touching and quickening them at all points of their inmost being. He literally occupies a throne of moral administration. Shall his subjects be angels or fiends? The danger of his making them the latter must not deprive him of whatever power he possesses of making them the former. And that he does possess such a power is evident from the hallowed history of many a family; a history which is happily perpetuating itself among their descendants, and which is still unfinished on earth and in heaven.

By the separation into families. Each family is a world apart. It gravitates to other families, indeed; has interests in common with them; can not exist without them. "Why, then, should they not all live in unrestricted intercourse, and in sight of each other?" Because each needs a free space for the free development of its own powers: whereas, the communism implied in the question would be only a new form of intolerable oppression, in which one kind of knowledge would outrun reflection, and another kind forestall experience, and many things would be disclosed and felt which would prove fatal to moral liberty and progress. Hence, each family instinctively draws apart from the rest. And, as darkness curtains off each man from his fellows, and puts him on a probation distinct from that of the day, so the local separation of the family, and the seclusion of the tent or the house, place each family on a probation of its own.*

réunis, et la guerre même, comparés au vice, qui est comme le mauvais principe, *homicide dès le commencement*, qui agit sur le possible, tue ce qui n'existe point encore, et ne cesse de veiller sur les sources de la vie pour les appauvrir ou les souiller," etc.—De Maistre, *Soirées de Saint-Pétersbourg*, i. 64. 65.

* Man Primeval, p. 400

By property and civilization.

Property and the progress of civilization brought indefinite enlargements of man's moral domain. They brought Nature to his side, and gave him the key to all its resources; multiplying his own powers by linking them on to those of his fellows; opening to him the unlimited advantage of being one of a race. But along with property came the opportunity of theft and injustice. Every new art and branch of industry, each opening field of activity, and every fresh subject of intercourse which the progress of civilization created, brought new occasions of fraud and oppression. Why, then, was not each tongue struck dumb in the first utterance of falsehood; each hand withered in the act of robbery; and each oppressor paralyzed in the midst of his spoliation? Because man is a voluntary being; and such coercion, by alighting only on his physical nature, might even exasperate his moral disease. Because he has the power of voluntarily withholding his hand from the evil deed; and, by every exertion of that power, augments it. Because man has the godlike prerogative of uttering His will, as law, on the subject; and all such laws possess, as expositions of human duty, a highly educating power for the whole community. Because physical coercion, by usurping the place of man's nature, would allow him to form no common stock of moral experience, no public opinion, no self-expanding sense of justice, and would allow no social progress from generation to generation.

Each advance enlarged the sphere of man's probation.

It is to be remarked, that at each stage of the development of the family, a new domain was added to the empire of the will, and, consequently, a new sphere in which man was placed on probation. His special probation in Paradise made it possible for him to bring his will into direct collision with the Divine will. In the expansion of the family a succession of similar collisions were made possible; but with this difference, that now the possibility related proximately and directly to a collision with other human wills, and with the Divine will only through them. Thus, marriage was meant to solve the problem, antecedently inexplicable, of two distinct human wills harmonizing so as to attain even their personal ends best in one and the same sphere, and to become practically one. Love, itself a profounder mystery, was to furnish the solution. But though this love admitted of perpetual increase, it always left the will at large. Man could not complain, on the one hand, that he had no adequate motives to observe the sanctity of the marriage-bond; a thousand considerations pressed on him to that effect: nor could he urge, on the other, that he was compelled to observe it; for if he pleased he could burst through them all. Education placed him in a relation to the wills of his children most formative and unique. Will he train them to the right use of their wills—to true freedom? This he can do only by training them to obedience; for law and liberty are truly correlative. Interest, affection, and duty, all combine to urge such training. But all history, postdiluvian as well as antediluvian, unites to show how free man is to neglect it, even though the effect be to arm the filial will against the parental. Property and civilization placed him face to face with the wills of other heads of families. Will he respect or violate their rights? He has only to be just. And, in order to this, he has only to will. For justice, as the Roman law truly defines it, is but a "constans et perpetua *voluntas* jus suum cuique tribuendi."* How easy, yet how difficult the task! Let man

* *Corp. Jur. Civ. Instit.* I. i.

only do unto others as he would they should do unto him, and the earth will be a social paradise. Let the obligation be disregarded, and a fierce anarchy of selfish wills must ensue. And "the earth was filled with violence through them."

The unfolding of the individual and the family supposes a scheme of mercy.

If the well-being of the race presupposes the family constitution, the very existence of the family presupposes a dispensation of mercy. The moment that guilt became a fact of man's consciousness and history, his relation to the government of God was changed. Equity could award him only the punishment due to his guilt. The remission of that punishment, and his restoration to God, could come only from a Divine arrangement of mercy. The first promise and the institution of sacrifice announced that arrangement, and symbolized its method. Only thus could RELIGION be made possible—the religion of penitence, faith, and loving obedience. The *subjective* conditions of religion, indeed, belonged to man's constitution; and sin, though it might pervert, could not destroy them. And here, now, in the means of mercy, were its *objective* conditions. By the Divine arrangement that the promise should be fulfilled through the medium of the woman, and that sacrifice should be offered by the man, while each was alike interested in both, a new and sacred character was given to the bond which made them one; and *the religion of the family* became possible. While the unique arrangement by which every thing calculated to impress in the parents found a counterpart susceptibility of impression in the children; by which they were retained, year after year, in the parental hand; the head of the family leading them all the time to the altar as their representative with God made possible the transmission of religion from generation to generation.

Why was religion made possible only?

And here, again, if the question recurs, Why was not all this made more than possible? the reply recurs also, Because man was endowed with the power of making it actual, and of benefiting himself by the effort; and because any necessitating force acting on that power would have altered its character, and have made religion impossible. True, if he chose, he could desert the altar and disregard the Promise, violate the sanctity of home, arm his children in the general revolt against God, and reduce the family organization to a wreck. The event proved the fatal easiness of the process. But what an unknown weight of motive lay in the opposite direction! The beseeching sacredness of conjugal love; the strength of parental affection yearning for the highest happiness of its objects; the fact that to train their wills to a harmony with God's will was the only guarantee for keeping them in accordance with the parental will. Regard for the law and character of God, whose representative the parent was. These were considerations by which many a Patriarch was actually induced for centuries to "walk with God," and "to command his household after him."

What motives more cogent could have been brought to bear, consistently with freedom, on man's moral nature? Antecedently, and to other orders of being, these motives might have appeared even too forceful. "What (it might have been asked) can counterbalance them? The family constitution is all but necessitated to work well. It is wanting in liberty of action." On the supposition that some other mode of developing and training humanity had been tried and failed, and that the family constitution was now Divinely propounded for the first time, who could survey its exquisite framework and strong tendencies for good, without concluding that had it been resorted to at the first, no failure could have ensued, and that it would only be necessary to resort to it now, in order to render the well-being of the race secure ?

Why was the economy continued after its failure became apparent?

But why was the economy continued even after it threatened to fail as a Divine manifestation by man ? The preceding law—the law of change—is supposed to contain the reason. Man, if treated as a free being, must be allowed a sufficient period for repairing the past by turning to account his dear-bought experience. Had the era of the family economy, in its probationary and dispensational form, been closed while appearances were yet promising, or when as yet they were only doubtful, man " would have had whereof to glory," and history would have pronounced the experiment unfinished and unsatisfactory. Had it been brought to an end, even speedily after the instances of failure formed a decided majority, it would still have been fancied that, had space been given to man, those failures might have been converted by him into the very means of his recovery. The force of motives fluctuates with circumstances. The experiment must be varied. Accordingly, no two days of patriarchal longevity were precisely alike. The situation of each patriarch differed from that of every other. Every family had its own distinctive history. Generation differed from generation. The experiment never paused, and was ever varying.*

Motives to recovery always on the increase.

In connection with its prolonged duration, too, two facts are to be remembered : that the accumulating evils attending the family apostasy were always accumulating motives for reformation

* Chapter xvii.

and return to God; and that motives to the same effect were added, age after age, by positive Divine calls and interventions suited to the times. So that, at the eve of the deluge, the "preacher of righteousness" had grounds of appeal, exceeding in number and weight those of any previous age. Nor was it until it appeared as if motives became subjectively weak in proportion as they were objecjectively multiplied and strong, that the great experiment was quenched in the deluge. Morally, as an experiment of and for man, it had ceased long before; for other and higher considerations it was high time that it should now cease historically also.

SECTION II.—THE REASON WHICH RELATES TO THE MANIFESTATION OF THE DIVINE ALL-SUFFICIENCY, AND SO INCLUDES MAN'S DESTINY.

Reason of man's well-being.

In the preceding section we saw so much of the reason of the Divine method as relates to man's well-being; here, we advance further, and seek for the reason of that well-being itself. There, he might be viewed as an end to himself; here, we regard him as a means to an end beyond. His well-being is necessary, even if he is to be only the means of Divine manifestation to other orders of being—just as the mere animal creation is to us; but if, beyond this, he is to be a manifestation of the Divine all-sufficiency to himself, he must be able to trace his well-being to its source, and to live in the consciousness of his high destiny. And if man's well-being accounts for the existence of the remedial and family economy, his destiny equally accounts for much in the form and method of that economy which would otherwise appear inexplicable.

Reason of method.

If the constitution of the family is to be construed by man so as to point him to its ultimate design, all the "laws of the method" might be shown to be indispensable. In the entire absence of law it would be impossible for the mind to infer a Lawgiver. In the absence of all signs of a plan, the family would not be known to have a constitution; and, evincing no design, could whisper no hint of the mind which framed it. But the laws of relation and order, of uniformity and analogy, are modes by which the great Pater-familias reflects His mind, and says, in effect: Let such a plan be apparent.*

Why its evidence is limited.

Why, then, it may be inconsiderately asked, were not these laws made to force themselves, Sinai-like, on man's involuntary notice? Because they were designed to report themselves as the chosen arrangements of a Being infinitely free; and this they could do only as they developed and respected the idea of freedom in man's own nature. Proof of a Divine agency so cogent as to leave man no option whatever as to his conclusions respecting it, would be as unsuited to his moral freedom as the absence of all, or of adequate, proof would be to his rational conviction.

The family arranged to teach dependence on God.

If the family did not exhibit marks of arrangement, dependent on the will of God, it would be regarded as proclaiming its independence. Instead of being the means of the Divine manifestation, it would only manifest itself and absorb attention in its own nature. So far from referring the human mind to God, it would literally stand between man and his Creator, and would tend to inclose him in its own mechanism. Here, then, is the profoundest reason which

* Chapters vii. viii. xi. xvi.

can be conceived of for the law of dependence. Even if man had not sinned, this principle would have been of the highest importance. But the fact that he has not only sinned, but that it was at this very point of dependence that he fell, invests this law with transcendent interest. The question now involved is no less than this, whether—man having violated the law of dependence in his own individual person—there are adequate safeguards against his repeating, diffusing, and perpetuating the same evil in the family? That such safeguards do exist we have shown. In the complementary characteristics of the sexes and in their numerical proportion; in the selected mode for continuing the race, for long retaining the child in the parental hand, and for securing the possible progress of the species from age to age; in the adaptedness of the region assigned to antediluvian man; in the mutual dependence and instinctive co-operation of distinct families, as well as in the plan for his recovery, direct from Heaven;—in these and other respects, choice and adjustment are every where visible. Every helpless little one that lives on his smile was meant to memorialize him, in the manner most likely to affect him, on the fact of his own dependence. From the first a Voice and a Hand, not to be mistaken, had "called a little child, and set him in the midst of" every family, as a symbol of humility and dependence to all its members. The entire constitution was inter-dependent, and an embodiment of dependence on God. It was a God-like method of saying: Let man have ever before his eyes a welcome symbol and a memorial of my Fatherhood and of his loving dependence on me.* Still, if the right interpretation of the symbol is to be either useful to man or acceptable to God,

* Chapter xiv.

it must be voluntary. His recognition of his dependence is simply the recognition of a fact, and, as such, adds to his knowledge; but it is the knowledge of his highest moral relation, and as such it involves both his well-being and his destiny more vitally than all his other relations put together. Let the evidence of his dependence sink below a given point, and his ignorance of it would be pardonable; let it rise to the point of compelling belief, and all the moral part of his nature—the very part to which it relates—would be ignored, and its highest end unattained.

The ultimate facts of the family teach dependence.

In the absence, again, of all ultimate facts and necessary truths from the sphere of the family—supposing their absence possible—man might have moved forever in the mill-horse circle of secondary causes, and have blindly regarded it as of unaccountable self-origination. But the several arrangements just enumerated were all ultimate facts. By these contingencies the family is characterized and made unique. Man himself did not originate them. They could not explain themselves. Nothing in nature accounted for them. To the listening ear, they distinctly reported themselves as Divine appointments. If man looked behind and beneath them, he could find nothing supporting them but the will of God. Where was the Fountain of the love which flowed through the family, and which it always seems laboring to express? Whose mind conceived the idea which the family embodies? What Will assigned and maintained the laws which made it what it was? In every conception of what man *ought* to do, an eternal distinction underlies his sense of duty—the immutable difference between right and wrong. Even on the eve of the flood, man had to take but a few backward steps, in order to reach historically the

18*

first family, and to find himself standing face to face with its Divine Creator. Reflection, consciousness, history, alike pointed him to the Hand from which it was suspended.*

Man is to recognize his dependence voluntarily.

Still, if man is to recognize that hand as the free and fatherly Hand of God, he must be able to do it freely. The ultimate facts and necessary truths involved in the constitution of the family must not declare themselves so as to prejudice his responsible freedom. Accordingly, though they can not but act as laws of thought, they neither select the objects of his attention nor determine the extent of his mental operations. Even the evidence that there was a first family, and that Adam was the father of the whole antediluvian community, must not be such as to make every opposite theory impossible. Nor was it. From the very make of the mind, the strength of the evidence, so far from being felt necessarily, could be appreciated only according to the degree of attention given to it; and attention is a voluntary act of the mind. Thus, every law of the family constitution was a test and discipline of man's sense of dependence; while the whole was the Divine mode of saying: Let the manifestation of my Fatherhood be made to the family through the family itself.

The remedial economy aims at the same effect.

But man has sinned; that is, has brought his will into collision with the will of God. If, then, there was reason for testing and developing the sense of dependence in unfallen man, as the only condition of his being a medium of Divine manifestation to himself, surely every act of disobedience strengthens the reason for continuing to aim at the same end through every successive stage of the Divine dispensations. Ac-

* Chapter xv.

cordingly, the remedial economy was the Divine contrivance to deepen the sense of dependence in sinful man, and to increase his motives to obedience. It gave him a promise of deliverance, which required his belief; and appointed the institute of sacrifice, which required his obedience. He could not believe the promise without consciously admitting that the pure mercy of God had saved him from destruction. While at the altar of sacrifice, where he surrendered as a penitent to the justice of God, he was simply replacing himself in the position which he ought never to have left, and throwing himself unconditionally on the grace of God. Here was the Divine method of saying: Let man, in his own person and experience, be a conscious manifestation that God is merciful.

"Why, then, was not a power brought to bear upon man which should make the recognition of this display inevitable?" Because coercion is the opposite of freedom, not its manifestation. Had the scheme of mercy been forced on the Divine Being, man's compelled reception of it would have been the appropriate sequel. No grace, no gratitude. But man is the free subject of a free Sovereign. And the first promise and the institution of sacrifice are the instruments of his government, as much as the tree of life and the tree of knowledge were in the probation of the first man. The Promise was a newly-planted tree of life; the Altar was another tree of the knowledge of good and evil—a discriminating test of man's sense of dependence and obligation. Believing obedience in relation to the altar of sacrifice entitled man to all the blessings included in the promise; disobedience involved the confirmation and prolongation of the original curse.*

* Chapter iii.

As well as all subsequent Divine interventions.

But what (it might be said) if the same Mercy which introduced the dispensation had continued to supplement it from time to time, as depravity advanced, with Divine disclosures and striking interpositions, who can say but that the tide of evil might have ebbed? Not only did such interventions take place, they were even in selected accordance with the character of the times when they were made. From the nature of the one we may safely infer that of the other. When the antediluvian population were threatened with a deluge, they had, most probably, reached the point of a pantheistic polytheism or of confirmed practical atheism. Now, history warrants the conclusion that this condition would be attained gradually. What are the stages by which it would be reached? Beginning with the denial of *future* retribution as the least revolting form of disbelief, it would extend next to the denial of God's *present* providential government, and end in questioning the fact of the Divine existence itself. This is the order which error observes from bad to worse. To meet the first error, we find Enoch commissioned to prophesy, "Behold, the Lord cometh with ten thousand of his saints, to execute judgment." After a season of continued but neglected warning, the startling event of his translation was admirably fitted to meet the infidelity of the second stage. And when, "because judgment against an evil work was not speedily executed, the hearts of the sons of men were set in them to do evil," then, and not till then, did outraged Goodness accept the challenge of man's impiety and significantly command the construction of the prophetic ark.* And thus God said: Let the history of man become a manifestation of mercy drawn out into long-suffering.†

* Heb. xi. 7.

† Chapter iv.

Man's moral freedom respected.

But even these signs of the preternatural, meant to preserve the balance between man's trial and his strength, and to keep him in mind of his high and ultimate end, must be kept within certain limits; or he himself will complain that his freedom is overborne. Accordingly, they were only in analogy with the Divine method from the beginning. Whether the Almighty chose to address us by things or by words, each method alike had to be originated by Himself. Each geological stage through which the earth had passed beheld Him "coming out of his place," to add a new section to the great system of signs by which He prepared eventually to reveal Himself to man. The creation of man was a recent miracle. Some of the elementary truths of civilization had doubtless been Divinely and directly imparted to him. The cherubic symbol of the Divine presence, probably, had not yet faded from his horizon, but still visibly lingered at the gates of Eden; its very familiarity depriving it of its supernatural significance. So impervious had man's moral nature become, that little danger would there have been of his being too roughly roused from his fatal slumber, "even though one rose from the dead."

Every increase of power an increase of responsibility.

Thus every fact and law of the economy, while it enlarged man's power of attaining his highest end, in being a distinct manifestation of God as the Father of Mercies, proportionally enlarged his responsible liberty and danger of becoming his own end, and so involving the race in ruin. An Abel and a Seth, an Enoch and a Noah—every antediluvian who recognized his new remedial relations to God, who became conscious of his consequent obligations, and yielded obedience to his new motives—became once more capable of answering the ultimate end of his existence. Were all the laws of nature, physical and social, the contingent but chosen appointment of the Divine will? The same state of mind which made him sensible of his entire dependence for mercy on the sovereign will of God, would tend also to keep him in harmony with these laws. For instead of presuming to dictate to them, he would recognize in them the unvarying expressions of their Maker's will, and find that he could employ them only as he moved in harmony with them. Had he, by placing himself in hostility to God, virtually enlisted in the quarrel all the kingdoms of nature which had been given into his hands? In every sacrifice he offers, he brings them all back again; for in the altar, the fruit, and the victim, they are all present—present as the witnesses of his guilt in having abused them to sinful purposes; and present as expressions of his penitence and dependence, in restoring them again to their great Proprietor, and in thus giving the glory of the whole to God.

Domestic government brings the highest power and responsibility.

But that which armed man with greater power than even his dominion over the kingdoms of nature was his domestic and social relations. Through these, he could alienate the entire race from God; and, by his voluntary transgression, he had prospectively done so. But the same motives which bring *him* back to God, induce him to consecrate his influence to the recovery of his children and dependents also. Having discovered the grand secret that happiness and honor can be found only in accordance with the laws and purposes of God, all the sympathies of his social nature are enlisted in persevering endeavor to harmonize the character and conduct of his household with the will of God. The prolonged period of filial impressibleness and docility affords him the most precious facilities for the attainment of this end. It seems impossible to conceive of a situation more favorable to the right development of that distinctive prerogative of humanity, the will, than that which the family affords. On the one hand, what temptation could there be to crush or oppress the individuality and free agency of the young human being, where affection itself administers law, and finds much of its happiness in the freedom of its subjects. On the other hand, if the preservation of parental authority is essential to the well-being of the family, the parent discovers that in training his children to piety, he is both best securing their love for himself, and is advancing his own conformity to the Divine will. How eminently calculated is the position of the parent to occasion gratitude for his domestic enjoyment and deep anxiety for the future and lasting welfare of the objects so dear to him; and how natural for him to appeal to the Being who alone can befriend him on the only scale commensurate with his wishes—to the Father "of all the families that call upon His name!" And in conducting the worship of the assembled family, he appears in the Divine presence with all his individual powers and social relations restored; and thus prepared to answer the ultimate end of his existence by appreciating and voluntarily subserving the advancement of the Divine manifestation. While each patriarch, by being placed at the head of a new generation, was afforded the opportunity of carrying the manifestation beyond all who had gone before, and of thus approaching a stage nearer to perfection.

The explosive power of sin.

The explosive power of sin, as selfishness, indeed, prevailed. The first man was not content to derive from a source that lay out of himself, the ultimate ground and reason, and the definite criterion of his acts. And the same repellent power appeared in every member of his antediluvian family. "It constituted as many new centers, as many rebellious and divided systems of action as there were human beings; atomic centers of limited and petty influence, but without subordination to Him from whom they had derived the power to rise in revolt against Him. Nay, even more. So long as man was obedient to God, the whole being of man was obedient to his controlling faculties; but when he ceased to be the servant of the Lord, he ceased also to be the master of himself. Thus, therefore, in the midst of God's fair creation was there planted, wherever there stood a man, a perpetually prolific principle of derangement, of separate, self-centered action, spent ineffectually upon objects that did not enter into the design of the universe, nor contribute, unless by opposition and revulsion, to the fulfillment of its appointed work. God, however, ordained certain conditions of human existence which, as intermediate expedients, and instruments of a secondary discipline, should both check the progress of selfishness by establishing a counteracting principle, and should likewise prepare men to recognize the higher truths taught in Divine revelation, and supply them with real, though partial, approximations to the true law of their being. These were various in shape; but their pervading character was the same; it was that of a *κοινωνία*, a common life. A common life in the family, in the tribe, in the nation was, apart from direct manifestations of the Divine will, the grand counteractor of the disorganizing agency of the law of self-worship." *

* Gladstone, *The State in relation to the Church*, vol. i. pp. 46–50.

The family, God's natural ordinance against selfishness.

During the whole antediluvian period, the family was God's great natural protest and ordinance against the dissevering power of sin. "One blood" circulated through the veins of humanity. Each individual will stood in the midst of a number of related wills, whose separate ends could be best gained by the union of each with all. The only atmosphere proper to the community was love. The family should have been the "schoolmaster to lead" them to the altar; where one sacrifice would have availed them all, and one promise have addressed them all. But, in ceasing to love the blessed God, man lost the great unitive principle of the race. In arming himself against God, he becomes, more or less, a center of repulsion to the universe.*

The event, however, proved that at every step of the process the balance was maintained between man's freedom and his duty, between his condition and his destiny. That the means of answering the high end of the economy were adequately supplied, appears from this, that many adoringly recognized and employed them. They were "preachers of righteousness;" enforcing the laws and claims of the dispensation. They pointed to the preternatural events that occurred as warning angels sent from God. They received or assumed significant names, like medallions struck to save from oblivion the Divine element and object of the dispensation. The altars which "by faith" they reared, were so many points of friendly contact with Heaven, and protests against the world's apostasy. While the great mass was moving in a contrary direction, they "walked with God," so as to reflect and radiate his presence. They pointed to His awful "coming" to vindicate the economy,

* Chapter xvii.

and to punish all who had resisted the faithful in their endeavors to answer its end. In a word, they were living moral manifestations of God. Even at last, the faith and practical obedience of Noah "condemned the world;" convicting it of self-destruction under an economy which might have saved the race as well as an individual. On the other hand, that the means employed for attaining this end left man's moral freedom unimpaired is mournfully clear. The family, like the individual, fell through the abuse of that freedom, and continued falling. The altar was not a fort to compel submission; and Cain forsook the altar. The affections were not constrained; and "the sons of God took them wives of all which they chose;" and the great moral distinction of the economy between the obedient and the disobedient was confounded—the church was merged in the world. Right was not armed with the bolts of heaven, and might overcame it, "filling the earth with violence." The church was destroyed by the world. The high end of the family constitution could be attained only by moral means; and man, instead of being a manifestation of God, became a manifestation of selfishness. From first to last, the contest which he maintained was this—whether God's will should prevail for good, or his own will for evil; whether God should be the chief good and ultimate end of his own creation, or whether man should wrest it from Him, use it for his own selfish purposes, and so become his own end. This is the key to the entire economy. Was it strange that all human distinctions should be merged in that one which marked off the few who in any degree answered the end of the dispensation from the masses who spent life in the violation of its laws?

FOURTH PART.

THE ULTIMATE END OF THE FAMILY PROBATION AND ECONOMY AS A MEANS OF DIVINE MANIFESTATION.

CHAPTER XIX.

SECTION I.—POWER.

The economy a display of Divine Power.

THOUGH the patriarchal dispensation had failed, as a voluntary manifestation of God by man, not the less did the wonderful constitution of the family contain, quite irrespectively of the human will, a manifestation of God to him; while his perversion of it was made the occasion of bringing to light new aspects of the Divine character, especially patience and long-suffering.

All the illustrations of Power in nature continued.

All the preceding manifestations of the Divine Power in the material world were brought forward into the period of the family economy. Life, in its unnumbered forms, was continued. The seasons revolved. The earth silently and smoothly rolled on in space. All the laws of nature, animate and inanimate, were maintained in ceaseless activity, combined with undeviating uniformity. For about two thousand years, notwithstanding the elemental conflicts which then, doubtless, as now, seemed to threaten at times the stability of the system, "all things continued as they were at the beginning." Now, if the first hour of creation continued a display of boundless power, every moment which prolonged that display was calculated to render man's conceptions of it more enlarged and impressive; just as our sense of the force of the arm which projected a heavy body ten yards, would go on increasing as we saw the distance prolonged and the velocity undiminished.

And enlarged in the multiplication of the human race.

In a similar manner, if the production of a single human being, capable of voluntary effort, furnished a surpassing illustration of the Divine Power, the continuance and multiplication of the human race, during so long a period, proportionally increased the force of the illustration. And this would be true, even if each of the race had lived and moved in isolation from all the rest. But all the power which they gained by combination was so much gained to the argument for the power of God. Every latent force elicited from matter by antediluvian progress in the arts; every natural instinct which kept its ground in defiance of a perverted intellect; and, still more, every social law voluntarily agreed to and obeyed, despite the importunities of depraved propensities—all combined to proclaim: "Thou hast a mighty arm: strong is Thy hand, and high is Thy right hand."*

Laws and forces of the domestic constitution.

The power residing in the domestic constitution loudly proclaimed the same truth. The power of authority, of opinion, of example, of union—indeed, all the various modifications of influence which are elsewhere found in separation, and which

* Psalm lxxxix. 13.

yet separately move the societies they affect—are all united in the family as in their fountain-head. In truth, so powerful are they in the family for evil or for good, that all other forms of social power can do little more than take advantage of them or direct them. So invincible is the moral energy which inheres in this constitution, that, where it operates, every force of evil from without is repelled like waves from a rock. During the antediluvian period, indeed, that moral power declined from causes within the family; but the very "violence which filled the earth" in consequence, was only the measure of the power which had been let loose and lawless from the salutary restraints and guidance of family government. Even then, however, the physical framework of the family continued to stand, though it had ceased to answer its higher social and moral ends, and though an ocean of licentiousness surged around it; and, by standing, it presented a lofty monument of the power which had reared it.

Every holy character an instance of power.

Every instance of virtue and piety which adorned that early period, was a striking illustration of the Divine Power. The production of a holy character under the most favorable circumstances evinces the operation of the Divine energy; for its existence is a triumph over antagonistic powers in the man himself. But where, in addition to this, the foes of his piety are those of his own household; and where every thing beyond his family circle, turn which way he will, presents a threatening aspect also—the origination and maintenance of a holy character in such circumstances exhibits the energy of a perpetual triumph. Such a character is "an organized victory." Lamentable it is that the decision of character and indomitable purpose which men so profoundly admire, should so seldom be seen on the side of piety. The antediluvian world resounded, probably, with the fame of many distinguished for those qualities, as human engines of destruction. But so much the more loftily did the character of a Seth, of an Enoch, and a Noah tower above them all in monumental strength; inasmuch as each of them stood like an Abdiel among an apostate host. The silent admiration they excited in some, the uncontrolable fears with which they inspired others, and the hatred and active hostility which beset their onward course—all attested an energy of character which, if put forth in some popular cause, would have awed the wild into homage at its daring and power. While the *faith* by which Enoch walked with God, and the *prayer* which distinguished a Noah, evinced their own conviction, that the power which enabled them "to stand"* was ultimately traceable to God. "He giveth power to the faint, and to them that have no might He increaseth strength."

The deluge was to be a new display of power.

The prediction which threatened the destruction of the world, too, was, in effect, a prediction of a new display of power. On this account, probably, it was partly that the world withheld their belief from it. Their immoral condition prepared them to believe that they did not deserve such a punishment; and this again prepared them to believe any one who chose to assert that it could not be inflicted. When, therefore, it actually occurred, "the voice of many waters" proclaimed, "He ruleth by His power forever; His eyes behold the nations; let not the rebellious exalt themselves."†

* Romans, xiv. 5.

† Psalm lxvi. 7.

SECTION II.—WISDOM.

The whole of the period during which the development of the Family Constitution took place, was stored with illustrations of the Divine Wisdom. Proofs of this fact are so numerous that we must limit ourselves to a selection; and most of these even we can do little more than name.

The family an unfolding of Divine design.

During the entire period, the progress of civilization in any one department was, in effect, a cumulative argument for that provident wisdom which had made such progress possible. Every application of physical means to human ends, every addition made to human knowledge and comfort, was only a new discovery of relations instituted by Him who had forelaid the entire plan, and who designed to benefit man by the same means by which He educated him.

Maternal affection.

But entering the domestic circle itself, what marks of benevolent design appear in the arrangement by which the tender remembrances and yearning associations which "accumulate in the maternal mind during the period of gestation, should all be summed up amid the throes of parturition," and go to augment the affection which she is henceforth to feel for her offspring; by which the necessary aliment is secreted in the maternal bosom, and the mouth of the suckling is provided with the means of abstracting and imbibing it; and in that by which the strength of the maternal regard is proportioned to the helplessness and wants of her child, not waiting for its power of appreciating and returning her affection, but meeting it with caresses in the hour of its weakness and unconsciousness.

Simplicity of parental office.

As to the parents themselves—the simplicity of the office assigned them in the government of the family, compared with the magnitude of its results, is a marked display of the Divine Wisdom. The task to be accomplished is difficult and momentous; so arduous that human legislation has never touched it without more or less marring it. But the whole is devolved, by Providence, on two persons. These, from their mutual relations, are in various respects better qualified for the office, and have a deeper interest in its right discharge, than any other parties in the world. Their task is made easy by having to begin, not with many, but with one; and still easier by having to attend at first only to its physical wants. The experience thus acquired is carried forward with advantage to the treatment of the younger children, and facilitates their training. As their activity for their children's welfare is purely voluntary, and as that voluntariness is derived from gratitude and love, it leads to affectionate emulation; so that the increase of parental duties, instead of diminishing their mutual regard, serves to multiply and draw closer their bonds of reliance, helpfulness, and love. And yet from this diminutive constitution, so simple in its plan and quiet in its operations, proceed effects on which all society is dependent, and which no expedient of society could ever produce.

Special correspondences between parent and child.

Elsewhere I have remarked on the striking coincidence between the ability of the parents to teach, and the disposition of the child implicitly to receive and believe their instructions; between their authority and power, and the readiness of the child to obey; and between the influence of their example, and the susceptibility of the child to receive the corresponding impression and to follow it out in imitation. How useless would the parental properties be if they were not met by the corresponding filial dispositions. How invaluable the advantages resulting from the co-existence of the two; for thus the child is enabled to avail itself of all the wisdom and experience of its parents, and of all which their affection can prompt them to do for its well-being.

Influence of conjugal love.

But here let me call attention to the wisdom apparent in the benevolent arrangement by which the example of the parents' regard for each other is made to distill a happy influence on their children. "Should their mutual love be grounded on esteem, there is a secret and instituted virtue in their example, which will descend on a constitution of things Divinely adapted to receive it." Equally striking is that appointment by which example is made more influential than teaching. Oral instruction can only be imparted at distant intervals; but example is a perpetual ordinance, imparting power to verbal lessons, and filling up all the intervals of formal instruction besides.

Variety of character with mutual dependence.

Wisdom appears also in the variety of character observable in a family, when viewed in connection with the mutual dependence and union resulting from it. We can conceive of a normal human mind, in which all the faculties are perfectly proportioned and balanced. Now, as far as variety of character is independent of outward condition, all the shades of difference observable in adult society are owing to slight departures from that normal mind; and this variety it is, chiefly, which occasions that mutual dependence and tendency to combination, so productive of advantage to society at large. That dependence and reciprocity of services, however, receive their earliest development in the domestic circle. Here inferiors and superiors of every kind and degree mingle and co-operate—youth and age, weakness and strength, ignorance and knowledge, male and female, affection and authority, are blended together into one compact society. None is entirely independent of the others; each has his place and value in the little community, and the loss of one would be felt to be a loss to the whole. Now, the community of feeling and close relationship produced by this variety of character, would form an attractive illustration of Divine design even if they terminated within the inclosure of each separate family.

The family a rehearsal for society.

But the same arrangement prepares for the still wider community of collective families, and thus increases the force of the illustration. Here I may remark on the advantages of that Divine appointment which defers the season of marriage till the parties have reached maturity. By this means they are enabled to avail themselves of all their parents' experience before they sustain the parental relation themselves—to begin with a stock of household knowledge. But the advantages which the family constitution confers on society, are co-extensive with the relations and duties of society. Here, in the feeling of property which begins with their toys, children take their first lessons on that great and original doctrine of *meum* and *tuum* which is essential to the wealth of society and conducive to its comfort and progress. Here, in the familiar intercourse of brothers and sisters, that affection, with sexual separation, is developed which is the best safeguard for the laws of chastity and honor in social life. Here the laws of reciprocity are educed under circumstances most favorable to their full development; laws by which each is led to recognize in every other man, the same rights which he claims for himself, and even to respect, and sympathize with, the claim. Here, every coming relation of life, every future form of duty, and every subsequent social affection, are seen virtually put in rehearsal for the more public scenes of after life. As if with a direct view to all the affairs of active life, the children are placed in the family in the most advantageous situation for preparing to assume their important duties in civil society.

Union of seniors and juniors in a generation.

The advantages arising from the arrangement by which the seniors and juniors of families intermingle, and by which one generation is appointed to give place to another gradually and imperceptibly, are numerous and important. Had the senior members of each family been removed by death at the same age; or had the elders of each generation died at about the same time; or, if during the latter part of their course they had lived entirely apart, and been lost to society, the result could only have been a one-sided development of society. "Two principles govern the moral and intellectual world. One is perpetual progress, the other the necessary limitations of that progress." * Now, it will be admitted that, generally speaking, the principle of progress is that to which men most naturally commit themselves in early life; while the principle of permanence is that—still speaking generally—which is most in favor toward the close of life. The arrangement, therefore, which provides that a proportion of each class shall occupy the stage of life together, provides that the principles they respectively represent shall be held in salutary counterpoise; that "one party shall see the importance of holding

* *Genz* (*Briefe an Johannes* v. *Müller*).

the rein while urging forward; and the other shall not forget to urge onward while keeping a steady rein."

Easy would it be to multiply illustrations of the wisdom of God in the arrangements of the Family constitution.*

Self-accommodating power of the family.

Were this the place, we might especially call attention to the self-accommodating power of the family constitution to the different forms of human society. And, from the facts of history, it could be shown that every change or attempted refinement on that constitution has ended in failure, and the deterioration of that which it was meant to amend; leaving us to infer that the family, as divinely constituted, is incapable of improvement.

Special illustrations of wisdom.

Three facts, however, may here be appropriately noticed. First, the Divine arrangement that conjugal love should not diminish, but increase in proportion to the demands made on it. "One of the consequences of having children (it might have been reasoned antecedently) will be the multiplication of the cares and duties of the parents, and the consequent multiplication of the points on which they will be liable to differ. Besides, what other effect can the introduction of new objects of affection, in the persons of their children, produce, than to diminish the regard of the husband and wife for each other?" On the contrary, however, they become increasingly endeared to each other. Now, if any thing analogous to this occurred in the working of a complicated piece of human mechanism; if the union of its parts, and its strength as a whole, became the more apparent in proportion as its springs were pressed on and all its machinery

* See Chapters v. vii. xi. xii. xiii.

put in stress, not only would the result be ascribed to design on the part of him who planned it, but it would be regarded as reflecting great honor on the penetration of his views and on the power of combining them into one. How much more, then, does a similar result demonstrate the existence of a plan when it is found obtaining, not in a piece of machinery, but in the history of living, intellectual, moral beings!

Secondly; that all the diversified effects which the family exhibits, flow from the application of a single principle—that of parental love. In the material world, where an abstraction called Nature is deified, we are often invited to mark how sparing she is in causes and how prolific in effects, and to admire the wisdom which is thus displayed. Here, however, in the family circle, the same principle obtains. A single affection receives such various application, that, notwithstanding the diversity of age and character which the family exhibits, it presents the spectacle of liberty united with subordination, love with authority, permanence with progress, and in which, while each keeps his appropriate sphere, every one is active for all, and the whole is preparing for and advancing toward the larger sphere of families yet to come.

And thirdly; that the effects thus produced, and the compound good resulting from it, as they were not foreseen by the first human pair, and as they do not form the primary inducements of their descendants to assume the conjugal relation, refer us for their origination to a higher will and a higher wisdom than man's. It has been well observed, that "when by natural principles we are led to advance those ends which a refined and enlightened reason would recommend to us, we are very apt to impute to that reason, as to their efficient cause, the sentiments and actions by which we advance those ends; and to imagine that to be the wisdom of man, which is in reality the wisdom of God."* All the complex and beneficial effects flowing from the family constitution presupposes a plan, and illustrate the wisdom of its Divine designer.

SECTION III.—GOODNESS.

Here, wisdom is Goodness. All the instances adduced in illustration of the wisdom of God, are adducible also in exemplification of his goodness; their tendency being the production of human happiness. But the proofs of benevolence are so numerous that we need not have recourse to such a repetition.

Every onward step meant to minister to man's happiness.

During the antediluvian period, every onward step in material civilization was Divinely meant to minister to human enjoyment. This is true of the domestication of every animal, and of the new application of every material substance and law. But independently of the direct utility of such events, the pleasure arising from the consciousness of power, from the discovery of facts, and from the attainment of success, with which it was accompanied—all is to be taken into account. Nor was this pleasure confined to the first ages of time when man was comparatively new to the world; for the earth is as fresh to the childhood of to-day as it was to the childhood of six thousand years ago. Every sound and perfume, every color and movement in creation, is a source of wonder and delight.

* Dr. A. Smith's Theory of the Moral Sentiments.

Love, the basis of the family, another name for enjoyment.

As to the family economy; its very foundation is laid in that love which is but another name for the purest enjoyment. Who can imagine the amount of happiness which has resulted to man from this source alone! The exquisite delight of Eve, when she exclaimed, "I have gotten a man-child from the Lord!" was only a specimen of the emotion which has filled the maternal bosom on every similar occasion, "with joy that a man-child was born into the world." Add to this, the stream of enjoyment constantly flowing through the parental heart generation after generation, at witnessing the health, the growth, the union, the intellectual and moral progress, and the happiness of his children, especially the happiness resulting from parental effort; all this is traceable to the Divine benevolence as to its fountain-head.

Parental instincts subservient to the child's highest welfare.

Remarkable is the manner in which the parental instincts are made to subserve the highest well-being of the children. Thus, if it be necessary to the welfare of children that provision should be made for their preservation, support, and education, the Divine arrangement which devolves this provision, partly on the instinct of parental affection, is not less benevolent than that which refers it partly to reason and conscience. Were it devolved entirely on our sense of duty, the probability is that, in a great majority of cases, the necessary provision would be quite neglected. On the other hand, were it referred exclusively to parental affection, the sphere of parental virtue would be contracted to a point. But by arranging that a strong natural instinct should come to the aid of conscience, the latter is relieved considerably in its responsibilities, in a way which exempts the children from innumerable evils; while that natural instinct, in ministering to their welfare is a source of enjoyment to the parental heart. Besides which, if this arrangement illustrates the Divine benevolence, the illustration increases in value in proportion as the period of this natural affection is prolonged. In the case supposed, it is prolonged indefinitely. And still further is it increased, if we remember the longevity of antediluvian life.

Happy effects of family sympathies.

Akin to this is that principle of sympathy by which the members of a family not only fly instinctively to each others' aid, but by which their various dispositions and emotions are regulated and equalized. "By the mere principle of sympathy," remarks Dr. T. Brown, "all the discord in the social feelings become accordant. The sad, unconsciously become gay; the gay are softened into a joy, that has less perhaps of mirth, but not less of delight; and though there is still a diversity of cheerfulness, all is cheerfulness." "How much more admirable, however, is the providence of the Creator's bounty in that instant diffusion to others of the grief which is felt only by one, that makes the relief of this suffering not a duty merely, which we coldly perform, but a *want*, which is almost like the necessity of some moral appetite." Now, in the family, the occasions for this aid, and the pleasure arising from its exercise, are of daily occurrence. Memory recalls and repeats those pleasures in after life. And thus the family provides for the perpetuation and diffusion of our sympathy, and for all the delights attending it. Not only do the family affections survive every benevolent act to which they give expression; they gather strength from such activity, and would fain immortalize the objects of their regard.

And of family opinion.

Most wise and benevolent, too, is that arrangement by which every member of the family is constantly living and moving under the influence of opinion—the opinion of those to whom he is the most nearly related and tenderly attached. By this means, an ever-present motive to merit approbation is kept in constant activity, as well as a silent and salutary counteractive of evil, more efficacious than a perpetual lecture on morality, and quietly doing the work of chastisement without its pain. But besides the goodness which appears in the great outlines of the family constitution, we recognize the same profuse benevolence in all the innocent interchanges of humor, and the little pleasantries of the domestic circle. By these it is, partly, that, in the absence of those occasions for excitement which can but rarely occur, the large interspaces of time are pervaded with tranquil enjoyment. How much more readily, too, children love than hate! How quickly they forget and forgive! How much less retentive their memory is of sorrows than of joys! And how hallowed and beneficent the arrangement that the critical period when youth begins to become conscious of sex is the age at which it first dreams of the greatest and the best, and sees visions of ideal excellence.

Each family and generation unconsciously preparing happiness for others.

But not only does every separate aspect of the domestic economy display the goodness of the Creator: viewed as a whole, it assumes the character of an institution designed to convey an ever-increasing stream of enjoyment from generation to generation. The gradual development of the first family brought to light, at every step, some new provision which the benevolent Creator had made and reserved for its arrival at each successive step. Similar illustrations of the Divine goodness were repeated and multiplied in the progress of each of the families which branched off from the first. How incalculably was the display of that goodness increased, then, when it was seen that in addition to the happiness secured to the family while each member of it had, to a certain extent, been thinking mainly of his own interest, provision had also been made that each family, while thinking mainly of its own interest, should be unconsciously multiplying the enjoyments of all the other families. For, by this peculiar constitution, the knowledge and experience of the earlier families were accumulated, and devolved on the generation succeeding, to receive additions from them, and to be devolved on the next. A virtuous and distinguished name, by being regarded as the heraldry of the family, would awaken emulation and multiply itself in those who came after. The increase of comforts attending the ever-advancing civilization which would result from the swelling stream of wisdom and virtue would, sooner or later, become common property. So that each family, while chiefly occupied with its own aggrandizement, was, in reality, creating new reciprocities in the great community of families, and ministering unconsciously to the good of the whole; and thus bringing to light the comprehensive benevolence of Him who had designed and sustained the whole.

SECTION IV.—HOLINESS.

Home a new paradise and probation.

Much as God willed the happiness of His human family, He willed its holiness still more. Accordingly, as Paradise was the home of man in innocence, so home was meant to be the paradise of childhood, where the family should pass through a moral probation. Here man was to have a moral government of his own; the very image of the Divine government, and aiming at the same high end.

Hence, as we have seen, the basis of the family life is laid, not in sexual desire, but in love. Sense—desire—is consecrated in marriage, and is raised to a moral office. Ideas which are but corporeally expressed in the lower orders of life, are here seen to be symbols of spiritual facts, and the facts themselves are realized. "Singly and solely on the supposition that the spiritual life of the parents is transplanted into the children, does the communication of corporeal life become a blessing." The family was God's first Church.*

Family relations, facilities for training to virtue.

All the relations between parent and child are so many natural facilities for training the young to virtue. They are committed to him while yet free from the blots and stains of actual transgression, to be preoccupied as quickly and fully as possible with the writing and signature of Heaven. Would a state of great susceptibility to impression facilitate their training? The age of childhood is the age of impressibleness; and God commits them to the parent in that state, to receive, through his instrumentality, the imprint of the Divine image. Would it conduce to their training if the parent found them not inclined to dispute his testimony, not requiring him logically to believe every thing, but disposed readily to believe his word? He enjoys this advantage. Belief is natural to the child. When first it has to suspect or disbelieve it suffers violence. But prior to this, it asks not for evidence; waits not for proof; but believes

* Tholuck's Exposition of the Sermon on the Mount. Bib. Cab. p. 316.

on the simple testimony of those it loves. Would it add to the probability of parental success if children were permitted to remain for a considerable time in this impressible and improvable state? It is wisely ordered that the young of the human kind should remain in a state of comparative helplessness longer than the young of any other kind. The poet of ancient skepticism sang of this long period of infantine dependence as a state of supposed inferiority to the young of the brute creation; and, therefore, as a proof that there is no Providence; whereas, it supplies one of the strongest proofs of the contrary. Had the child remained dependent on its parents only as long as the brood remains with the parent bird, the endearing names of father and mother would have been empty sounds; and justly might the parents have pleaded that the brevity of the term afforded them no opportunity of training their offspring to walk with God. But wisely ordered as it is, they have not only an opportunity of inscribing on their children's heart the first impressions which it receives, and of molding their character while it is in its most impressible state, but of continuing to retouch and deepen their best impressions for a succession of years. And, in the instance of the first families, this opportunity, of course, was extended in proportion to the period of antediluvian longevity.

Means possessed by the antediluvian parent.

The moral facilities which the parent possesses for training his offspring to spiritual excellence correspond with the natural; and, with it, tend to illustrate the Divine holiness. These facilities, indeed, have gone on increasing with the increase of Divine revelation. But even the antediluvian parent enjoyed them, in such a manner, and to such an amount, as to render his neglect of them inexcusable. They consisted (in the instance of Noah, for example, and of each cotemporary parent), in the institution of the Sabbath; in the hallowed and interesting nature of the knowledge he had to impart—relating, as it did, to the recent creation—the glories of Paradise—the first command—its violation, and the fearful consequences—the mercy which spared the offenders and which animated their hope with the first promise—the institution of sacrifice—the symbolic cherubim—the mortality of man—the translation of Enoch—and the threatening of a deluge in punishment of man's disobedience, together with the preparation of the ark; in the attractive and impressive manner in which He had conveyed this knowledge; in the affecting rite of public sacrifice; and in the power of prayer. Here every thing proclaimed the hostility of God to sin, and His design to facilitate and reward obedience. What could the purpose of God be, in all these successive revelations and appointments, but to induce men to "keep His commandments, and that they might not be as their fathers, a stubborn and rebellious generation, a generation that set not their hearts aright, and whose spirit was not steadfast with God?" And what could the character of such a Being be but holy?

Natural instincts made subservient to morality.

The remarkable manner in which the natural instincts and affections are modified and pressed into the service of morality, attest the same truth. Fear, and anger, and maternal affection, are evinced by the animal tribes, which are utterly incapable of morality. With them they answer the beneficent purpose of self-preservation and the continuance of their kind. But with man, besides subserving his safety and comfort, they subserve his character and become elements of his moral excellence. If the sexual desires are an instance of physical adaptation, illustrative of the Divine wisdom and goodness, not less is that sense of shame which checks and regulates the passions, and that trembling delicacy which, even in early childhood, becomes the guardian of chastity, an evidence of the holiness of the government of which they are laws. And if the desire of the good opinion of others, by restraining our selfishness, evinces the presence of a Divine design, not less does the same desire—operating as it does most powerfully where we love most, or entertain the highest veneration—illustrate the Divine regard for virtue, by begetting in the children the very excellence they suppose their parents admire.

The child has the best opportunity for knowing man at his best.

Not only has the parent the best opportunity of training man for God, but the child has also the best opportunity of studying God in man. "It is a wise ordination of Providence, that, at our outset in life, we should come in contact with human nature under its best aspect; that, under the relation of parent and child, we should form our first acquaintance with humanity."* By this arrangement it is that the child—finding itself an object of tender regard to a being in whom interest and self-love combine with the parental instinct to render the watchful guardian of its highest welfare—learns to recognize, in his affectionate solicitude, a copy of the love of its Father who is in heaven, and becomes conscious of those corresponding emotions of benevolence which in after-life prove the strongest auxiliaries of conscience and duty.

In training the child to love God, the parent is best training it to love himself.

Equally emphatic for the holy designs of the great Parent is that arrangement by which the parent, in teaching the child to love virtue, is found to be best securing its

* Parkinson's Hulsean Lectures, 1838, p. 62.

moral affection for himself. Earlier in life than is commonly supposed, the child begins to distinguish between that instinctive affection which would deny it nothing, and that higher moral regard which studies its welfare. And from the moment it makes the important distinction, it begins to respect and love the latter most, though necessarily less indulgent than the former. A higher part of his nature is appealed to, and responds to the appeal. And thus, in teaching it to respect virtue, the parent is securing its affection more effectually than if he sought the object directly and exclusively; and is at the same time obtaining an additional proof that the author of the parental relation and the patron of holiness is one and the same.

The occasion on which all the family is harmonized into one.

How beautifully illustrative of the same truth is the fact that the particular occasions on which all the members of the family are assembled in one spot, harmonized in one act, and represented by one mind, should be at the altar of God. It matters not whether the duty there consisted of sacrifice or of prayer—for prayer is the sacrifice and offering of the heart, and sacrifice is an acted prayer. Whichever it might be—there, where sin is confessed and forgiven; where the conscience is quickened and strengthened for duty; where holy resolutions are formed, and aid obtained to fulfill them —there He makes it their duty and privilege to come, "that with one mind and one mouth they might glorify God." A numerous patriarchal family thus collected at "the place of the altar," while its aged priest and head performed the solemn rites, presented one of the most attractive illustrations which the mind can conceive of the hallowed design of the domestic constitution. For there where all were one with each other, and only in proportion as they were one with each other, were they one with God. The same act which brought them nearest to the source of excellence, drew closer their family ties, and made them love as brethren.

The virtue of a family essential to its well-being.

The virtue of a family is essential to its well-being The first sin of our first parents led to mutual accusations. The first sin recorded of their offspring led to the death of one child, the exile of another, and the wretchedness of the parents. Every act of immorality in the member of a family is a seed which only requires time in order to become "a root of bitterness." And while the same spirit of impiety which revolts from God introduces an insubordinate and disorganizing spirit into the family, the recovery of its members to their allegiance to God is the only restorative process for the family. He has thus "revealed from heaven His hostility against all impiety and unrighteousness of men"—revealed it by an "ordinance"* "shown to them ever since the creation of the world;" and most emphatically shown in the laws of the family constitution. For we know not how a more conclusive demonstration could be given of the holiness of God, than that the domestic economy should have been so framed by His hands that its welfare is made to depend on its virtue; so that for its members to be right socially, or as a family, it is indispensable that they should be right virtuously, or in their relations to morality.

Depraved parents in favor of their children's moral training.

Even depraved parents are, generally speaking, in favor of the moral training of their children. Though hourly polluting their family by their own evil example, their sympathies

* δικαίωμα, Romans, i. 32.

are on the side of any effort made by benevolence to counteract the influence of such example; thus silently intimating the original design of the parental relation. So indestructibly did God interweave into the texture of the family constitution the law of "Holiness to the Lord."

The holy design of the family avowed.

During the theocratic period, this high aim of the family was very variously and distinctly affirmed. When vindicating the inviolable sanctity of the conjugal tie, the prophet* asks. "Did He not make one? though He had the residue of the Spirit. And why the one? That He might seek a godly seed." The original formation of one man and one woman into "one flesh" or conjugal body, contemplated the rearing of a pious offspring. Other and inferior ends were to be secured by it, but this was its ultimate design. "He did not design it (remarks Howe†) merely that there might be a continual descent of human nature, but that religion might still be transmitted from age to age; and this design He never quits." Marriage was a Divinely-conceived idea for the manifestation of God in man.

Every new family, a new call to aim at this end.

And the arrangement by which children come, *successively*, to form new families, and families to form new generations, was an ever-recurring call to man to resume the original design of the family. Every child in its innocence was a new vindication of the family constitution, and a "living witness against all who had been babes." The great possibilities which came with the first-born of the race, reappeared with every subsequent birth. Each family brought with it the means of retrieving the past. Each generation might have begun the history of the world anew. By this constant incoming

* Mal. ii. 15. † Vol. v. p. 396.

of new life and power, man was ever summoned to recommence the great experiment, to reconstruct society on the basis of love, and to consecrate the family to God. The very last birth that preceded the flood was a virtual renewal of the first Promise. And does not the significant manner in which the fulfillment of that promise was inwoven with the family constitution imply that the recovery of the family is essential to the recovery of the race; that the restoration of the family to its original functions is necessary in order to the full effect of the remedial economy?

Justice, the enforcement and vindication of holiness.

Justice is but a mode or phase of holiness. If the latter utters itself in laws expressive of Divine Perfection, the former administers their righteous sanctions. If holiness flows forth in a family constitution, justice, animadverts on all the infractions of that constitution. From the day of man's first transgression "till the day that the flood came," the justice of God had shown itself in active hostility against sin. The first offenders had been expelled from Paradise. Even the promise of a Deliverer contained an intimation that the deliverance would be obtained by suffering; while the institution of sacrifice proclaimed that "without the shedding of blood there is no remission of sins." Mercy itself must be based on equity. "Death had passed upon all men, for that all had sinned." The solitary exception—the translation of Enoch—had, combined with his prophecy of the Lord's coming to judge the ungodly, to corroborate their forebodings of a state after death; a state in which character and the consequences of character would be both resumed. In the family constitution, especially, the Divine justice had declared war against sin, by "visiting the sins of the fathers upon the children unto the third and fourth generation."* When, amid the thunders of Sinai, He described himself as doing this, the language denoted that it was no new law, but that it had characterized His government from the beginning. During the entire antediluvian period it had been in force, infants had died. Diseases, the fruit of sin, had been propagated. Poverty had been entailed. Indulged and neglected children had been judgments to their parents. Bad families had been curses to society. Sin was literally made a family quarrel. And in thus punishing the parent in the person of the child, the Divine Governor was simply allowing the known and settled laws of the family constitution to take their course. Laws—which, if complied with, would have rewarded the parent in the person of the child—were not to be repealed by the Divine Legislator when, and simply because, they were disobeyed. To the parent himself, therefore, this was only an arrangement of strict equity. He could not justly complain; for both the law and its self-executing sanction were foreknown to him. Besides which, its original tendency was one of unmixed good; nor could it be withdrawn without withdrawing also all the good of which it was still, and ever would be, the channel.

But when the family constitution had existed about two thousand years, the persistency of mankind in a course of sin, drew forth a new and appalling intimation of God's just displeasure against it. "He said that he would destroy them." When the guilty race had either forgotten or denied His government: or was flattering itself that he was "altogether such an one as itself," the tremendous proclamation went forth, "the end of all flesh is come be-

* Exodus, xx. 5.

fore me; for the earth is filled with violence through them; and, behold, I will destroy them from the earth." So far from reducing the just and natural sanctions of virtue belonging to the domestic economy, here was a special infliction impending, on the largest scale, with a view to reinforce those sanctions as of Divine appointment.

Divine faithfulness illustrated.

Faithfulness is an element of holiness. If truth is the expression of the holy mind and will of God, faithfulness is adherence to that expression. As an attribute requiring for its development the lapse of time and a succession of events, every successive part of the antediluvian period enlarged the field of its manifestation. The first transgression was the first occasion for its display. The Satanic suggestion that the threatened penalty would not be inflicted, was a guilty experiment on the Divine veracity. But even before "the voice of the Lord God was heard in the garden in the cool of the day," the shame, the conscious guilt, and the attendant pain, of which man forthwith became the subject, showed that "God is not a man that He should lie." But will God rigidly adhere to the sentence, "dust thou art, and unto dust shalt thou return?" With what deep intetest must the first practical reply to this momentous question have been waited for by the first men! The death of Abel, indeed, came early in the history of the race, as if in solemn anticipation of the truth. But while human foreboding would one while view the event in this impressive light, hope would, doubtless, at other times, awaken the idea that, as far as that event was concerned, it only showed that death might occur by violence. And then, as the life of the great progenitor of the race was drawn out century after century, while his "eye was not dim, nor his natural force abated," the hope that the sentence of mortality was remitted, would often rise toward certainty. But, at length, the long-suspended stroke fell; and the father of the race was buried by his children. Every subsequent instance of dissolution confirmed the Divine veracity, and showed that sinful man had nothing to expect from that quarter "but a certain fearful looking for" of the threatened judgment; while all the sufferings, physical and mental, which went on increasing with the increasing guilt of the species, demonstrated that sin and misery are linked together with the invariableness of cause and effect.

But the same faithfulness which bound together guilt and punishment by a law, was manifested also in the fulfillment of promise and the reward of obedience. The faithfulness of God was reflected in the faith of his worshipers. "By faith Abel offered unto God a more excellent sacrifice than Cain, by which he obtained witness that he was righteous; God testifying of his gifts." Believing the testimony he had received respecting sin and sacrifice, he confessed at the altar his personal unworthiness, and looked to God for the pardon he sought. And the Divine acceptance of his offering showed that "He is faithful who hath promised. Enoch "walked with God;" and the consequence was that even "before his translation he had this testimony, that he pleased God." His translation itself was the surpassing proof of the Divine complacency in his faith. "Noah being warned of God of things not seen as yet, moved with fear, prepared an ark to the saving of his house." Every part of the patriarch's conduct evinced his reliance on the Divine veracity. The subject of the Divine communication related to "things not seen as yet"—unprecedented both as to the judgment which should destroy the world, and as to the mercy which should select and save a single family; as well as to the peculiar manner in which both the judgment and the mercy should attain their ends. Yet, by a faith which "moved him with fear"—penetrated him with a conviction of the Divine veracity, he "prepared an ark to the saving of his house." And by this confidence of his in the faithfulness of God, "he condemned the world"—convicted it of guilty unbelief in not believing God on the evidence on which he believed; "and became an heir of the righteousness which is by faith."

SECTION V.—MERCY.

Mercy made the dispensation possible.

Much and variously as the preceding aspects of the Divine nature were illustrated during the patriarchal economy, they were not first made known by it. Man, either as unfallen or fallen, had exemplified them all. Whereas Mercy alone could make the dispensation possible. Mercy both introduced it, and was introduced by it. Then first mercy became known to man; perhaps to the universe.

From the moment man sinned and incurred condemnation, it is difficult to conceive on what ground the human race could have been perpetuated, apart from a remedial scheme. For justice to have taken its direct course would have involved the destruction of the transgressors. The dispensation of mercy literally caught man in the very act of falling, arrested his descent to perdition, and placed him on an entirely new footing. Hence, the entire constitution of things by which humanity subsists is represented in Scripture as resting on a basis of mediation. And although this great fact may have only dimly dawned on the antediluvian believer, he must have been often amazed at that outburst of grace which was ever flowing onward in a dispensation of good, encircling him and all his race.

Mercy, the utterance of a purpose

This mercy was evidently the utterance of a Divine purpose. The believer of that day could not have looked back on the mode of its original announcement without recognizing this exhilarating fact. The close connection in time between man's guilty fall and God's hand outstretched to save, showed that sin is not to be viewed as an unforeseen frustration of Divine plans, nor mercy as a Divine afterthought. The fact that man's hope was suspended on a promise, whose fullfilment was placed in the future, showed that it was no mere device or sudden expedient for supplying a defect in the scheme of Divine procedure, but that it belonged to a far-reaching plan; while the institution of sacrifice not only pointed to the same plan, but dimly foreshadowed the mode of its accomplishment.

Not less efficacious because not then fulfilled.

And as the means of mercy were thus based on a Divine purpose, it needed not to wait for the actual appearance of those means—the personal advent of the Deliverer. Moral causes, unlike physical, operate prospectively; and therefore mercy proceeded to act from the first on the forelaid ground of His coming. He is the "lamb without blemish and without spot, who verily was foreordained before the foundations of the world."* And as there never was a point in past

* "St. Peter, in the words above (says Warburton), distinguishes between the *advent* of our Redeemer, and the *efficacy* of His death, in teaching us, that though His *manifestation* was late, yet the virtue of His *foreordained* redemption operated from the most early times. For it would

duration in which the atonement was not present to the Divine mind as *a fact* unchangeable in its value and relations, so there never has been a moment, since man fell, in which mercy, on the ground of that fact, was not awaiting his acceptance.

Its aspect universal.

And for the same reason that mercy was free for any, it was free for all. The promise challenged universal belief. It was "the Gospel preached before" to the antediluvian world. The Protevangelium was "to every creature." The altar was unfenced. The Divine remonstrance with Cain showed that God was "waiting to be gracious." The various interpositions of Heaven to reinforce its means of winning attention were so many devices of mercy. The "preachers of righteousness" were its agents. The period of respite, during the building of the ark, was one long wail of mercy.

The saved, themselves manifestations of mercy.

But besides this outward apparatus of mercy, there were men who so opened their hearts to its saving influence that they themselves became living manifestations of Divine compassion. That apparatus was an earlier ark for saving men from the surges of a spiritual flood; and, as it floated down the stream of time, they who availed themselves of its ever-open door became at once monuments of the grace which had saved them and living arks for the rescue of others. They "could not but speak the things which they had seen

be trifling to speak of a *pre-ordination* which was not to be understood of a *pre-operation;* since those to whom the Apostle wrote well understood, from the attributes of the Godhead, that all things *that were*, had been *pre-ordained*, in the mere simple sense of the word. The *other* sense, of a *pre-operation*, St. John more forcibly expresses by 'the Lamb *slain* from the foundation of the world.'"—*Divine Legation*, Book ix. c. 2.

and heard." They were saved, partly, that "in them God might show forth all long-suffering," as an encouragement to others. As men, "who had found mercy of the Lord," their character was a reflection of the Divine character; and their condition was a proclamation of mercy to all who would accept it.

The ark a symbol of mercy.

Even the deluge was an event in which "mercy rejoiced against judgment." For though "few, that is, eight souls, were saved by water," their temporal rescue was but a symbol of the higher deliverance which had been offered to the race, and was effected in order to resume, under new auspices and in a wider theater, the great experiment of mercy which the family had failed to improve. As the ark rose and floated solitarily over the world's grave, it might have spoken to other worlds, both of the past and of the future; but in each respect it testified to the mercy of God. In its relation to the past, it was the memorial of a world that would not be saved; while in relation to the future, it was freighted with the means of mercy to a new world.

SECTION VI.—LONG-SUFFERING.

The economy pre-eminently a display of long-suffering.

The family constitution introduced the dispensation of mercy for all time. But that aspect of the Divine character, which was especially illustrated during the antediluvian period, was the long-suffering of God. Long-suffering, indeed, is historically and in fact only a mode of mercy. But this is by no means a necessary fact. The long-suffering is as truly contingent on the will of God as the mercy. On the one hand, there might have been mercy without long-suffering; for salvation might have been made dependent on the instant acceptance of its conditions. Its language might have been: "In the day that thou declinest to accept them thou shalt surely die." On the other hand, there might have been long-suffering, hypothetically, without any dispensation of mercy. The race, that is, by a suspension of strict justice, might have been left to die out, without any hope of mercy. Or there might have been both mercy and long-suffering during the term of the family probation, and no longer. Both forms of Divine manifestation might have ended with the flood. As it was, mercy was offered to all, long-suffering was experienced by all.

That long-suffering estimated by the capabilities of the family.

In order to estimate the patience of which that economy was the special manifestation, we must try to compute the vast capabilities of the family as a means of reflecting the paternal character of God. Man, for example, is an assertion of Divine Power. In the family, his individual energies for good were to be indefinitely increased by combination; and the whole to be put forth as a moral leverage for lifting earth nearer to heaven. Man is an illustration of the Divine Wisdom. Besides being an epitome of all the complicated relations with which nature abounds, he includes a multitude of others which transcend nature, and which ally him to the supernatural. In the family, entirely new relations are added, of a nature so tender and sacred, so profound and indissoluble, that they are employed as the fittest symbols of the life-and-spirit relations between the soul and God, and of the union between the Church and Him "of whom the whole family in heaven and earth is named." Here was the promise of a union so helpful, hallowed, and close as to represent and rival the union of the blessed above. The Divine Goodness finds its highest reflection in man's capacity for enjoyment; but in the family that capacity was to be more than doubled. Commencing in marriage—in "the idea of an entire disposal of self by the one party to the other in love"—no member of the society was to live to himself. It needed the parental relation to help man to a vivid sense of the goodness of God. A father's heart alone, with its yearning, expanding, self-giving affection can truly apprehend it. So ocean-like is it, that it required the channels of unnumbered hearts—generations of them—in order to represent it. Its depth and strength could not be made apparent except as it was divided among myriads of fathers' hearts, all overflowing like itself; and all pouring that overflow into the open channels of the family, waiting like a vast capacity to receive and reflect it.

But all the happiness which thus came down from the great Fountain-head, the family was meant to send back to it again in loving obedience and moral excellence. The government, set up for God in the individual breast, was externalized in the family; made collective and social; and he who had instrumentally given life to its subjects ruled in the name of God. Its only bonds were "cords of love." Its infant members came into it as the symbols of celestial purity. It had no adequate explanation except as it prepared them for that state which they symbolized. If the earth was a temple, the family was its "holiest of all;" and all its divinely selected arrangements and influences were meant to be ever crying to each other, "holy, holy, holy is the Lord God Almighty," as the continuous service of love and worship trained up its members for heaven.

Rich in possibilities.

How rich was the family in Divine possibilities! How large its capacity for reflecting the holy Fatherhood of God! Each father surrounded by his offspring—an exponent of the life-giving Creator. Each child, losing its first vernal freshness, only to replace it by beauty of a higher order—the very image of God; and each gradually enfolding a different aspect of that image! Every family an epitome of the government of God; headed by its own father in the threefold relation of prophet, priest, and king; complete in itself; but seeking and reciprocating the love of every other. A community interlaced and bound together by ties too sacred and strong for selfishness to rupture or impair. Every generation inheriting the excellence of the past, only to enlarge and carry them forward for all the future. The whole community, when at its highest and its best, feeling that the Divine qualities which it embodied and reflected, even if the reflection were spread over ten thousand such communities, would but faintly represent the Fatherhood of God. Had this sublime possibility been realized, and could the first man—the patriarch of the race—have come back to survey the blessed scene when at its best, what a heaven would he have found upon earth! But could his large heart have taken into itself all the paternal emotions of love, and hope, and joy to which the family constitution had ever given rise, how feebly, after all, would it have represented the Divine complacency of that Mind which had given birth to the whole, and which alone could see all the rich possibilities and endless consequences which it inclosed!

Nearly the whole wasted and perverted.

Now, though there was no controlling necessity to prevent the realization of this scene to the utmost, the conduct of the antediluvian world involved the perversion and waste of well-nigh the whole. All the powers inclosed in the family economy for good broke lose for evil.

If the family had yet to be set up, how much would be expected from it?

Had that economy itself been known only as a thing possible, what lofty ideas of man's perfectibility would have swelled the human breast on the supposition that the possible could be made actual. Now here it was actually set up; and as it had unfolded, one generous provision after another came to light; and one wise and holy law after another disclosed its existence. But each provision by its perversion, and each law by its transgression, seemed only to furnish man with an occasion for developing his disregard for the will of its Divine originator. Had children come at length to be only bright possibilities; had they ceased to be born when the family had reached a certain pitch of disorganization and depravity, what visions of improvement man would have indulged in, if he might but have a new generation once more to begin with! But the stream of humanity never ceased to flow, and never ceased to deepen its pollution. Generation followed generation; and every new-born infant came like a fresh witness for God and a protest against man. But the multiplication of the species was the measure of their progress in evil.

Hope often kindled, but uniformly quenched.

Were other orders of beings looking on? Supposing such to have been the fact, occasions were not wanting, at times, to kindle and rekindle their hopes for the issue. When they saw that human life was to be drawn out, century after century, they might surely have expected that "years would teach wisdom;" for this doubtless was the moral reason of man's longevity. When they saw one generation of infant human beings succeed another, each affording a new opportunity for retrieving the past, they could hardly fail to look with a feeling of certainty for new results. When certain crises arrived, and the heart of society was smitten with a sense of misgiving and gloom, they might surely have looked for a gathering of venerable men on the great subjects which concerned them in common. When every law involving the well-being of the family had been fairly worked out, what more natural than that these laws should have been affirmed by a *consensus familiarum*, and have henceforth secured the general obedience? Alas for such expectations! The sun was gone from the center of the system, and each little planet and satellite was jostling every other in a struggle to take the vacant place. The great principle which alone can give repose to the individual heart which unites man to man, and family to family, was lost. Man knew no higher end than himself. And they saw his long life spent in a laborious multiplication of means to serve this end. They saw generation after generation of new-born souls devoted and destroyed for this end; while every great gathering of human families took place, not from any principle of love to each other, but for the subjugation or destruction of other families standing in the way of their selfish ends.

Judgments often anticipated.

Doubtless, too, there were epochs, when, if such beings were looking on, they might justly have lost all hope for man, and have assumed that he had at length exhausted long-suffering. When, for example, the number of the families that stood for God came to be in the minority, and still continued to dwindle. When it was seen that each generation accepted the disorganized state of things inherited from all the past, concerned only to carry the guilty experiment still further. Especially when the two classes of character which had stood confronting each other, the righteous and the wicked, came to mingle and unite, showing that they had not only lost all sense of this moral distinction, but had replaced it by the passing differences which end with life. This, in truth, was the only distinction which the economy recognized. It drew but one line; that which divided those who lived to promote the ultimate purpose of the Divine manifestation, from those who lived to frustrate it. It knew but of two families; those who remained on the side of the great Pater-familias and who aimed to carry up the economy to the height of His design, and those who combined to reduce it to their own selfish ends. Among the latter, there might have been numerous grades, and distinctions, and occupations; some high in intellect, others devoted to the æsthetic service of the emotions, and others known for their conquests of nature or of their fellow-men; but all ultimately failing of the great end of existence. And, among the former, there may have been those who at times were tempted to regard some of those artificial distinctions, for a moment, as if they were all-important. But they had only to reflect, in order to feel that to be "the sons of God" was the only substantial and enduring distinction. And as the process of human deterioration advanced from stage to stage, the imaginary spectators may have often looked for the sudden descent of judgment, and have been ready to say: "Here, surely, the process will end. We must now have seen the utmost of Divine long-suffering." But again their apprehensions were met by some new interposition which spoke of the unexhausted "riches of His goodness and forbearance" yet in store.

God repented man's creation.

At length, however, the state of the world had reached a pitch of guilt so enormous that it is actually said, "It repented the Lord that He had made man upon the earth." The language, of course, is figurative; exhibiting what ancient philosophy called συγκατάβασις, a condescension to the views and capacities of men. Nor is there any book that can so well afford to indulge in such language as the Bible; not only on account of its compassionate aim in employing it, but because of the precautions it employs to guard against the only danger to which it exposes. For it both solemnly forbids any artistic image of God, and it distinctly teaches that, strictly speaking, "God is not a man that He should repent." * To say, then, that *it repented God that He had made man*, is to tax and exhaust language in an effort to express the depth of human degradation and the utterness of the manner in which the family constitution had failed to answer its primary and proper end. Even "He that made them will not have mercy on them; and He that formed them will show them no favor." † From the depths of the preceding eternity, when contemplating the bright possibilities of such a world, He had "rejoiced in the habitable parts of the earth, and his delights were with the sons of men." ‡ That was the Divine idea: here was the human reality; so foul that it must be swept from the face of the earth!

Every man, family, and age tried the Divine patience differently.

But what a manifestation of the Divine forbearance had it led to; for by what long travail in sin had man reached his fearful climax! Every sinful man that had lived

* 1 Sam. xv. 29. † Isaiah, xxvii. 11. ‡ Proverbs, viii. 31.

had tried the patience of God "in his own way," in a manner different from all the rest. Every godless family had varied the great experiment on his long-suffering. What lessons, warnings, and significant intimations each man of many centuries had unconsciously sown broad-cast as he walked through life; and what vital seeds, numerous as the spores shed in autumn, had others unconsciously scattered in his path—to be all trodden into the general mire! What myriads of children had come age after age, bringing with them traces of their Divine origin and mission—to be all wrought up into the great organization of evil! What an amount of resistance man must have offered to Divine remonstrances and restraints, in order to break through them all! What miseries he had been content to endure in his prolonged hostility against God! What misrepresentations—caricatures—of the Divine Being had come to pass for portraits! What perversions of humanity, for normal man—the image of God! What object in nature had he not wrested from its rightful purpose, and selfishly appropriated? What law of the family constitution had he not violated, and what violation had he not misnamed liberty—an improvement on the Divine plan? What sins did that constitution make possible, which he had not perpetrated? What promise or possibility of amendment was there at any point of the process which had not been waited for, and which he had not disappointed? What interposition of mercy which he had not turned into an occasion for new acts of presumption? What delay of judgment, from which he had not taken heart to believe that no excess of depravity will ever arouse the Divine displeasure? Of all the evil which his state admitted, what stage of evil had he not passed through, and what depths had he not reached? Yet of what regret was he conscious, except that he could not descend deeper; that the laws of his nature, and the limitation of even his many-centuried life, placed bounds to his powers for evil which he could not exceed? But that which he could not perpetrate he could imagine; and, having exhausted the present and the actual, what worlds of possible evil and Titanic daring did not his imagination create and revel in? For, "God saw that the wickedness of man was great in the earth, and that every imagination of the thoughts of his heart was only evil continually." In addition to the wrecks of a Divine economy which he had strewn around him, there were undeveloped powers of evil within him; springs which only wanted room to uncoil, in order to desolate other worlds. And all this was ever present to the Divine eye, standing side by side with the possible heaven which might have occupied its place. Yet, for all this, the Divine forbearance proves itself sufficient.

Punishment deferred for a hundred and twenty years.

"And God said unto Noah, The end of all flesh is come before me." But still the Divine patience "endured with much long-suffering the vessels of wrath fit for destruction." For a hundred and twenty years longer the seasons revolved. No storm gathered in the heavens. All things appeared to "continue as they were from the beginning of the creation." Only the prophetic ark arose; proclaiming that every added day was a winged messenger from the mercy-seat inviting men to repent. As if lingering to see whether some ground might not yet appear for withdrawing the doom; whether the world's last consummating sin might not be indefinitely delayed; whether their manifestation to themselves as incarnations of evil might not bring them to a pause, "the long-suffering of God waited in the days of Noah while the ark was a preparing."* "The Lord is not slack concerning His promise; but He is long-suffering, not willing that any should perish, but that all should come to repentance."† It was His mode of expressing, for more than a century, His reluctance to close the door of hope.

The entire period a display of long-suffering.

But man's intense depravity was more than a match for even such patience. "They did eat, they drank, they married wives, they were given in marriage, until the day that Noah entered into the ark, and the flood came and destroyed them all."‡ The ark uprose; the monument and memorial of a departed race. At the beginning of the dispensation God had said, in effect: "Let the family be a voluntary manifestation by man, and to him of my Fatherhood;" nor had the natural unfolding of its Divine constitution failed to place in a stronger light than ever the various attributes of the Divine character. But this, as far as man was concerned, was an involuntary process. He had selfishly perverted the family constitution itself in which God was meant to be seen. Even the intellectual and social development which it had occasioned, only increased his moral disqualification for appreciating the character of God. And, therefore, from the moment man had shown himself regardless of the Divine design of the constitution, and had set himself to pervert the working and application of it to his own selfish ends, God had said, in effect: "Let his conduct be the occasion of making a manifestation to him of My Long-suffering—an aspect of My character as yet

* 1 Peter, iii. 20. † 2 Peter, iii. 9. ‡ Luke, xvii. 27.

unknown. As he becomes to himself a manifestation of evil, I will make to him a new manifestation of good." And now the time had come when the evil must be swept from the earth to make way for yet greater good. The planet over which "the morning stars had sang together," and which might still have been floating through the heavens to the same strains—the ark of space—now showed only a solitary vessel in the midst of a shoreless waste of waters, freighted with the hardly-saved wreck of a world departed. But that vessel was conveying into the future the precious germs of a new era of the Divine manifestation. For the human incarnation of the Divine—the great manifestation of God by man, as well as to him—is yet to come.

INDEX.

VALUABLE WORKS

PUBLISHED BY

GOULD AND LINCOLN,

59 WASHINGTON STREET, BOSTON.

SACRED RHETORIC: Or, Composition and Delivery of Sermons. By HENRY J. RIPLEY, Prof. in Newton Theological Institution. Including Ware's Hints on Extemporaneous Preaching. Second thousand. 12mo, 75 cts.

An admirable work, clear and succint in its positions and recommendations, soundly based on good authority, and well supported by a variety of reading and illustrations. — *N. Y. Literary World.*

We have looked over this work with a lively interest. The arrangement is easy and natural, and the selection of thoughts under each topic very happy. The work is one that will command readers. It is a comprehensive manual of great practical utility. — *Phil. Ch. Chronicle.*

The author contemplates a man *preparing to compose a discourse* to promote the great ends of preaching, and unfolds to him the process through which his mind ought to pass. We commend the work to ministers, and to those preparing for the sacred office, as a book that will efficiently aid them in studying thoroughly the subject it brings before them. — *Phil. Ch. Observer.*

It presents a rich variety of rules for the practical use of the clergyman, and evinces the good sense, the large experience, and the excellent spirit of Dr. Ripley; and the whole volume is well fitted to instruct and stimulate the writer of sermons. — *Bibliotheca Sacra.*

An excellent work is here offered to theological students and clergymen. It is not a compilation, but is an original treatise, fresh, practical, and comprehensive, and adapted to the pulpit offices of the present day. It is full of valuable suggestions, and abounds with clear illustrations. — *Zion's Herald.*

It cannot be too frequently perused by those whose duty it is to *persuade* men. — *Congregationalist.*

Prof. Ripley possesses the highest qualifications for a work of this kind. His position has given him great experience in the peculiar wants of theological students. — *Providence Journal.*

His canons on selecting texts, stating the proposition, collecting and arranging materials, style, delivery, etc., are just and well stated. Every theological student to whom this volume is *accessible* will be likely to procure it. — *Christian Mirror, Portland.*

It is manifestly the fruit of mature thought and large observation; it is pervaded by a manly tone, and abounds in judicious counsels; it is compactly written and admirably arranged, both for study and reference. It will become a text book for theological students, we have no doubt; that it deserves to be read by all ministers is thus as clear. — *N. Y. Recorder.*

THE CHRISTIAN WORLD UNMASKED. By JOHN BERRIDGE, A. M., Vicar of Everton, Bedfordshire, Chaplain to the Right Hon. The Earl of Buchan, etc. *New Edition.* With Life of the Author, by the REV. THOMAS GUTHRIE, D. D., Minister of Free St. John's, Edinburgh. 16mo, cloth.

"The book," says DR. GUTHRIE, in his Introduction, "which we introduce anew to the public, has survived the test of years, and still stands towering above things of inferior growth like a cedar of Lebanon. Its subject is all important; in doctrine it is sound to the core; it glows with fervent piety; it exhibits a most skilful and unsparing dissection of the dead professor; while its style is so remarkable, that he who could *preach* as Berridge has *written*, would hold any congregation by the ears."

THE CHRISTIAN REVIEW. Edited by JAMES D. KNOWLES, BARNAS SEARS, and S. F. SMITH. 8 vols. Commencing with vol. one. Half cl. lettered, 8,00. Single volumes, (except the first,) may be had in numbers, 1,00.

These first eight volumes of the Christian Review contain valuable contributions from the leading men of the Baptist and several other denominations, and will be found a valuable acquisition to any library.

WORKS OF JOHN HARRIS, D. D.

THE GREAT COMMISSION; Or, the Christian Church constituted and charged to convey the Gospel to the World. With an Introductory Essay, by WILLIAM R. WILLIAMS, D. D. Seventh thousand. 12mo, cloth, 1,00.

Of the several productions of Dr. Harris, — all of them of great value, — this is destined to exert the most powerful influence in forming the religious and missionary character of the coming generations. But the vast fund of argument and instruction will excite the admiration and inspire the gratitude of thousands in our own land as well as in Europe. Every clergyman and pious and reflecting layman ought to possess the volume, and make it familiar by repeated perusal. — *Puritan Recorder.*

His plan is original and comprehensive. In filling it up, the author has interwoven facts with rich and glowing illustrations, and with trains of thought that are sometimes almost resistless in their appeals to the conscience. The work is not more distinguished for its arguments and its genius than for the spirit of deep and fervent piety that pervades it. — *Day-Spring.*

This work comes forth in circumstances which give and promise extraordinary interest and value. Its general circulation will do much good. — *N. Y. Evangelist.*

To recommend this work to the friends of all denominations would be but faint praise; the author deserves, and will undoubtedly receive, the credit of having applied a new lever to that great moral machine which, by the blessing of God, is destined to evangelize the world. — *Ch. Secretary.*

"Have you read the Great Commission, by Harris?" I answer promptly, *No.* I have often attempted it, but have as often failed. Before I can go through with a single page, the book is laid down, and my mind is lost in thought; and yet so profitably and pleasantly lost, that one almost wishes to continue so. *I have* THOUGHT *it nearly through!* The book is made up *of* thought, and made *for* thought, and consequent action. — REV. A. WILLIAMS.

THE GREAT TEACHER; Or, Characteristics of our Lord's Ministry. With an Introductory Essay, by HEMAN HUMPHREY, D. D., late President of Amherst College. Twelfth thousand. 12mo, cloth, 85 cts.

Its style is, like the country which gave it birth, beautiful, varied, finished, and every where delightful. But the style of this work is its smallest excellence. It will be read; it ought to be read. It will find its way to many parlors, and add to the comforts of many a happy fireside. The writer pours forth a clear and beautiful light, like that of the evening light-house, when it sheds its rays upon the sleeping waters, and covers them with a surface of gold. We can have no sympathy with a heart which yields not to impressions delicate and holy, which the perusal of this work will naturally make. — DR. TODD, *Hampshire Gazette.*

He writes like one who has long been accustomed to "sit at the feet of Jesus," and has eminently profited under his teaching. I do not wonder at the avidity which is hastening its wide circulation in England; nor at the high terms in which it is recommended by so many of the best judges. I am sure that it deserves an equally rapid and wide circulation here. — DR. HUMPHREY'S *Introduction.*

To praise the work itself would be a work of supererogation. All Christians know it; all read and admire it. Harris is, to our view, incomparably the greatest religious writer now living — more particularly of practical works. His pages are a storehouse of "weighty and well-digested thoughts, imbued with deep Christian feeling, and clothed in perspicuous and polished language." — *Weekly Rev.*

MISCELLANIES; Consisting Principally of Sermons and Essays. With an Introductory Essay and Notes, by JOSEPH BELCHER, D. D. 12mo, cloth, 75 cts.

These essays are among the finest in the language; and the warmth and energy of religious feeling manifested will render them the treasure of the closet and the Christian fireside. — *Bangor Merc.*

DR. HARRIS is one of the best writers of the age, and this volume will not in the least detract from his well-merited reputation. — *American Pulpit.*

The contents of this volume will afford the reader an intellectual and spiritual banquet of the highest order. — *Philadelphia Ch. Observer.*

ZEBULON; Or the Moral Claims of Seamen stated and enforced. Edited by REV. W. M. ROGERS and DANIEL M. LORD. 18mo, cloth, 25 cts.

☞ A well-written and spirit-stirring appeal to Christians in behalf of that numerous, useful, generous-hearted, though long-neglected class, *seamen.*

THE PREACHER AND THE KING;

OR, BOURDALOUE IN THE COURT OF LOUIS XIV.

Being an Account of that distinguished Era. Translated from the French of L. BUNGENER. Paris, fourteenth edition. With an Introduction, by the REV. GEORGE POTTS, D. D., New York. 12mo, cloth, 1,25.

It combines *substantial history with the highest charm of romance;* the most rigid philosophical criticism with a thorough analysis of human character and faithful representation of the spirit and manners of the age to which it relates. We regard the book as a valuable contribution to the cause not merely of general literature, but especially of pulpit eloquence. Its attractions are so various that it can hardly fail to find readers of almost every description. — *Puritan Recorder.*

A very delightful book. It is full of interest, and equally replete with sound thought and profitable sentiment. — *N. Y. Commercial.*

It is a volume at once curious, instructive, and fascinating. The interviews of Bourdaloue, and Claude, and those of Bossuet, Fenelon, and others, are remarkably attractive, and of finished taste. Other high personages of France are brought in to figure in the narrative, while rhetorical rules are exemplified in a manner altogether new. Its extensive sale in France is evidence enough of its extraordinary merit and its peculiarly attractive qualities. — *Ch. Advocate.*

It is full of life and animation, and conveys a graphic idea of the state of morals and religion in the Augustan age of French literature. — *N. Y. Recorder.*

This book will attract by its novelty, and prove particularly engaging to those interested in the pulpit eloquence of an age characterized by the flagrant wickedness of Louis XIV. The author has exhibited singular skill in weaving into his narrative sketches of the remarkable men who flourished at that period, with original and striking remarks on the subject of preaching. — *Presbyterian.*

Its historical and biographical portions are valuable; its comments excellent, and its effect pure and benignant. A work which we recommend to all, as possessing rare interest. — *Buffalo Morn. Exp.*

A book of rare interest, not only for the singular ability with which it is written, but for the graphic account which it gives of the state of pulpit eloquence during the celebrated era of which it treats. It is perhaps the best biography extant of the distinguished and eloquent preacher, who above all others most pleased the king; while it also furnishes many interesting particulars in the lives of his professional contemporaries. We content ourself with warmly commending it. — *Savannah Journal.*

The author is a minister of the Reformed Church. In the forms of narrative and conversations, he portrays the features and character of that remarkable age, and illustrates the claims and duties of the sacred office, and the important ends to be secured by the eloquence of the pulpit. — *Phil. Ch. Obs.*

A book which unfolds to us the private conversation, the interior life and habits of study of such men as Claude, Bossuet, Bourdaloue, Massillon, and Bridaine, cannot but be a precious gift to the American church and ministers. It is a book full of historical facts of great value, sparkling with gems of thought, polished scholarship, and genuine piety. — *Cin. Ch. Advocate.*

This volume presents a phase of French life with which we have never met in any other work. The author is a minister of the Reformed Church in Paris, where his work has been received with unexampled popularity, having already gone through *fourteen* editions. The writer has studied not only the divinity and general literature of the age of Louis XIV., but also the memories of that period, until he is able to reproduce a life-like picture of society at the Court of the Grand Monarch. — *Alb. Trans.*

A work which we recommend to all, as possessing rare interest. — *Buffalo Ev. Express.*

In form it is descriptive and dramatic, presenting the reader with animated conversations between some of the most famous preachers and philosophers of the Augustan age of France. The work will be read with interest by all intelligent men; but it will be of especial service to the ministry, who cannot afford to be ignorant of the facts and suggestions of this instructive volume. — *N. Y. Ch. Intel.*

The work is very fascinating, and the lesson under its spangled robe is of the gravest moment to every pulpit and every age. — *Ch. Intelligencer.*

THE PRIEST AND THE HUGUENOT; or Persecution in the Age of Louis XV. Part I., A Sermon at Court; Part II., A Sermon in the City; Part III., A Sermon in the Desert. Translated from the French of L. BUNGENER, author of "The Preacher and the King." 2 vols. 12mo, cloth. ☞ *A new Work.*

☞ This is truly a masterly production, full of interest, and may be set down as one of the greatest Protestant works of the age.

IMPORTANT NEW WORKS.

THE CHRISTIAN LIFE: Social and Individual. By PETER BAYNE, A. M. 12mo. Cloth. $1.25.

Contents.—PART I. STATEMENT. I. The Individual Life. II. The Social Life. PART II. EXPOSITION AND ILLUSTRATION. *Book I. Christianity the Basis of Social Life.* I. First Principles. II. Howard; and the rise of Philanthropy. III. Wilberforce; and the development of Philanthropy. IV. Budgett; the Christian Freeman. V. The social problem of the age, and one or two hints towards its solution. *Book II. Christianity the Basis of Individual Character.* I. Introductory: a few Words on Modern Doubt. II. John Foster. III. Thomas Arnold. IV. Thomas Chalmers. PART III. OUTLOOK. I. The Positive Philosophy. II. Pantheistic Spiritualism. III. General Conclusion.

PARTICULAR attention is invited to this work. In Scotland, its publication, during the last winter, produced a great sensation. Hugh Miller made it the subject of an elaborate review in his paper, the Edinburgh *Witness*, and gave his readers to understand that it was an extraordinary work. The "*News of the Churches*," the monthly organ of the Scottish Free Church, was equally emphatic in its praise, pronouncing it "the religious book of the season." Strikingly original in plan and brilliant in execution, it far surpasses the expectations raised by the somewhat familiar title. It is, in truth, a bold onslaught (and the first of the kind) upon the Pantheism of Carlyle, Fichte, etc., by an ardent admirer of Carlyle; and at the same time an exhibition of the Christian Life, in its inner principle, and as illustrated in the lives of Howard, Wilberforce, Budgett, Foster, Chalmers, etc. The brilliancy and vigor of the author's style are remarkable.

PATRIARCHY; or, the Family, its Constitution and Probation. By JOHN HARRIS, D. D., President of "New College," London, and author of "The Great Teacher," "Mammon," "Pre-Adamite Earth," "Man Primeval," etc. 12mo. Cloth. $1.25.

THIS is the third and last of a series, by the same author, entitled "Contributions to Theological Science." The plan of this series is highly original, and thus far has been most successfully executed. Of the first two in the series, "Pre-Adamite Earth," and "Man Primeval," we have already issued four and five editions, and the demand still continues. The immense sale of all Dr. Harris's works attest their intrinsic popularity. The present work has long been expected, but was delayed owing to the author's illness, and the pressure of his duties as President of New College, St. John's Wood. We shall issue it from advanced sheets (a large portion of which have already been received) simultaneously with its publication in England.

GOD REVEALED IN NATURE AND IN CHRIST: Including a Refutation of the Development Theory contained in the "Vestiges of the Natural History of Creation." By the Author of "THE PHILOSOPHY OF THE PLAN OF SALVATION." 12mo. Cloth. $1.25.

THE author of that remarkable book, "The Philosophy of the Plan of Salvation," has devoted several years of incessant labor to the preparation of this work. Without being specifically controversial, its aim is to overthrow several of the popular errors of the day, by establishing the antagonist truth upon an impregnable basis of reason and logic. In opposition to the doctrine of a mere subjective revelation, now so plausibly inculcated by certain eminent writers, it demonstrates the necessity of an external, objective revelation. Especially, it furnishes a new, and as it is conceived, a conclusive argument against the "*development theory*" so ingeniously maintained in the "Vestiges of the Natural History of Creation." As this author does not publish except when he has something to say, there is good reason to anticipate that the work will be one of unusual interest and value. His former book has met with the most signal success in both hemispheres, having passed through numerous editions in England and Scotland, and been translated into four of the European languages besides. It is also about to be translated into the Hindoostanee tongue. (m)

WORKS JUST ISSUED.

VISITS TO EUROPEAN CELEBRITIES. By WILLIAM B. SPRAGUE, D D. 12mo. Cloth. $1.00. Second Edition.

THE first edition of this work was exhausted within a short time after its publication. It consists of a series of Personal Sketches, *drawn from life*, of many of the most distinguished men and women of Europe, with whom the author became acquainted in the course of several European tours: Edward Irving, Rowland Hill, Wilberforce, Jay, Robert Hall, John Foster, Hannah More, Guizot, Louis Philippe, Sismondi, Tholuck, Gesenius, Neander, Humboldt, Encke, Rogers, Campbell, Joanna Baillie, John Pye Smith, Amelia Opie, Dr. Pusey, Mrs. Sherwood, Maria Edgeworth, John Galt, Dr Wardlaw, Dr. Chalmers, Sir David Brewster, Lord Jeffrey, Professor Wilson, (Kit North,) Southey, and others, are here portrayed as the author saw them in their own homes, and under the most advantageous circumstances. Accompanying the Sketches are the AUTOGRAPHS of each of the personages described. This unique feature of the work adds in no small degree to its attractions. For the social circle, for the traveller by railroad and steamboat, for all who desire to be refreshed and not weared by reading, the book will prove to be a most agreeable companion. The public press of all shades of opinion, North and South, have given it a most flattering reception.

THE STORY OF THE CAMPAIGN. A Complete Narrative of the War in Southern Russia. Written in a Tent in the Crimea. By Major E. BRUCE HAMLEY, Author of "Lady Lee's Widowhood." 12mo. Thick. Printed Paper Covers. 37½ Cents.

Contents.—The Rendezvous—The Movement to the Crimea—First Operations in the Crimea—Battle of the Alma—The Battle-field—The Katcha and the Balbek—The Flank March—Occupation of Balaklava—The Position before Sebastopol—Commencement of the Siege—Attack on Balaklava—First Action of Inkermann—Battle of Inkermann—Winter on the Plains—Circumspective—The Hospitals on the Bosphorus—Exculpatory—Progress of the Siege—The Burial Truce—View of the Works.

THIS was first published in *Blackwood's Magazine*, in which form it has attracted general attention. It is the only connected and continuous narrative of the War in Europe that has yet appeared. The author is an officer of rank in the British army, and has borne an active part in the campaign; he has also won a brilliant reputation as the author of the fascinating story of "Lady Lee's Widowhood." By his profession of arms, by his actual participation in the conflict, and by his literary abilities, he is qualified in a rare degree, for the task he has undertaken. The expectations thus raised will not be disappointed. To those who have been dependent on the brief, fragmentary, interrupted, and irresponsible newspaper notices of the war, this book will furnish a full, complete, graphic, and perfectly reliable account from the beginning. Should the author's life be spared, his history of future operations will follow, and will be issued by the publishers uniform with the present volume.

ROGET'S THESAURUS OF ENGLISH WORDS. A New and Improved Edition. 12mo. Cloth. $1.50.

THIS edition is based on the last London edition (just issued.) The first American edition having been prepared by Dr. Sears, for strictly educational purposes, those words and phrases, properly termed "vulgar," incorporated into the original work, were omitted. Regret having been expressed by critics and scholars, whose opinions are entitled to respect, at this omission, in the present new edition the expurgated portions have been restored, but by such an arrangement of matter as not to interfere with the educational purpose of the American editor. Besides this, there will be important additions of words and phrases not in the English edition, making this, therefore, in all respects, more full and perfect than the author's edition.

RECENT PUBLICATIONS.

THE EVIDENCES OF CHRISTIANITY, as exhibited in the writings of its apologists, down to Augustine, by W. J. BOLTON, of Gonville and Caius College, Cambridge. 12mo, cloth. 80 cents.

The essay contained in this volume received the Hulsean prize (about $500) in England. The author is a professor in Gonville and Caius College, Cambridge, and evidently a very learned student of the patristic writings and the whole circle of ecclesiastical history. He has presented to the world in this essay an admirable compendium of the arguments for the truth of Christianity advanced in the works of the Apologetic Fathers during the third, fourth, and fifth centuries of the Christian era. These arguments are classified as being deduced from antecedent probability, from antiquity, from prophecy, from miracles, from the reasonableness of doctrine, from superior morality, and from the success of the Gospel. — *N. Y. Commercial.*

This is a work of deep research, and of great value to the theological student. — *Transcript.*

We had occasion, some time since, to notice this work, when we expressed a high estimate of its merits. We can only say that, in looking through it a second time, our appreciation of both the learning and the ingenuity which it discovers is heightened rather than diminished We thankfully accept such an effort as this of a profound and highly-cultivated mind. — *Puritan Recorder.*

The work bears the marks of great research, and must command the attention and confidence of the Christian world. — *Mercantile Journal.*

THE BETTER LAND; or, Thoughts on Heaven. By A. C. THOMPSON, Pastor of the Eliot Church, Roxbury. 12mo, cloth. $1.00. *Just published.*

THE MISSION OF THE COMFORTER; with copious Notes. By JULIUS CHARLES HARE. Notes translated for the American edition. 12mo, cl. $1.25.

We hardly remember any treatise which is so well calculated to be useful in general circulation among ministers, and the more educated laity, than this, which is rich in spirituality, strong and sound in theology, comprehensive in thought, vigorous and beautiful in imagination, and affluent in learning. — *Congregationalist.*

We have seldom read a book with greater interest. — *N. Y. Evangelist.*

The volume is one of rare value, and will be welcomed as an eloquent and Scriptural exposition of some of the fundamental doctrines of our faith. — *New York Recorder.*

THE VICTORY OF FAITH. By JULIUS CHARLES HARE, author of "The Mission of the Comforter," etc. 12mo, cloth. *In press.*

FIRST LINES OF CHRISTIAN THEOLOGY. In the form of a Syllabus, prepared for the use of Students, with subsequent Additions and Elucidations. By Rev. JOHN PYE SMITH. Edited from the author's manuscripts, with Additional Notes and References, etc. 1 vol. Royal octavo. $5.00.

☞ A most important work for ministers and theological students.

THE RELIGIONS OF THE WORLD, and their relations to Christianity. By FREDERICK DENISON MAURICE, A. M., Professor of Divinity in King's College, London. 16mo, cloth. 60 cents.

The effort we deem masterly, and, in any event, must prove highly interesting by the comparisons which it institutes with the false and the true. His investigations into the Hindoo and Budhist mythologies will itself repay the reader's trouble. — *Methodist Quarterly.*

GUIDO AND JULIUS. THE DOCTRINE OF SIN AND THE PROPITIATOR; or, the True Consecration of the Doubter. Exhibited in the Correspondence of two Friends. By FREDERIS AUGUSTUT O. THOLUCH, D. D. Translated from the German, by JONATHAN EDWARDS RYLAND. With an Introduction by JOHN PYE SMITH, D. D. 16mo, cloth. 60 cents.

☞ It might naturally be expected that a work by authors so distinguished in the literary and religious world would prove one of great interest and value. This expectation will not be disappointed. It is pre-eminently a book for the times — full of interest, and of great power.

NEW WORKS

THE TEACHER'S LAST LESSON. A MEMOIR OF MARTHA WHITING, late of the Charlestown Female Seminary, consisting chiefly of Extracts from her Journal, interspersed with Reminisences and Suggestive Reflections. By CATHARINE N. BADGER, an Associate Teacher. With a Portrait, and an Engraving of the Seminary. 12mo. Cloth. $1.00. Second Edition.

THE subject of this Memoir was, for a quarter of a century, at the head of one of the most celebrated Female Seminaries in the country. During that period she educated more than *three thousand* young ladies. She was a kindred spirit to Mary Lyon, the celebrated founder of Mount Holyoke Seminary, with whom, for strength of character, eminent piety, devotion to her calling, and extraordinary success therein, she well deserves to be ranked.

MY MOTHER: or Recollections of Maternal Influence. By a NEW ENGLAND CLERGYMAN. 12mo. Cloth. 75 Cents.

THIS is a new and enlarged edition of a work that was first published in 1849. It passed rapidly through three editions, when the sale was arrested by the embarrassment of the publisher. The author has now revised it, and added another chapter, so that it comes before the public with the essential claims of a new work. . . . It is the picture of a quiet New England family, so drawn and colored as to subserve the ends of *domestic education*. The central figure is the author's mother, around whom are grouped the various members of the family. Biographical sketches and lessons of practical wisdom are so intermingled, that while the former relieve the latter, these in turn give force and significance to the sketches. . . . . . . The author has already distinguished himself in various walks of literature, but from motives of delicacy towards the still surviving characters of the book, he chooses for the present to conceal his name. . . . . . A writer of wide celebrity says of the book, in a note to the publisher — "It is one of those rare pictures, painted from life, with the exquisite skill of one of the *old masters*, which so seldom present themselves to the amateur."

WORKS IN PREPARATION.

MEMOIR OF OLD HUMPHREY. With Gleanings from his Portfolio, and a Portrait.

KNOWLEDGE IS POWER. A View of the Productive Forces of Modern Society, and the Results of Labor, Capital and Skill. By CHARLES KNIGHT. With numerous Illustrations. American Edition. Revised, with additions, by DAVID A. WELLS, Editor of the "Annual of Scientific Discovery."

SACRED LATIN POETRY. CHIEFLY LYRICAL. Selected and arranged for use. With Notes and an Introduction by RICHARD CHENEVIX TRENCH. Revised, with important Additions by J. L. LINCOLN, Professor of the Latin Language in Brown University.

EXPOSITION OF THE SERMON ON THE MOUNT. Drawn from the Writings of St. Augustine, with Observations. By RICHARD CHENEVIX TRENCH.

☞ G. & L. would call attention to their extensive list of publications, embracing valuable works in THEOLOGY, SCIENCE, LITERATURE AND ART; TEXT BOOKS FOR SCHOOLS AND COLLEGES, and MISCELLANEOUS, etc., in large variety, the productions of some of the ablest writers and most scientific men of the age, among which will be found those of Chambers, Hugh Miller, Agassiz, Gould, Guyot, Marcou, Dr. Harris, Dr. Wayland, Dr. Williams, Dr. Ripley, Dr. Kitto, Dr. Tweedie, Dr. Choules, Dr. Sprague, Newcomb, Banvard, "Walter Aimwell," Bungener, Miall, Archdeacon Hare, and others of like standing and popularity, and to this list they are constantly adding. (o)

www.ingramcontent.com/pod-product-compliance
Lightning Source LLC
LaVergne TN
LVHW020927110826
845150LV00004B/787